# DATE DUE

| DE 16 06 | | | |
|---|---|---|---|
| | | | |
| | | | |
| | | | |
| | | | |
| | | | |
| | | | |
| | | | |
| | | | |
| | | | |
| | | | |
| | | | |
| | | | |
| | | | |
| | | | |
| | | | |
| | | | |

DEMCO 38-296

U.S.-MEXICO CONTEMPORARY PERSPECTIVES SERIES, 5
CENTER FOR U.S.-MEXICAN STUDIES
UNIVERSITY OF CALIFORNIA, SAN DIEGO

PRINTED WITH THE ASSISTANCE
OF THE TINKER FOUNDATION

# Assembling for Development

## The maquila industry in Mexico and the United States

**Leslie Sklair**

*London School of Economics*

Updated and Expanded Edition
Center for U.S.-Mexican Studies, UCSD

Printed in the United States of America by
the Center for U.S.-Mexican Studies
University of California, San Diego

1993

Cover: Detail from *The Mechanization of the Countryside*, panel in the
series of murals by Diego Rivera, in the Court of Labor, Ministry of
Education Building, Mexico City.

ISBN 1-878367-12-9

This is an updated and expanded edition of *Assembling for Development*, published in hardcover in 1989 by Unwin Hyman Inc., London.

For Doro, Jessie, Aphra, and Tillie

# Contents

# List of Tables

# List of Abbreviations

| | |
|---|---|
| AFL-CIO | American Federation of Labor-Congress of Industrial Organizations |
| AMCHAM | American Chamber of Commerce in Mexico |
| Banamex | Banco Nacional de México |
| BIP | Border Industrialization Program |
| CAD/CAM | Computer-aided design/Computer-aided manufacturing |
| CANACINTRA | Cámara Nacional de la Industria de Transformación |
| CIM | Computer-integrated manufacturing |
| COLEF | El Colegio de la Frontera Norte |
| CTM | Confederación de Trabajadores de México |
| ELI | Export-led industrialization |
| ELIFFIT | ELI fueled by foreign investment and technology |
| EPA | Environmental Protection Agency |
| EPZ | Export-processing zone |
| INEGI | Instituto Nacional de Estadística, Geografía e Informática |
| MN | Maquiladora Newsletter |
| NAFTA | North American Free Trade Agreement |
| NIC | Newly industrializing country |
| PAN | Partido de Acción Nacional |
| PEMEX | Petróleos Mexicanos |
| PRI | Partido Revolucionario Institucional |
| PRONAF | Programa Nacional Fronterizo |
| SECOFI | Secretaría de Comercio y Fomento Industrial |
| SEDESOL | Secretaría de Desarrollo Social |
| SEDUE | Secretaría de Desarrollo Urbano y Ecología |
| SIC | Secretaría de Industria y Comercio |
| TCC | Transnational capitalist class |
| TNC | Transnational corporation |
| TPN | *Twin Plant News* |
| TSUS | Tariff Schedule of the United States |
| USITC | United States International Trade Commission |
| UTEP | University of Texas at El Paso |

# Preface

Whatever else, a book about the maquila industry in Mexico is, inevitably, a book about women working in factories. Most of what has so far been written on the maquilas has had the effect of marginalizing women, either consciously as an orthodox way of coping with a difficult issue, or unconsciously as a way of trying to convey feminist principles. Accordingly, in this book whenever "worker" appears in the text it is to be understood to mean "woman worker"; "labor," "female labor"; "employee," "female employee"; except where the context indicates otherwise. In this way, the men working in the maquilas are marginalized, for this is traditionally where they have been, on the margins. As will be shown, this has been changing as the maquilas employ more men in the 1980s.

Another stylistic peculiarity should be pointed out. Though maquilas are to be found in a wide variety of industrial sectors, it is convenient to refer to the whole as "the maquila industry." As long as it is understood that what unites them is that they operate under the maquila regulations rather than what they produce, this convenient label does no great harm.

This book is part of a larger project on the developmental effects (or lack of them) of transnational capital in the Third World. It started off as an attempt to analyze the processes and dynamics at work in a group of export oriented assembly industries: the Shenzhen Special Economic Zone in China, just across the border from Hong Kong; the Shannon free zone in the midwest region of Ireland; and the Egyptian free zones. My strategy in each of these studies was to work out a set of criteria against which the developmental effects of foreign investment in these zones could be measured and an answer to the pressing if crude question about whether or not the zones were "a good thing" could be offered. This strategy proved to be increasingly unsatisfactory for the simple reason that a judgement on the zones could not be made in isolation from a judgement of the developmental effects of transnational capital on the whole country. It was at that point that I began to see the zones not only as an interesting phenomenon in their own right, but also as *symbolic* of something far more important that

[ xi ]

was happening in the relations between the countries of the capitalist center and the countries of the Third World, especially those aspiring to the status of newly industrializing countries (NICs). Whereas most of the new international division of labor and world systems analyses quite correctly concentrated on what was happening at the core of the global capitalist system, it seemed to me that insufficient attention was being paid to the new policies that were being produced in the countries of the Third World to accommodate the needs of the center. This is the origin of the idea of the "reformation" of capitalism.

The actual field work on which this book is partly based was carried out while I was a visiting research fellow at the Center for U.S.-Mexican Studies, at the University of California, San Diego. For a non-Mexicanist like myself, the opportunity to spend nine months at the Center was invaluable insofar as it exposed me to the expertise, opinions, and sense of fun of a wonderfully diverse group of Mexican, North American and European Mexicanists. I am very grateful to Wayne Cornelius and all at the Center and to Joseph Grunwald at the adjoining Institute of the Americas for their benign tolerance of a generalist in a hotbed of specialization. The years 1986 and 1987 were particularly active and exciting in the maquila industry in Mexico and in the United States, in terms of the unprecedented growth of the industry along the border and in the interior, the renewal of political attacks on it in the U.S., and the establishment of a maquila defence organization. I was fortunate to be able to closely observe many of these events.

I have accumulated an unusually large collection of debts in the writing of this book. The first is to my family who, through a succession of negotiated settlements, made it possible for me to prepare the ground, do the research, and write it up, within a loving and stimulating environment. The many friends we made in San Diego played an important part in all of this.

Funds from the Social Research Division at the London School of Economics, and a small grant from the Center at UCSD met most of the travel costs incurred in the course of my research. Logistical support from both of these institutions facilitated the research. I am particularly grateful to my erstwhile secretary, Yvonne Brown, and my part time research assistant, Georgia Morgan.

Literally dozens of people in Mexico and the U.S. assisted me in the research, either academically, practically, or both. Moving from west to east along the border, in addition to those at the Center, I am indebted to other colleagues at UCSD (especially Larry Herzog) and at San Diego State University, both in the Sociology Department and at the Institute for the Regional Studies of the Californias (notably Norris Clement). In Tijuana, Carlos Graizbord and Alejandro Mungaray at the Universidad

Autonomía de Baja California, and Bernardo Gonzalez-Arechiga at El Colegio de la Frontera Norte were especially generous in sharing research materials with me. My two trips to El Paso and Ciudad Juárez were made productive and enjoyable through the friendly cooperation of researchers and staff attached to the Center for Inter-American and Border Studies at the University of Texas, El Paso, particularly its past and present directors, Oscar Martínez and Jeff Brannon. In Juárez and Matamoros, the regional offices of COLEF also generously offered assistance. Patricia Wilson of the University of Texas, Austin, procured unpublished materials for me. A subsequent visit to the University of New Mexico at Albuquerque, and discussion with Susan Tiano and Bob Fiala was extremely valuable in clarifying many points in the first draft of the manuscript.

I had the opportunity to visit many maquilas and discuss the maquila industry with a variety of people actively involved in it all along the border and in Chihuahua City. Although they frequently disagreed with my interpretations, those whom I have labelled the public and private "facilitators" invariably gave me the opportunity to see what was going on for myself. I am especially indebted to the following people: in Tijuana/San Diego, Terri Cardot of Assemble in Mexico, and Howard Boysen of IMEC; in Mexicali, Francisco Xavier Rivas M. of Parque Industrial Mexicali, Manuel Rubio of El Vigia Industrial Park, officials of the Industrial Development Commission, and the state government (arranged by Carlos Graizbord); in Juárez/El Paso, C.P. Cesar Alarcón of AMAC, Joanne Gouge of ELAMEX, Lucinda Vargas of Grupo Bermúdez, Rex Maingot of American Industries, and Wayne McClintock of Mexico Communications; in Matamoros/Brownsville, Lindsey Rhodes and Jim Ebersole of the Brownsville Chamber of Commerce, Jaime Martínez of FINSA Industrial Park, and Haskell Knight of Fisher Price de México; in Reynosa/McAllen, Peter Pranis of COSTEP, and Frank Birkhead of the McAllen Industrial Board; in Chihuahua City, Alejandro Paz Facio of the Maquila Association, and the local staffs of American Industries and Las Americas Industrial Parks. Many other managers of individual maquilas and the officials of the local maquila associations and chambers of commerce and their Mexican equivalents gave me access to mountains of unpublished materials on the past and present of the industry. Particularly helpful in this respect were the maquila associations in the states of Baja California and Chihuahua; the Chambers of Commerce and/or the economic development agencies of San Diego, El Paso, Brownsville, and McAllen. The American Chamber of Commerce of Mexico, Mexican and U.S. government agencies, the AFL-CIO in Washington D.C., Victor Urquidi of El Colegio de México, Dennis Bixler-Marquéz of UTEP, and the office of congressman Jim Kolbe of Arizona also provided useful material; as did Elena Wingate, formerly at the Mexican Embassy, and Jane Thomson of Banamex, both in London. In the final preparation of the manuscript the comments of Gil Merkx, the Series Editor, were very helpful. To all many thanks, and the usual disclaimers apply.

London, *August 1988.*

# Preface to the
# Updated Paperback Edition

The invitation of the Office of Technology Assessment of the U.S. Congress to write a report on the likely impact of a NAFTA on the maquila industry, as a contribution to their research program on the NAFTA, and the stimulating discussion I had with the OTA team in Washington in December 1991 persuaded me that there was real value in updating this study of the maquila industry for the early 1990s. The number of items in the additional bibliography for the update chapter (around seventy), most published since 1988, indicates that maquila-related research continues apace.

I have also had the good fortune to renew my contacts with the Center for U.S.-Mexican Studies several times since 1988, and I am grateful to Wayne Cornelius and his staff for the opportunity to update the book and issue it in paperback. As before, many colleagues and friends in Mexico and the United States have sent me mounds of material and I could not easily continue to work on the maquilas without their generous support. In addition to those mentioned in the preface to the first edition, I would like to thank Lucinda Vargas, of CIEMEX-WEFA, for sending me the latest INEGI data, and Alejandra Salas-Porras, of CIDE (presently at the London School of Economics), for a critical reading of chapter 11. A brief but intensive visit to Mexico City in September 1992 to discuss the new CIDE-CEPAL research project on maquilas in Mexico and Central America was useful in locating some recent materials.

London, *November 1992.*

# 1

# The Maquilas in
# Global Perspective

In all but the very poorest Third World countries the belief in export-led industrialization fuelled by foreign investment and technology (hereafter ELIFFIT) has begun to challenge the other available strategies for economic and social development. Although more traditional development strategies, such as import substitution, varying degrees of autarky, or exporting primary products persist in practice, few countries continue to believe that they offer a realistic path to development. The reasons for the global hegemony of ELIFFIT are many, and the peculiar circumstances of some countries have often been as important as the universal forces nudging the Third World towards the gradual or rapid adoption of such a strategy.

This book has two main objectives. First, it tries to establish the thesis that the ELIFFIT strategy represents a fundamental coming together of the interests of the transnational corporations (TNCs) and some key elites in the countries of the Third World. This increasing coincidence of interests is a result of the rapid rise in the globalization of production that has taken place since the 1950s, the absolute growth of world trade in manufactured goods, and the changing nature of the relationship between the TNCs and the countries of the Third World.[1]

These changes in the global political economy constitute a new phase in the history of capitalism and, concurrently, a new ideology is emerging to sustain it. The ELIFFIT strategy is a central part of the new ideology that the TNCs which direct global capitalism are constructing in their relations with the countries of the Third World. This new phase represents a "reformation of capitalism," the latest

[1]

readjustment that capitalism has been forced to make to ward off the economic, political, and ideological crises with which it is continually faced. "Political" imperialism marked the phase of capitalist expansion when the states of the capitalist centers exercised sovereignty over their colonies. "Economic" imperialism marks the present phase as the states of the capitalist and noncapitalist centers exercise economic control over their "clients." The reformation of capitalism marks the next phase in the relations between dominant powers and the countries of the Third World. The hallmark of global capitalism has always been its ability to ensure the continued accumulation of capital at home and abroad. The reformation of capitalism is one more attempt to achieve this end in difficult circumstances. The second main objective of this book is to analyze the trajectory and consequences of the reformation of capitalism in a specific place and over a specific period of time, namely the maquila, or export oriented assembly industry, in Mexico and in the United States over its first 20 years of existence.

The capitalist reformation of the late twentieth century is both a re-formation of national and global capitals at home and abroad, and a re-formation of capitalism on a world-scale to cope with the problems presented by the struggles of Third World countries to achieve a level of development that will afford their citizens decent lives. There are several interlocking processes at work, and in the last decade they have all begun to be identified, analyzed, and theorized. This reformation of capitalism has at its heart the quest to ensure the perpetual continuation of world trade, primarily in the interests of the countries of the capitalist center, of which the most important by far is still the United States. Trade relations with the Third World present special problems for the operation of the leading TNCs and the reformation of capitalism is their strategy for solving them. It is both an economic problem and a question of right and wrong. As one commentator asserts: "It is not an overstatement to describe this basis of American trade policy as being almost religious. Protectionism is seen as an evil. . . . There is still a strong moralistic opposition to the use of trade measures" (Wolff in Scott and Lodge 1985:302). This sentiment should be borne in mind when we come to identify the main processes at work in the reformation of capitalism and begin to integrate them into a more or less coherent theory to explain the rise of the maquilas as a local and ultimately a global phenomenon.

## *The Reformation of Capitalism: Identifying the Processes*

There are several key processes at work in the reformation of capitalism. They are all connected to the economic consequences of the revolutions that swept across the Third World after World War II. These revolutions signalled the end of formal colonial rule in much of Africa and Asia and the emergence of many newly independent nations on these continents. In Latin America, struggles for political independence had taken place mostly in the nineteenth century, but none of the nations of the region achieved the status of an advanced industrial society of the western European or North American type. Other countries outside western Europe and the Americas, variously described as poor, undeveloped, or underdeveloped, that had been formally independent for some time, were eventually lumped together with these "new nations" and the Latin American countries, as the Third World.[2] Most Third World countries set themselves goals of industrialization and sociopolitical modernization. Many of them adopted First World industrialization strategies rather uncritically, trying to build iron and steel, textile, engineering industries, and so on, with little regard for economies of scale or international competitiveness. These industries were bound to be highly inefficient because they were rarely integrated into systems of rational backward and forward linkages, and they tended to rely on a captive domestic market, highly protected from outside competition. Colonies had exchanged their natural resources, food and industrial crops, and minerals for the manufactures on which the west prospered. By the time the countries of what was to become the Third World reached the stage when they could have started to export their own manufactured goods, there was substantial competition in place from the advanced industrial societies. The theory of international trade based on the concept of comparative advantage justified this state of affairs, arguing that the First World was doing what it did best and most efficiently, namely producing and exporting manufactured goods, and the Third World was doing what it did best and most efficiently, namely producing and exporting raw materials. On this basis, it is difficult to see how the Third World could ever industrialize, and the system of formal political imperialism ensured that Third World countries rarely had the opportunity to compete in global markets for manufactures with the countries of the capitalist core.

Some Latin America countries, independent nations since the nineteenth century, did manage to build a good mix of substantial industries. By 1945, Argentina, Brazil, and Mexico had all passed through the first phase of industrialization, had all entered the world economy as exporters of manufactured goods, and all managed to combine highly protected domestic economies with large amounts of foreign investment from Europe and the U.S. The strategy that these countries used to promote their industrial growth was misleadingly termed "import substitution industrialization" (ISI). There

[3]

was nothing misleading about the intention to substitute domestically produced goods for imported goods. However, instead of importing finished goods, these countries tended to import the machinery and components from which the finished goods were manufactured. So, the substitution was not between imported and domestic goods, but between imported finished goods and imported capital and intermediate goods. ISI created many manufacturing jobs in Latin America, but at a double price. Imports rose rather than fell, causing balance of payments problems; and the industries that were at the center of the ISI strategy were often foreign owned. ISI, thus, profited the TNCs as much as the developing countries themselves.

U.S. and European TNCs had been involved since the nineteenth century in a variety of industries in richer and poorer countries all over the world. This involvement was mainly in the extraction and processing of natural resources, like food and industrial crops, petroleum, and other minerals, though a few U.S. firms did venture into manufacturing abroad. In the twentieth century, more and more U.S. and European companies saw the benefits of locating their production facilities near their prospective export markets, and following this logic some more adventurous entrepreneurs began to manufacture in Latin America, Asia, and Africa. For some the savings in labor costs did compensate for the lower productivity and logistical penalties of operating in what were basically nonindustrial societies.

TNC manufacturing in the Third World spread rapidly in Latin America and to a group of East Asian countries in the 1950s and 1960s. By the 1970s, these processes were so far advanced that a new terminology was necessary to distinguish the developing countries in which they were most profitably taking place. Thus, the Newly Industrializing Countries were born. The Third World was no longer capable of simple characterization. The East Asian NICs (originally Hong Kong, Singapore, Taiwan, and South Korea), did not pursue the same ISI strategies as their Latin American predecessors (see Jenkins 1984; Gereffi and Wyman 1986). For them, the future lay not only in substituting imports but also in promoting manufactured exports. They reasoned that they could industrialize by becoming internationally competitive in some products, and thereby earn sufficient foreign currency to pay for ambitious programs of industrial and infrastructural growth. This was known as "export led industrialization" (ELI).

From the 1950s on, the TNCs began to explore in a systematic fashion the possibilities of splitting up their processes of production not just in the traditional manner of the division of labor on the shop floor, but in a geographical sense. Thus, "offshore sourcing," where the materials and components of a final product were assembled or processed not in one plant or even in several plants in one country,

[4]

but in several plants in different countries, began to account for an increasing proportion of TNC activity. Frobel and his colleagues (1980), in their widely discussed book, *The New International Division of Labour* (NIDL), connected this with the domination of capital over labor on a global scale. Not everyone was willing to accept their political conclusions, but as Grunwald and Flamm (1985:6) assert, those like Frobel: "who claim that the 1960s and 1970s marked a new stage in the evolution of the world capitalist system appear to be correct, insofar as the operations of U.S. multinational firms seem to have switched, on a fairly large scale for the first time, to overseas production of manufactured exports for the home market."[3]

Offshore sourcing was largely, though not exclusively, about labor costs. For products that required straightforward assembly of standard parts in a series of simple operations that could be minutely broken down, and that were small and light enough to fly back to the home country, there was no geographical obstacle to offshore sourcing. The factory could be built anywhere that the foreign investment regime of the host nation permitted. However, in the 1950s there were few countries that combined cheap labor, unrestricted access for foreign capital, and the modicum of political stability that the TNCs always deemed necessary for their overseas operations. Many Third World countries demanded that the TNCs establish companies that were jointly owned with host nationals, and some, like Mexico and India, even insisted that all foreign investment should be through companies in which over half of the equity was held by host nationals. For the majority of TNCs in the Third World, producing for the domestic market and acting to some extent like domestic companies, such regulations were not always entirely unwelcome insofar as they offered some measure of protection against expropriation or nationalization, and as long as the remittance of profits to the parent company was not interfered with, this arrangement suited the TNCs quite well.[4]

For corporations wishing to construct chains of production based on offshore sourcing, this was not always satisfactory. These corporations needed total control and immediate response and, more importantly, they needed to be able to organize the accounts of their operations with the maximum of flexibility. A central requirement was the ability to practice "transfer pricing" or "intragroup settlement prices," substituting for the real market prices of goods and services, artificial prices to maximize fiscal benefits, profits, and cost adjustments over all the countries in which the TNC was doing business. Though by no means impossible to achieve in a joint venture, transfer pricing is much easier in a wholly owned subsidiary and TNCs producing in and for Third World markets had long practiced it (Lall 1980: chapters 5 and 6). The combination of transfer pricing with offshore sourcing introduced a new dimension into TNC operations. Transfer pricing could bring substantial benefits to TNCs that were using cheap labor in the Third World to assemble products.

Offshore sourcing and transfer pricing are what the TNCs brought to the reformation of capitalism. The response of a group of Third World countries was, simply, to make it easier for the TNCs to operate within their borders. These were the countries, the NICs, whose development strategies were versions of export-led industrialization. Starting with Hong Kong and Singapore, enclaves that were almost entirely open to foreign direct investment, a network of export processing zones (EPZ) was created in Asia, in Africa, and in Latin America.[5] These zones were often purpose built industrial parks, geared to the offshore sourcing needs of foreign TNCs. Typically, equipment, materials and components would be shipped into the zone and held in bonded warehouses until needed. These imports were duty free on condition that the products assembled or manufactured from them were exported out of the host country. The advantage in relocating production from an advanced industrial economy to a Third World economy for the TNC was that labor costs were considerably reduced. For the host country, the advantage lay in the jobs created and foreign currency earnings by requiring the TNC to exchange hard currency for local currency at official rates to pay wages and other costs. Some NICs had ambitious goals for their EPZs, and in all of them the entry into global markets that they represented had a symbolism that far outweighed their actual industrial contribution. An important part of the explanation for this is that the consumer electronics industry, virtually created from scratch in the 1950s, used techniques of offshore sourcing extensively and thus introduced the products of the most modern technologies under conditions of perpetual dynamic change into many countries that were barely industrial.[6]

Though most EPZs failed to achieve their primary goals of creating large numbers of jobs and generating substantial amounts of foreign exchange, in a few countries the EPZs were extremely successful in both of these objectives. Among them were Hong Kong, Singapore, Taiwan, and South Korea (wryly labelled the "East Asian gang of four"), economies that generated balance of payments surpluses through sub-stantial and frankly astonishing levels of manufactured exports. Thus, the connection between EPZs, established specifically to promote exports of manufactured goods, and the success of the ELI strategy in the East Asian gang of four, gradually came to occupy a significant place in the thinking of those in other Third World countries who were desperately trying to find the key to the door of competitiveness in global markets for manufactured goods. In one country after another, EPZs began to be established for the benefit of the TNCs and the indigenous companies that wished to join them, and new partnerships between the TNCs, domestic bourgeoisies, and state bureaucracies began to evolve. The regulations specific to these export enclaves were often extended outside the spatial limits of the EPZs, in some cases to the whole country. The cost savings and ease with which the TNCs were able to operate in the Third World caused some major rethinking at corporate headquarters about how best to exploit the commercial opportunities of the global economy. The reformation of capitalism was under way.

Technological change and a determination on the part of most of the world's major trading nations to avoid a recurrence of the collapse of the 1930s, combined to produce a belief that ELI was the most certain path to industrialization and subsequent all round development. The problem was that most countries have tariff barriers (duties) on imports, and nontariff barriers (like quotas, licenses, and unusual customs or product requirements) to discourage imports.[7] The major colonial powers had created special trade arrangements between themselves and their former colonies after independence. With the establishment of the United Nations' continuing Conference on Trade and Development (UNCTAD) in 1964, a sentiment gained ground amongst the rich nations of the world that the poor nations did need help if they were ever to be able to provide a decent standard of living for their rapidly expanding populations. In 1968, UNCTAD created the General System of Preferences (GSP) to facilitate the export of Third World manufactures to the First World. Lying behind this commendable humanitarian sentiment was the undeniable fact that the rich countries could sell very many more products if people in the Third World were able to buy them. The interest of the rich, and particularly of the TNCs, in the development of the Third World was a paradigm case of enlightened self interest.

Consequently, many special trade agreements were concluded between the advanced industrial countries and the countries of the Third World. The U.S. enacted its own GSP regulations in 1976 by which certain noncommunist developing countries were permitted duty free access to the U.S. for several thousand products on condition that at least 35 percent of the value of the goods was produced in a beneficiary country. Imports under the GSP are not unlimited; dollar and percentage restrictions are set and are adjusted to discourage the most successful of the NICs from relying excessively on exports to the United States market.

The role of the U.S. in the reformation of capitalism is central. Despite its relative decline since the 1950s as the global leader in almost all branches of economic activity, it continues to be by far the richest economy in the world and, most significantly, the largest and

[7]

most sought after consumer market. In the bulky Harvard Business School 75th Anniversary compendium on *U.S. Competitiveness in the World Economy* (or the lack of it), Wolff succinctly describes the history of U.S. trade policy as follows: "The primary objective of American trade policy has been to create a single world market, free of barriers, discrimination, and subsidies. To this end, the U.S. government has devoted fifty years of unrelenting effort" (in Scott and Lodge, eds., 1985:301). It is important to distinguish in principle between protectionism and a defensive trade strategy, though it is often difficult to do so in practice. Whereas protectionism is the deliberate policy of excluding foreign competition, defensive trade strategies, like antidumping laws, may coexist easily with a substantial degree of free trade. Offshore sourcing, based on cheap labor in the countries of the Third World substituting for expensive labor in the U.S., immediately ran into this problem. As far as the TNCs were concerned, competition from Europe and the emerging countries of Asia and Latin America was making offshore sourcing necessary to maintain profitability and employment at home. For the U.S. labor movement, any foreign competition based on cheap labor was unfair, and since the 1960s it has continually campaigned against offshore sourcing on the grounds that it caused the loss of U.S. jobs.

There has been sufficient pressure from the labor movement and public opinion on the question of the relationship between cheap imports and job losses in the U.S. to necessitate a defence of offshore sourcing and the practice of direct foreign investment. The idea of "production sharing" or "coproduction" had been floating around the offices of the more sophisticated TNCs and their friends during the 1960s, and it was first popularized to the corporate masses in the pages of the *Wall Street Journal* in 1977 by Peter Drucker.[8] "Production sharing" is based on the simple idea that the interests of both the First World and the Third World are best served if each concentrates on those parts of the production process for which it is most suited. At this point in history, and for the forseeable future, the countries of the First World are best suited to provide the high tech requirements of modern production and the science based services that keep the wheels of international trade turning, i.e., high skill jobs and capital intensive operations. The rest of the world, and particularly the NICs and near NICs, would assemble the high tech components and materials produced by their "coproducers" in the advanced industrial societies. The Third World, thus, was to specialize in the low to medium skill and labor intensive operations. In this way global production would be "shared" to the mutual benefit and satisfaction of all.

One further factor in the offshore sourcing equation, that strengthens the case for "production sharing" very considerably, is items

[8]

806.30 and 807.00 (806/807) of the Tariff Schedule of the United States (TSUS). Item 806.30 permits the export, processing and reentry into the U.S. of any nonprecious metal article of U.S. origin for further processing, with duty levied only on the value of the processing carried out abroad. This accounts for a very small proportion of U.S. manufactured imports. The value of imports under 807 is much more significant. Item 807 comprises:

> Articles assembled abroad in whole or in part of fabricated components, the product of the United States, which (a) were exported in condition ready for assembly without further fabrication, (b) have not lost their physical identity in such articles by change in form, shape, or otherwise, and (c) have not been advanced in value or improved in condition abroad except by being assembled and except by operations incidental to the assembly process such as cleaning, lubricating, and painting . . . [are liable to] . . . A duty upon the full value of the imported article, less the cost or value of such products of the United States. (United States International Trade Commission [USITC] 1986:82).

Put simply, goods assembled abroad from U.S. components could be brought back into the U.S. with duty only on the value added, mainly the (cheap) labor and overhead costs. Items 806/807, in effect since September 1962 but derived from similar provisions in the Tariff Act of 1930, were not specifically legislated to promote either offshore sourcing or "production sharing," but they have facilitated these trends along the U.S. border, through a process that I shall label the "maquila effect." This has come to occupy a central place in the reformation of capitalism.[9]

## The "Maquila" Effect: Assembling for Development

The main problem for U.S. manufacturers operating in Asia is, obviously, logistical. It is expensive to ship equipment and components and tiresome for personnel to commute to the Far East. In the 1960s, many U.S. companies began to buy their materials and components in Asia, and in Japan and in the East Asian "gang of four" they found willing and capable suppliers. This meant that the advantages of 806/807 were lost to the extent that manufacturers assembled goods with materials and components that were not made in the United States. In the 1950s and 1960s, the wage differentials between Asia and the U.S. for assembly and similar work were so substantial that the loss to compliance with 806/807 was vastly outweighed by the savings in production costs.[10] Some logistical problems remained, however. For many executives and technicians, the romance of the East wore off after a few trips, and for some items the lag time between production and delivery to the U.S. market became problematic.

Mexico introduced an export oriented assembly industry program in 1965 to encourage foreign firms to build factories along the U.S.-Mexico border. For U.S. companies, this would simplify the logistics of supplying U.S. equipment, materials, and components, and reduce costs by taking full advantage of items 806/807. The Mexican factories were first identified as "in-bond" plants, but they have become better known by their Spanish name, the *maquiladoras* (or, in the abbreviated form used in this book, maquilas). In colonial times, the *maquila* was the portion of flour that the miller kept after grinding the corn. The U.S. companies provide the corn (for example, cut cloth or electronic components), Mexico keeps its portion (U.S. dollars changed into pesos for wages and production costs), and the assembled goods (garments or TVs or auto parts) return to the U.S., sometimes for sale to maquila workers who regularly spend part of their wages in the United States. The Mexican government expected (or hoped) that the maquilas would be buying local materials and components where these were available. In the early 1970s, the maquila strategy was extended to other parts of the country and can now be found all over Mexico.[11]

Foreign investment in Mexico has been very substantial since the late nineteenth century. Though its foreign investment regime has always been considered to be on the "strict" side, this has not prevented massive U.S., British, and, latterly, European and Japanese investment in a wide variety of Mexican industries.[12] The maquila program was specifically designed to make foreign investment easy and painless, particularly for U.S. companies. Fernández (1977: 134) reports that the idea came from Mexican Treasury Secretary Campos Salas who had seen U.S. assembly plants in the Far East and realized the potential of Mexican labor on the border. He did not advocate the creation of EPZs on the Taiwan or South Korean models, but saw the strategy in a more regional context. What was needed was not a few foreign currency earning enclaves providing some low-level assembly jobs for the unemployed of Tijuana or Juárez, but rather a development and industrialization strategy in which the maquilas could play a catalytic role in the takeoff of the whole border region.

The connection between the maquilas and the reformation of capitalism is precisely that an important group of TNCs based in the United States gradually came to see that the opportunities offered by the maquila industry were both typical in terms of the global embryonic reformation of capitalism (like the EPZs in east Asia) and also unique in terms of the interests of particular TNCs in a position to exploit the logistical advantages of the U.S.-Mexico border region. The embryonic reformation of capitalism can be perceived in both quantitative and qualitative terms. Technological changes in processes of production in the advanced industrial countries and changes in the political economy of foreign trade and investment in both First and Third World countries are beginning to alter the ways in which global capitalism works, albeit in an as yet quite limited fashion. The qualitative effects of the ELIFFIT strategy as expressed in the existence of export processing zones are far greater than the quantitative impact that they presently have in the economies of most countries. The concrete manifestations of the globalization of capital are apparent in the export oriented assembly zones, but their effects are being felt much more widely in politics and culture (for example, through *comprador* groups and consumerism), as well as in the sphere of economics.

Most international trade and investment is still conducted among the countries of the capitalist center and near center. However, the proportion of world exports of manufactured goods coming from the developing countries has increased rapidly over the last 20 years. In 1963, the developing countries accounted for only 4.3 percent of the world's manufactured exports; by 1985 this had risen to 16 percent (calculated from World Bank 1988). Almost two thirds of these exports go to the advanced industrial societies, the United States being the most important market for some of these products. An increasing proportion of U.S. imports of manufactured goods from the Third World is a result of offshore production of one type or another. The role of the U.S. Tariff Code in the growth of the assembly part of these manufactures has been substantial.

Between 1970 and 1987, total U.S. imports increased ten-fold, from about $40 billion to $400 billion, but imports under 806/807 increased more than thirty-fold, from about $2 billion to over $68 billion. In this period, 806/807 imports increased from 5.5 percent to about 17 percent of *total* U.S. imports, and from under 10 percent to around 20 percent of U.S. *manufactured* imports. According to the USITC (1986:84), this upward trend is likely to continue. Similarly, some GSP imports are a direct result of "production sharing" and, under the Multifiber Arrangement, cloth can be manufactured abroad, cut in the U.S., exported for making up, and reimported for final sale in the U.S. with reduced tariffs. "Production sharing" now constitutes a significant part of U.S. manufactured imports. The value of the

*Table 1.1*
Mexico's share of U.S. 806/807 imports, 1965–1987.

| YEAR | 806/807 IMPORTS TOTAL | 806/807 IMPORTS MEXICO | MEXICAN PERCENT OF 806/807 IMPORTS | 806/807 AS PERCENT OF MANUFACTURED IMPORTS |
|------|------|------|------|------|
| 1965 | 577 | 3 | 0.52 | 5.5 |
| 1968 | 1,432 | 73 | 5.10 | 7.4 |
| 1970 | 2,208 | 219 | 9.92 | 4.9 |
| 1976 | 5,722 | 1,135 | 19.84 | 9.5 |
| 1980 | 14,017 | 2,342 | 16.66 | 12.0 |
| 1984 | 28,573 | 4,808 | 16.83 | 13.8 |
| 1986 | 36,497 | 6,450 | 17.67 | 13.7 |
| 1987 | 68,549 | 8,689 | 12.68 | 2000/(est.) |

NOTE: 806/807 figures are in millions of dollars.
SOURCES: USITC data; *Statistical Abstract of the United States,* various years.

U.S. product in these 806/807 imports (the nondutiable value), has remained around 25 percent of the total, although imports from Mexico under 806/807 have always had a much higher proportion of U.S. product (around 50 percent).

As table 1.1 shows, Mexico's rise from 806/807 obscurity to prominence began in the late 1960s. In 1965, Mexico provided less than one percent of total 807 imports, rising to five percent by 1968 (Ericson 1970:36). By 1976 it provided almost 20 percent. Although Mexico's share slipped in the 1980s, in 1986 it was second only to Japan, and well ahead of any other Third World country.[13] Mexico's product mix in the early 1970s was dominated by garments, but in the 1980s it became more varied, with electronic and electrical goods, auto parts, and office machines and parts all prominent. Grunwald (in Grunwald and Flamm 1985: table 4–4) shows that in 1970–71, out of 16 806/807 product categories, Mexico was the number one supplier in only 3 (semiconductors and parts, textiles, electric circuit equipment). By 1980, Mexico was the primary supplier in no fewer than 12 product categories. If we section out the two main industrial branches, textiles and apparel (T&A) and machinery and equipment (M&E), the pivotal role of 806/807, GSP, and Mexico's place in global assembly, is apparent. In 1985 T&A and M&E accounted for over 20 percent of U.S. imports, compared with 14 percent in 1976. GSP plus 806/807 in T&A and M&E was around 25 percent of the total imports of these two sectors. In M&E, now the leading edge of the maquila industry, Mexico's part is most clearly seen. In 1985, Mexico accounted for 15 percent of all 806/807 M&E imports to the

U.S. For the U.S., the most significant fact is that over half of the dollar value of these imports was duty free, reflecting the heavy use of U.S. materials and components, compared with the average duty free value under 806/807 of countries other than Mexico of less than one quarter. In dollar terms, "production sharing" in Mexico utilized more than twice as much U.S. materials and components than in other countries.

Offshore production, transfer pricing, production sharing, locational choices in EPZs, and international trade incentives like 806/807 and GSP, can be organized into a relatively coherent Third World development strategy, albeit emanating from external and hardly disinterested sources. The reformation of capitalism is the TNC-led response to the problem of creating development in the Third World. Its corollary, the strategy of "export-led industrialization fuelled by foreign investment and technology," is the Third World response to the global reformation of capitalism. The "maquila effect" is the set of consequences at the economic, political, and ideological levels of the ELIFFIT strategy, manifest in the relations between the transnational corporations of the capitalist core and the countries of the Third World. While the economies of the countries of the Third World are still very much dominated by production for the home market, whether by domestic or foreign owned companies, political and economic elites in these countries are becoming increasingly locked into the global capitalist system. Mexico, a country traditionally dominated by a high degree of political and economic nationalism, is a good test case for this proposition. Though "production sharing" accounts for a small proportion of First World imports, these are concentrated in some of the most important manufacturing sectors, and there are powerful forces in the First World whose interests are bound up with the ELIFFIT strategy. Because the U.S. is still the leading capitalist power, and the reformation of capitalism has gone as far in the maquila industry along the U.S.-Mexico border as anywhere else, it is appropriate to label this phenomenon the "maquila" effect, inside and outside Mexico.

There are three main categories of actors involved in the reformation of capitalism. They are the capitalist class, the state and quasistate functionaries, and the working class. These are labels of convenience based on fundamental theoretical and political choices about how all industrial and industrializing societies are organized. Many groups in capitalist societies do not neatly fit into one or another of these categories, but the basic framework, the metatheory, can survive as long as the anomalies do not swamp the regularities. The concept of the "triple alliance" of the TNCs, the host state bureaucracy, and the local comprador bourgeoisie (see Evans 1979), helps to make the class issues of exactly who benefits from foreign investment and who pays the costs quite specific. It is difficult to avoid the tendency to reify the capitalist class in the abstractions of TNC, comprador bourgeoisie, and state bureaucracy, while trying to construct a theoretical explanation of why things happen and why people act in patterned and predictable ways.[14] Genuine representatives of the laboring masses are usually conspicuous by their absence. This framework raises many eminently researchable questions for which Mexico provides rich mines of information and theoretical promise. Wherever we find the ELIFFIT strategy at work, we also find an alliance between transnational capital, the host state bureaucracy, and a comprador bourgeoisie which produces the class that is mainly responsible for the reformation of capitalism at the local level.

Along the U.S.-Mexico border, the maquila industry—the local manifestation of the reformation of capitalism—is directed by a specific version of the triple alliance. The members of the capitalist class, those who own and/or control the maquilas, are divided into several groups, and while their interests usually coincide, they do not always do so.[15] These groups are the major transnational corporations, those that have investments in many foreign countries; and those who have investments in Mexico or one or two other countries and can be regarded as TNCs only in a formal sense. There are also many small and a few large Mexican capitalists who run maquilas, sometimes independently, but often in joint ventures with U.S. capital. These compose the comprador bourgeoisie insofar as they see their best interests served by their continued alliance with foreign capital, though this does not necessarily mean that their nationalism is compromised in any way. There is also a very important group of people who operate within the maquila industry without owning maquilas in the normal fashion. They typically offer a variety of subcontracting or legal services to those manufacturers who wish to use a maquila, but do not wish to own one directly. There are also many individual professionals who gain a large part of their livelihoods from serving the needs of the maquila industry. These groups help people to take advantage of the maquilas, and because they do it for private profit, I label them "private facilitators."

State and quasistate bureaucracies operate on both sides of the border. Originally, the Mexican government administered the maquila program, like most other entities in Mexico, from Mexico City, but recently there has been a significant measure of decentralization. This has given the local representatives of central government and the representatives of the governments of the separate states more autonomy in their dealings with the maquila industry. At the local level, in communities on both sides of the border, there are numerous organizations devoted to industrial development in general, and the progress of the maquilas in particular. Though the maquila industry has no legal status in the U.S., it has many powerful supporters among government officials, in chambers of commerce, and affiliated industrial development agencies which are usually part funded with public money. Their counterparts on the Mexican side are often straightforward agencies of the local state. Maquila associations are quasipublic bodies through their connection with the National Maquila Association and the National Association of Transformation Industries (CANACINTRA), a statutory body that is a major political forum provided by the state for the expression of the interests of Mexican private capital. These groups are more or less committed to the continuation and expansion of the maquila industry, and I label them "public facilitators." The common border naturally gives the triple alliance that runs the maquila industry a quite distinctive character, and the activities and energy of the private and public facilitators help to explain the extraordinary growth of the industry. The triple alliance in other Third World countries not contiguous with the U.S. will clearly differ to the extent that this unique "border" phenomenon is absent, but it will be composed of similar elements.

The work force of the maquila industry is mostly female. Though this is unusual for manufacturing industry as a whole anywhere in the world, it is very common for the export oriented assembly industries of the Third World (see Lim 1985). Issues of gender and the maquila labor force are intrinsically linked along the U.S.-Mexico border. The labor force of the maquila industry is a creation of the foreign investment that has taken place as mediated through the patriarchal structures that dominate Mexico, like all other countries, though not necessarily in the same way. The fact that export assembly industries tend to employ mainly young women is well known, though most of the literature merely records it without exploring its significance in any detail (for example, Frobel et al. 1980). A growing volume of feminist theory and research, however, is beginning to demonstrate that, far from being a byproduct, the sexual division of labor and the changing relations of patriarchy are fundamental components of some new tendencies in capitalism (see Nash and Fernández Kelly eds. 1982; Lim 1985). The argument to be advanced here is that the reformation of capitalism simultaneously produces a new sexual division of labor and reproduces a traditional sexual division of labor, often in contradictory ways. The prospects for development itself may, in some cases, hinge on the ways in which patriarchal social relations, particularly those surrounding the sexual division of labor, will change. In this sphere, as in others, there is substantial potential for conflicts between the forces promoting foreign investment and those resisting it. This question will be taken up again specifically in chapters 8 and 9, when some conclusions about the developmental effects of the maquilas are discussed.

## The Maquila Effect and Development Theory

The relationship between development and foreign investment has been characterized in several ways, but the one that is most useful for our purposes is the debate surrounding the controversial question of dependency. There are many excellent critiques of the idea of dependency and how it has been used and misused in the development literature.[16] Here I wish to use the term in a specific and dispassionate sense to refer to the differential power relations that exist between two formally or informally contracting parties when foreign investment takes place. Of particular interest is the case where a transnational corporation invests in a Third World country. Any dependency that is created is the result of two quite specific factors that presently obtain in the global economy. First, there are many more sites for low-cost offshore assembly and fabrication than there are TNCs wishing to go overseas. Second, large (and even some relatively small) TNCs in specialized market niches may exert control of global production and distribution in ways that those in Less Developed Countries (LDCs) cannot hope to match. It is a long way from these two quite specific considerations to a generalized theory of dependency of the poor country on rich country type. What I am suggesting here is something far more restricted in order to tap the relationship between TNCs and those they impact in the LDCs in which they invest. One outcome of such a relationship has been conceptualized as "dependent development" (see Evans 1979), and this book sets out to investigate the potential for dependent development to be reversed, a process that has been termed "dependency reversal" (Doran et al. eds 1983). This is a crucial test of the developmental effects of transnational capital in the Third World insofar as progressive development will only take place when the needs and interests of the populations of the LDCs begin to displace the needs and interests of the TNCs and their local allies—that is when dependency reversal begins to displace dependent development. The issue for the reformation of capitalism is whether specific foreign investments strengthen or weaken global capitalism in its struggle to maintain its hegemony over competing forces, and whether First World TNCs can maintain their hegemony over the Third World countries who presently depend upon them. This initial

[16]

formulation clearly leaves many vital questions hanging, principally the class struggle in the LDCs, the logic of transnational capital's organization of global production, and conflicts between the leading capitalist powers.

In order to approach these questions concretely I have selected four countries for detailed study, and this book focusses on one of them—Mexico.[17] Mexico has for some time been a prime location for U.S. foreign investment. While less than 3 percent of Mexican firms are foreign owned or controlled, more than 30 percent of Mexican manufactured exports derive from them, and they are principally U.S. companies (as reported in *La Jornada*, 18 June 1985:11). This gives the TNCs a considerable implicit power on questions of Mexico's foreign trade. TNCs, with some notable exceptions, do not instruct foreign governments how to act, but rather rely on more subtle methods to secure and advance their interests. To hold and extend foreign direct investment, the host government must ensure that the investment climate, as defined by the TNCs, is favorable, i.e., conducive to the production of maximum easily repatriated profits. Host governments are not, of course, constantly being forced to act against their better judgements due to TNC pressure. Where they can, TNCs in countries like Mexico tend to influence the limits of host government action in indirect ways.[18]

The interests of TNCs and their local agents (the comprador bourgeoisie) frequently come into conflict with the interests of the indigenous capitalist class. As far back as the Porfiriato, the Mexican government was criticized for favoring foreign owned over domestically owned industry in the allocation of scarce resources, and such criticisms continue to the present.[19] The maquila industry was introduced along the geographically remote northern border and did not seem to pose much of a threat to Mexican national industry. However, when it was extended to the rest of Mexico and began to be more important in Mexico's strategy of industrialization and development, serious questions were asked about the contribution that the maquilas could make to national development. What started out as a set of economic zones, became something much more. The maquilas were established to create jobs and earn foreign currency like all other economic zones, but they were in time transformed into strategic centers with the potential to stimulate development throughout the regions in which they were located and, ultimately, throughout the whole country. The criteria on which their success or failure could be properly judged had to change with the change in their status. Though the precise ways in which this happened in Mexico were distinctive due to its unique proximity to the U.S., the phenomenon is not uncommon in the Third World. The analysis of dependency reversal is predicated on the assumptions of a prior dependency and criteria for measuring nondependent development. Therefore, it is necessary to generate a method to evaluate such zones and, by implication, foreign investment in the Third World in general.

## From Economic Zones to Development Zones

In their book *Territory and Function*, Friedmann and Weaver demonstrate the salience of regional planning for development. They show how the doctrines of growth poles which captured the imagination of academics and planners alike from the 1960s proved to be, in their own no nonsense words, "quite useless as a tool for regional development" (1979:175). Foreign investment has to go somewhere, and from the 1960s onwards, some of it that flowed to Third World countries was directed into specially constructed zones on the basis of these apparently useless doctrines. Even relatively large investments produced few "spread" or "trickle down" effects in the economies of the host countries. The growth of some indigenous subcontracting industries in the East Asian "gang of four" are exceptions rather than the rule.

The study of "economic zones" is important because they have often been the physical expressions of industrial development policies in Third World countries; and they have invariably been set up to attract foreign investment. They have always tended to concentrate the effects of the global capitalist system in a particularly intense manner. For example, in the EPZs the profitability of the TNCs operating within them often actually depends on their degree of intracorporate global integration. Thus, "spread" effects or "trickles down" might interfere with the corporate plan, inhibit transfer pricing, and eventually reduce the rationale for such investment. Foreign investment often does bring economic growth in the sense of increased economic activity, and foreign trade is said to increase, irrespective of the balance between exports and imports, as long as its volume increases. What EPZs have failed to do, with few exceptions, is to transform this economic growth into development. In order to explain why this is the case and to show how it might be changed, it is necessary to examine further the concept of "economic zone" and to relate it to the problems of how the reformation of capitalism in some ways makes it more difficult —and in other ways less difficult—for Third World countries to embark on genuine development paths. The concept of "development zone"

[18]

denotes the successful transition of an economic zone to a status where it begins to have genuine developmental effects for the region in which it is located. The connection with the "maquila effect" is that the criteria for this transition specify how export oriented assembly zones could work in practice to produce economic growth and development. The connection with the reformation of capitalism is that capital is sometimes forced to give opportunities for genuine development to sustain its own interests. In this sense, capitalism might be sowing the seeds of its own destruction in order to survive.

The criteria for measuring the extent to which an economic zone is becoming a development zone test dependency reversal under the actually existing conditions of the reformation of capitalism. They are intended as a concrete contribution to development policy and a theoretical contribution to the fierce arguments surrounding development. A methodology to evaluate development effects is necessarily a normative exercise, though it need not be an arbitrary one. International comparisons of the developmental effects of foreign investment, particularly in "maquila like" zones, have generated a methodology based on a set of criteria both logically and sociologically related to a general theory of development and underdevelopment. The "maquila effect" originates from the Mexican experience, but the phenomena it conceptualizes are universal effects of the global reformation of capitalism in its relations with the countries of the Third World. This methodology is intended to give the capacity to decide concretely where an export oriented assembly zone is in the process of transformation to a "development zone." There are six dimensions along which the developmental success or failure of a zone can be measured:

1. **Linkages**. The share of imports (backward) of a firm's inputs and the share of exports (forward) of a firm's products that come from and go to the host economy are its linkages. The greater the extent of backward linkages (raw materials, components, services) and the greater the extent of forward linkages (sales to intermediate goods industries) achieved with the host economy, then the more likely is the creation of a development zone.[20] ("Exports" of finished consumer goods to the host economy are emphatically excluded from forward linkages as used here.)

2. **Retention of foreign exchange**. The more value added and the higher the level of foreign currency retained in the host economy, the more likely is the creation of a development zone.

[19]

3. **Upgrading of personnel**. The greater the proportion of indigenous to expatriate managers, technicians, and highly trained personnel, the more likely is the creation of a development zone.

4. **Genuine technology transfer**. The greater the degree of genuine technology transfer in contrast to technology relocation, the more likely is the creation of a development zone.

5. **Conditions of labor**. The more favorable the day-to-day conditions of work are for the labor force in relation to prevailing conditions in the rest of the host society, the more likely is the creation of a development zone.

6. **Distribution**. The more equitable the distribution of the costs and benefits between foreign investors, competing strata among the local population, and the host government, the more likely is the creation of a development zone.[21]

These six criteria for the evolution of a development zone are not all or nothing conditions, but continua on six constantly changing spectra. Linkages, foreign currency, upgrading of local personnel, technology, conditions of labor, and distribution of benefits, therefore, can all have positive or negative values in consequence of the policies that are put to work to produce regional development. In the worst case, existing backward and/or forward linkages might be destroyed as a result of the creation of an economic zone, currency retention might decline, local skills might be lost, local technology might be displaced, the exploitation of labor might intensify, and distribution might become more inequitable than before. This would mean that there is no development zone being created however much "economic growth" (for example, rising GNP per capita or increasing foreign trade), and thus no development. Under such circumstances, the problems of development in the region in question and, by implication, in the whole country, might be expected to intensify.

The neutral case, where there is little change in the criteria, signifies that there may exist the potential for the evolution of a development zone but that changes in policy and practice are required to bring out the potential. The positive case, where all the criteria are improving, speaks for itself. Clearly, the criteria may change at different rates over time and space, and the substantive problems that this methodology throws up principally involves such questions.

This chapter has set out the theoretical objectives of the book. Underlying what follows is the contention that the reformation of capitalism is slowly gathering pace, and that as a strategy for solving some new problems in the relations between the countries of the capitalist center and the Third World it operates through the "maquila effect." As a case study of the Mexican maquila industry, the book has two substantive goals. The first is to document the actual history of the maquila industry from its modest beginnings in the mid-1960s to its present position, namely the second largest source of foreign exchange earnings for Mexico after petroleum and a major provider of one category of imports to the most important consumer market in the world. This will involve a study of maquilas, their workers, managers, and owners in the main maquila centers in Mexico, and an examination of the effects that the industry has had on each of these places and on their U.S. counterparts on the other side of the border.

The second goal is to begin to evaluate what the maquila industry means for Mexico, particularly as a development strategy. This implies two main questions, namely how does the actual growth of the industry measure up to the stated objectives of the Mexican government over time? And, do these stated objectives constitute a viable development strategy? I shall attempt to unravel the complex issue of whether or not the maquilas have improved the developmental prospects for Mexico as a whole, for its border communities, and for the U.S. and its border communities. Of course, everything has its costs and its benefits (real and/or imagined), and the maquila program is no exception. This is the point of the methodology for measuring costs and benefits, the six criteria introduced to help reach concrete conclusions about the overall worth of such development strategies as well as the particular costs and benefits they may have for different interest groups in each of the affected communities. The communities in this case are not only the Mexican and U.S. towns strung out along a two thousand-mile border stretching from the Pacific to the Gulf of Mexico, but many other communities in the rest of Mexico and the United States. However, it is along the border that the "maquila effect"—the clearest illustration of the reformation of capitalism—is to be found.

## Notes

1. The literature on this is enormous. Good places to start for data and discussion are the quinquennial *Survey* of the United Nations Centre on Transnational Corporations (1988) and the World Bank's annual *World Development Report* (1976 to the present).

2. The other two worlds were, of course, the industrially advanced capitalist countries, the First World, and the communist states of eastern Europe, the Second World. A Fourth World of very poor countries has recently been added.

3. The NIDL thesis has been widely criticized (see, for example, Cor-

bridge 1986:146–155). While acknowledging its seminal contribution, I am attempting to move beyond it and elaborate the "new stage in the evolution of the world capitalist system" of Grunwald and Flamm.

4. There are several theoretical frameworks within which these developments have been located. Leading the field are the "law of uneven development" (Hymer 1975), and the "product life cycle hypothesis" (Vernon 1971). In what follows the reference is mainly to United States based TNCs. Though the U.S. share of global TNC investment has been declining since the 1950s, it is still the largest single foreign investor.

5. There are similar zones in Europe (actually the first modern EPZ was in Shannon, Ireland) and in North America (like the McAllen Foreign Trade Zone on the Texas-Mexico border, see chapter 6 below). The evolution of EPZs is discussed in my 1988a (153–57).

6. For the development of the international electronics industry and the pivotal role of semiconductors see Flamm (in Grunwald and Flamm 1985: chapter 3).

7. For example, the 1982 French stipulation, subsequently rescinded, that all VCR imports be processed at Poitiers, a small town distant from seaports and major retail outlets. This and other cases are discussed in World Bank (1987:133–67).

8. As Drucker later wrote (1980:97), "production sharing has been the fastest-growing segment of international trade these last ten years. Production sharing—a term I coined a few years ago and still not in wide use—is increasingly becoming the dominant mode of economic integration throughout the non-Communist world."

9. Special legislation came into effect in 1984 which provided duty free treatment for imports into the U.S. from the Caribbean—the Caribbean Basin Initiative. This applies the GSP 35 percent local content rule, but up to 15 percent of this "local" content can be of U.S. origin, a clear invitation to "production sharing" and the use of 806/807. The "maquila effect" is not restricted to Mexico.

10. In the late 1960s the average "export processing" worker in Asia was earning the equivalent of about 25 cents per hour, compared to a minimum wage in the U.S. of $1.60 per hour, and a Mexican maquila wage of about 40 cents per hour (see McClelland 1979).

11. This phenomenon of the extension of economic zones (based on incentives to attract foreign investment) from their original localities to include much wider areas is one that is by no means exclusive to Mexico, as my studies of China, Ireland, and Egypt show (1985; 1988a; 1988b).

12. See Wright (1971); Fajnzylber and Martinez (1976); and Unger (1985). Baird and McCaughan (1979:190–205) list "the major foreign investments in Mexico from 1940–1978 by company" from a database compiled by Marc Herold.

13. Japan's lead in the 1980s is almost totally due to the success of Japanese automobiles in the U.S. market. Vehicles and vehicle parts make up over two-thirds of 807 imports by value but only the vehicle parts sector operates in maquilas. The auto industry is a larger part by value of the "production sharing" complex in Mexico than the whole of the maquila industry as such (see Bennett in Rosenthal-Urey, ed., 1986).

14. "Comprador" in this context implies that there is a section of the bourgeoisie that considers the national interest best served in alliance with foreign, usually Westernizing forces (see Sklar 1976).

15. Here I refer only to U.S. and Mexican maquila interests. Though there are other countries, principally Japan, involved in the maquila industry they are, as yet, minor players. The most comprehensive listing of maquilas and their parent companies is Wayne McClintock's annual *Maquiladora Directory*.

16. See, for example, the special issue of the journal *International Organization* 32 (Winter 1978).

17. The other three are China, Ireland and Egypt. A composite work comparing the four cases is in progress. The epistemology on which this attempt to link theory and practice is based is presented in my earlier study (1988c).

18. According to Baird and McCaughan (1975:9), "Any attempt by the Mexican Government to boost corporate taxes has been met with organized resistance of the U.S. *maquiladoras*, through organizations such as the American Chamber of Commerce in Mexico." The Chamber's *Maquiladora Newsletter* confirms this impression.

19. These criticisms come from both academic and business sources. For example, the UNAM economist Blanco Mejia (1983) argues that the maquilas receive preferential treatment over national industries in the areas of labour and fiscal legislation, while Bojorquéz (1987) reports an ex-president of CANACINTRA in Baja California as saying that the state government gives preferential treatment to the maquila industry and that this discriminates against national industry in the state.

20. This formulation borrows from Hirschman (1958:chapter 6). In some combination most of these criteria have been discussed in the maquila context by, for example, Carrillo and Hernández (1985); Grunwald (in Gibson and Corona Rentería 1985); and Dillman (1983). The only originality claimed here is in the ways in which they are combined to evaluate the creation of development zones as a part of the reformation of capitalism.

21. These criteria are all discussed in detail in chapter 9, below. For the application of earlier versions of this methodology to the cases of China and Ireland see my studies (1985; 1988a).

# 2
# The Border Context

In *Where North Meets South*, Herzog (1989:60) nicely understates the central dilemma of the border: "The boundary that separates the two nations today is hardly a logical one in terms of ecology, culture, and history." This illogicality encourages us to look at the two thousand mile international border vertically as well as horizontally. Horizontally, it divides the richest country in the world from a country that is by no means the poorest, but by common consent has been in a state of profound economic and deepening sociopolitical crisis for most of the 1980s. While the ruling party hangs on to power by electoral manipulation, the currency has all but collapsed,[1] real wages are in serious decline,[2] and annual rates of inflation in high double digits appear to be setting in.

However, if we look at the northern border states of Mexico and the southwest border states of the U.S. vertically—Baja California and California; Chihuahua and west Texas; Tamaulipas and south Texas; for example—some of the richest communities in Mexico in per capita income terms (Peach 1984: table XVII) face some of the poorest communities in the U.S. (Peach in Gibson and Corona Rentería 1985: chapter 5). Even the exception of San Diego, a very rich community, is misleading, as the actual border with Mexico is not San Diego proper, which is about 15 miles from Tijuana, but San Ysidro, a poor mainly Hispanic settlement (see Herzog 1989:265–72). For Mexico City and Washington D.C. there is one border, the line that marks the extent of national sovereignty, but it is a line that is closely guarded only on one side. For the border communities, the border exists for some practical purposes, but the borderlands within which they live out their daily lives facilitate and constrain what they do and how they do it. For nation-states, borderland communities are secondary to national borders, in fact and in symbol, while for borderland communities, the borders may be secondary to their borderlands, the economy, polity and culture, the total social formation of that part of their borderland that happens to lie on both sides of the national frontier (see Ross, ed., 1978).

For those of a constitutionalist or nationalist frame of mind, this assertion may seem unconvincing. Nevertheless, as the long and stealthy fingers of the past reach into the immediate present, the international border dissolves and reconstitutes at the levels of economy, polity, and culture. My particular purpose here is to show how the creation of the maquila program and its history to the present were a result of the conjuncture of economic, political, and cultural forces acting horizontally along the border, but vertically through these borderlands. Thus, in order to explain how the maquila industry grew into what it is today, we must pose both national and regional questions and anticipate both national and regional answers.

## One Border, Many Borderlands

Mexico's *frontera norte* has always been as much connected with the southwest borderlands of the U.S. as it has with the rest of Mexico, and it has always been considered to be remote from Mexico City in more than a geographical sense. The borderlands are meaningful sociocultural entities in their own right and their isolation from Mexico City and from Washington is sometimes self inflicted and a true reflection of what the peoples who inhabit them consider to be in their own best interests. This has resulted in a long standing neglect of these regions by their respective central governments, broken spasmodically by commissions, delegations, reports, flurries of official statements, and then further periods of benign and sometimes not so benign neglect. The history of these events and nonevents is, of course, complicated by the successive acts of conquest by which Spain, France, and the United States and its various constituent parts acquired large tracts of northern Mexico, successfully pushed the Texas border to the Rio Grande, and split the Californias to the Pacific ocean.[3]

The U.S.-Mexican borderlands operate through several politico-administrative systems, each with its own degree of autonomy and institutional structures. Below the level of the nation-states, the local states and the so-called twin cities that face each other across the border constitute a variety of interlocking, sometimes complementary and sometimes antagonistic, social systems. It is all too easy to imagine that the whole border is characterized by the same set of economic, political, and cultural forces and that any local peculiarities are swamped by these. There is some truth in this, but there are also distinct social formations that have arisen to give the evolution of the maquila industry rather different characteristics in different areas of settlement along the border. This book focusses on five pairs of border cities in three regions. The cities are Tijuana and Mexicali in Baja California and San Diego and Calexico in California (the Californias); Ciudad Juárez in Chihuahua and El Paso in West Texas (Paso del Norte); Reynosa and Matamoros in Tamaulipas and McAllen and Brownsville in South Texas (the Valley).[4] The most highly developed interior maquila location, Chihuahua City, which is not very far from the border, and other interior sites will also be considered. These areas account for about three-quarters of total maquila employment and plants.

Before the advent of the maquila industry, few of the cities on either side of the border could be characterized as industrial, although the states in which they were located did have some industry. The communities north of the border were for the most part traditionally poor and backward. In his thorough study of the economy of the U.S.-Mexico borderlands from the U.S. side, Hansen shows that, with the exception of San Diego, some of the least industrialized areas in the U.S. are to be found along the border (1981: chapter 3).

The regional distribution of Mexican industry has always been unbalanced. Reynolds has estimated that over half the total value of Mexican manufacturing output from 1930 to 1950 took place in Mexico City and the surrounding central region, while the states of the north and the gulf had the bulk of what remained. Of the 25 cities whose industrial production in 1955 exceeded 250 million pesos (about $20 million), 13 were located in the states of the *frontera norte*, and three of these (Reynosa and Matamoros in Tamaulipas, and Mexicali in Baja California) were actually on the border (1970:171 and chapter 5 *passim*). But the industries on which this was based were raw materials processing for export mainly to the U.S., and those supplying the mines and farms of the region (see Bassols Batalla 1972; Reynolds 1970:174). The backwardness of most of the Mexican borderlands in comparison with the northern and central regions had long been recognized. Despite the obvious benefits from the export trade to the U.S., there was a good deal of consensus in Mexico that it was the dependence of the frontera norte on the rich and powerful neighbor to the north that was at the root of the problem (Xirau Icaza and Díaz 1976). This was a theme that was to exercise the Mexican government with particular force from the 1960s onwards and was to be instrumental in the creation of a series of innovative administrative vehicles to promote border development.

[26]

Mexico introduced the Border Industrialization Program (BIP) in 1965 with the stated intention of creating jobs to replace the employment opportunities that had vanished when the U.S. ended the bracero program (for which see below), by attracting foreign (mainly U.S.) investment and the industrial upgrading that was expected to accompany the jobs. Behind the program lay the hope that the BIP would really work as a full blown regional policy that would turn the traditionally backward and isolated frontera norte, dependent as it was on supplies from north of the border, into a dynamic growth pole for the whole northern region, if not the whole country.[5] What happened on Mexico's northern border throws considerable light on the fate of what was clearly the main force in the global capitalist system in the 1960s, the United States, and why it no longer has such an unambiguous claim to this title today. This can help to clarify some of the complex dynamics of the capitalist system in its unending quest for markets, profits, and the domination of labor. The significance of a global perspective is that it adds to and does not take anything away from the analysis of the Mexican domestic situation. The reformation of capitalism acknowledges national frontiers, but it operates on a global scale.

## *The Antecedents of the Border Industrialization Program*

While the respective governments could do little to control socioeconomic and cultural structures that ignored the international frontier, they sporadically attempted to influence the economies of the borderlands, attempts often resisted by the local populations. In the words of Raúl Fernández: "though the period from 1848 to 1914 is known as one of world peace, it is precisely during this period that the newly formed border between the United States and Mexico became a bloody arena of cultural, racial, economic, political, and military conflict" (1977: 76). Fernández convincingly shows that the roots of these conflicts lay in the clash between the two economic systems that characterized both sides of the border. On the U.S. side a free-wheeling version of the capitalist mode of production was ever extending its hegemonic grasp into the most peripheral areas of the country. This contrasted with the highly protectionist and highly taxed Mexican side, where many daily necessities were more expensive (and remained so until the spectacular devaluations of the 1980s). One consequence of such a situation was widespread smuggling of goods from the cheaper to the dearer marketplace. From the 1860s onwards, the Mexican government, in a series of gestures to try to stop the smuggling, to bring some order into the region, and to tie its northern frontier more closely into the national economy, authorized Free Zones, some form of which eventually extended along the whole of the border. A predictable consequence was to increase illegal economic transactions between the border and the Mexican interior (Fernández 1976: chapter 4, passim.). There was also a substantial migration of Mexicans into the U.S. border states and beyond, and it was partly to stem this flow and to retain population in Mexico that the Free Zone was established. One economic effect of the Free Zone along the border was to inhibit the development of a Mexican industrial base in the region.

A more serious regional development strategy was introduced in 1933 when federal legislation established a Free Perimeter in the towns of Tijuana and Ensenada, and by 1937 the whole of Baja California Norte was declared a Free Zone. In 1939, the Free Zone was further extended to include Baja California Sur and, later, part of Sonora (see Mendoza Berrueto 1982:47–50). The purpose of the Free Zone was to facilitate the supply of products not available locally and too expensive to import from the interior of Mexico. The Zone permitted duty free imports of raw materials and other industrial necessities from the U.S. for local processing. Unsurprisingly, the main result of the Zone was to open up Baja to even greater quantities of U.S. products rather than to stimulate local Mexican producers.

In August 1942, the U.S. and Mexican governments formally agreed to the introduction of a migrant labor mechanism, the bracero program, designed to alleviate labor shortages for agricultural and other workers in the U.S. brought on by the war. For generations Mexicans had come across the border, legally and illegally, to seek work, and by no means only in the border states. The bracero program gave a legal basis to this traditional labor migration (Galarza 1964), and involved over four million Mexican workers until it was unilaterally cancelled by Washington in December 1964 (Briggs 1973:4–6).

The Mexican government realized that the bracero program could not continue forever. As early as 1961 President López Mateos established the *Programa Nacional Fronterizo* (PRONAF), an ambitious scheme to promote social and economic development all along the border and to turn the frontera norte into a veritable "window on Mexico" through which the rich northern neighbour might gaze, presumably with admiration. PRONAF was intended to range widely from the provision of cultural facilities and social services, to the virtual creation of an industrial base along the border. While there were a few laudable concrete results, notably the creation of PRONAF Centers in Tijuana and Ciudad Juárez, across the bridge from El Paso, Texas, there were never sufficient resources either in money or skills to permit the program to take off in any substantial manner. Of the 41 million pesos (about $3.28 million) originally allocated in the early 1960s, almost one-third went to Juárez, Ensenada and Nogales received 16 percent each, and Tijuana, at that time a relatively small border town, only 10 percent (Bermúdez 1968: chapter 4; Mungaray and Moctezuma 1984).

PRONAF revolved around the person of Antonio J. Bermúdez. Born in Ciudad Juárez, Bermúdez had been Director General of PEMEX, the Mexican national oil company, and had served as a senator in the Mexican parliament. A former president of the Juárez Chamber of Commerce in the 1920s, he had personal knowledge of the extent to which U.S. goods flooded the frontera norte market to the detriment of the local Mexican producers and retailers.[6] Bermúdez was approached by President López Mateos at the end of 1960 to head an organization to transform the northern border. From Bermúdez' own account it is clear that the government had a somewhat vague idea of how to go about this perennial and daunting task, even to the extent that the name and location of the new body were left to Bermúdez himself. He rejected "The Frontier Movement" as smacking too much of politics, and chose "El Programa Nacional Fronterizo." The choice of the location of PRONAF headquarters is also interesting and significant: Bermúdez turned down offices in government buildings and chose "the Centre of Industry so as to be near this group, to work along with these people and to further, day by day, the success of the new undertaking; I should thus be working hand in glove with them" (Bermúdez 1968:26). This was a key theme of PRONAF (and, some might add, postrevolutionary Mexico), namely the coordination between government and private enterprise for their mutual benefit. The relationships between public and private sectors have always been extraordinarily complex in Mexico, not least because of the peculiar mix of a corporatist state, a highly protected but fiercely capitalistic domestic bourgeoisie, and an increasingly foreign dominated manufactured export sector (Shafer 1973; Maxfield and Anzaldua M., eds., 1987).

The centers of Mexican economic and political power are far from the frontera norte, and neither economic nor political elites have ever put the border high on their list of priorities. The Bermúdez strategy in locating PRONAF in the Centre of Industry, therefore, was a direct challenge to Mexican business to wake up to the fact that there were substantial profits to be made along the border, but that it was the U.S. and not the Mexican business community that was reaping them. Bermúdez had the facts on his side. In the 1950s, Mexican border communities retained only 40 cents out of each dollar spent by U.S. visitors, i.e., out of each dollar that came into Mexico, on average 60 cents were taken back across the border and spent in the United States. Obviously, some of the cross-border dollars were bound to return to the U.S., but Bermúdez believed that Mexican businesses could capture a much larger proportion of them if they tried harder. Despite the apparent economic stagnation of the border, cross-border monetary transactions were growing rapidly, from about $122 million in 1950 to $354 million in 1959 (Martínez 1978: chapter 7 *passim*).

There was, however, not only a regional motivation behind Bermúdez' strategy for PRONAF, but the issue of national survival. At many points in his book, Bermúdez quotes from a speech by President Díaz Ordaz, delivered in 1965: "Let us make our country economically free so that it may be politically free."[7] The context leaves no doubt from whom Mexico must free herself economically and politically. Since the Mexican-American War in the middle of the nineteenth century, the power of the United States has always been seen as a real or potential threat to the wellbeing of Mexico, and this perception continues to the present day. Nevertheless, there are important strata in Mexican society that are clearly not anti-American or whose anti-Americanism is issue-specific rather than general. Bermúdez cleverly points out that President Johnson had exhorted U.S. citizens at home and abroad to buy U.S. made goods, and that the point of "recovering our frontier market" is precisely to ensure that Mexicans likewise have the opportunity to buy goods made in Mexico.

By the 1960s the Mexican border towns, especially Tijuana and Juárez, had extremely sleazy reputations in the U.S.,[8] and the Mexican authorities were naturally worried that such places were attracting the wrong people and repelling a potentially more lucrative family tourist trade. Accordingly, one part of the PRONAF brief was to clean up the border physically (beautifying the "Gateways to Mexico," by building modern shopping malls and cultural centers), and socially (by eradicating the vice and crime for which many of the border towns were notorious). It was soon obvious that the money available was swamped by the enormity of the tasks and that the funds at PRONAF's disposal would hardly transform one border town, let alone all of them. PRONAF's plans remained largely on paper gathering dust (physically as well as metaphorically, for these borderlands are for the most part desert). PRONAF was quietly allowed to die in 1971, by which time it had been overtaken by the BIP, the framework within which the maquila industry was created.

There were several borderlands initiatives in the U.S., but none had the scope of PRONAF, and most of them were intended to apply to both sides of the international boundary. Prime amongst them was the U.S.-Mexico Commission for Border Development and Friendship, established in 1967 as a result of a meeting in the previous year between the two presidents in Mexico City. Plagued by uncertainties over funding, presumably because the Nixon administration did not feel bound by agreements reached on a rather personal level by President Johnson, it was unable to achieve anything very concrete apart from binational planning commissions in Matamoros/Brownsville and in Juárez/El Paso to work on transportation and environmental problems. The combined effects of "Operation Intercept," an attempt to stop transborder drug trafficking that was bitterly resented in Mexico, and the discontinuation of the Commission in 1970, effectively put an end to these binational commissions. Also, in the 1960s a Border Cities Association was formed by the chambers of commerce on both sides with the purpose of lobbying the respective governments and improving business along the border. Although this particular organization faded out by the end of the decade, informal and, in some cases, formal connections between the Mexican and the U.S. business communities along the border were created during this period, many surviving to the present. Some of these grew into influential economic and political organizations, many concerned with the maquila industry.[9]

Environmental questions frequently created problems along the border. The allocation of the waters of the Rio Grande/Río Bravo del Norte, the river that makes the international boundary from El Paso/Ciudad Juárez to the Gulf of Mexico, is at the root of many of these problems. An International Boundary and Water Commission was established in 1889 to oversee boundary disputes, but its work in recent years has focussed on water and, increasingly, on pollution.[10] Public health has also loomed large in the concerns of border officials. As early as 1903 the authorities in El Paso required all cars crossing the border from Juárez to be fumigated (Bath 1982:379). In the 1940s, a Border Health Association was set up to moniter public health issues between the U.S. and Mexico. This developed into the Pan American Health Organization, based in El Paso/Juárez and, according to Bath, it is beset with problems of lack of resources and credibility in the respective seats of national government.

There have also been attempts in the U.S. to create regional organizations along the border. The most important of these has been the Southwest Border Regional Commission (SBRC), one of the eight "Title V" economic development regions established to provide a vehicle for socioeconomic development in backward areas of the U.S. (Tocups 1980:638ff.). Each of the border states had its own commission, and they worked with the SBRC in identifying projects and in researching development plans. When the Title V Commission was terminated in 1981, the SBRC was replaced by the Governors Southwest Border Regional Commission, which formalized the crossborder contacts that the SBRC had been making with a conference in Ciudad Juárez in June 1980. This was the first time that crossborder diplomacy had been conducted by local rather than central government officials and the meeting was called "historic" in the *New York Times* (Tocups 1980:640). This Commission was supported by the Organization of U.S. Border Cities (a resuscitated version from the 1960s), federally funded from the Commerce Department. From the 1970s onwards, therefore, there were several organizations on the U.S. side of the border devoted to socioeconomic development.

## Developing the Frontera Norte

As PRONAF was being wound down in the early 1970s, several other national and regional organizations in Mexico were established to collect data and to stimulate socioeconomic development along the border. Most influential was the Intersecretarial Commission for the Development of the Northern Frontier and Free Zones, set up in 1971 at a high-level meeting in Nogales attended by President Echeverría, members of the federal government, all the border state governors, the municipal presidents (mayors) of the main border towns and representatives of local and national business and finance. Its purpose was to "bring the border region economically closer to the rest of the country, alleviate the unemployment situation, and encourage the Mexican consumer to shop at home," all unfulfilled aims of PRONAF (Urquidi and Méndez Villarreal 1978:157). Border businesses were given more freedom to import U.S. consumer and capital goods and the duties on these goods sold along the border were reimbursed; there were subsidies to offset federal income tax derived from sales of new goods and the costs of transporting goods to the border for sale; lure items (*artículos gancho*) were introduced; and trusts were created to finance industrial and commercial construction.

Most of these measures were designed to encourage Mexican consumers to spend their money in Mexico and Mexican businesses to make it desirable for them to do so. Merchants in the Mexican interior were offered Tax Exemption Certificates (CEDIS) and freight subsidies to encourage them to supply the border market. Over the whole border, Tamayo and Fernández (1983) estimated that Mexican shopping in the U.S. represented an annual leakage of more than half a billion dollars in the early 1970s. The lure items were intended to bring some of this business back to Mexico by permitting local retailers to import a certain amount of U.S. goods and sell them at a price equal to or less than their cost in the U.S. From the end of 1971 to the beginning of 1974, over 900 million pesos (almost $100 million) worth of lure items were brought into Mexico, over 80 percent of which were consumer goods, and more than half of which were traded in Juárez (Urquidi and Méndez Villarreal 1978:157–59). Research revealed that two thirds of the families in Baja California regularly shopped in the U.S., and that in Tijuana, on average almost 40 percent of monthly family expenditure took place across the border, mostly on food (78 percent) and apparel (16.5 percent). For half the items bought in the U.S., comparable Mexican products were available more cheaply in the local market, so there was obviously a measure of consumer resistance, much encouraged from north of the border, at work in the Tijuana population when it came to buying Mexican goods.[11]

Despite the fact that Baja is a Free Zone and most items are available duty free, Urquidi and Méndez Villarreal (1978:179) are correct to point out that the lure items was poorly thought out strategy because it encouraged smuggling (not that smuggling actually needed much encouragement across a notoriously porous border), the imported goods still had to be paid for in dollars at some point, import oriented consumerism was intensified and, most important, it discouraged the production of local goods to compete with the lure items.

This last shortcoming clearly worried the Mexican government, for it introduced a program in March 1974 to stimulate small and medium sized industry—capital stock, reserves, and undistributed profit less than five million pesos ($400,000)—along the border to produce goods for domestic consumption. The idea was to permit domestic firms to share in the fiscal benefits that the maquilas already enjoyed, mainly duty free import of machinery, materials, and components, with the proviso that the "import duty on raw materials is subsidized only when domestic supplies are inadequate or not competitive in quality, price and delivery."[12] To qualify for these subsidies, firms had to be Mexican owned, the products had to have a minimum of 20 percent local content, and their retail prices could not be higher than the international price. Further, firms who benefited from the program could sell in the rest of Mexico if they could prove that they were not exploiting an artificial advantage and paid the import duties. Up to about 1978, only 33 such applications had been received, of which 13 had been approved, 7 were pending, and 13 had been refused because they failed to meet the criteria (Mendoza Berrueto in Ross 1978:169). It must be concluded that the incentives offered by the small and medium enterprises program were insufficient to stimulate the growth of a domestic industry that could seriously challenge the sales of U.S. goods along the border.

Between 1971 and 1975, there were seven national work meetings for border development to assess the progress of the border program in its various ramifications (Mendoza Berrueto 1982:58). Under President

Echeverría, these meetings were held regularly in border towns and continued to attract the participation of high-level personnel from Mexico City, including the president. They acted as vehicles for the promotion of border policy and ensured ongoing frequent contact between the local elites and those who were making the decisions in Mexico City. These work meetings were not simply talking shops for federal and local government officials to congratulate each other on their administrative initiatives, but they reached out to people active in the border communities themselves. Economic promotion committees were set up to popularize official policy in the border cities, and these committees, by combining representatives of the federal and state governments and private entrepreneurs, seemed at last to be bringing to fruition the vision of PRONAF as expressed by Antonio Bermúdez: "the perfect coordination between government and private enterprise" (Bermúdez 1968:30).

A substantial program of public works along the border was also set in motion under the Echeverría administration. *Ciudades Industriales* (literally "Industrial Cities") and industrial zones were planned in Tijuana, Nuevo Laredo, Ciudad Juárez, Piedras Negras, and Acuna, construction works on the northern border highway and the Benito Juárez transpeninsular highway in Baja California were stepped up, airstrips were built, and many sewage and drinking water projects were inaugurated. In 1972, a program for the construction of commercial centers was started, continuing the work of PRONAF. At the work meeting held in Nuevo Laredo in June 1974, a spokesman for Mexican industry was moved to proclaim that "never in the history of Mexico has so much been done in so little time on behalf of the 8 million Mexicans living in this border zone of our country" (*Mexican Newsletter*, 31 July 1974:4). Nevertheless, the government was fast running out of the resources necessary to fulfil its promises. In 1973, inflation began to rise, and the peso-dollar exchange rate which had been held steady since the 1950s (and, of course, was a continuing incentive to Mexicans along the border to shop in the U.S.), came under intense pressure. This was when the "economic miracle" of the 1950s and 1960s definitely came to an end (Clement and Green 1978) and the country entered the series of painful crises from which it has yet to emerge.

It is not surprising that the marginal border areas would fail to attract special treatment in the distribution of resources under such circumstances, but the flurry of administrative activity that had started with the Nogales meeting of 1971 continued throughout the decade. In 1977, when Echeverría had been succeeded by López Portillo, a new organization, *La Comisión Coordinadora del Programa Nacional de Desarrollo de las Franjas Fronterizas y Zonas Libras del Pais* (CODEF) was established, to indicate that the incoming administration had its own policies for the development of the frontera norte. CODEF operated as a coordinating agency for all the interdepartmental policies that might affect the border (and the Free Trade Zones not on the border) and was intended to reflect the interests of the border in national development planning (Mendoza Berrueto 1982:69ff.). This was exemplified in the inclusion of the principal border towns in the top priority group for industrial decentralization in the National Industrial Development Plan of 1979 (México 1979:153ff.). CODEF also set up economic promotion committees in the main border cities to coordinate planning at the local level. The new president, Miguel de la Madrid, replaced CODEF with a revamped Intersecretarial Commission in August 1983, specifically to implement the border policy outlined in the 1983–1988 National Development Plan. The Commission was placed firmly under the control of the industry ministry (SECOFI) and along with a new set of regulations for the maquila industry promulgated at the same time (to be discussed in the next chapter), represented yet another attempt to develop the frontera norte and to integrate it into the national economy and society.

While all this administrative activity was proceeding, the communities of the border were growing apace. Despite their isolation from the rest of Mexico, the border towns experienced substantial growth in population. Recent data suggest that this has been uneven from place to place along the border, and that the very high growth rates of the 1940s, 1950s, and 1960s may have given way to average rates of growth compared with the rest of Mexico in the 1970s (Peach

Table 2.1

Population growth in Mexican and U.S. border cities, 1940–1980.

| CITY | 1940 | 1950 | 1960 | 1970 | 1980 | 1980: 1940 |
|---|---|---|---|---|---|---|
| Tijuana | 21,977 | 65,364 | 165,690 | 340,600 | 461,254 | 21:1 |
| San Diego | 203,000 | 334,000 | 573,000 | 697,000 | 876,000 | 4:1 |
| Mexicali | 44,399 | 124,362 | 281,333 | 396,324 | 510,664 | 12:1 |
| Calexico | 5,415 | 6,433 | 7,992 | 10,625 | 14,412 | 3:1 |
| Ciudad Juárez | 55,024 | 131,308 | 276,995 | 424,135 | 567,365 | 10:1 |
| El Paso | 96,810 | 130,485 | 276,687 | 322,261 | 425,259 | 4:1 |
| Reynosa | 23,137 | 69,428 | 134,869 | 150,786 | 211,412 | 9:1 |
| McAllen | 11,877 | 20,067 | 32,728 | 37,636 | 68,569 | 6:1 |
| Matamoros | 54,133 | 128,347 | 143,043 | 186,146 | 238,840 | 4:1 |
| Brownsville | 22,083 | 36,066 | 48,040 | 52,522 | 84,997 | 4:1 |
| Mexico (m.) | 19.8 | 26.6 | 34.0 | 48.2 | 66.8 | 3.4:1 |
| U.S. (m.) | 131.7 | 150.7 | 178.5 | 203.3 | 226.5 | 1.7:1 |

SOURCES: Mexican census; *Statistical Abstract of the United States*, various years.

1984). There is a good deal of controversy over whether these earlier high growth rates (high even by booming Mexican standards) simply reflected the position of the border towns as jumping off points for emigration to the United States, or whether the border cities attracted and held population in their own right. Certainly, all the research points to very high in-migration rates for most of the border towns, both from the surrounding rural areas and from much farther afield in central and southern Mexico (see, for example, Corona 1986: especially *Anexo* C). Table 2.1 presents population data for Mexican and U.S. border cities and indicates their growth rates as compared with the national averages.

Two things are clear from table 2.1. First, the populations of the border cities on both sides have increased more rapidly than their respective national populations between 1940 and 1980, but the increases on the Mexican side have tended to outstrip the increases on the U.S. side. Second, the Hollywood image of sleepy border towns in the middle of the desert no longer catches the reality of the main border settlements. Absolute population sizes along the border were in many places in excess of 100,000 from the 1950s onwards. Tijuana, Mexicali, and Ciudad Juárez are now certainly cities of at least one million, and Reynosa and Matamoros are both approaching half a million. One of the goals of PRONAF and the organizations that succeeded it (on both sides of the border) was to improve the social and physical services available to the people living along the border, for it always had been obvious that local resources were entirely inadequate to provide the necessary services. In Mexico—a much poorer country overall than the U.S.—the problem of the main border communities was one of basic poverty and lack of amenities compounded by rapidly growing population, both natural and migratory, that was putting even more strain on the inadequate infrastructures all the time. PRONAF's dilemma, which it never came to terms with, was that the people of Tijuana and Juárez and so on along the border needed housing, clean running water, and sewers rather than beautification schemes and shopping malls.[13] On the U.S. side, although resources were more plentiful than in Mexico, the border communities were among the poorest in the whole of the U.S. Their problems were compounded by the use that Mexican citizens made of their schools, hospitals and social services, and the downward pressure that Mexican labor (legal and illegal) exerted on working class wages. Although Mexican workers and consumers paid a variety of direct and indirect taxes in the U.S., the feeling along the north side of the border was that the federal government derived most of the benefits, while the local communities picked up most of the cost. The fact that almost all of these U.S. border communities had large hispanic minorities (and in some cases hispanic majorities) made for an extraordinarily complex set of social, economic, and cultural transborder forces.

Even though the communities north of the border are very poor, the states in which they are located are not particularly characterized by poverty (see Peach in Gibson and Corona Rentería 1985: chapter 5); the main border communities to the south, on the other hand, are amongst the richest in Mexico, though some of the states in which they are located are not particularly well off.[14] In 1960, the average per capita income of the main Mexican border cities was 135 percent of the Mexican national average (Dillman 1970a:491), and in 1980 it stood at 120 percent of the national average in Nuevo Laredo, 130 percent in Ciudad Juárez, 140 percent in Tamaulipas, and over 150 percent in Baja California and Nogales (Peach 1984: table XVII). Economic opportunities north of the border for most people, and certainly for the most disadvantaged groups, have always been better than those south of the border. That this has traditionally been well known throughout Mexico is shown by the fact that large numbers of people are attracted to the frontera norte, particularly to Tijuana and Ciudad Juárez, both to take advantage of these prosperous cities and to cross the border. The reasons for this migration to and across the border are clear. The scarcity of jobs, low wages, and the steeply rising population that puts pressure on jobs and wages, conspire with Mexican perceptions of U.S. wages to draw people from towns and villages all over Mexico to the border and into the United States. These conditions have led to "an ever-expanding absolute number of persons living in abject poverty, who are presumably candidates for migration" (Evans and James 1979:9).

Minimum wage legislation was first introduced into Mexico in 1917, mainly as a device by the public and the private sector to ensure the creation of the maximum number of jobs at the minimum level of wages. Accordingly, increases in the minimum wage have more often been attempts to restore purchasing power to offset inflation than to raise the standard of living of the workers and peasants (Macarthy 1983). Table 2.2 illustrates the movement of minimum wages from the 1960s to the present. Until 1980, the highest minimum wage rates were to be found in Baja California, with Juárez some distance behind, and Nogales and the maquila locations in Tamaulipas a little lower. In 1964, the top daily minimum wage for industrial workers could be found in Tijuana and Mexicali (32 pesos), followed by Juárez (24.5), while in Mexico City it was 21.5 pesos and 19 pesos in Guadalajara. The national average daily minimum wage in 1964 was 16 pesos, but along the border the average was 24.4 pesos, a differential of about 50 percent (a national average of not quite $1.30 per day, and a border average of $1.95 per day). By 1980, devaluation, inflation, and annual increases had brought the national average up to 136 pesos per day, and the border average up to 160, a differential of less than 20 percent (see Van Waas 1981: table 10,

*Table 2.2*
Daily minimum wages for selected wage zones in pesos, 1964–1988.

| YEAR | JUÁREZ | TIJUANA | NATIONAL AVERAGE |
|------|--------|---------|------------------|
| 1964 | 24.58 | 32.00 | 16.00 |
| 1966 | 29.00 | 35.70 | 18.69 |
| 1968 | 31.90 | 40.00 | 21.55 |
| 1969 | 36.00 | 46.00 | 24.91 |
| 1972 | 42.30 | 53.85 | 28.20 |
| 1973 (Sep) | 49.90 | 63.55 | 34.56 |
| 1974 | | | |
| (Jan) | 57.90 | 69.60 | 39.38 |
| (Oct) | 70.60 | 74.90 | 48.04 |
| 1976 | | | |
| (Jan) | 83.00 | 99.80 | 50.64 |
| (Oct) | 102.30 | 122.80 | 72.18 |
| 1977 | 111.30 | 133.80 | 79.37 |
| 1978 | 125.00 | 147.00 | 90.50 |
| 1979 | 143.00 | 162.00 | 116.00 |
| 1980 | 160.00 | 180.00 | 136.62 |
| 1981 | | 210.00 | 178.87 |
| 1982 | | | |
| (Jan) | | 280.00 | |
| (Nov) | | 364.00 | |
| 1983 | | 455.00 | |
| 1984 | | | |
| (Jan) | | 680.00 | |
| (July) | | 816.00 | |
| 1985 | | | |
| (Jan) | | 1,060.00 | |
| (July) | | 1,250.00 | |
| 1986 | | | |
| (Jan) | | 1,650.00 | |
| (July) | | 2,065.00 | |
| (Oct) | | 2,480.00 | |
| 1987 | | | |
| (Jan) | | 3,050.00 | |
| (April) | | 3,660.00 | |
| (July) | | 4,500.00 | |
| (Oct) | | 5,625.00 | |
| 1988 | | | |
| (Jan) | | 7,765.00 | |
| (March) | | 8,000.00 | |

NOTE: In 1980 the differentials were abolished. The rate was temporarily fixed in March 1988.
SOURCE: Mexican national commission for minimum wages: Mexico City.

based on data from the *Comisión Nacional de los Salarios Mínimos*). Van Waas has calculated the minimum wage weighted by the percentage of economically active population in each zone, and on this basis the differentials between the whole country and the border reduce even further, from about 40 percent in 1964 to barely 16 percent in 1980. At this point the differentials between the main border maquila sites and Mexico City were abolished. With the rapid increases in devaluation, inflation, and minimum wages of the 1980s, the differentials between the border and the rest of the country floated around 20 percent until 1986 when the wage zoning system was restructured. This was brought about by the need to adjust wages more often to cope with inflation of over 100 percent and a reduction in the value of the peso from 300 to the dollar at the end of 1985 to 1,000 to the dollar in 1987.

Mexico is divided into three wage zones. Zone 1, at the lowest wage level, consists of most of the 28 out of the 30 states of Mexico; zone 2 covers Guadalajara, Monterrey and a few other cities. Zone 3, at the highest level of minimum wages, covers mainly the frontera norte, Baja California (north and south), Juárez, Nogales, Nuevo Laredo, Reynosa and Matamoros, and also Mexico City, Acapulco, and some parts of Veracruz. In the October 1986 minimum wage setting, the general and farm worker daily rate for zone 1 was 2,060 pesos, for zone 2 2,290 pesos, and for zone 3 2,480 pesos. The differentials, therefore, were 20 percent between zones 3 and 1, and 8 percent between zones 3 and 2. Exactly the same differentials were retained for the January 1987 minimum wage settings, with zone 3 increasing to 3,050 pesos per day, zone 2 to 2,820, and zone 1 to 2,535 pesos (*Twin Plant News*, November 1986:43; and January 1987:46). We can conclude from this that differentials between the minimum wage on the border and most of the rest of Mexico will continue, but at a lower rate than before, and that minimum wages on other parts of the border (and in Mexico City and a few other special cases) are being brought into line with those in Baja California, hitherto the area of highest minimum wages in Mexico.

Rises in minimum wages cannot be seen as a victory for labor on the border because the trend of wage increases over the whole country in recent years has been below the rate of inflation, and the rate of inflation on the border has tended to be somewhat higher than the national average. Therefore, wage differentials between the border (plus, from 1981, Mexico City and a few other places) and the rest of the country may not even compensate for the differentials in inflation. Much of the Mexican economy is tied to the economy of the U.S.[15] It is, therefore, not at all surprising that the devaluations of the peso relative to the dollar that began in 1976, continued in 1982, and accelerated dramatically in 1986—as detailed in table 2.3—affected the Mexican economy adversely. The cost to Mexico of its imports

*Table 2.3*
Peso to dollar exchange rates, 1948–1988.

| YEAR | AVERAGE PESOS PER DOLLAR | YEAR | AVERAGE PESOS PER DOLLAR |
|------|--------------------------|------|--------------------------|
| 1948 | 5 | 1980 | 23.0 |
| 1949 | 9 | 1981 | 24.6 |
| 1954 | 12 | 1982 | 57.4 |
| 1965 | 12 | 1983 | 120.7 |
| 1975 | 12.5 | 1984 | 167.8 |
| 1976 | 15.4 | 1985 | 257.0 |
| 1977 | 22.6 | 1986 | 611.4 |
| 1978 | 22.8 | 1987 | 1,421.4 |
| 1979 | 22.8 | 1988[a] | 2,257.0 |

[a] The rate was temporarily fixed at the end of February 1988.
SOURCE: Banco de México (Mexico City).

rose steeply as the international purchasing power of its currency declined and many Mexican firms went out of business because they could no longer afford to import what they needed. The effects of the 1976 devaluation, brought on by the U.S. slump, were to some extent softened by the economic recovery in the United States, and although the border economy was damaged, it recovered fairly quickly. The 1982 devaluations were much more serious, both in absolute loss of value and in terms of the general economic situation. The price of the main Mexican export by value—petroleum—tumbled, and the government had fewer dollars with which to finance imports. Domestic inflation resulted as Mexico strove to keep trading internationally. Along the border the situation tended to be worse than in the interior for the simple reason that the Mexican border communities were all much more tied to the communities in the U.S., economically, socially, and culturally, than those in the interior. The workers, who had spent a good deal of their wages across the border before 1982, were suddenly faced with what was in reality a massive wage cut (in dollars that is), disguised by less massive wage rises in pesos. This forced them and their families to spend a greater proportion of their reduced real income in Mexico in a way that no amount of lure items or tax rebates to Mexican merchants could ever have done. Out of the currency debacle, therefore, has come something of a windfall for Mexican shopping mall developers who have capitalized on this exchange rate induced opportunity to modernize retail trade all along the border. Mexican shoppers continue to come across to U.S. border towns to purchase some foodstuffs and clothes, less than previously but still in substantial numbers, but the U.S. shoppers in the Mexican border towns are shopping for more than touristic items, and many are to be seen in Mexico's new U.S.-style malls buying groceries and apparel. For them, Mexican inflation is generally lagging behind the slide of the peso.

The U.S. merchants who had been selling to Mexican consumers in cities all along the border (much to the chagrin of Mexicans like Bermúdez at PRONAF) saw their trade progressively wiped out as the pesos that their customers offered in exchange for goods were worth fewer and fewer dollars. As one perceptive border scholar has argued, the days of "cheap dollars" for the *norteños* were over (Tamayo, in Gibson and Corona Rentería, eds., 1985: chapter 6). The peso was devalued three times in 1982. It began the year at less than 27 to the dollar and ended the year at around 100. Strict exchange controls were imposed by the government to stop the massive outflow of funds from Mexico into U.S. banks, a trend that had been gathering pace over the preceding years. The combined effects of the exchange controls and the fall in the value of the peso were disastrous for many residents in the U.S. border cities and beyond. From San Diego in the west to Brownsville in the east, retail sales plunged, businesses failed, and unemployment rose (USITC 1986:17–19). The situation was so serious that the Small Business Administration "recognized the peso devaluations as an area disaster and instituted a program of special loans for businesses that had been impacted by the devaluation. Through August 1983 they had approved 590 loans for a total of $45,595,754" (Prock 1983:86–87). Border towns in Texas were worse affected. Unemployment in Texas as a whole increased from 5.9 percent in 1982 to 8.5 percent in 1983, but in Laredo where the retail trade almost collapsed, it increased from 11.0 percent to 27.3 percent; in Brownsville it increased from 11.4 percent to 17.7 percent; and in McAllen the increase was from 14.0 percent to 20.5 percent (Prock 1983:81). The lowest increase in unemployment along the Texas-Mexico border was in El Paso (from 9.2 percent in 1982 to 13.3 percent in 1983). Those who saw a connection between Juárez's booming maquila industry and El Paso's employment base during this difficult period suggested that U.S. border communities could best protect themselves from "exchange rate shocks" by expanding their own manufacturing industries and by encouraging the maquila industry across the border (for example, Davila et al. 1984).

This is, of course, what the public and private maquila facilitators of the border cities had been so assiduously trying to do since the late 1960s when the BIP was getting off the ground. It remains to examine how they went about this task, analyze their successes and failures, and evaluate their impact on Mexico's quest for development and the creation of an industrial economy and society along the border.

# Notes

1. At the beginning of 1982, one U.S. dollar bought about 25 pesos, in 1988 it bought more than 2000 pesos. See table 2.3.

2. In his survey of "the crisis" Cornelius reports that "By the end of 1985, real wages had fallen to mid-1960s levels . . . [and that of a sample survey of workers in Mexico's 16 largest cities] 62 percent had incomes below the official minimum wage" (1986:32).

3. Hall (1986) is an interesting attempt to deal with this in terms of a critical reevaluation of world system theory. For a review of borderlands literature see Stoddard et al. eds. (1983).

4. The other main maquila sites are Nogales (about 50 plants and 22,000 employees in 1988) and Agua Prieta (26 and 6,500), in Sonora; Cd. Acuna (34 and 10,000) and Piedras Negras (25 and 6,000) in Coahuila; and Nuevo Laredo, Tamaulipas (40 and 8,500).

5. Pena (1981:A-10 to A-17) lists more than twenty papers on the frontera norte in the important Mexican journal *Comercio Exterior* in the late 1960s and early 1970s on this theme.

6. As Shafer says in his study of Mexican business, "A lengthy essay could be composed on Mexican business organization efforts over the decades to penetrate the psychology of Mexican preference for foreign goods" (Shafer 1973:300).

7. Bermúdez was so impressed with this sentiment that he circulated it to 500 institutions and businesses (Bermúdez 1968:142ff.).

8. Compare, for example, Demaris (1970), and the eloquent essay by Carlos Monsivais (in Ross, ed., 1978:50–67).

9. As Jamail points out: "in almost every [U.S. border] community there is a group concerned with the maquiladora industry" (in Purcell, ed., 1981:84). *See also* Tocups (1980).

10. There is a considerable literature on these issues. For example, *The Natural Resources Journal* ran special issues on environmental problems along the border in 1977–1978 and 1982.

11. This research, published in *Comercio Exterior* (August 1970), is summarized in Pena (1981:A-60).

12. *Mexican Newsletter* (30 April 1974:3). This government magazine has many useful pieces on border legislation in the 1970s.

13. See the evidence on this from a school principal in Ensenada, quoted by Ugalde (in Ross, ed., 1978:112). It is still true.

14. Both sides of the border generally share the same disadvantages of physical geography (*see* House 1982).

15. This may be decreasing somewhat. In 1979, for example, 68 percent of Mexican exports went to the U.S. and the U.S. accounted for 71 percent of Mexico's imports, while in 1985 the respective figures were 61 percent and 66 percent (Banamex data).

# 3

# Phases of Maquila Expansion

There are several versions of the origins and development of the maquila industry. My own view is that it is most useful to distinguish three phases. The first phase is from the mid-1960s to the crash of 1973–1974; the second is from 1975 to the collapse of the peso in 1982; and the third is from 1982 to the present.[1] While the details of these phases are specific to Mexico and to the frontera norte, the broad processes involved are typical of the reformation of capitalism and the efforts of the TNCs from the capitalist center to deal with their global problems.

## Phase 1

The origins of the maquilas are partly bound up with the PRONAF. Antonio Bermúdez, in his book on the early years of the program, recounts that the PRONAF Advisory Committee, made up of prominent businessmen and bureaucrats, itself set up a committee to study the prospects for border industrialization. Their deliberations eventually led to the commissioning of studies by Arthur D. Little de México (ADL), a firm of industrial consultants specializing in economic development. The gist of these studies was that the brightest prospects for industrial employment along the border lay in manufacturing in Mexico for the U.S. market. In some accounts of the origins of the maquila industry, particularly those from the U.S., Richard Bolin, who conducted the ADL study, is credited with the idea of the maquilas (see, for example, Beebe, 12 March 1987:A-10). Bolin, in fact, claims the idea himself (see below).

On the surface, one would be forgiven for assuming that the ADL studies could not have greatly pleased Bermúdez and others in PRONAF, as they appeared to undermine the goal of recovering the Mexican market for Mexican goods. At that time PRONAF was trying to promote border industry and was involved in such projects as an olive packing plant in Tijuana, a coffee company in Tecate, various factories in Juárez, and a milk products plant in Matamoros (Bermúdez 1968:52–53). All of these supplied goods for the local market and for U.S. customers coming across the border, for example people from south Texas who bought milk in Mexico. In these small ways PRONAF was helping to bring in dollars and stem the flow of Mexican funds across the border. However, Bermúdez and PRONAF were at the same time buying up land for the creation of industrial parks.

In May 1965, Campos Salas of the Ministry of Industry and Commerce (SIC), announced a new scheme to allow the temporary duty free importation of materials and components for assembly and subsequent reexport, on condition that they remained in-bond while in Mexico. From this the label "in-bond industry" came into use. In June 1966, the Ministry of Finance and Public Credit issued a set of rules for the in-bond industry which gave it a quasilegal status (see Davis 1985:23–34; Villalobos C. 1973:5–9).

The origins of the maquila industry are complicated by the prior existence of free zones in various parts of Mexico where the strict rules covering foreign investment were considerably relaxed. The most important of these was in Baja California Norte, and particularly around Tijuana. Ugalde (in Ross, ed., 1978:109–111) argues that U.S. and Mexican influentials with interests in the borderlands kept the free zones in existence and prepared the ground for the maquila industry. Export oriented assembly plants, U.S. owned and sourced, are reported in Tijuana from the 1950s (Mungaray 1983), and there are several claims, not necessarily mutually exclusive, to parenthood of the maquila idea in Mexico. The most popular and widely circulated is that of Campos Salas himself and the crucial event is his tour of the Far East in 1964 where he saw U.S. manufacturing industry in action. By the 1960s, the U.S. was importing substantial amounts of goods assembled in the Far East, often from U.S.-made components. Offshore sourcing and "production sharing" were becoming quite common for U.S. and European TNCs, particularly in the apparel industries and in the newly booming electronics field. Asian producers were increasingly willing and able to provide the materials and components that went into the goods destined for the U.S. market, and logistically it made very good sense to use local materials and components. Such products did not qualify for 806/807 tariff concessions, but with wage costs so low in the Far East compared with the U.S., this did not appear to worry many

U.S. corporations unduly. Nevertheless, all other things being equal, those producers who could take advantage of 806/807 would clearly have a competitive edge. For Mexico, this was an idea whose time had come! On 25 May 1967 Campos Salas was quoted on the front page of the *Wall Street Journal* to the effect that the intention of the BIP was to offer a Mexican alternative to Hong Kong, Japan, and Puerto Rico.

A different account of the origins of the maquila industry involves an attorney in Ciudad Juárez, Javier Álvarez Moreno, who was approached in 1962 by two Boston lawyers on behalf of a U.S. client who wished to utilize Mexico's pool of cheap labor to set up a factory. Álvarez researched the problem and came up with the idea of taking advantage of 806/807 to assemble U.S. parts with cheap Mexican labor for reexport to the United States. Eventually his idea came to the attention of the President, Díaz Ordaz, and Campos Salas, and they built the BIP and the maquila industry around it.[2]

The rules of the BIP were set out in various forms. The Mexican government published a Spanish language version of the program (México, SIC 1968), and an English language version soon followed (Farías Negrete 1969). However, a legal framework did not appear until March 1971, by which time there were more than 200 maquilas employing about 30,000 workers. By amending the Customs Code to permit in-bond manufacturing, President Echeverría symbolically located the maquila industry within the orbit of foreign trade relations, but by designating SIC to handle the maquilas, he inserted it into the Mexican industrial structure. The 1971 regulations are quite clear cut, and I shall set them out as they are usefully summarized in the official translation:

WHAT IS THE PROCESSING PLANTS PROGRAM? According to the respective Regulations, it is a promotional program granting assistance to investors to establish industrial units within a 20 kilometer strip parallel to the international border line or to the coast line. It authorizes tax free importations of raw materials, parts, components, machinery, tooling equipment, and everything else needed for the transformation or processing, assembly and finishing of products to be entirely exported.
WHO MAY BE INTERESTED IN THE PROGRAM? All those businessmen who wish to obtain a substantial reduction in their production costs, such as labor, transportation, financing, etc., as well as other comparative advantages arising from close location, which are promptness, time, ease of transportation of technicians and supervising of processing operations.
WHY IS IT ADVANTAGEOUS FOR BUSINESSMEN TO ESTABLISH PROCESSING PLANTS IN MEXICO? It is a Country with political stability in the process of economic development. Its labor is inexpensive and easily adaptable to productive processes and with a high productive rate. Its proximity to the United States and the closeness to important cities

permits the operation of twin plants. Its cities have all necessary services and are characterized by their pleasant way of life, great variety of tourist attractions, resorts, bull rings, race tracks, archeological areas, restaurants with typical and international cuisine, etc.
HOW CAN ONE PARTICIPATE IN THE PROGRAM?   Through the approval of the Mexican government after filling the initial (EF-14) and final (EF-15) application forms for approval of the program. Interested parties, based on their own interests, may choose the structure of the capital of the company and the productive processes to be carried out.
WHERE SHOULD THE INDUSTRIAL UNIT BE ESTABLISHED?   There is the possibility of establishing it in any of the following cities in the northern border of Mexico. Tijuana, Tecate, Mexicali, San Luis Río Colorado, Nogales, Naco, Agua Prieta, Las Palomas, Ciudad Juárez, Ojinaga, Ciudad, Acuna, Piedras Negras, Nuevo Laredo, Ciudad Alemán, Reynosa and Matamoros.
WHEN IS THE OPERATION OF THE INDUSTRIAL UNIT STARTED AND TERMINATED?   It is started at the time the authorization from the Mexican Government is obtained: With regard to the termination, the operating term is indefinite.
WHICH ITEMS MAY BE PROCESSED?   There is no limitation under the laws and government of Mexico, except for those items which may be dangerous to health (México, SIC 1971:1–2).

Once the investor, who could of course be foreign or Mexican or a combination of both, had decided to establish a maquila, a Mexican corporation was formed, registered with the Ministry of Finance (for tax purposes), with the General Bureau of Statistics, and with the Mexican Social Security Institute (as an employer). The maquila application form could then be sent to the Ministry of Industry and Commerce. Additional forms were needed to authorize importation of goods and to secure the in-bond status for them that was required by the program. Although there were representatives of SIC in the border cities, it was still necessary to pursue most of this administrative process through Mexico City, and veterans of the early days of the maquila industry never tire of relaying stories of bureaucratic delays in the capital, though it was certainly a more pleasant place in which to be kept waiting then than it is now.

As noted earlier, the BIP was introduced to combat the unemployment that the cancellation of the bracero program had produced, though of course there had been unemployment on the border before the bracero program had attracted masses of potential workers to the borderlands. Due to the increasing mechanization of agriculture in the U.S. southwest, the bracero program had in fact been running down for some years—from a peak of almost half a million contract laborers in 1956, there were less than 200,000 in the last official year of the program (1964) (Fouts 1973:4). Accordingly, the Mexican government had known for some time that there was a critical unemployment problem on the frontera norte. The BIP extended the free zone concept in scope and distance by effectively turning the whole of the Mexican side of the border into such a zone. The regulations of March 1971 also allowed for the establishment of maquilas outside the border and free zones, at first in the coastal areas but, before long, in the whole of Mexico with the exception of a few already highly industrialized areas.

The attitude of the Echeverría government towards the maquila industry was ambiguous. On the one hand, Echeverría and his ministers were responsible for putting it on a secure legal footing for the first time and for many administrative initiatives that extended the work of PRONAF. The maquila industry clearly did benefit from infrastructure improvements in some of the main maquila locations. On the other hand, Echeverría's bid for leadership of the Third World often led him to make criticisms of global capitalism, the United States, and the maquila industry. Torres Manzo, his Secretary of Industry and Commerce, is said to have called the maquila program "a necessary evil" (U.S. Department of State, "Airgram" 4 June 1971:9).

Another fly in the ointment for the maquila industry then, as now, was the U.S. labor movement, and the issue then, as now, was the export of jobs. The union case was straightforward: cheap labor combined with generous U.S. import legislation was pricing U.S. workers out of jobs. The overseas production of U.S. firms, the unions argued, represented job losses for U.S. workers and set up pressures for wage cuts in the jobs that remained in the U.S. The maquila industry and its friends were ready with a three-pronged defence. First, those who established production or assembly facilities abroad had no real alternative. The spokespersons of the once globally hegemonic U.S. manufacturing industries plaintively argued that it was survival, not super profits, that was at issue. Competition from low wage areas, principally the Far East, meant that U.S. corporations either had to take advantage of cheap labor in their own labor intensive operations or be eliminated. The next two prongs of the defence were specific to Mexico. The proximity of Mexican border towns meant that it made very good sense to use U.S. materials, equipment, components, and services for the offshore industries. Therefore, far from causing job losses in the U.S., the maquila industry could save U.S. jobs that might otherwise be lost, namely in the production of materials, equipment, components, and services for the maquilas. The U.S. proponents of the maquila industry even argued that the maquilas created jobs in the U.S.

In light of the almost total failure of the unions in the U.S. and other investing countries to stop the relentless march of offshore production—the key process in the reformation of capitalism since the 1960s—it is difficult to take the AFL-CIO campaign very seriously. Nevertheless, there is evidence that both the Mexican government and the maquila industry did take it seriously at the time.[3] In 1968, according to the Department of State, "In no instance has a border industry been identified as a runaway firm . . . and the Mexican Government has declared its intention not to accept any such industry; Mexican officials state that they have refused to accept one such U.S. firm" ("Airgram" 4 February 1968:3). Ericson (1970:40) adds: "Following complaints that Mexico was encouraging U.S. 'runaway' plants on its northern border, the Mexican Government reported that it is carefully reviewing applications . . . to make certain that they do not shut down the sources of primary employment in the United States when the firm decides to locate in Mexico." As we shall see, neither the Mexican government nor the private and public facilitators of the maquila industry permitted such concerns to stand in their way, and many plant closures and even more plant reductions have contributed to the growth of the maquila industry. The Mexican government, like all the others involved in the maquila industry, obviously did not wish to be seen as destroying U.S. jobs. This sentiment led the industry to develop strategies that would permit it to go from the defensive to the offensive on the issue of jobs. The central point in this was the prospect of "twin plants."

The concept of twin plant was reportedly invented by Richard Bolin, the general manager of ADL between 1961 and 1972, whom Bermúdez had invited to research the industrial potential of the border. Bolin also worked closely with the American Chamber of Commerce in Mexico City and was involved in the creation of the BIP.[4] The twin plant idea was that each Mexican maquila might have a twin, preferably in the city on the U.S. side of the border. The U.S. twin would supply materials and components and provide technical services, while the Mexican twin would provide cheap labor, essential to keep U.S. manufacturing industry competitive with cost cutting rivals in the Far East.[5] Bolin had an early opportunity to put his ideas into practice in the Nogales industrial park, which he developed with Richard Campbell in 1968. Here, Campbell and Bolin pioneered the "Nogales Shelter Plan," a form of subcontracting in which the client provided the materials and components while the shelter operator provided the plant, labor, and administration. This avoided legal involvement in Mexico because the client was contracted with the U.S. arm of the shelter operator, which was, in turn, "contracted" with its own Mexican company. Shelter plans (as well as more conventional subcontracting operations) have flourished in the maquila industry, particularly in the 1980s. The maquila industry in Nogales grew rapidly (Overstreet 1981). Nevertheless, there were very few actual twin plants, and those that were established to service maquilas tended to be warehouses and offices rather than the high technology, capital intensive facilities that had been promised.

Unsurprisingly, the AFL-CIO were not convinced of the benefits of the maquila industry for U.S. workers through twin plants. However, rather than confront the maquilas head on, the AFL-CIO devoted their campaigning efforts to the repeal of items 806/807 which they believed were at the bottom of the job flight from the U.S. to foreign countries that had raised U.S. unemployment rates in the late 1960s and 1970s.[6] From 1967 on, the union called for the repeal of 806/807, and in 1969 Congressmen Green and Mills introduced bills to this effect. As Green shrewdly commented in 1970, "The United States has fostered policies of expanded trade for better living standards and building world markets. Item 807.00 merely promotes competition between Hong Kong and Haiti for lower wage labor to serve this market without building markets worldwide" (Goldfinger 1975:97). The unions and their congressional allies capitalized on public fears about rising unemployment, and were able to bring pressure on President Nixon to order the U.S. Tariff Commission (USTC) to report on 806/807. USTC got to work with commendable speed, and in 1970 it produced a document detailing the history and practices attached to the implementation of 806/807. The main findings were that most of the near doubling of imports under these items between 1966 and 1969 were due to 807 (products with U.S. components); foreign governments tended to consider 806/807 to be more crucial than U.S. manufacturers did; few jobs would be saved or repatriated if the items were repealed; and the U.S. would lose more from lost exports of components than would be gained from reduced imports of foreign goods. Although some of the figures that the Tariff Commission used to prove its case are rather dubious—for example they estimate that 806/807 had been responsible for creating 121,000 jobs abroad and for saving 37,000 jobs in component manufacture in the U.S. without any real inquiry into alternatives to 806/807 related employment—the report did provide a powerful defence of the maquila industry. Despite the USTC imprimatur, opposition pressure generated over the issue led to the Burke-Hartke foreign trade and investment bill, introduced in Congress in 1971. The AFL-CIO campaigned for this until 1973 when President Nixon persuaded the executive council of the union to drop the bill and support his own foreign trade bill of 1973. Baird and McCaughan (1975:25), not without reason, label this "The Sell-Out." Neither the Nixon trade bill nor the report did much about the question that was at the center of the opposition case, namely, why are the jobs being exported in the first place? The answer to this will throw light on the reformation of capitalism in general, and the maquila industry in Mexico and the U.S. in its first phase in particular.

For Mexico, the success of the BIP was measured not just by the numbers of plants, or even jobs, that were created, but by the nature and quality of these plants and jobs. Although they were not discouraged, small *maquilas de ropa* (clothing factories, often of the sweatshop type), scrap metal works, and other low capital enterprises, were not what Mexico really wanted.[7] From the beginning, the average number of workers per plant, a measure of the graduation of the maquilas from small shops to entities of industrial significance, was a statistic of importance for the planners, just as the landing of Fortune 500 corporations was a major symbol of success for the public and private facilitators. This meant that the BIP was directed at particular types of companies, preferably large and prestigious corporations, but as they were few and far between along the border, solid, dependable companies that were long-term prospects were also very welcome. By the nature of the program, the assembly of U.S. materials and components to take advantage of the tariff provisions, much of the available industrial activity that was liable to be attracted into the maquilas was in the consumer products sector.

In consumer goods industries it is generally the case that the manufacturer and the retailer are different organizations. The United States is rather distinctive in having a retail sector that is dominated by a few enormously powerful chains. The leading chain is Sears Roebuck, which has also been active abroad for decades. Sears has always been renowned for the attention it devotes to its suppliers. The equation is simple. The cheaper Sears can sell its goods, the more goods it will sell, and if it has done its sums right, the more profit it will make. The cheapness of its goods depends largely on the prices it has to pay to its suppliers, some of whom are captive, some not. By the 1960s, Sears' executives were noting with anxiety the number of goods on its shelves that were of foreign origin, though the public were sometimes not aware of this because the laws on country of origin labels were less strict than today. The reason why there were so many consumer goods from abroad, particularly from the Far East, on the shelves of their stores was, of course, because the Sears' purchasing agents were buying them in preference to domestic alternatives which were, on the whole, more expensive. The maquila industry, therefore, seemed to be a good idea to Sears long before some of their suppliers had even heard of it. To be sure, Sears may have developed the essential idea of the maquila industry. In the 1930s, as the biographer of General Wood, the *eminence grise* of Sears, states, "Wood's strategy converted the design and development of goods into a joint undertaking between Sears and its sources. In a sense, he reintroduced the practice—which predated the industrial revolution—whereby 'merchants' farmed out the fabrication of goods and later assembled them for transport and resale" (Worthy 1984:69).

There are many cases of Sears' purchasing agents introducing U.S. suppliers, or potential suppliers, to the maquila industry and its advantages for high wage cost producers caught by low wage cost competition.[8] Direct evidence of this comes from a report of a trip organized for a Sears buyer, H. E. McCoy, by the Central Power and Light Company of San Antonio, Texas, to evaluate the potential for locating Sears suppliers factories in Mexican border cities. It precisely summarizes the whole issue:

> Mr McCoy stated that Sears is becoming more and more concerned about the number of items on their shelves stamped made in Japan, Hong Kong, Tai Wan, and other remote foreign locations. Sears is also concerned about the stability of some of these foreign governments and the possibility of some of their suppliers possibly losing their investments in these countries. Due to the labor shortage in the East and North East, manufacturers and processors are having to move West or South or to foreign countries to find the necessary competitive labor to meet the demands for their products and to make the necessary profit. Due to this situation, Sears is looking at the towns along the Mexican border as well as the 12 mile Mexican zone along the Rio Grande that they had designed as an industrial area with certain advantages on the duty paid on the finished product when it reenters the United States.[9]

From California to Texas, Sears executives were observing what was going on just across the border and working out how it might fit into their own corporate plan. A not unusual case concerns the relationship between Sears and companies that supplied its stores with television sets. The influx of sets from the Far East threatened to drive U.S. made TVs from Sears' shelves, and this was something that the management wished to prevent where commercially possible. In the 1960s, Warwick Electronics, which Sears partially owned, was one of only two U.S. companies that supplied Sears with TVs for the western states. In order to rationalize its own supply network, Sears strongly suggested that Warwick combine with the other company. Sears decided to divest from Warwick and encouraged the Whirlpool Corporation to buy it up.[10] Sears introduced Warwick to the maquila industry to help it survive as a U.S. firm by being able to compete for price with Asian imports. Warwick entered the maquila industry as a wholly owned subsidiary of the Whirlpool Corporation, supplying Sears with TVs, operating under the name of Electrónica de Baja California in Tijuana from 1970, and from another maquila in Reynosa, in 1974. There were also Warwick TV plants in Arkansas, Tennessee, and Louisiana, captive suppliers in the sense that all of their production went to Sears under contract. Whirlpool was a more diversified company, well known in American utility rooms, and after an abortive attempt to manufacture its own TVs, it abandoned this market. In 1978, Sears helped dissolve Warwick, which was sold to Sanyo, with whom Sears had been doing business for some time. Warwick, once a formidable presence, disappeared from the maquila industry.

Another telling example of Sears' influence is in the needle trades. The early involvement of Sears in the establishment of such a maquila is described by the head of the McAllen Industrial Board. He recounts the genesis of one of Reynosa's most solid maquilas in 1967, when he was, "first approached by Sears buyers who were carrying out a top Sears corporate policy to attempt to distribute and disperse their various manufacturing operations and merchandise sources out into the various territories where there were in fact Sears retail units" (Birkhead 1984:2). This is interesting in that Hidalgo county, in which McAllen is situated, is one of the poorest counties in the whole of the U.S. but, in the 1960s and 1970s, the Sears store in McAllen recorded excellent business largely due to the regular influx of Mexican shoppers, both maquila workers and workers from the PEMEX plant in Reynosa. However, it is safe to speculate that Mr. McCoy's trip to McAllen and Reynosa had less to do with a local supplier for the Sears store in McAllen than with a cheap labor source that would permit its suppliers to compete with goods from the Far East, as was made clear in the report quoted above.

This maquila, Rey-Mex Bra, whose story will be taken up in chapter 6, had an arrangement with Sears for the distribution of its annual production of half a million brassieres. In 1968, the U.S. imported 40 million brassieres, mostly from the Phillipines, Hong Kong, and the Caribbean, and Sears' aim was to replace as many of the foreign imports as possible with "U.S. goods," that happened to be sewn just across the border in Mexico. As Goldfinger comments, when Rockwell International reports that its "American operations have already been cut in half to 1,000 employees, including the 550 in Juárez" the company appears to forget that Juárez is in Mexico. "Thus, U.S. jobs are slopped into overall company reports" (Goldfinger 1975:98).[11]

This leads to an important truth about the maquila industry, and one that the private and public facilitators have always seen with far more clarity than either the Mexican government or the AFL-CIO. The maquila industry is, genuinely, a binational industry and one in which the domestic operations of U.S. firms and their "foreign" operations along the Mexico-U.S. border are very much more difficult to separate than when the foreign operations are in noncontiguous countries. Both the locational features of the maquila industry along the border and its logistical organization (its materials and components are almost all from the U.S.), combine to draw the maquilas closer to the U.S. economy and society than to the Mexican economy and society, particularly as seen from Mexico City. In the first phase of the industry, from 1966 to 1974, the seeds of this relationship with the U.S. were definitively sown. As it was originally conceived as an export processing industry, naturally it would be oriented to foreign export markets, and so forward linkages were not on the agenda. There was, however, a real expectation that backward linkages, and therefore solid and ongoing connections with Mexican manufacturers, might be created, but the anticipated use of Mexican materials and components never occurred in these early years, and still has not happened.

The PRONAF strategy consisted not only in beautifying border cities, but in building a commercial and industrial base that would serve to counterbalance the U.S. influence in the frontera norte. Bermúdez was not hostile to the U.S., but he wanted to increase the Mexican share in border business while decreasing the U.S. share. Supplying goods and services to the maquila industry (as well as engaging in maquila production itself) would appear to be an excellent base from which Mexican entrepreneurs might start. This has happened only to a limited extent. The Mexican government, in the role of public facilitator, and Mexican entrepreneurs, in the role of private facilitators, secured a less substantial part of the profits of the maquilas than those from north of the border. Neither federal nor state governments played any very profitable part in the promotion of the maquilas. Most of the profits from shelter and subcontract operations went to private facilitators, the majority of whom were U.S. citizens. Even the Mexican private facilitators were involved in the property development side rather than in the manufacturing side of the maquila industry. Property development is, of course, a lucrative activity, and many Mexican fortunes along the border were based on supplying land and factories for the maquilas, but this did not create many long-term jobs or multiplier effects for local businesses.

BIP administration was in the hands of several different ministries, and startups and closures were often inadequately documented during the early years. Surveying the industry in 1969, the American Chamber of Commerce of Mexico commented that it was difficult to get accurate maquila lists because they were constantly changing. Starting from government lists, "it was found that many of the plants listed had already closed down and others, not included, had opened up. The greatest attrition was in the Tijuana area. Since . . . November 1967, almost 50 percent of the companies . . . had closed their doors" (quoted in Fernández 1977:141–142).[12] Administrative records either lagged behind the reality of plant operation or anticipated them too freely, as when maquilas were included in the figures but plants never actually opened. Much maquila work is of a seasonal nature, and employment can vary during any given year, so job creation can be inflated or deflated according to the point in time when the data are recorded. Further, in Baja California many plants did not register as maquilas because it was easier to import foreign goods under the free zone system. This led to an undercount of up to 300 maquilas in the mid-1970s. From 1972 onwards, maquilas operating in free zones were legally obliged to register under the maquila legislation, though it is not certain how many actually did this (see Mendoza Berrueto in Ross 1978:168).

Bearing all these strictures in mind,[13] table 3.1 shows the growth of the maquila industry for the years of the first phase, 1967 to 1974. The growth of plants and the growth of employment did not occur in parallel. In some years there were substantial increases in numbers of plants, while in other years relatively few plant startups brought substantial numbers of new jobs. This varied from place to place, as the following chapters will illustrate. Nevertheless, from 1970 the maquila industry began to have a significant impact on manufacturing industry along Mexico's northern border. As Dillman shows in his analysis of the industrial census for 1970, "The absence of the electrical/electronic industries from the border zone [most of which were maquilas] would have reduced the number of employees in manufacturing by 25 percent, the value of production by just under 29 percent, but the number of establishments by only 3 percent" (in Stoddard et al. 1982:145). Between 1971 and 1972, the excess of startups over closures was over 100, and employment increased by almost 20,000.

On the surface, this seems a very unlikely time for any sort of progress in the maquila industry. On 1 May 1970, the Mexican government passed a new federal labor law which was widely seen as a measure that would increase costs for the maquilas. Apprenticeship

*Table 3.1*
Maquila industry by plants, employees, labor costs, and value added, 1967–1974.

| YEAR | NUMBER OF PLANTS | NUMBER OF EMPLOYEES | LABOR COSTS | VALUE ADDED |
|------|--------|-----------|-------|-------|
| 1967 | 72  | 4,000  | n.a.   | 925   |
| 1968 | 112 | 10,927 | n.a.   | 975   |
| 1969 | 149 | 15,900 | n.a.   | 973   |
| 1970 | 160 | 20,327 | n.a.   | 1,035 |
| 1971 | 205 | 28,483 | 16,460 | 1,227 |
| 1972 | 339 | 48,060 | 17,388 | 1,820 |
| 1973 | 400 | 64,330 | 17,808 | 2,415 |
| 1974 | 455 | 75,977 | 32,082 | 2,610 |

NOTE: labor costs are average annual costs per employee in pesos; value added is annual total in millions of pesos.
SOURCE: Grunwald (in Grunwald and Flamm 1985): 140, amended.

contracts, used to employ young workers for less than the minimum wage, were abolished; workers would now be entitled to paid vacations; mandatory Christmas bonuses were introduced; death, termination, and retirement compensation were to be paid by employers; workers' schools and training and recreation programs were to be established; and employers were to share in the responsibility of providing housing for their workers. All maquilas with more than 100 employees were obliged to introduce these measures in three years (Tansik and Tapia, cited in Pena 1981:A-84-5, from *Comercio Exterior*, April 1971). In a series of interviews with maquila managers on the effects of the new labor regulations (and 806/807 too), Tansik and Tapia reported that the managers, though objecting to the housing requirement, did not consider that the new fringe benefits would raise the cost of labor to a point at which the maquilas would lose their competitive edge in the world offshore production market. For the U.S. manufacturer, then, the combination of proximity and cheap labor made the maquilas in 1970 and 1971 such a good bargain that even one of the most progressive Third World labor codes presented no real threat to future profitability.[14]

Although the government was making progress in regularizing the legal basis for the maquilas, those who were establishing them were very much left to their own devices, and many recruited the services of Mexican professionals in the border cities. Attorneys, customs brokers, and facilitators of all sorts were available to the incoming manufacturers. There were also many jobs for builders, carpenters, electricians, and other trades when the plants were being built and furbished.

Reports of the experiences of workers and employers in the maquila industry tended to differ according to source. David Lopez, a field worker for the AFL-CIO along the border, quotes a worker at Transitron, in Nuevo Laredo, and the sentiment expressed is quite typical: "I work on these small things under a microscope, and they get very angry if we make any mistake or if we don't work fast enough. The foreman is always trying to date us, and if we say no, we have problems, or we can get fired" (López 1969:5). The publications of the Mexican left also carried reports on "las maquiladoras como explotación neocolonial" (to quote the title of a particularly bitter attack in the magazine *Punto Critico* of February-March 1974). It was also in the early and mid-1970s that the radical Mexican academics in the universities and research institutes began to take a serious interest in the maquilas, several research projects being set up to assess the industry and its affects on Mexican labor and the developmental prospects for the country.[15]

The point of view of the employer can be gleaned from the account of the manager of Boss Manufacturing, a small twin plant, employing 40 people to cut work gloves in El Paso and 70 to sew them in Juárez at this time. Permits for importing equipment and machinery had to be meticulously completed, as the slightest inaccuracy could delay a shipment. For example, if motors and the tables to which they were fixed were itemized separately they would have to be separated to be allowed entry into Mexico. (Mexico did not then and does not now have the monopoly on such absurdities.) Maquilas had to buy their own electric transformers and run the supply to the plant, and in order to have a telephone it was necessary to buy shares in the telephone company (which turned out to be a good investment). Hiring and testing of workers was a revelation. The first advertisement that Boss put in the local paper attracted hundreds of applicants, and when they were given peg tests for dexterity, 288 out of the first 300 scored over 20 on the test, a level that about one percent of U.S. workers would normally achieve. This was reflected in excellent productivity and quality in the work. Turnover, a problem that would become chronic in Juárez in the 1980s, as we shall see in chapter 5, was almost nonexistent in the Boss maquila, and there was very little absenteeism (Wende 1969).

The management picture, therefore, was one of a certain level of material difficulty, but nothing that could not be solved with a little patience. A capable and undemanding workforce, that cost much less than in the U.S., seemed to achieve comparable if not better standards of work. It is no wonder that the maquila industry was booming. On 3 April 1973 the Mexican Institute of Foreign Trade placed a full page advertisement in the *Times* (London) extolling the virtues, and listing the progress of the "in-bond" industries in Mexico, with a view to encouraging British and European investment. What was to happen next, in 1974, was to take most people by surprise and the explanation for it is still being hotly disputed.

## The First Crisis

The quarterly breakdown of numbers of maquilas and total employment in 1973–1974, shows an unprecedented increase in plants, 248 for the final quarter of 1973 to 464 for the first quarter of 1974. This was matched by a substantial rise in employees, from 60,356 to 78,025 in the same period.[16] In the following quarter, to June 1974, the total of plants had barely increased (to 467) and exactly 2,000 more jobs had been created. It was then that the slide began. By the end of September, plant numbers were back to 464 but, more seriously, employment had declined by almost 4,000, to 76,232; and by the end of 1974, the maquila total had dropped to 455 and the jobs total had plunged to 69,512. In 1975 the number of plants hovered around the 450 mark, and the job total declined to a low point of 64,650 in the first quarter, from where it steadily recovered to 70,000 by the end of the year. While jobs increased over the next few years, the number of plants remained around 450 until 1979, when almost 100 more plants were added and employment reached 100,000 for the first time. So, the average maquila was employing more labor as time went by and, as a corollary, the crisis had shaken out many small and less stable firms from the maquila industry. Some large firms did not survive. In Tijuana, Rohr Industries closed two of its three maquilas. In Mexicali, the Mattel subsidiary, Mextel, and in Nuevo Laredo, Transitron, closed down, both with the loss of several thousand jobs. Here, bitter struggles took place in which the workers were pitted not only against the employers but also against the union (Baird and McCaughan 1975).

There is no doubt that part of the reason for the closures and the layoffs was the recession in the U.S. economy of 1974 and 1975. Clearly, an industry oriented to exports to the U.S. could not fail to be affected by the sharp downturn in demand that was experienced in these years, especially in the consumer electronics industry, which was particularly hard hit along the border. While most of the big corporations, like RCA, Zenith, General Motors, and General Electric had the resources to weather the storm, some of the smaller and more marginal maquilas did not, and they either went under or curtailed their activities. However, as the official quarterly figures reveal, even allowing for a little promotional embellishment, the vast majority of maquilas survived, and those that laid off workers were rehiring by 1976, by which time the U.S. recovery was well under way. It may not be a total explanation, but the argument that the crisis and the recovery were caused by the U.S. recession and the subsequent miniboom does not conflict with the facts (see Amozurrutia, 1987).

The second main explanation is that the crisis was brought on by the increasing militancy of the labor force. Baird and McCaughan, whose NACLA report has done more than any other single piece of research to popularize this theory, quote the American Chamber of Commerce *"Maquiladora" Newsletter* (*MN*) of November 1974 to the effect that "Mexican labor today—as did U.S. labor a few years ago—is killing the goose" by their excessive demands (1975:16). This theory needs to be unpacked because there are two elements in it that are certainly related, but by no means identical. The first element is labor militancy as organized by the official labor movement, in most cases the CTM; the second element is labor militancy that is outside official

[57]

channels, and sometimes directed against the CTM as much as against the employers. Carrillo (1985) has shown that, to put it succinctly, the CTM has not always acted in the best interests of its members in the maquilas. The evidence from major maquila disputes during these years supports the view that attempts to create a workers' movement independent from the CTM (or other quasiofficial unions) was a key ingredient in the struggle, and in every case was suppressed by the union, with or without the help of the employers. It is difficult to disagree with the conclusion that, on the whole, maquila workers have lost faith in the official unions. Thus, having failed to create independent unions along the border some groups of workers organized their own resistance, while others relied on the goodwill of their employers.

The argument on the militancy of labor begs a very important question, namely whether the militancy was a consequence of the crisis, or whether the crisis was a consequence of the militancy. Transitron, for example, was taken by surprise at the intensity of the workers' response to its decision to curtail production in Nuevo Laredo, but this very response intensified the crisis, and no doubt contributed to the company's decision to close down completely.[17] In Mextel, on the other hand, the evidence suggests that Mattel's problems were far wider than those in the plant in Mexicali, and that the militancy of the workers had very little effect on the decision to close down.[18] In the absence of access to confidential company records, one cannot be sure about any of this. The only certainty was that in the early and mid-1970s, maquila workers were becoming more militant, and that this coincided with the economic crisis that the U.S. recession had provoked for companies along the border.

Why were the maquila workers, hitherto noted for their docility, becoming so militant? The answer lies in the economic conditions of the industry, and in particular the movement of wages and prices in the border communities. The frontera norte has become one of the richest parts of Mexico. Table 2.2 showed that the northern border areas have the highest level of minimum wages in the country. This is, of course, extremely important for the people who live along the border, but for the maquila industry, dominated as it is by U.S. capital, the important wage factors are first, the differences between maquila and U.S. wages for comparable jobs; and second, the differences between Mexican maquila wages and the wages in other Third World countries for comparable jobs. These differences are only relevant in terms of U.S. dollars, and so it is as well to bear in mind that the exchange rate for maquila transactions was 12.5 pesos to the dollar all through the 1960s and up to September of 1976.

The business press in the U.S. and in Mexico was in no doubt that U.S. companies were using maquilas for cheap labor, but by 1974 maquila workers were said to be pricing themselves out of their jobs. For example, at the national level *Industry Week* drew attention to the fact that wages in the maquilas rose yearly and, ominously, that, "The union wanted a 33 percent increase in late 1973 and got about a 20 percent boost" (4 March 1974:37). In Mexico, the president of CANACINTRA's consultative council on the maquila industry argued that "exaggerated" wage increases entitled the maquila operators to tax relief because the maquilas had been created to reduce unemployment not primarily as a source of revenue for Mexico (Rubio del Cueto 1974:17–19).

The border minimum wage almost trebled in dollar terms from the late 1960s to the first devaluation of the peso in 1976, and the fully burdened wage could be up to 50 percent above the minimum wage. It is also the case that as the maquila wage increased so did the duty paid by U.S. manufacturers who were using 806/807 on the value added (mainly wage cost) element of the goods they were bringing back into the U.S. Van Waas (1981) has computed the differences between the minimum and average manufacturing wages for the U.S. and the Mexican border region from 1965 to 1979 with some very interesting results. For all manufacturing industry, the difference between the U.S. average and the Mexican border minimum hourly wage rate was $2.33 in 1965 and $5.70 in 1979, but the really significant fact is that this difference rose in every single year. Breakdowns for the apparel industry and the electrical industry, where much of the production in the maquilas lay, showed the same results with, interestingly, the electrical industry average wage marginally below the average for all manufacturing in the U.S., and the average in the apparel industry well below. But in both cases, the differences between U.S. and Mexican border minimum wage rates increased in every single year. The trend of the difference between the U.S. and Mexican border minimum wages was more complex. In 1965 the minimum in the U.S. was $1.25 per hour, while on the Mexican border it was 28 cents per hour, a difference of 97 cents. By 1975, the last full year before devaluation, the difference was $1.29, and by 1979 the difference was $2.00. Between 1969 and 1974 the U.S. minimum wage had in fact stagnated, at $1.60 per hour, while the border minimum almost doubled, but the absolute difference never fell below $1.08 (where it was in 1973).

It is possible that some maquilas that had come in at the end of the 1960s when the difference between the U.S. and the border minimum wage was over $1.20 per hour, found that the reduction of 15 cents per hour in their wage costs savings was too much to bear, and went out of business. This is possible but unlikely, because the alternative labor pool for such manufacturers would in all probability be earning manufacturing wages rather than minimum wages in the U.S. and, as has been demonstrated, even in the low paid apparel industry in the

U.S., the difference between U.S. and border wages increased every single year. On the basis of this evidence, one would have to conclude that the economics of wages along the border was not the prime cause of the crisis in the maquila industry in 1974 and 1975. This is not to say that wages were unimportant, but to argue that in the corporate boardrooms of the U.S. where decisions about most of the substantial maquilas were being taken, rising labor costs did not often indicate the need for closure.

It is in the *politics* of wages that the answer is to be found. The maquila industry perceived itself to be under a dual threat in 1974. First, the Mexican currency was widely acknowledged to be seriously overvalued with respect to the dollar, which was very good news for U.S. businesses along the border that existed to sell goods and services to Mexican crossborder customers, and to Mexican businesses that imported foreign goods. However, it was becoming very bad news to Mexican exporters, and especially to the maquila industry whose wage costs were rising along with all their other costs of operation, particularly rents and utilities. In 1975, nonlabor costs in the maquila industry amounted to more than one-quarter of the total operating costs (INEGI 1988: table 1). So while wages alone, relative to U.S. wages, were not in themselves critical, as an indicator of exchange rates that were getting more and more out of line with economic realities, they were starting to ring alarm bells in corporate headquarters. The second threat was the aforementioned militancy of labor, one of whose concomitants was the continuing pressure in the maquilas for wage increases.

The maquila industry can be seen as a further phase in the general movement of manufacturing industry in the U.S. from the rustbelt to the sunbelt (Ende and Haring 1983). It is generally accepted that one key reason for this industrial relocation within the U.S. is the wish of corporations to rid themselves of the necessity to deal with unionized labor (Bluestone and Harrison 1982), and the sunbelt states do have a much lower proportion of workers in unions than the rustbelt states. The nature of assembly work, particularly in electronics and some of the needle trades where precision is of the essence, increases management's reliance on close control and supervision of the workforce. Any deviation from the extremely high quality standards that are required in such industries can lead to loss of the subcontract work for a prestigious client—the bread and butter of a large number of maquilas.[19] For many maquilas, therefore, the difference between strict and loose management control of the shop floor was literally the difference between survival and destruction. Though the official unions did oppose management on behalf of the workers and organized strikes and other forms of protest in the early 1970s, they were frequently to be seen to be turning the workers away from confrontation, whether in the guise of mature negotiators trying to protect jobs, as those in defence of the interests of capital saw it, or as corrupt union bosses (*charros*) anxious to protect their bribes from the companies, as the left and the workers trying to establish independent unions saw it.

By 1974, the official unions seemed to be losing their grip and massive strikes in Nogales and Nuevo Laredo encouraged *Punto Crítico* to speculate (February–March 1974:24–28) that what was happening along the border could show workers in the rest of Mexico that the CTM was incapable of defending their interests against foreign, domestic or state employers. This must have been as alarming for the Mexican government and Mexican capital as it was for the maquila industry, and as plant closures took place (even though they were not numerous), and job losses started to mount, an atmosphere of crisis was engendered in the maquila industry.

All these events came at a particularly bad time for Mexico. Not only was the U.S. domestic recession beginning to bite by the end of 1974, but there was increasing evidence that Mexico was rapidly losing its labor cost advantages. Mexican wages were significantly higher than those of its competitors in the Far East and the Caribbean, and even with its logistical advantages many TNCs were said to be considering relocation out of Mexico (see Banamex's *Review of the Economic Situation of Mexico* for August 1975:283). Victor Muñoz, an El Paso union leader, reports that U.S. Chamber of Commerce and maquila representatives met Mexican officials in Chihuahua City at this time and presented them with an ultimatum: reduce production costs and control the workers or the maquilas would leave Mexico (Muñoz 1987:4). Whether this was a bluff or not, it achieved its ends. As we have seen very few firms did relocate, but the pressure worked in three ways. The government and the maquila industry entered into an "Alliance for Production," the CTM regained control of a workforce increasingly worried that its jobs really might all be lost (see Baird and McCaughan 1975), and in September 1976 the Mexican government devalued the peso from 12.5 to the dollar to over 26 to the dollar. The first crisis was over.

## Phase 2

There is good, if circumstantial, evidence that all parties had learned a lesson from the crisis of 1974. The workers had seen plants close, massive layoffs, their official unions often hand in glove with the employers to break strikes, and attempts to create unofficial unions defeated. It was not difficult to take seriously threats that the maquila industry might actually fold up altogether and go to Haiti or Korea if you had worked for Transitron or Mextel, or knew someone who had. The employers had learned that making profits along the Mexican border was not as painless as it had seemed in the heady days at the turn of the decade. Buffeted by the storms of inflation, wage rises, and labor unrest, and contemplating its global choices, the industry had discovered that it had more influence in Mexico than it had believed. To put it crudely, the workers and the government needed them more than they needed to have maquilas in Mexico. The Mexican government, too, had learned to take seriously the signs of the fragility of the maquila industry, and the years of benign neglect that had marked the first decade of the industry ended with an "Alliance for Production" between the government and representatives of the maquilas.

The "Alliance for Production" was part of a development strategy worked out by the incoming President, López Portillo, who was determined to show the world, and particularly the U.S., that the radical policies of his predecessor, Echeverría, were not to be continued by the new government. One spinoff of this was an agreement between the Mexican government and the maquila industry. The government agreed to step up its maquila promotional activities, to streamline maquila administration, to finance industrial parks and look into their fiscal position, to ease the quota problems of textile maquilas, and to establish "a single channel of communication for the treatment of all in-bond industry problems"; while the maquila owners agreed on goals of 175,000 new jobs over the next 6 years, $1.5 billion dollars in exports and 3 billion pesos worth of Mexican components and raw materials by 1982, to use the maquilas as import substitution industries through joint ventures, and to promote maquila investment in general with an emphasis on industrial parks (cited in Van Waas 1981:190–191).

However, the most important aspects of the new government's more positive attitude to the maquilas were not contained in the agreement. First, the decision to devalue the peso, which had taken place some months earlier under the outgoing president had underpinned the whole economic exercise and cut dollar wages at a stroke. Second, the atmosphere of labor relations and the government's willingness to stand up for the maquila workers began to change, and a new order gradually emerged. The progressive measures of the 1970 federal labor law, some admittedly honored more in the breach than in the observance, were slowly whittled away under López Portillo and the maquilas were given much more freedom of action. Workers who were deemed

[62]

inefficient could be fired without severance pay;[20] management was empowered to alter pay and conditions of employment much more freely than before; the 30-day probationary period for new workers at rates of pay below the minimum wage was extended to 90 days; and the social security fund payments of the maquilas were eased (Baird and McCaughan 1979; Carrillo and Hernández 1985). The second phase of the maquila industry was characterized by the increasing use of these powers to discipline a labor force that was being squeezed between domestic inflation and the intensification of production in the factory.

Table 3.2 shows the slow recovery followed by the rapid growth of the industry from 1975 to 1981, roughly a doubling of employees to over 130,000, and more than 600 plants, and foreign currency earnings which rose from just over 4 billion pesos to almost 24 billion pesos, that is (as the peso-dollar rate had remained around 23 until 1981) from $170 million to the magic one billion dollar mark.[21] There are various simple explanations for what it was that, in the words of one banker commentator, put "U.S.-Mexico Border Industry back on fast-growth track" (McClelland 1979). McClelland himself strongly favors the international competitiveness of Mexican wage costs relative to other Third World countries, or lack of it, as the key factor, and this thesis shines a strong light on rates of exchange. Unlike many others who argue along these lines, McClelland does note the rising differential between Mexican and U.S. wage rates and, interestingly, shows that in countries like West Germany and Japan average manufacturing wages were fast approaching those of the U.S. and that this might stimulate Japanese and European companies to establish maquilas.

Table 3.2
Maquila industry by plants, employees, labor costs, and value added, 1975–1981.

| YEAR | NUMBER OF | | LABOR COSTS | VALUE ADDED |
|------|-----------|-----------|-------------|-------------|
|      | PLANTS | EMPLOYEES | | |
| 1975 | 454 | 67,214 | 36,153 | 4,015 |
| 1976 | 448 | 74,496 | 44,579 | 5,425 |
| 1977 | 443 | 78,433 | 57,731 | 7,118 |
| 1978 | 457 | 90,704 | 66,006 | 10,000 |
| 1979 | 540 | 111,365 | 76,030 | 14,543 |
| 1980 | 620 | 119,546 | 87,816 | 17,729 |
| 1981 | 605 | 130,973 | 111,809 | 23,957 |

NOTE: labor costs are average annual costs per employee in pesos; value added is annual total in millions of pesos.
SOURCE: INEGI (1988: table 1).

Banamex's *Review of the Economic Situation of Mexico* of August 1977 summarizes the views of Mexican finance capital on the revival of the industry. In addition to the peso devaluation of 1976, the U.S. boom of 1977 (when GNP increased by 7 percent in the first six months) had a dramatic effect on the maquila industry. The order books of the apparel and electronics plants were bulging. The U.S. electronics industry was also recovering from the blows dealt to it over the previous years by Japanese competition by introducing various cost saving technological innovations. Although these tended to be capital rather than labor intensive, the market volume recaptured as a result had increased employment along the border. The final reason offered by Banamex for the maquila revival was that, although wages had been rising, wage demands had been very moderate, and investors' confidence had been encouraged by the lessening of labor conflict.

The second phase of the maquila industry saw consolidation at both the national and the local levels. The government of López Portillo was coming to terms with the necessity of creating a unified administrative structure for the maquila industry. A maquila department was set up within the Industry ministry with Dr. Guillermo Teutli as director. The maquila industry, however, still had to wait some years for genuine administrative reform (see Ojeda, ed., 1982).

The Maquiladora Industry Council (CNIME), an organ of CANACINTRA, was beginning to assert itself as the industry was forging for itself a more secure place in the Mexican economic structure. CNIME had been formed in 1965, but its activities had been rather low key, and the U.S.-dominated maquila industry on the border had largely bypassed it. The events of 1974 and 1975, and the decentralization of administrative power to facilitate the work of the industry promised in the Alliance for Production, had given it an opportunity to play a fuller part. The CNIME annual convention became a major event for the maquila industry, often used by important government officials to sound out opinion and to discuss official policy.

In the border cities, the maquila managers were beginning to organize themselves into local maquila associations, sometimes in direct connection with CNIME, and sometimes independently. In Tijuana, for example, the U.S. maquila managers considered that they would be better off with their own organization, being unimpressed with Mexican official efforts to organize the industry, while in other places, like Juárez, U.S. managers and Mexican officials appeared to have somewhat closer working relationships. The organization of the maquila industry was furthest advanced in the state of Chihuahua, where Juárez was by far the leading border location.

The American Chamber of Commerce of Mexico (AmCham) had been involved with the maquila industry since the mid-1960s, and was one of its strongest advocates. Founded in 1917, the Chamber represented all U.S. business interests in Mexico, including many TNCs that had happily been producing for the heavily protected Mexican domestic market since the nineteenth century. It is now the largest U.S. chamber of commerce outside the United States, and claims to represent more than 90 percent of U.S. investment in Mexico.[22] In 1974 the Chamber began to produce a monthly *Maquiladora Newsletter* (*MN*) which has appeared regularly since then and is a mine of information and opinion on the whole industry. AmCham organized its maquila industry activities through a special development committee, which had a specific "Maquiladora Advisory Council" with representatives from the various maquila sites. It organizes the AmCham annual seminar on the in-bond industry, which started off in a small way in 1975, and has grown to be one of the major social and political events in the maquila calendar. These seminars often feature officials and legislators from Washington, as in 1981 when the acting U.S. ambassador to Mexico proclaimed that "the maquiladora plant system is an element of exceptional importance in the relationship between Mexico and the U.S." (*Mexican-American Review*, May 1981:35). Hyperbole aside, not all business meetings in Mexico (this one was in Guadalajara) attract the U.S. ambassador, even if he is only acting!

Wages continued to rise in pesos, but the impact in dollar terms was delayed because of the devaluation of 1976. In Juárez, for example, the minimum daily wage rose from 102 pesos at the end of 1976, to 160 in 1980, but leapt to 210 in 1981, reflecting the worsening inflation in the country, especially along the border. In dollars, this represented an hourly rate of 57 cents in 1976, about half the rate immediately before devaluation. By 1980 it had reached 89 cents per hour, and for the first time ever broke the one dollar an hour barrier in 1981, when it reached $1.12. In 1982, responding to intense public pressure, the minimum wage was again increased, this time by an unprecedented 70 pesos per day to 280, and with a small adjustment to the exchange rate, the dollar value of the minimum wage for maquila workers in Juárez reached $1.53 per hour, the highest level ever (*Twin Plant News*, January 1987:48).

Unlike the period before the 1976 devaluation, there were few strikes, and labor unrest was directed more against the government than the maquila employers. For the first time since the mid-1970s, the maquila industry experienced net losses of plants (down from 620 in 1980 to 585 in 1982) and jobs (almost 4,000 between 1981 and 1982). The second crisis had arrived.

## The Second Crisis

For some parts of the border, Ciudad Juárez for example, there was really no second crisis at all, only a short interruption to explosive growth. In other parts, however, Mexicali for example, the downturn lasted longer. But taking the maquila industry as a whole, along the border (and now in the interior), although 1981–1982 was a year of difficulties, these appear to have been quickly resolved. It is tempting to argue that as the recession in the U.S. in the late 1970s and early 1980s was less severe than the recession of the mid-1970s, so the effects on the maquila industry would be less serious, and there is certainly some truth in this. What does seem more important, however, is that not only were wages rising in dollar terms, almost tripling in five years, but the differential between maquila wages and wages in competing Third World countries were growing at an alarming rate. By 1982, maquila wages had raced ahead of wages in Hong Kong, South Korea, and Taiwan, and were even higher than Singapore and Brazil (see Pranis 1987).[23] Anecdotal evidence strongly suggests that many companies were threatening to close down their maquilas at this time. From 1980 until the devaluations of 1982, there was more and more talk of the "uncompetitiveness" of the maquila program, of the necessity to curb wages, and of the likelihood that large numbers of maquilas would be forced by economic circumstances to find some other Third World location, of which there were plenty beckoning.

President López Portillo went out with a bang in 1982. In February he began to devalue the peso, which had the effect of cutting dollar wage costs at a stroke. The exchange rate was raised from 26 pesos to the dollar to 45 pesos, and later in the year it was raised again to 70 pesos to the dollar. These measures automatically reduced the maquila minimum wage from the historic high of $1.53 to about 76 cents per hour. Then, on 1 September 1982 he stunned the world by nationalizing the banks and imposing exchange controls. These controls included a multi-tier peso-to-dollar rate, and established an "official" rate for maquila transactions.[24]

Before 1982, there was always the feeling that maquila wages were, however inadequately, related to U.S. minimum wages, but after the devaluations of 1982, maquila wage rates seemed much more related to those prevailing in Asia and other competing offshore sites in the Third World. When the new president, Miguel de la Madrid, widely seen as technocractic and pro-U.S., took office, he continued the peso devaluations, mainly to stimulate exports to service foreign debt. One immediate effect, of course, was to relieve the wage pressure that the maquilas were finding so intolerable. Mexico was once more competitive. The maquila industry again was saved, and in 1983, the biggest annual rise in maquila employment—almost 24,000 jobs—was recorded.

The usual assessment of this situation, the straightforward connection between the rise in dollar wages, the devaluation, the subsequent drop in dollar wages, and recovery, is unconvincing largely because there is no evidence whatsoever to suggest that more than a very few of the U.S. corporations that were involved in the maquilas had any serious intention of pulling out of Mexico. For some marginal producers, the increase in dollar wages might have been significant, but for the majority of efficient maquilas, the 25 percent of total operating costs represented by wages and salaries did not make the difference between survival and closure, and there is nothing to show that what was acceptable from 1975, after the first crisis, was not acceptable in 1982. The drop in the proportion of wages to total operating costs after the devaluation, to about 17 percent in 1985 (INEGI 1988:1), was a bonus for the employers not a lifeline for the industry.

The difference, again, was the *politics* of wages rather than the *economics* of wages. The pressures on U.S. manufacturers to use U.S. materials and components, to organize the logistics of supply in line with the methods of "just in time," to make life easier for their "expatriate" managers and technicians, and to produce as near as possible to the marketplace, none decisive in itself, have had a cumulative effect in the locational choice of the Mexican border for offshore assembly. There is no other area anywhere in the Third World that comes near to matching the Mexican maquila industry along the border in these respects. What caused the closures in the mid-1970s was not rising wages, but rather the loss of control of the labor force. This did not happen to any great extent in the crisis of 1981–1982 because of negative experiences of the workers with attempts to create alternative vehicles for the expression of their interests, which were widely felt to be neglected or actually opposed by the unions. Further, the inflation had made it even more important for the workers to hold on to their jobs, particularly where the maquila wage was the only money coming into the household.

Average plant size and probably average level of amenities was rising, and many maquilas were introducing new systems of labor relations to forestall worker unrest and interruptions to production. For the workers, the realization that their unions did not do much to help them and that the road to independent formal organization was blocked by the combined might of the employers, the official unions, and, sometimes, the state, there were three alternatives. Either they could (1) lapse into quiescence; (2) generate collective informal modes of shop floor organization to make their jobs more tolerable;

or (3) throw their lot in with the employers and join in the "maquila family." The third phase was to see all of these amid astonishing growth of the industry.

## Phase 3

The effects of the 1982 devaluations and the regular devaluations that followed were immediate and spectacular. As table 3.3 shows, the performance of the maquila industry fully merited the designation of "star performer" enthusiastically bestowed upon it by the magazine *Business Mexico* in a highly informative promotional article (February 1986:76–95).

The prospect that the new exchange rates and the continuation of industrial peace would secure the future of those maquilas already in production and encourage many more, made it imperative that the government fulfil its regular promises to simplify the administration of the maquila system. Legislation had long been anticipated, and President de la Madrid had been making supportive remarks about the maquilas ever since he came to power. The "Decree for the Promotion and Operation of the In Bond Industry for Export" of 15 August 1983 contained few surprises, but much that reassured the industry. Mandatory local content requirement had been rumored but was not imposed, and the Ministry of Industrial Development (SECOFI) was confirmed as responsible for the maquilas. The employers were

*Table 3.3*
Maquila industry by plants, employees, labor costs, and value added, 1982–1988.

| YEAR | NUMBER OF PLANTS | NUMBER OF EMPLOYEES | LABOR COSTS | VALUE ADDED |
|------|------|------|------|------|
| 1982 | 585 | 127,048 | 192,998 | 46,588 |
| 1983 | 600 | 150,867 | 311,055 | 99,521 |
| 1984 | 672 | 199,684 | 504,418 | 194,756 |
| 1985 | 760 | 211,968 | 790,992 | 325,250 |
| 1986 | 890 | 249,833 | 1,440,850 | 792,018 |
| 1987 | 1,125 | 305,253 | 3,397,044 | 2,235,150 |
| 1988 (Jan.) | 1,279 | 329,413 | 45,894 | 305,012 |

NOTE: labor costs are average annual costs per employee in pesos; value added is annual total in millions of pesos.
SOURCE: INEGI (1988: table 1) and *Avances*.

relieved that a suggestion that control should pass to the Treasury had been rejected. Presumably the Treasury would be more likely to raise taxes than SECOFI (*MN*, September 1983:1).

These were the things that the decree had not done for which the industry was grateful, and there were also things that the decree did do for which the industry was equally grateful. Conditions under which maquilas could sell their products in the Mexican domestic market, something that some maquilas had been keen to do for some time, were codified. Generally, up to 20 percent of production could be sold in Mexico (and more in special circumstances) as long as there were no available competing Mexican goods, and where a local content requirement was met (the actual figure was not specified but it was usually 35 percent). As direct labor and fuel were included in this local content requirement, some maquilas who actually bought nothing in the way of materials or components in Mexico satisfied the requirement. An interesting rider to this is that the decree stipulated that the maquilas must render technical assistance to current or potential suppliers. Although many in the industry had campaigned for the right to sell in the Mexican domestic market, the new regulation did not open any floodgates for maquila products in Mexico.[25] It is not entirely clear whether the authorities were putting obstacles in the way of maquilas wishing to sell in Mexico, or whether the maquilas were not interested in doing so. The virtual collapse of nonessential domestic consumption in Mexico due to the combined effects of inflation and devaluation suggests that the latter reason was as important as the former.

The most important innovation was the creation of a single administrative organ—a revamped Intersecretarial Commission for the Promotion of the In-Bond Industry—to promote, nurture and supervise the maquila industry, a measure that was long overdue. In this manner the government was beginning to clear up some of the confusion that had bedevilled the maquilas by putting the whole industry under a strong minister with a certain amount of transdepartmental authority. The commission was made up of representatives from various ministries, including the Interior, Treasury, Planning and Budget, SECOFI, and Labor and Social Security. The commission was serviced by a technical secretariat to collect information and organized an advisory committee for the maquila industry. This provided a forum where the national and local maquila associations and other relevant bodies (for example the AmCham maquila committee) and individuals (for example, plant managers) could discuss matters of mutual interest in centers of the maquila industry as well as places where the industry was just emerging. Mauricio de María y Campos, who had negotiated a series of tax breaks for the maquilas while in the Ministry of Finance

[69]

in the 1970s, was appointed under secretary of industrial development and chairman of the commission. A certain amount of success has been achieved in at last bringing a more uniform administrative structure to the maquila industry and decentralizing the regulation of the maquilas from Mexico City.

Between 1979 and 1985, maquilas increased by 40 percent and employees almost doubled. There were significant variations in the rate of increase between the different industrial branches represented in the maquila industry as a whole. Table 3.4 details the changes in the sectoral composition of the maquila industry in this period.[26] The apparel sector was the only one that actually had fewer plants in 1985 than in 1979, and although it did increase its workforce by about 20 percent, this was the smallest increase of any sector. Nevertheless, in 1985 it still acounted for 14 percent of plants and about 10 percent of total maquila employment. The major sectors in terms of employment were electric and electronic components and equipment, which have always been large maquila employers, and transport equipment, by far the fastest growing sector.[27]

It is clear that a good deal of thought went into the problem of the "enclave" nature of the maquilas at this time, and the relationships

*Table 3.4*
Maquila industry by sector, 1979–1985.

| SECTOR | PLANTS | | PERCENT CHANGE | EMPLOYEES | | PERCENT CHANGE |
|---|---|---|---|---|---|---|
| | 1979 | 1985 | | 1979 | 1985 | |
| Food | 12 | 12 | 0 | 1,481 | 1,855 | 30 |
| Apparel | 122 | 108 | −10 | 17,631 | 21,473 | 20 |
| Leather | 20 | 36 | 80 | 1,655 | 4,531 | 70 |
| Furniture | 54 | 74 | 40 | 3,515 | 6,522 | 90 |
| Chemical | – | 3 | – | – | 92 | – |
| Transport Equipment | 38 | 63 | 70 | 5,035 | 40,145 | 700 |
| Non-electrical Equipment | 14 | 21 | 50 | 18,034 | 2,386 | 30 |
| Electronic Equipment | 56 | 81 | 40 | 28,664 | 44,776 | 60 |
| Electronic Components | 124 | 193 | 60 | 34,797 | 57,083 | 60 |
| Toys, Sports | 16 | 26 | 60 | 2,454 | 7,265 | 200 |
| Other Manufactures | 54 | 105 | 90 | 7,775 | 13,904 | 80 |
| Services | 30 | 38 | 30 | 6,524 | 12,936 | 100 |
| Total | 540 | 760 | (40) | 111,365 | 211,968 | (90) |

SOURCE: Calculated from INEGI (1988: table 7) rounded.

between the center in Mexico City and the regions, particularly the frontera norte. Distinguished Mexican scholars, some quite sympathetic to the maquila program, had been calling emphatically since the 1970s for the integration of the maquilas, and by implication the whole of the frontera norte, more productively into the national economy. Jorge Bustamante, who was to be the leading figure in the establishment of COLEF, a group of research centers along the border, and Victor Urquidi (the then President of *El Colegio de México*), with Sofia Mendez Villarreal, had argued this case persuasively in two influential articles in *Foro Internacional* in 1975 which criticized the Mexican government's naive optimism on the industry.[28] By the 1980s, this theme had been taken up by almost every Mexican commentator on the maquilas, and many were beginning to draw the conclusion that it was something inherent in the maquila industry rather than something inherent in the nature of Mexico that was preventing this from happening.

The development of the maquila industry in the 1980s has fed the purveyors of fact and propaganda alike with rich pickings. On the one side there were those who have always been implacable in their opposition to the maquilas, primarily because they were seen to represent the long and greedy fingers of U.S. imperialism and to promote ever greater degrees of Mexican dependency. Such vehicles of radical opinion as *Punto Critico* and *UnomasUno* almost always portray foreign capital and its works in a negative light, and any attention they give to the maquila industry is usually intended to expose the exploitation of the workers and highlight the damage that the maquilas do to Mexico. On the other side, the Mexican facilitators, whether paid advocates for the industry or independents convinced of its benefits for the country, rarely acknowledge any drawbacks of the maquilas, tending to interpret all problems of the industry in terms of militant labor and bureaucratic inefficiencies at the local and national levels. Some, however, who generally see the industry in a positive though not entirely uncritical light have begun to question some of its fundamental characteristics. This questioning is a logical consequence of the paradoxical condition of the industry in the 1980s, and the options for the future that it suggests.

The paradox of the maquila industry is encapsulated in the relationship among the growth of maquila jobs, the rate of devaluation of the Mexican peso, and the dollars that it brings to Mexico. The raw data in pesos present an apparently unambiguous picture. Between 1980 and 1982, maquila value added increased from about 18 billion pesos to nearly 200 billion, and by 1987, to over 2,000 billion pesos. But the figure that matters most to the Mexican economy (if not always to the Mexican worker) is what the maquilas earn in U.S. dollars. The value added in 1980 was $770 million, $1.16 billion in 1982, and

$1.57 billion in 1986. Clearly the maquila industry was doing more than standing still, but it was having to run faster and faster for every increment in its dollar revenues. The same can be said for wages. Table 3.5 documents average wages and value added between 1970 and 1988.

The implications of the constant devaluation of the peso has led such publications as *El Financiero*, an important mouthpiece of the financial and business community in Mexico, to complain that as the dollar buys more and more labor, electricity, and other services in Mexico, the maquila industry brings in relatively fewer and fewer dollars.[29] The nub of the problem is that the maquila industry, though it is growing, is growing less quickly than the fall in the value of the peso. *Maquiladora Newsletter*, in a rare examination of this effect, calculated that in the first quarter of 1986 the value added in dollar terms grew only 2 percent over the first quarter of 1985 (the 1984 to 1985 increase had been 15.5 percent), but to achieve this the maquilas had to increase their value added growth by 34 percent in constant pesos between the first quarters of 1985 and 1986 (August 1986:2).

Mexico is caught in a dilemma of its own making, though hardly one that it would have freely chosen. In national terms, the decline in foreign earnings as a result of the falling price of oil dislocated all the economic calculations of the early 1980s. As the foreign debt passed 100 billion dollars (no one is certain where the

*Table 3.5*
Wages and value added in the maquila industry, 1970–1988.

| YEAR | AVERAGE HOURLY OPERATIVE WAGE | | VALUE ADDED | |
|---|---|---|---|---|
| | IN PESOS | IN U.S.$ | IN BILLIONS OF PESOS | IN MILLIONS OF U.S. DOLLARS |
| 1970 | 8 | 0.63 | 0.104 | 86.7 |
| 1975 | 10 | 0.78 | 4.015 | 321.2 |
| 1980 | 23 | 1.00 | 17.729 | 770.8 |
| 1981 | 36 | 1.46 | 23.957 | 974.6 |
| 1982 | 76 | 1.32 | 46.588 | 811.6 |
| 1983 | 84 | 0.70 | 99.521 | 824.5 |
| 1984 | 126 | 0.75 | 194.757 | 1,160.6 |
| 1985 | 190 | 0.74 | 325.250 | 1,265.6 |
| 1986 | 577 | 0.94 | 792.018 | 1,295.4 |
| 1987 | 1,003 | 0.75 | 2,235.149 | 1,572.5 |
| 1988* | 1,825 | 0.80 | 3,650.000 | 1,600.0 |

NOTE: average rounded peso-dollar exchange rates used.
* my own estimate.
SOURCES: 1970, Banamex; 1975–1987, INEGI (1988) and *Avances*.

money is, but a good part of it is undoubtedly in personal accounts in U.S. and European banks), and demographic and political pressures intensified the necessity to create new jobs, the maquila sector, the most "dynamic" in the economy, could not be allowed to flounder. The need to keep wages low in dollar terms came into unbearable tension with the realities of inflation, and permanent devaluation of the currency seemed the only possible strategy for survival. The inevitable consequence was that for Mexico the dollar earning capacity of the industry has actually declined dramatically in relative terms.

Under the presidency of de la Madrid, the maquila industry certainly enjoyed more official expressions of support than under any previous incumbent. The 1983 legislation and initiatives to foster foreign investment outside the areas of greatest industrial concentration in Mexico encouraged the industry to believe that the government was genuinely concerned to further the interests of the maquilas. This belief was enhanced by a meeting in 1985 of the president and the managers of industrial parks from eight Mexican cities to discuss the maquila industry. Shortly after this meeting de la Madrid declared that the maquila industry was a "priority sector" for the economy (*Business Mexico*, February 1986:86–87), and he set in motion yet another round of SECOFI surveys to determine how the industry could be released from its shackles. In August 1986, SECOFI once again committed itself to bring the maquilas into closer interaction with domestic industry, encourage national industry to participate in subcontracting programs or in supplying maquilas, and promote the establishment of high technology maquila plants. There was, however, a set of concrete targets for the industry (*MN*, Sept. 1986:2–6), a welcome change from the generalities of previous official statements, including an annual average growth rate of 15 percent for new plants though none for jobs. The implication is that fewer large plants were preferable to more small plants. Machinery, electric and electronic supplies, and automotive equipment were identified as priority sectors. Some locational recommendations were also made to attract maquilas to areas with available infrastructure and labor, and with idle capacity. In the first category, of the main maquila sites only Matamoros, Reynosa, Nuevo Laredo, and Chihuahua City were listed, and in the second category only Mexicali, indicating the official view that Tijuana and Juárez were not among the places where further maquila development was deemed desirable. Targets for increasing local sourcing of maquila inputs (backward linkages) from the 1985–1986 level of 1.5 percent to 5 percent over the following two years were set. It is difficult to see how the Mexican authorities could have achieved these goals by persuasion alone, and they did not.

The third phase of the maquila industry, particularly after 1986 when peso devaluation began to accelerate, has been full of contradiction.

[73]

Although maquila dollar earnings have increased, as a proportion of Mexico's debt repayments they account for a smaller and smaller part. Therefore, the more the industry grows, the less it appears to contribute to the solution of Mexico's most desperate problems.[30] The only area in which this could be disputed is in the creation of jobs, and even here the previous assumption that the maquila industry brought Mexico almost costless jobs has to be reexamined.

The costs and benefits of the maquilas are not, of course, exclusively of concern to Mexico. Although the U.S. government has officially done nothing to encourage the industry, and it has no legal status in the U.S.[31] some interest groups in the U.S. have presented the maquila industry as a crucial component in the industrial progress of the nation. Thus, for some it is not only the welfare and prosperity of Mexican and U.S. communities along the border that the maquila industry is said to promote, but also the competitive position of the U.S. in the global marketplace.

## Notes

1. Barajas (in González-Arechiga, ed., 1987) identifies four stages: 1965 to 1970, 1971 to 1976, 1977 to 1981, and 1982 to 1986.

2. This information comes from an interview with Wayne McClintock, in April 1987 in El Paso. The maquila idea, of course, could have been invented/discovered independently by several people, as were many of the great ideas of science.

3. One writer concluded, rather prematurely, that by the late 1960s the "negative reaction of the two big trade unions in the United States has put a stop to this promising development," that is, the maquila industry (Derossi 1971:95).

4. Mr Bolin's resumé states: "1964 Started the Mexican Border Industrialization Program—provided 100,000 jobs in ten years." Grunwald (1985:139, n.5) asserts that Bolin introduced the "twin plant" concept in his ADL report on Juárez in 1964.

5. This contained the germ of the idea of "production sharing" that was popularized some years later by Peter Drucker in the *Wall Street Journal* (1977), discussed in chapter 1.

6. The GSP Rules are also relevant to the issue, but the controversy has always focussed around 806/807.

7. It is as well to note that the term maquila is used in Mexico in the sense of "small workshop," without any implication of in-bond activity. For an interesting discussion of the definition of "maquila" see Tamayo and Fernández (1983:221–223).

8. For the more general phenomenon of the regional distribution of industry involving the move from snowbelt (rustbelt) to sunbelt in the U.S. (Sawers and Tabb, eds., 1984).

9. C. C. Whitworth, "Memorandum: Whitworth to Price," Central Power and Light Co., San Antonio, Texas (4 December 1967:1).

10. Whirlpool, which is now a major Fortune 500 Corporation, was actually brought into existence by Sears' need for someone to manufacture refrigerators for them. It grew out of a company making steam locomotive parts that General Wood persuaded to retool, with Sears supplying the finance (Worthy 1984:70–71).

11. It is possible, though unlikely, that Rockwell was demonstrating a commendable pan American consciousness, and not appropriating the title "America" for the territory occupied by the U.S.

12. A Department of State "Airgram" in 1971 noted that since June, 37 maquilas in Tijuana had closed and 53 had been established. "The Embassy is aware of one family, for example, which has operated at least seven different textile assembly firms during the past three years" (17 December 1971:3).

13. Since *Instituto Nacional de Estadistica Geográfia e Informatica* (INEGI) took over responsibility for maquila industry data in the 1980s, a commendable uniformity has been introduced. INEGI (1988) has data from 1975 to 1986, updated periodically by "Avance de Información Económica. Industria Maquiladora de Exportación." In my tables all the pre-1975 data are estimates derived from a variety of published and unpublished sources, not always consistent, and must be regarded with caution. Post-1975 figures are all yearly averages, but pre-1975 figures may not be.

14. It must also be noted that some corrupt Mexican unions made agreements with maquila employers that violated the labor law. On the case of Acapulco Fashions and the unions in Juárez see Carrillo and Hernández (1985:158–164).

15. Pena's bibliography (1981) indicates that most Mexican researchers were hostile to the maquilas in the 1970s.

16. These figures (and those to follow) are taken from Van Waas' excellent thesis (1981:172ff.), citing official sources.

17. The maquila industry in Nuevo Laredo took many years to recover. The workforce declined from about 8,000 in 1974 to a low of around 2,000. By 1988 it had reached about 8,000 again.

18. Goldfinger (1975) reports U.S. Customs demands for $30 million from Mattel for concealment of foreign components in reimported maquila goods, and the general malaise of the company.

19. For example, Sears has a "Partners in Progress" award that it presents to suppliers that have achieved top levels of quality and delivery; and General Motors circulates "quality audit" performance ratings to its eight (1987) maquila contractors, presumably *"pour encourager les autres."*

20. The Chinese in the Shenzhen Special Economic Zone have made similar concessions to foreign capital (Sklair 1985:588).

21. The basis on which value added was worked out was altered in 1980 and this resulted in a substantial reduction in the total. This is allowed for in the INEGI data (see below, chapter 9).

22. Total U.S. fixed investment in Mexico is estimated at over $10 billion. Rivero (in Lee, ed., 1988:35–36) asserts that the maquila industry, traditionally a labor rather than capital intensive sector, had $5 billion in fixed assets, about one-quarter of Mexico's total foreign investment. U.S. TNCs have traditionally accounted for around 90 percent of maquila investment.

23. Despite the difficulties of exact comparisons in terms of varying rates of pay along the border and hours worked, these generalizations appear firmly based.

24. For a useful account of the effects of all of this on Border Banks, see Prock (1985). On the related question of capital flight, see de Murguia (1986).

25. A booklet issued by the U.S.-Mexico Chamber of Commerce in 1987, "Doing Business in Mexico," lists (Appendix F) 55 maquilas authorized to sell in the Mexican market and their products.

26. Sector names in full are *selección, preparación, empaque y enlatado de alimentos* (food); *ensamble de prendas de vestir y otros productos confeccionados con textiles y otros materiales* (apparel); *fabricación de calzado e indústria del cuero* (shoes and leather); *ensamble de muebles, sus accesorios y otros productos de madera y metal* (furniture); *productos químicos* (chemicals); *construcción, reconstrucción y ensamble de equipo de transporte y sus accesorios* (transport equipment); *ensamble y reparación de herramienta, equipo y sus partes, excepto eléctrico* (nonelectrical tools); *ensamble de maquinaria, equipo, aparatos y artículos eléctricos y electrónicos* (electrical and electronic equipment); *materiales y accesorios eléctricos y electrónicos* (electrical and electronic components); *ensamble de juguetes y artículos deportivos* (toys and sports goods); *otras industrias manufactureres* (other manufactures); *servicios* (services).

27. Of relevance here is Suárez-Villa's (1985) concept of the "urban-manufacturing life cycle." On the basis of rapid increases in manufacturing employment in some sectors he sees a bright future for the maquila industry. This work is marked by great empirical richness and conceptual originality.

28. See also, the papers that later appeared in English, Bustamante (1983); and Urquidi and Mendez Villarreal (1978). A more recent paper by Urquidi and Carrillo Huerta (of July 1988) reached me too late for consideration here.

29. See Muñoz Ríos (1987:1,31), a commentary on a SECOFI study suggesting in part that the maquila growth due to devaluation is being bought too dearly. I return to this issue in chapter 9.

30. A public debt conversion program (debt equity swap scheme) was introduced as a temporary expedient in 1986. Up to January 1988, over $2 billion of debt had been converted, 13 percent of which went into the maquila industry, and most of the rest into automobile and tourist investment.

31. Government employees, however, are often to be seen promoting the maquilas (see Turner 1983; the chief of the U.S Trade Center in Mexico City; and others discussed in chapter 8, below).

# 4

## The Californias

Although Mexicali is the state capital, most popular and scholarly attention has been focussed on Tijuana. The reasons for this are not difficult to understand. While Mexicali is far from any major U.S. population center, Tijuana is a short distance from San Diego, which houses the largest naval base in the United States and, more symbolically, a scenic drive from Camp Pendleton (a huge marine base), Orange County, and Los Angeles. Indeed, Tijuana's dubious reputation is due to its capacity to provide "recreation" for temporary or permanent Californians whose lives used to be constrained by morally repressive laws and mores (see Demaris 1970; Price 1973).

The northern border states have always been characterized by a high rate of inmigration from the rest of Mexico and the introduction of the bracero program in the 1940s undoubtedly attracted many Mexicans to the border areas. The Mexican census indicates that the population of the municipio of Tijuana almost tripled from 1940 to 1950 (see table 2.1). The real population of Tijuana is today estimated to be well in excess of one million people, and it is now "one of the fastest growing metropolitan areas on the continent, and the site of the largest international border crossing in the world" (Herzog 1985:297). The growth and prosperity of San Diego and its agricultural hinterland was the necessary corollary to the growth of Tijuana. Commerce and trade over the international border had always been brisk, if not always entirely legal. Successive Mexican governments had realized that, as Antonio Bermúdez argued when he went about the task of establishing PRONAF, to recapture the northern market the Mexicans would have to create an industrial society along the northern border. Looking northwards from Tijuana, while the vertical borderland section might extend the 100 or so miles to the heavily Mexicanized areas of east Los Angeles, the whole of

California from San Diego to the Bay Area around San Francisco may now be regarded as one long industrial corridor and this, naturally, has not gone unnoticed in Mexico. The phenomenon of California, one of the paradigm cases of "sunbelt" development, is obviously an important part of the Baja California-California relationship.

This is particularly the case for the high tech industries that catapulted Silicon Valley into a permanent place in the industrial archeology of the planet after the 1960s, and rapidly moved south through Los Angeles and to San Diego thereafter. While not the only industry to have a significant impact on the Mexican side of the Californias borderlands, the electronics industry did play a peculiarly central role in the drama that was to unfold along the border as a result of the technology of the production of electronic goods and the division of labor that this technology makes possible. Simply put, there is a great deal of relatively simple labor intensive hand work involved in the production of electronic goods, so the cost of labor has always been of significance. However, the cheapness of labor does not explain everything. Governments in countries where there is a large supply of cheap labor must accommodate the needs of the potential investors before systems of global production can be set up. By the mid-1960s many countries were providing substantial incentives to attract "production sharing" foreign investment. Californian corporations, particularly the electronics firms that were mushrooming all along the west coast, were quick to see the advantages of global production. It was at this point that the Mexican government began to ask why these Californian corporations were looking to the Far East and not south. The answer was simple enough. There was no administrative structure in Mexico, such as the export processing zones in Taiwan and South Korea, or the virtual free zones in Hong Kong and Singapore, within which the foreign corporation might feel safe to operate. For Baja California the "production sharing" idea seemed both logical and convenient. For California, U.S., the reformation of capitalism was coming closer to home.

Baja California, therefore, was doubly receptive to the maquiladora program. It shared with the rest of the border the factors that made global production in Mexico an attractive option, and its proximity to one of the world's fastest growing centers of high tech industry meant that it started with a comparative advantage over other border locations.

## The Maquila Industry in Tijuana and San Diego[1]

The first "maquila type" plants were established in Tijuana years before the official program got under way (see Mungaray 1983:26). From the mid-1960s, private facilitators in California, principally the Cal

Pacifico company, began to develop the shelter plan concept. Many of those who were to become influential players in the maquila industry, like Richard Campbell who founded the successful maquila park in Nogales, Richard Bolin, of Arthur D. Little, and Enrique Esparza, whose firm eventually became the leading facilitator in Tijuana, had worked for Cal Pacifico.

Although there were numbers of small companies running maquilas in the early 1960s, in 1966 when the BIP was introduced, some larger and more notable corporations began to look seriously at Tijuana. The electronics industry was well represented in this early inflow. Litton Industries, operating under the name Triad de México, opened two plants. The larger made memory cores for computers, and the smaller made transformers. Fairchild, one of the pioneers of the global electronics industry, also opened a component assembly plant in Tijuana in 1966. The company already had electronics plants in Hong Kong, Korea, and other low-wage sites. In 1967, a Fairchild official was quoted as saying that wages in the Far East were less than two-thirds those in Tijuana, "But on heavier components where freight cost is important, the higher Mexican wage is offset by low freight charges, so the advantage is with Tijuana" (*Wall Street Journal*, 25 May 1967:10). This operation was typical of the electronics maquila industry in the Californias. Fairchild shipped all the components from its plant in Mountain View, Silicon Valley to Tijuana (see *Business Abroad*, 11 December 1967:20–21).

By the end of 1971 Tijuana had 36 maquilas, about the same number as Mexicali and Matamoros, but lagging behind the 52 that Ciudad Juárez had attracted. Tijuana had fewer employees (4,400) than Mexicali (nearly 6,000) or Juárez (more than 5,600), but the really significant figure was for the value of equipment and machinery in Tijuana's maquila industry. There were 5 substantial maquila sites in 1971, the 3 already mentioned, plus Matamoros and Nuevo Laredo all of whom had more than 20 plants. Though Tijuana had the second largest number of plants, and the third highest employment total, it was bottom of the list for fixed capital (data from SIC, cited in Villalobos 1973: table 1). This can be explained by the fact that Tijuana had attracted a disproportionate share of two categories of maquilas—needle trades subcontracting for the apparel industry in California, mostly small shops using secondhand sewing machines of low value; and simple electronics assembly plants, often operating under shelter or subcontracting plans, which utilized low levels of skill but physically very demanding and sometimes dangerous hand work. Such plants had little capital equipment relative to the value of the final product, the key to maquila profitability.

The U.S. labor unions did not sit idly by as these maquilas were beginning to dot the industrial landscape of the frontera norte, and the

AFL-CIO in San Diego did try to defend its interests and the jobs of its members locally. There were attempts to forge an anti-maquila alliance between the San Diego County Federation of Labor and the CTM in Baja California, but it foundered for the stark reason that the CTM officials wanted maquila jobs to come to Mexico as much as the San Diego AFL-CIO wanted them to stay north of the border. The unions in Tijuana recruited very few members from the local maquilas, though the CTM in Tecate was a little more successful. The complaints of the AFL-CIO were entirely justified in at least one particular. The promise that the maquila industry would create "twin plants" was totally unrealized in the case of San Diego and Tijuana. Most of the maquilas at this time in Tijuana were typically offshoots of parent companies in Silicon Valley, for electronics, and Los Angeles, for the needle trades. San Diego itself had seen few if any manufacturing jobs from the maquilas in Tijuana. There is no report at this period of a company establishing a maquila in Tijuana and any sort of support facility, other than an office or a freight depot, in San Diego. This was a development for which San Diego would have to wait some time, although it was happening in a few other locations along the border at the turn of the 1970s, particularly where there were industrial parks on both sides of the border.

Tijuana did, in fact, have a small industrial park at this time, the *Centro Industrial Barranquita*, established in the mid-1960s by a Mexican developer. This was not an industrial park in the accepted sense of the term, certainly nothing like the parks being created in Nogales or in Ciudad Juárez. It was more like a zoning device to encourage factories to locate near each other, and few services were provided beyond the provision of industrial space. The lack of proper industrial parks meant that certain types of U.S. corporations were less likely to establish maquilas in Tijuana and, conversely, certain types were more likely to do so.[2]

Apart from the lack of a real industrial park, Tijuana's main competitive disadvantage, which it shared with Mexicali, was that it had the highest minimum wage levels in the whole of Mexico. As I have already presented some comparative wage figures in table 2.3, let it suffice to say that the general minimum daily wage in Baja California Norte in 1970–1971 was the equivalent of $3.68, compared with $2.88 in Ciudad Juárez, $2.70 in Nogales and Matamoros, $2.64 in Laredo, and $2.56 in Mexico City itself (Ericson 1970: table 1). The maquilas were obliged to pay fringe benefits and most added some company benefits, which generally averaged out at around 50 percent of the minimum wage, and so the absolute wage differentials between Tijuana and Mexicali and the rest of the border were even greater than the minimum wage figures suggest.

For the "true believers" of the maquila movement, the experience of the first five years in Tijuana must have been rather disappointing.

Both in terms of absolute numbers of maquilas, about 7 per year on average, and in terms of jobs created, less than 1,000 per year, the industry clearly had not even begun to make a significant impact on Tijuana's critical unemployment and underemployment problems. Nevertheless, something had been achieved. A small, but expanding U.S. owned industrial base was being established to stand beside, and sometimes to join in ventures with domestic industry in Tijuana. From Tijuana, through San Diego and up to Los Angeles and beyond, groups of dedicated entrepreneurs were slowly beginning to realize that the maquila industry did have some very concrete benefits to offer, particularly in the needle trades, and in electronics. However, few people, even the most optimistic, could have predicted that, as table 4.1 shows, the maquila industry in Tijuana was about to take off.

By 1974, Tijuana had 100 maquilas (and Tecate had increased its total to 14). There is some confusion about the exact timing of this growth, due to the anomaly that before 1972 maquilas operating in free zones were not legally required to register under the maquila legislation. Internal checks of the names of maquilas around this time show that many of the original companies had dropped out, but the inflow more than made up for the outflow. For a time, employment exceeded 10,000, but this was badly affected by the first crisis. Half of the maquilas were producing electrical or electronic goods, about one-quarter were in apparel of various kinds, and the rest were in a variety of products from plastic bags to orthopaedic appliances.

Tijuana's record on fixed capital and value added per worker did not change greatly in the early 1970s, despite the increase in the numbers of

*Table 4.1*
Tijuana by maquilas and employees, 1970–1988.

| YEAR | NUMBER OF PLANTS | NUMBER OF EMPLOYEES | YEAR | NUMBER OF PLANTS | NUMBER OF EMPLOYEES |
|------|--------|-----------|------|--------|-----------|
| 1970 | 16 | 2,000 | 1980 | 123 | 12,343 |
| 1971 | 36 | 4,400 | 1981 | 127 | 14,482 |
| 1972 | 54 | 5,250 | 1982 | 124 | 14,959 |
| 1973 | 94 | 8,000 | 1983 | 131 | 17,423 |
| 1974 | 101 | 10,000 | 1984 | 147 | 23,047 |
| 1975 | 99 | 7,844 | 1985 | 192 | 25,913 |
| 1976 | 93 | 7,795 | 1986 | 238 | 30,248 |
| 1977 | 92 | 7,111 | 1987 | 317 | 40,409 |
| 1978 | 95 | 8,778 | 1988 (Jan.) | 324 | 40,965 |
| 1979 | 101 | 10,889 | | | |

SOURCES: 1970–1974, my own estimates; 1975–1988, INEGI (1988: table 3), and *Avances*.

maquilas. Phenomenal growth of the industry in Nogales because of the industrial park had increased the maquila big league to six by 1973, but Tijuana still had the lowest level of fixed capital per worker of these six locations, and the maquilas of Tijuana were producing a much higher rate of value added per worker than the average along the border. This suggests that the maquila industry in Tijuana in the early 1970s was rather different to the industry elsewhere, particularly in Ciudad Juárez where the fixed capital per worker was three times greater than in Tijuana, and where the fixed capital per plant was between five and six times greater (calculated from Baird and McCaughan 1975:9). This was not only because Juárez had more employees per plant than Tijuana, but more importantly, because Juárez was already attracting some major Fortune 500 corporations who were making substantial capital investments in the well managed industrial parks of the city (see chapter 5).

Tijuana's response was *Ciudad Industrial Nueva Tijuana* (CIN), an initiative of the state government of Baja California, located on the eastern flank of Tijuana at the Mesa de Otay, and intended to draw off some of the existing maquilas from the most congested parts of the city and to provide a new site for incoming maquilas. CIN recruited its first foreign maquilas in 1976, but although many domestic public and private enterprises came in and land speculation in and around the area gained momentum, there were very few U.S. maquilas on the ground until the early 1980s. Slowly, corporations began to realize the advantages of the relatively wide open spaces of the Mesa de Otay compared with downtown Tijuana, and as customs facilities were located nearby and the promise of a new border crossing came to fruition, the center of gravity of the Tijuana maquila industry gradually began to shift from the areas of traditional maquila concentration to the *Ciudad Industrial Nueva*. The main reason why most maquilas did prefer the traditional areas, despite the fact that they were becoming more and more congested, was that they were near to the main centers of working-class housing. The authorities began to build public housing schemes near to the factory sites on the Mesa de Otay and to provide shops, schools, and clinics in the area, but these tended to be for middle-class rather than working-class families. The decision in 1979 by Matsushita (one of the first Japanese maquilas) to locate its new TV assembly operation in the CIN was a definite coup both for Tijuana and for CIN, and other substantial maquilas followed.[3] Housing continues to be a major problem and this contributes to a high rate of labor turnover.

The traumas of 1974 and 1975 swept over the maquilas of Tijuana, but almost in slow motion compared to what was happening in other parts of the border, with temporary layoffs rather than permanent plant closures between 1974 and 1978. Maquila employment increased every single year since 1978, even in 1981–1982 when the number of maquilas declined nationally, the only major maquila center for which this is the case. The crisis and its passing highlight the special circumstances of Tijuana. The substantial increases in the minimum wage rates had a relatively greater impact in Baja California, where minimum wages were always the highest in the country, than elsewhere along the border. It is therefore not surprising that employment losses were greater in Tijuana and Mexicali, than in the areas of lower minimum wages like Ciudad Juárez, Reynosa, and Matamoros where, despite some closures, total year-end to year-end maquila employment actually increased from 1974 onwards. There may also have been some disadvantage in having fewer large corporations that might be prepared to absorb losses and weather the storm, than some other places, though it is also true that there were some very large corporations who pulled out, leaving thousands of workers stranded over this period (see Baird and McCaughan 1975). The mid-1970s were a baptism of fire for the Tijuana maquila industry, but the optimism of the "true believers" was unabated while everyone around them, including some Mexican government officials, were anticipating the collapse and even the total disappearance of the maquila industry.

The employers' association in Tijuana and CANACINTRA (to which all maquilas are obliged to belong), both tried to impose some unity of action and purpose on the industry in the latter part of the 1960s, but neither of these bodies was very successful. The maquila association emerged gradually in the 1970s, but it lacked muscle due to the fact that so few of the maquilas were willing to play an active part in its work. The absence of industrial parks (partly explained by the shortage of suitable flat terrain in Tijuana), is responsible to some extent for the relative lack of unity of the maquila community there. It was around this time that the San Diego Economic Development Corporation (EDC) began to play a more active role in the maquila industry. The EDC, a nonprofit organization funded mainly by the City and the County of San Diego, exists to attract jobs to the area. The organization was established in 1965 in order to help in the task of diversifying the manufacturing industry of San Diego which was then seen to be over-dependent on the rather unstable aerospace industry.[4] The EDC was radically reorganized in 1977, and one of its new tasks, and a task that was to become more and more central in the late 1970s and the 1980s, was to support the maquila industry in Tijuana (just emerging from the slump) and to ensure that San Diego derived all possible benefits from the anticipated boom in "twin plants."

In 1980 a Baja California development council was established. The President of the Tijuana branch was Carlos Bustamante Anchondo, the owner of the local gas company, and through his powerful Grupo Bustamante, the developer of the Tijuana International Industrial Park. The council brought together the local chambers of industry and commerce, bankers, and the state government. The council and the EDC worked together but, for reasons that were probably more to do with the internal politics of Baja California than its effectiveness, the organization was abolished in the mid-1980s.

The maquila association in Tijuana had always been seen by the U.S. part of the maquila industry to be a Mexican, Spanish language organization, unable to organize the maquilas in the city for any concerted action at all. This prompted some of the largest U.S. owned maquilas to create their own organization. In 1982, under the stimulus of the devaluation of the peso, 18 maquilas formed the Western Maquila Coordinating Council. This became the Western Maquila Trade Association (WMTA) which, since then, has represented the interests of most of the important owners and facilitators of the maquila industry in Tijuana and San Diego. The first task of the WMTA was to deal with what many saw to be a growing danger of an anarchic wage spiral in the maquilas of Tijuana. As maquila employment rose dramatically in the 1980s, and particularly after the devaluations of 1982, some maquilas were finding it more and more difficult to attract skilled workers.[5] In order to retain and recruit skilled workers, some maquilas had proposed to raise wages to hold their dollar value and a wages survey carried out by the WMTA revealed little pattern or consistency in wage levels. The results of this survey and the ensuing discussions persuaded most of the maquilas in Tijuana that their interests would be best served by a common if not uniform wages policy. Though not all the maquilas were in the WMTA, most of the big employers were members, and since 1982 they have been able to exert sufficient influence over those that counted in the industry to prevent the runaway wage inflation that some feared as labor shortages began to be reported.

The WMTA grew in numbers and influence and, by 1986, its members employed about three-quarters of the maquila labor force in Tijuana. One of the most important differences between the organization of the maquilas in Tijuana and, for example, in Matamoros, is that in Matamoros the maquila association executive is usually dominated by U.S. managers (see chapter 6), while in Tijuana it is Mexican officials and managers who are most active. It is this that explains the perceived need for the creation of a separate body, the WMTA, to represent the interests of U.S. capital in Tijuana/San Diego.

1986 was a record year for the maquila industry in Mexico, and nowhere was this more marked than in Tijuana. As the *Los Angeles Times* reported on its front page on 10 March 1987, no less than 79 new maquilas opened in Tijuana in 1986, the highest single year total since the inception of the BIP, and 7 of these were major Japanese companies. One, the Sony Corporation, had previously had a maquila in Tijuana, a subcontract operation with Cal Pacifico in the mid-1970s, but had pulled out of Mexico in the late 1970s. Their return was a response to the success of the Matsushita maquila in Tijuana and highly symbolic.[6]

The influence of Mexican facilitators in Tijuana has grown appreciably in the 1980s. Salas-Porras identifies 12 main groups or individuals active in the maquila industry in Baja California in her study of the impact of the maquilas on Mexico's regional bourgeoisie (1987:57–58) and most of these operate in Tijuana. Many are involved in leasing industrial sites, and some are involved in the lucrative subcontracting. One of these is Jorge Salman Haddad, an ex-president of the National Maquila Council and owner of Industrias Salman, the largest garment maquila in Tijuana. An outspoken defender of the industry he is often quoted in the Californian press.[7] Salman, and other maquila activists in the Californias, were subject to criticism and attack from the U.S. side of the border as well as from Mexico. The San Diego Labor Council joined in a national AFL-CIO antimaquila campaign at the end of 1986 (see chapter 8), and in early 1987 the head of the local AFL-CIO, Joseph Francis, circulated a letter to all the key local government officials in San Diego criticizing the role of the publicly funded EDC in the promotion of the maquilas and the export of U.S. jobs (*San Diego Union*, 12 February 1987:D1,2). This was not the first time that the San Diego/Tijuana maquila industry had come under attack, and to the facilitators the resurgence of labor union opposition must have seemed quite ominous.

The economic impact of the maquilas of Baja California on California, U.S. is an important local political issue. The commerce department of the state of California sponsored a study of it which discovered that almost 8 out of every 10 U.S. parent corporations of Baja maquilas were, in fact, located in southern California, and about two-thirds employed fewer than 1,000 workers north of the border (Clement and Jenner 1987). The foreign owned Baja California maquila industry consists of a large group of small to medium size U.S. corporations and a smaller but still significant group of large corporations, mostly based in southern California. There are two complicating factors and it is difficult to say whether they are a function of the sample, which turned out not to be random,[8] or a true reflection of the Baja California maquila industry. First, the official statistics indicate that in 1986 well over half of the maquilas in Baja California were wholly or majority Mexican owned, and less than 40 percent were wholly or majority U.S. owned. Most of these Mexican owned maquilas were very small and tended to have much shorter business lives than the U.S. owned maquilas. However, it would be just as misleading to characterize the maquila industry here (or elsewhere) as if it were composed entirely of large and stable U.S. owned plants, as it would be to characterize it as if it were entirely composed of small and unstable Mexican owned plants. Second, as Clement and Jenner clearly point out, the sample was heavily biased toward U.S. corporations involved in shelter and subcontracting arrangements. Two-thirds of the sample by number of firms were in shelter or subcontract operations while it is unlikely that as much as one-third of the U.S. maquilas in Baja California in 1986 were shelter or subcontract operations. There are good reasons for this sample bias. In the course of maquila research, one facilitator usually leads to several maquilas; and the shelter and subcontract facilitators, who rely on high profiles and maximum publicity to drum up business, are exceptions in an industry that has traditionally shunned publicity. They, and by default the corporations they represent, are thus most likely to cooperate with researchers (and journalists, too) in the expectation that business opportunities may be created in the process. Shelter and subcontract operations are not the whole of the maquila industry, but they are certainly an important part of it, especially in Tijuana.

The upshot of the study was that the maquilas of Baja California, Mexico, were shown to have a significant economic impact on the economy of California, U.S. This was estimated for the year 1985 to be in the region of $83 million, made up of $32 million in salaries for over 1,200 "twin plant" employees in San Diego County (an average of around $25,000 per person), $24 million for maquila supplies bought in California, $12 million in management fees, another $12 million in rents in San Diego, and $3 million in salaries for the 245 maquila employees living in San Diego and working across the border (an average of $12,245 per person). An additional finding was that about half of the U.S. corporations that had established maquilas had managed to avoid net decreases of employment in their U.S. operations, but that those that had lost jobs in the U.S. tended to be the larger corporations (reported in the *San Diego Union*, 18 January 1987:I-11).

The maquila industry clearly does have positive consequences for some groups on the U.S. side of the border, particularly the facilitators (who account for some of the "twin plant" and transborder salaries, rents, and most of the management fees), but leaves the question of job loss and creation in the U.S. owing to the maquilas unresolved. U.S. corporations are understandably reluctant to discuss the issue in any detail, and where circumstances have forced them to do so (as in the case of Trico analyzed in chapter 6), the issue is perpetually confused by the argument that existing jobs might not in fact survive without the maquila option.

Another indication of the increasing importance of the maquila industry even to somewhere as affluent as San Diego, is the Otay Mesa International Center and the City's Foreign Trade Zone application.[9] There has always been a clear link between these schemes and the maquilas. Otay Mesa has been promoted as "ideal for twin plant operations" because it is directly opposite "Tijuana's 1,000 acre industrial park where several hundred maquiladoras are located [sic] with close to one hundred facilities opening within 1986 alone" (in International Center promotional materials). The evidence from the successful FTZ at McAllen, Texas shows that a properly run and promoted FTZ can improve the prospects of the maquila industry anywhere along the border, and San Diego and Tijuana are excellently placed to exploit these opportunities to the full. Despite the hyperbole, the words of a Trammell Crow leasing agent, quoted in the *Los Angeles Times* in late 1986, accurately express the hopes of the crossborder private and public maquila facilitators: "Tijuana is going to become the new Hong Kong, the new industrial hub of the world . . . as long as the Mexican government continues to encourage maquiladoras and San Diego has a foreign trade zone" (cited in Ray 1986:10). This is a clear, if somewhat optimistic, local expression of the centrality of the border for the reformation of capitalism.

There is a continuing feeling in Tijuana and San Diego that, for one reason or another, they are not the undisputed leaders of the maquila industry that they deserve to be and this is reflected in the suspicion that in Juárez/El Paso, commonly seen to be the leading maquila location, the industry is run more effectively. This feeling is best expressed by the professionals who largely organize the maquila industry, the facilitators.

## The Facilitators

I have discussed the role of the public facilitators in the previous section, so here I shall focus on the private sector. It has been estimated that there were about 60 maquilas in Tijuana in 1987 that were operating under shelter or subcontract arrangements, or some variation on these themes. These maquilas were said to employ between 6,000 and 7,000 workers, distributed between about a dozen main facilitators, with the top two facilitating companies accounting for almost one-half of the total.[10]

The first significant private maquila facilitator in the Californias was Ralph Girton, whose company Cal Pacifico ran at least 6 maquilas employing almost 1,000 people in the early 1970s. By all accounts, Cal Pacifico kept a low profile and rarely joined in any of the maquila association or wider industry activities, though it was instrumental in the creation of the WMTA. Several of those who were to become leaders of the industry began their maquila careers with Cal Pacifico. One such was Enrique Esparza, first as a factory manager and then as a general trouble shooter for the whole maquila operation. These were the years when the legislative basis of the maquilas was far from certain and shelter and subcontract operators were living by their wits. Esparza, in partnership with a Mexican lawyer, eventually founded his own business, Assemble in Mexico (AIM), in 1980. In 1975, Cal Pacifico had around 1,500 workers in shelter and subcontract operations; by 1988, AIM was responsible for around 2,000 workers in 35 maquilas, while the maquilas of Cal Pacifico employed about 500 workers.

AIM is organized as a California corporation in association with a wholly owned Mexican subsidiary which owns several corporations in Mexico, and these are the companies that are legally responsible in Mexico for the shelter and subcontract operations. AIM takes out long leases on industrial buildings in and around Tijuana, mostly as the contracts are won, but sometimes speculatively in anticipation of prospective business. Factories suitable for maquilas have been in short supply in Tijuana since the flood of new maquilas began in 1985, so facilitators now have to take rather more risks than was once the case to ensure that they are not caught without facilities when lucrative contracts appear on the horizon.

In contrast to Cal Pacifico's reticence, AIM lost no opportunity to promote itself and its services publicly and in 1985 Esparza was chosen as Stanford Business School Alumni Association Entrepreneur of the Year in recognition of his achievements in building AIM into the largest shelter and subcontract operation in Tijuana/San Diego, and possibly the whole border by 1987. AIM is, by any standards, a highly profitable business.[11] We may ask why some U.S. corporations pay companies like AIM to run their maquilas for them, when so many other U.S. corporations seem quite able to run their own maquilas? The answer would be simple if all of AIM's clients were small firms with little experience of offshore production. Then we could argue that the risks and problems involved in any offshore production, and they are real enough, are such as to make it worthwhile for these small and internationally inexperienced companies to pay for the protective umbrella of a specialist facilitator. This is certainly the case for some of AIM's clients, but not all of them. Some are companies with substantial offshore experience, and/or parts of very large corporations. For all companies coming into the maquila program for the first time, irrespective of size and experience, there are several common problems for which the services of a facilitator are, literally, invaluable. The facilitator can offer local expertise. Tijuana has developed a not entirely undeserved reputation for being difficult to do business in, even if it is a profitable location. A facilitator takes much of the anxiety out of relocation. Many corporations involved in "production sharing" require very rapid startups, and the experience of the facilitator can more or less guarantee this. The costs of the facilitator, though high, are almost totally predictable, and this predictability may be seen as more important than the uncertain savings that might be made by attempting to operate without a facilitator. Finally, the client is free to concentrate on problems of production and is usually not distracted by problems of administration.

Two of AIM's post-1985 boom clients are good cases in point. The first is a maquila that started up in December 1986, on contract for a New York based electronics company, that is part of a Fortune 100 conglomerate. The maquila fabricates an electronic training device for the U.S. military.[12] AIM, like most facilitators, has made a point of promoting technology and skill transfer through the maquilas, in theory if not always in practice. In this maquila, the client and AIM have developed an intrafirm soldering workmanship training program as an alternative to competing in the ever tightening Tijuana labor market for skilled workers. The training program has another important function in that it is used to sort out potential supervisors from the mass of assemblers. This is a 40-hour program for which the Spanish speaking instructors were recruited through advertisements in both Tijuana and San Diego.

On the surface, there appears to be no good reason why this maquila should have chosen to come to Tijuana under the umbrella of AIM. The parent corporation is large, internationally experienced, and the contract is relatively straightforward. However, the corporation's inexperience in Tijuana and its rapid startup requirements tilted the balance in favour of a facilitator. There is no doubt that AIM, and many similar companies, do offer an excellent service, and that some corporations are prepared to pay the high price that is asked. In some cases—those large transnational corporations who begin their maquila involvement in a shelter or subcontract relationship—graduate into their own independent operations. Therefore, the very success of companies like AIM, in organizing trouble free and profitable manufacturing for their clients, obviates the necessity for their services. Some famous names in the global industrial galaxy, like Honeywell and General Electric, started in shelter programs and now have substantial wholly owned maquilas of their own.

Not all AIM clients are large corporations with extensive U.S. operations, however. A small high tech company at the leading edge of dot matrix printer technology with no plants in the U.S., is also a recent client of AIM. This company had been manufacturing in Puerto Rico, but had decided to move to Mexico and establish a maquila. The reasons for this were quite predictable in the era of "global production sharing." Not only were the tax benefits in Puerto Rico that had attracted the company in the first place being phased out, but the cost of labor, another prime original incentive, had become internationally uncompetitive. And Puerto Rico does not have the advantage of a permanently devaluing currency! Having made the decision to relocate its head office from Silicon Valley to San Diego, the company with the assistance of AIM, had moved all its production facilities to Tijuana.[13] This case is of great interest for the question of the potential industrial impact of the maquilas on Mexican economy and society. There are hundreds of parts in a dot matrix printer, and many of them (moulded plastic, stamped sheet metal, cables, electronic components) could be sourced in Mexico. However, in 1987, no components were being sourced locally, and the print heads were being imported in kits at great expense from Europe. There may, of course, be technical reasons why these components are unavailable locally. There is no reason to doubt the sincerity of this company's wish to source locally, for if the components were available at satisfactory quality, price, and delivery in Mexico, the company would be able to reduce costs, and local content would permit sales in the Mexican market.

This maquila also provides one small piece of information on the subject of the relationship between the maquila industry and U.S. job destruction and creation. Originally, the printer heads were being shipped from Europe to San Diego in kit form and assembled there. A year of successful working in the maquila led the company to decide to carry out this work in Tijuana. This is clearly in the interests of the company, or else they would not be doing it, in the interests of AIM in the increased revenue that will accrue from the extra employees to do this work, and presumably in the interests of the Tijuana working class, who will provide the labor and possibly pick up some new and useful skills. (In early 1987 the plant had about 80 workers in a facility of 27,000 square feet, enough for the intended doubling of the workforce.) The only losers would appear to be the workers in San Diego who no longer have jobs assembling printer heads, and those who relied on their wages.

The main competitor of AIM in the Tijuana/San Diego maquila community is IMEC, a company that has specialized mainly in the electronics field. Howard Boysen, who built it up to its present position, worked for Fairchild, the first U.S. electronics corporation to go into offshore assembly in the 1960s. Boysen opened the Fairchild factory in Tijuana in the late 1960s, and at its peak it employed 350 people, but the technology it was using was said to be too advanced for its day and it could not sell its products, so the company closed it down. Nevertheless, Boysen saw clearly the great potential of the maquila program for the electronics industry and he eventually bought out his bosses and established IMEC (International Manufacturing, Engineering, and Consulting). By 1987, IMEC owned 7 maquilas, mostly in the electronics sector, and managed several more maquilas in shelter operations. In total it employed about 1,300 people, and the various plants occupied 225,000 square feet. Since 1967, as Boysen informed a maquila conference at SDSU in 1986, IMEC has processed high technology products in excess of $12 billion market value (in Ganster, ed., 1987:99).

IMEC, like AIM and most of the other facilitators, strives to maintain a balance between a U.S. head and a Mexican managerial and technical team in each of its plants. To this end it has trained and brought along many Mexican managers and technicians which is no doubt good for Mexico and tends to be cheaper and more convenient than hiring U.S. citizens. IMEC's involvement in the maquila industry is extensive. It has established its own maquilas in the normal fashion and also by buying out the interests of at least one client when a contract had come to an end. This seems to be a very practical strategy given the whole rationale of the facilitation process, namely to be able to facilitate anything within the company's range of expertise that will turn in a profit. There are circumstances under which a potential shelter or subcontract operation between a client and a facilitator might be more profitably and/or conveniently carried out as a straight contractual deal between the facilitator (acting as the assembler or fabricator of the product) and the client.

However it is done, the profits of shelter and subcontract operations can be substantial. The proliferation of private maquila facilitators not only in San Diego/Tijuana, but all along the border is sufficient evidence for the proposition and provokes the natural question: why does the Mexican government not try to capitalize on these opportunities itself, and thereby increase its share of maquila profits? I shall return to this question in my concluding chapter.

## The Maquilas of Mexicali

Mexicali and Calexico make an interesting contrast with Tijuana and San Diego. Calexico is a small and relatively poor town with almost none of the material and human resources of San Diego.[14] Two U.S. dependent firms began production in Mexicali as early as 1952 using components and materials imported from north of the border, one produced fruit juices and the other farm equipment under contract to a U.S. company. These firms began as suppliers for the local market, but after a few years, both began to export most of their production into the Mexican interior market. As Ladman notes, "Although the Free Zone worked to their advantage, however, it probably worked to the disadvantage of many industries [in Mexicali], which would have been able to produce for the local market had it not been for the low-priced competition from the United States" (1975:95–96). The traditional forms of foreign investment held out little hope for the creation of substantial industrial employment in Mexicali.

Between 1960 and 1970 unemployment in Mexicali rose to 40 percent (Whiteford in Rosenthal-Urey 1986:33), and nontraditional industrial employment, in the shape of the BIP, was thus extremely welcome in the city. As soon as the program was announced local entrepreneurs began to build an Industrial Park, and in 1967 the *Parque Industrial Mexicali* (PIMSA) opened its gates. PIMSA was owned by a private holding company, whose main shareholder was Eduardo Martínez Palomera, an important local businessman active in local politics.[15]

PIMSA, a wholly Mexican owned company, was started as a real estate business. The first maquila, a Mexican furniture factory, moved into the park in 1969, and the first U.S. maquila, Certron Audio, the subsidiary of a California audio cassette manufacturer, moved in shortly after. The early years of the park's existence were beset with difficulties. A natural wish to accommodate all comers and to keep the rents for the industrial facilities rolling in persuaded PIMSA to let in some bad risk companies. One of these, Diomex, got into serious financial trouble and without informing the park's managers, simply vanished one weekend, without paying its 83 workers their legal entitlements. Realizing the potential damage to its reputation, PIMSA pursued the company into California and, according to the park authorities, eventually negotiated 80 percent of the severance pay for the workers.

Many U.S. maquilas were also in operation in sites outside PIMSA in the 1960s. Kayser-Roth, for example, a large clothing manufacturer who already had offshore plants in the Far East and Puerto Rico, found that for goods made from expensive U.S. fabrics which qualified under 806/807, Mexico was cheaper than Hong Kong. It opened its Mexicali maquila in 1966, and by mid-1967 was employing more than 200 workers. Hughes Aircraft also set up a maquila in Mexicali, a pilot plant for semiconductor assembly in 1967, and this grew into a substantial facility. Both of these maquilas were still producing in Mexicali in the late 1980s. Table 4.2 traces the growth of the maquila industry in Mexicali.

At one point in 1971, Mexicali actually had more maquila jobs than anywhere else in Mexico. This was a testament to the promotional skills of the park developers and the local authorities, who worked closely with them. Being in Mexicali, the state capital, and being nearer to the state officials who were overseeing the maquila program in the

Table 4.2
Mexicali by maquilas and employees, 1970–1988.

| YEAR | NUMBER OF PLANTS | NUMBER OF EMPLOYEES | YEAR | NUMBER OF PLANTS | NUMBER OF EMPLOYEES |
|------|--------|-----------|------|--------|-----------|
| 1970 | 22 | 5,000 | 1980 | 79 | 7,146 |
| 1971 | 38 | 5,500 | 1981 | 64 | 7,628 |
| 1972 | 46 | 5,800 | 1982 | 54 | 6,268 |
| 1973 | 71 | 8,700 | 1983 | 55 | 7,392 |
| 1974 | 35 | 5,900 | 1984 | 67 | 10,264 |
| 1975 | 67 | 6,324 | 1985 | 75 | 10,876 |
| 1976 | 69 | 6,604 | 1986 | 86 | 12,727 |
| 1977 | 70 | 6,351 | 1987 | 123 | 17,572 |
| 1978 | 65 | 6,543 | 1988 (Jan.) | 125 | 17,656 |
| 1979 | 77 | 7,965 | | | |

SOURCES: 1970–1974, my own estimates; 1975–1988, INEGI (1988: table 3), and *Avances.*

early days, gave some U.S. corporations a feeling of greater security compared with the relative rough and tumble of Tijuana. The problem was to sell Mexicali, rather than a specific plant site.

Another prominent U.S. company that arrived to establish a maquila in Mexicali at this time, and that has gone down in the annals of the industry, was Mextel, the local subsidiary of the then largest toy manufacturer in the U.S., Mattel. The strike and subsequent closure of the Mextel maquila are well documented (see Baird and McCaughan 1975:16ff.), and it took many years for the maquila industry in Mexicali to recover in terms of both growth and reputation from these events. U.S. firms that were relocating—at least partly to escape the unions at home—would hardly welcome militant Mexican unions along the border. Mexicali, like Nuevo Laredo and later Nogales, was to suffer from the taint of the militant worker all the more because increasingly the maquila program was being sold to U.S. corporations on the basis of its plentiful supply of "docile" female labor.

Since the 1970s, the maquila industry in Mexicali has been tightly organized by an industrial development commission, combining the private sector, federal, and city government. It acts as the promoter, facilitator, and legal guarantor of maquilas in Mexicali. An industrial development committee, containing maquila operators, local entrepreneurs, Baja California state representatives, professionals, and academics, also has a representative of the Imperial Valley Private Industry Council, from El Centro, California.

A distinctive feature of the industry in Mexicali is the "cooperative" form of maquila that has evolved since the 1970s. These "cooperatives" grew out of the women's and children's clothing maquilas that dominated the industry in its early days in Mexicali. Many maquilas in the city took on this legal form to take advantage of the substantial incentives the Mexican Social Security System offered to cooperative enterprises, though, in most cases they were not genuine cooperatives. This was because those who were organizing the cooperatives were not able to ensure supplies of materials from the U.S. companies with whom the maquilas had previously been contracted, and so they were forced to turn to the original bosses who recreated the conditions of the original maquilas. But, as these firms were in the form of "cooperatives," the workers had lost most of their labor rights, and were once again at the mercy of the local contractor who controlled their access to materials. In 1980, there were reported to be at least 5 such contractors in Mexicali, controlling 33 clothing maquila "cooperatives," recognized by the authorities, and many more "clandestine" maquilas.[16] Although the garment sector still has more maquilas than any other in Mexicali, it has long since been overtaken by the electronics sector in terms of employment, and while the maquila "cooperatives" still exist in the city, they have declined in relative importance.

There are some more conventional small private facilitators operating in the city. These tend to be Mexican rather than U.S.-inspired, probably due to the fact that Calexico and El Centro, the nearest U.S. settlements, are economically undynamic places. Assembly de México is one such Mexican shelter and subcontract firm, established in Mexicali in 1980. By 1987, it was responsible for three maquila plants in Mexicali for U.S. clients, mainly in electronic assembly, assembling and fabricating such products as smoke detectors and computer components for some prestigious U.S. manufacturers, employing around 400 workers.

In addition to Assembly de México, there were other companies offering shelter and subcontract plans for prospective maquilas, though none on the scale of AIM or IMEC in Tijuana. Some established Mexicali maquilas have begun to release their surplus plant capacity for shelter-type operations. For example, Certron Audio, one of the first maquilas in PIMSA, and still one of the largest industrial employers in the city, advertises such a service. That this is quite a recent development is clear from the fact that while only 4 shelter/subcontract operators were listed in the 1983 edition of the Mexicali *Maquila Handbook*, in 1987 no fewer than 22 were listed. The word on the lucrative nature of this business had obviously spread along the border in these few short years.

By 1988, there were over 100 maquilas in Mexicali employing over 17,000 workers. More than 20 of these maquilas were in PIMSA, employing about 6,800 workers during the peak summer months. PIMSA operates on a minimum 5-year lease period, financed in U.S. dollars or in pesos depending on circumstances, around 30 percent in

U.S. dollars, and 70 percent in pesos. Several maquilas have terminated their operations in the park in recent years, but this has been done in a legal and orderly fashion to the extent that at least one maquila came back again to the park when the possibility of reestablishing a maquila occurred. A new maquila park, El Vigia, had attracted seven U.S. maquilas, and two other Mexicali firms by 1987, but only two of the maquilas, an electrical motor manufacturer with a number of other maquilas and an aircraft parts manufacturer with several other plants actually in Mexicali, had as many as 200 employees. Total employment in the park was around 1,000. The Cachanilla industrial park was being built in 1987 in the east of the city (Industrial Development Commission of Mexicali, 1987:28).

A notable feature of the maquila industry in Mexicali is that it has made a start in the provision of childcare facilities for its pre-dominantly female workforce. This is a development that is long overdue in the industry as a whole, and it is remarkable that Mexicali, which does not appear to have much of a labor turnover problem, should be relatively further advanced in this respect than Tijuana and Ciudad Juárez, who have been complaining about turnover and absenteeism for some time. There are three maquila supported child care centers in Mexicali. El Vigia park had the first child care center ever opened in Mexico for maquila workers in an industrial park as a joint venture between the maquilas themselves, the park authorities, and the Mexican Social Security System, the IMSS (reported in *MN*, November 1986:19).

Environmental pollution plagues most transborder communities, and it has been a major problem for the maquila industry in Mexicali for some time. Wilhelm reports that the U.S. Geological Survey, the state of California, and the Imperial County health department have labelled the New River, which flows from Mexicali and eventually ends up in the Salton Sea in California, "the dirtiest river in America." The two major sources of pollution that originate in Mexicali are, "millions of gallons of raw sewage and the industrial wastes dumped by Mexicali's industries. Some of the major polluters are U.S. businesses that have established maquiladora plants in Mexicali" (1987:7). The source of the problem is twofold. First, compared with Mexico, the U.S., and particularly California, has very strict environmental protection laws. Indeed, a growing trend in the maquila industry is for U.S. corporations to relocate along the border as much for the freedom to pollute as for the low labor costs. Second, even the weak environmental and public health laws which operate in Mexico are rarely enforced on industry in order not to endanger jobs. Research from both sides of the border confirms this grim picture of almost uncontrolled environmental degradation and risk to health due in large part to the rapid and largely unplanned industrial growth (see *El Colegio de México*/Center for U.S.-Mexican Studies, 1987: part VII), and Mexicali and its poor neighbors to the north are particularly vulnerable.

Mexicali, therefore, is caught in the now classical trap of rapid industrialization. Maquila jobs and their multiplier effects have brought an unexpected expansion of life chances to large numbers of workers and their families, some of whom have migrated to Mexicali from distant parts of Mexico. The industry has also brought additional prosperity to some of the traditional economically dominant groups and new prosperity to what Whiteford terms an "emerging regional bourgeoisie" (in Rosenthal-Urey, 1986:34)—more or less what I have identified as the private and public facilitators. On the other hand, as in the rest of Mexico, real wages for the workers are in decline, and in Mexicali a labor pool that appears to be much fuller than in Tijuana or Juárez generally has the effect of maintaining docility among the work force that at least some maquila managements have exploited. Environmental pollution and health and safety at work are all relatively uncontrolled, but this is not exclusive to the maquilas but characteristic of Mexican industry as a whole. The maquila industry has changed the face of Mexicali, as it has the northern border of Baja California as a whole.

## Notes

1. The maquila industry in Tijuana is often taken to include the nearby towns of Tecate, about 30 miles east along the border, and Ensenada, south of Tijuana. The post-1982 boom brought about 40 maquilas to Tecate, and about 20 to Ensenada by 1988.

2. The importance of industrial parks for the maquila industry has been insufficiently appreciated—an exception is the work of Salas-Porras (1986, 1987). In 1988, 44 percent of maquilas, but 75 percent of maquila jobs, were located in specialized maquila parks (Ochoa in Lee, ed., 1988:90).

3. On CIN see *MN* (July 1984:1–2); and Negrete (forthcoming). The new San Diego Foreign Trade Zone and International Center, directly across the border from CIN, are discussed below.

4. An ADL report of 1966 had estimated that between 1958 and 1965 San Diego County had lost almost 20,000 manufacturing jobs.

5. In 1983 some clothing maquilas in Baja California actually had to turn work away because of a lack of qualified labor. Industrial sewing courses for men and women were being established locally to meet the demand (*MN*, December 1983:4).

6. A Tijuana/San Diego maquila delegation visited the Far East in 1986, and at least 15 delegations from Asia visited San Diego and Tijuana during 1986 and 1987.

7. See, for example, " 'Assembled in Mexico' gets Respect" (*San Francisco Examiner*, 12 May 1986:F11); and "Mexico's cross-border factories attacked, defended" (*San Diego Tribune*, 26 January 1987:44) where Salman's praise for the industry is contrasted with the complaint of a "Disgruntled Mexican worker" (who declined to be named): "I work like a donkey six days a week just so that my two children can eat, but there is nothing left for anything else. I should have stayed back home." This was at a time

when there was a chronic labor shortage in the maquilas of Tijuana and rates of labor turnover of 100 percent per year were commonly reported.

8. About 40 percent of the estimated 300 maquilas in Baja California returned usable questionnaires but this 40 percent represented almost 70 percent of the maquila workforce (Clement and Jenner 1987: part II). Richard Kiy, of the San Diego EDC, has informed me that a joint SECOFI-EDC maquiladora directory for the Californias is being produced.

9. Otay Mesa refers to the area on the U.S. side of the border, while Mesa de Otay, in which CIN is located, refers to the Mexican side. For a remarkably clear guide to the complexities of geography and politics of land use planning in this area, see Herzog (1989).

10. Interview with Enrique Esparza in San Diego, May 1987. The figure of 99 subcontracted/sheltered firms given by Clement and Jenner (1987:47) includes those in Tecate and Mexicali, and may also include some marginal cases where U.S./Mexican ownership is uncertain. In 1986 Clement produced a resource guide, "Exploring the Mexican In-Bond/Maquiladora Option in Baja California" for the EDC, listing, among others, the facilitators. About 2,000 copies of this guide are in circulation and a new edition was planned for 1988.

11. This is partly due to its success in undercutting the competition on labor costs. I shall attempt to quantify just how profitable AIM and others like it are, in chapter 10 below.

12. Contracts for combat items usually stipulate that the work must be done in the U.S. with U.S. materials and components. I have observed other defence contracts in maquilas along the border operating within security stockades. See also USITC (1988:6–3).

13. The story of how this happened shows how the facilitators work. The *San Diego Union* rang Terri Cardot, AIM's Marketing V.P., for a comment on this company, which had just announced that it was leaving Silicon Valley. She had never heard of them, but immediately visited them to explain the services of AIM, winning the contract.

14. Calexico was the only U.S. border city that did not have a single twin plant by 1987. A proposal to create a foreign trade zone was made in order to improve Calexico's industrial employment prospects.

15. Martínez resigned from PIMSA in 1980 to become the PRI candidate and subsequently the mayor of Mexicali (*MN*, July 1980:6).

16. See Escamilla and Antonieta, "Consideraciones sociologicas del trabajo femenino en las maquiladoras fronterizas," (abstracted in Peña 1981:A-60, 61).

# 5

# Paso del Norte

In comparison with Baja California to the west, and Nuevo León and Tamaulipas to the east, Juárez and the whole of the state of Chihuahua were rightly considered to be underdeveloped and underprivileged. Martínez (1978) has characterized Juárez in historical terms as a "border boom town," but in the 1960s most commentators were rather pessimistic about the town's prospects. Now, about 20 years later, despite the social and economic problems that it shares with similar cities in Mexico (and, indeed, all over the Third World), Juárez is a "border boom town" once again, and this is widely considered to be a result of the tremendous growth of the maquila industry in the 1970s and 1980s.

## The Maquila Industry in Ciudad Juárez and El Paso

The maquila industry in Ciudad Juárez and El Paso began as one more swing on a pendulum that had measured the relative ascendence and decline of the two cities ever since Paso del Norte had been renamed for Benito Juárez, one of the liberators of Mexico, in 1888. By the 1960s, while Juárez languished, El Paso had enjoyed a decade of remarkable growth, due mainly to the contribution of the U.S. defence budget and to the nodal economic functions that it fulfilled for the surrounding area. However, El Paso was, in the words of one local researcher, "in the rather unique position of enjoying a higher growth rate in employment and income . . . but a decrease in its per capita income relative to the U.S. El Pasoans were earning more moderate incomes at the same time that they were making a less intensive use of the population in the labor force" (Richards 1964:53). This is a euphemistic social scientific way of saying that El Paso's relative "prosperity" was founded on cheap labor and low skill, a fact relevant to the growth of the maquilas.

From the discussion of the antecedents of the maquila industry and its link with PRONAF in chapter 2, it is clear that Ciudad Juárez had a special place in the affections and developmental plans of Bermúdez, a native of the city. The Arthur D. Little report on Juárez, like the one on Tijuana, predicted a rosy future for the city if it was prepared to offer facilities for U.S. companies to assemble labor intensive products in the in-bond plants. To this end, an industrial development board was established in Juárez with an office in El Paso, its membership composed of businessmen, bankers, lawyers, educators, and officials. The Juárez board made no bones about the specific attraction of the city in publicity material it distributed in El Paso in the late 1960s. The fully burdened weekly wage based on the January 1968 minimum, for example, was just over $20 for a 48-hour week. Even in 1968, this spoke for itself.

The competition between Mexican border cities for maquilas has always been intense, and in the mid to late 1960s it was not Juárez that attracted the bulk of the first wave of large maquilas, but cities like Mexicali and Nuevo Laredo. However, as table 5.1 shows,

*Table 5.1*
Ciudad Juárez by maquilas and employees, 1967–1988.

| | NUMBER OF | | | NUMBER OF | |
|---|---|---|---|---|---|
| YEAR | PLANTS | EMPLOYEES | YEAR | PLANTS | EMPLOYEES |
| 1967 | 9 | 925 | 1978 | 92 | 30,374 |
| 1968 | 10 | 1,502 | 1979 | 103 | 36,206 |
| 1969 | 17 | 2,093 | 1980 | 121 | 39,402 |
| 1970 | 22 | 3,135 | 1981 | 128 | 43,994 |
| 1971 | 52 | 5,617 | 1982 | 129 | 42,695 |
| 1972 | 75 | 9,988 | 1983 | 135 | 54,073 |
| 1973 | 72 | 12,058 | 1984 | 155 | 72,495 |
| 1974 | 85 | 18,483 | 1985 | 168 | 77,592 |
| 1975 | 86 | 19,775 | 1986 | 180 | 86,526 |
| 1976 | 81 | 23,580 | 1987 | 233 | 100,446 |
| 1977 | 80 | 26,972 | 1988 (Jan.) | 236 | 102,520 |

SOURCES: 1967–1974, Carrillo and Hernandez (1985): 92, amended; 1975–1988, INEGI (1988: table 3) and *Avances*.

after 1970 the maquila industry in Juárez took off, and although it lagged behind Tijuana in terms of the numbers of plants, from that time on Juárez was to have more maquila employees than any single city in Mexico. It also boasted the largest collection of Fortune 500 companies, an achievement that the public and private facilitators never tired of publicizing. In 1968 there were 10 maquila plants in Ciudad Juárez, employing a total of 1,502 workers. The largest plant was Acapulco Fashions which employed 450 workers, mainly women sewing garments, but the fixed capital of the firm was only $300,000.[1] At its peak, this firm employed more than 2,500 workers in Juárez. The next largest maquila was A. C. Nielson de México, one of the very first maquilas in Juárez, which employed 364 people, again almost exclusively women, to sort coupons. This was a prototypical labor intensive operation in which shopping coupons that are returned to stores and supermarkets all over the U.S. are sent to Mexico for sorting and then returned to the manufacturers. Although it had few workers, about 60 in 1968, the maquila with the highest fixed capital investment in Juárez ($3.5 million) was an assembler of piano and organ components by the name of Fabricantes Tecnicos, the Mexican subsidiary of the well known Ohio company, D. H. Baldwin. Altogether, up to 1968 something in excess of $10 million had been invested in the maquilas of Juárez, but only 3 out of the 10 maquilas in the city accounted for about 85 percent of the total capital investment. These were Fabricantes Tecnicos, and two local carpentry firms, one specializing in the wood mouldings for which much of the border is justly renowned, and the other a door manufacturer that went out of business in the 1970s.

Another feature of the Juárez maquila industry at this time was the apparent success of "twin plants" in El Paso. This is of great interest both in relation to the early growth of the industry in Paso del Norte, and in relation to the political struggles that have been and are still being fought over the maquilas in the U.S. The very fact that the city of El Paso devoted a section of its 1971 community renewal program to the maquila industry is itself significant. It quantified precisely the "manufacturing operations" established in El Paso and Juárez as a result of the maquila industry. The totals are impressive. Up to May 1970, 2,606 jobs had been created by the maquilas in Juárez, and 922 in El Paso; and the projections for job creation later in the year brought the Juárez total to 2,706, and jobs in El Paso to 1,527, a whopping 65 percent increase. However, when we examine the data presented, a curiosity arises. On the already existing employment list, 4 of the companies, accounting for 329 jobs in El Paso, have no jobs at all in Juárez, that is they appear to be companies that have a connection with the maquila industry but do not run a maquila. These four companies were in electronics, data processing, book publishing, and undergarments. One other electronics company was projected to be creating 200 jobs in El Paso but none in Juárez later in the year, and one of the original four was creating an additional 150 jobs (City of El Paso 1971). This is not to suggest that none of the jobs created by nonmaquilas in El Paso (or anywhere else) are unrelated to the BIP, and it is quite possible, indeed probable, that new El Paso firms might do business with maquilas in Juárez. However, these firms and the jobs they provide might also have been established without any maquila industry in El Paso or, at least, unless they are totally contracted with maquilas, not all of the jobs can be considered to have been established as a result of the BIP. If we subtract all the jobs in the El Paso-only firms, then the maquila job creation in the city drops from 922 to 593 actual jobs, and 1,527 to 846 projected jobs. The true figure, no doubt, lies somewhere between these two extremes, but the difference between 2,706 projected jobs in Juárez to 1,527 in El Paso compared with 2,706 and 846 is substantial, not only arithmetically but, more importantly, symbolically. The first, and in my view inflated, calculation of the ability of the maquilas to create jobs in El Paso (36 percent of the total maquila job creation) has the impact that the deflated figure (less than 20 percent) would not have. It is also relevant to look at which of the actual maquilas were providing most of the jobs in El Paso. Only 3 had more than 100 jobs: the wood moulding company mentioned above with a large capital investment in Juárez (sustaining 139 jobs in El Paso to 60 in Juárez), and a metal furniture company that employed 175 workers in El Paso and 100 in Juárez, plus a Western Boot manufacturer, charmingly called the Cowtown Boot Company, employing 225 workers in Juárez and anticipating 100 extra jobs in El Paso. However, the large U.S. maquila employers in Juárez created very few jobs in El Paso. Acapulco Fashions, reduced to 350 workers in Juárez in mid-1970, employed only 45 in El Paso, and others like Advance Ross Electronics (250 and 12), and A.C. Nielson (350 and 3) even less. RCA had 350 jobs in Juárez, but not one in El Paso (City of El Paso 1971:91).[2]

It is important to remember that behind each job statistic lies a human life and the lives of those around the actual worker. At this time both El Paso and Juárez were suffering from severe unemployment, and any job creation was more than welcome. My purpose, therefore, is not to diminish the job creation effects of the maquilas on either side of the border, but to put them into perspective. From the point of view of the AFL-CIO, for example, the true perspective of maquila employment was not the jobs it created, but the jobs it destroyed in the U.S. James Givens, the secretary of the Central Labor Union in El Paso, told a Texas newspaper in 1969, that for the U.S. worker the maquilas were "a bracero program in reverse. . . . Where we used to bring low-pay Mexican labor to our country, . . . we now take the work to them" (*San Antonio Express/News*, 9 November 1969:11-G). Givens and his members were right to feel aggrieved. The El Paso company Advance Ross Electronics had laid off more than 200 workers when it decided to take advantage of the low wage maquila option in Juárez. It was not only low wages that were attractive to U.S. corporations, but also, in many cases, the opportunity to escape from the union. Unionized apparel manufacturers from the southwest were relocating in Juárez, following the lead of those in the Californias (López 1969:2). This is an important domestic consequence of the reformation of capitalism.

At the turn of the decade the maquila industry in Juárez was poised for a dramatic surge. The Bermúdez family already had a construction company and saw the opportunity of building industrial parks for the maquilas along the border. The Antonio J. Bermúdez park, named for the patriarch of the family who had brought PRONAF to Juárez, employed a U.S. citizen, William Mitchell, to sell the "maquila in the park" idea to U.S. corporations. Mitchell saw very clearly that success lay with those who could attract the big players in the game, and he aggressively went after some Fortune 500 companies. His first major success was RCA, which already had a joint venture in Mexico City, but was convinced by Grupo Bermúdez to turn it into a maquila in the new park they were building in Juárez. (Actually the Park was built around RCA, rather than vice versa.) The first priority, consistent with the policy of attracting and retaining Fortune 500 companies, was to build a park to international standards with on-site facilities that would eliminate as much of the difficulty of operating in Mexico under the BIP as possible.

Also active in building industrial parks for the maquila industry from the 1970s on was a group of Mexican entrepreneurs who, like Bermúdez, expanded from purely domestic enterprise. The Grupo Omega, directed by Oscar Cantu Murguia, and the Grupo Juárez of Francisco Villareal, both established industrial parks for the maquila industry, offering a variety of services. Several other individuals and groups in Juárez also began to lease out factory space (see Salas-Porras 1987:55–56). These were joined by a substantial core of professional and commercial personnel who were able to service the growing maquila industry. The Juárez law firm, González Vargas et al. were the first legal experts in the city to take an active interest in the maquilas and they built up a thriving business in advising and representing U.S. and Mexican companies.[3] Other law firms followed suit. It would be incorrect, however, to suggest that the Mexican element from Juárez totally dominated the maquila industry in the early years, much less today.

Then as now the public facilitators in El Paso, those attached to the chamber of commerce and the industrial development corporation, and various other nonprofit making but profit oriented organizations, were quick to see the significance of the maquilas for the prosperity of El Paso and for the creation of economic opportunities for specific class fractions. Likewise, groups of private facilitators were emerging, not as manifestly as in San Diego and Tijuana, but influential all the same in the establishment and growth of the industry. These private facilitators were often men, and more recently some women, who usually began by working for the larger maquilas in Juárez and elsewhere. By dint of their vision for the industry as a whole, they became activists for the maquilas in the local and wider community. Some circulated between executive roles in industrial parks and specific maquilas and independent consultancy and quasiofficial state positions (though this was much more characteristic of the Mexican side), and back again.

The growth of the industry in Juárez in the early 1970s was tremendous, and far exceeded anything else along the border. By 1973, Juárez had more plants and far more workers, about 10,000, than any other maquila site in Mexico.[4] By the middle of 1974, Tijuana had overtaken Juárez in terms of plants, 101 to Juárez' 89, but the dominance of Juárez in terms of employment, 17,500 workers to Tijuana's 10,000, continued to be marked.

The crisis of 1974–1975 hit some parts of the border harder than others. Tijuana, Mexicali, Nogales, and Piedras Negras all suffered severe plant and job losses, and the maquila industry in Nuevo Laredo was devastated. Maquila employment actually increased in Ciudad Juárez through the crisis years, and whereas it took Tijuana until 1979 to recover its 1974 workforce, by 1979 Juárez had more than doubled its 1974 number of workers. How can we explain the differential effects of the crisis, or the nature of the "crisis" in Juárez at the time? From the fall of 1974 to the spring of 1975, there were massive layoffs in Juárez affecting more than 10,000 workers, and about a dozen plants closed down. However, it is clear that these were temporary dislocations and, as I have shown, the year end figures mask what happened.[5]

The first factor of importance was the presence of the thriving industrial parks. By 1975 there were 16 maquilas in operation in the Bermúdez park, and more in the pipeline. The Parque Industrial Juárez was also beginning to attract maquilas. Clearly, confidence in the industry locally was very high. The industrial parks gave a stable focus, provided a natural source of leadership, and provided centers for advice and sympathy for pressurized maquila management. All these qualities, none decisive in itself, might just have given the industry in Juárez a little extra confidence, while those to the west and some to the east panicked. The sectoral mix of maquilas in the city was also important. Although Juárez has always had a good number of apparel plants, there were fewer of the small sweatshop-type maquilas characteristic of the industry in the Californias. Carrillo and Hernández (1985:113) show that in 1979 20 percent of maquila employees in Juárez were in the clothing and footwear sector, compared with an average of only 16.7 percent for maquila employees as a whole. However, of 75 maquilas in Juárez in 1978, only 10 came into the category of "clothing and footwear" (13 percent), and for the maquilas in the Rio Grande cities as a whole, the figure was 25 out of 165 (15 percent), compared with Tijuana, where the garment maquilas (about 17 percent of the total) employed about 13 percent of the workforce.[6]

This suggests that the garment maquilas in Juárez tended to be larger than those elsewhere. There is, of course, an apparel industry in Texas, but its operating conditions were rather different to those in Los Angeles. As a so-called "right to work" state, industrial wages in Texas tend to be on the lower end of the national spectrum, and the needle trades tend to be among the lowest paying of all the manufacturing industries. In 1975, Texas had about 75,000 workers employed in the apparel industry (see *Fiscal Notes* [Texas], 1986:5–6), coincidentally almost the same number of workers as the total Mexican maquila workforce. The manufacture of jeans and work clothes had traditionally been concentrated along the border, where there was a plentiful supply of Mexican-American women in what was already a low wage sector. In El Paso itself, over 40 apparel plants (excluding firms with fewer than 10 employees) were established in the city in the 1960s and 1970s, about half before 1975, and some of these were engaged in subcontract work making them a form of "Texas maquila." About two-thirds of the 15,000 plus jobs in the El Paso apparel industry (in 1982) were accounted for by multiplant companies, some local (Ende and Haring 1983:19). So, relatively speaking, the Texas apparel industry had less need to go to Mexico for cheap labor than the higher wage Californian apparel industry, at least until the 1980s.

The level and nature of unionization in Juárez is also important. Carrillo and Hernández (1985:144, 151) report that in 1979 only 14 out of a total of 106 maquilas in the city were unionized, but these maquilas included some of the largest in Juárez. Thus, though only 13 percent of the maquilas were unionized, about one-third of the workforce was represented in these maquilas. Despite the bitter struggles around Acapulco Fashions, there were no major industrywide labor capital struggles to compare with the events in Nogales (where 6,000 maquila workers lost their jobs in 1974–1975) or Nuevo Laredo (where more than 8,000 maquila workers were made redundant). Where there was worker unrest, maquila management, often in collaboration with the official unions, was quite prepared to repress it by fair means or foul. There is also evidence that unions were positively discouraged by management, particularly in the industrial parks. Castellanos, in her evocative account of working class life in Juárez (1981: chapter 4), reports a wall notice at Comunicaciones Banda Grande (a large electronics plant in the Bermúdez park) which proclaimed: "workers attempting to contact unions will be fired."[7] Such evidence does not necessarily lead to the conclusion that the absence of militant labor saved Juárez from the adverse effects of the 1974 crisis, or the one that was to follow, as Tijuana had no substantial militant labor movement at this time and was still severely affected by the crisis. But the relative lack of labor unrest in Juárez was yet another factor that would reassure nervous maquila operators.

Not only was there no substantial labor unrest in Juárez, but in El Paso, just across the border, 4,000 garment workers had been on strike against the Farah company for almost 2 years, between 1972 and 1974, over the right to unionize. Farah was a local clothing company that had become the second largest employer in El Paso, employing mainly Mexican-American women. The strike developed into a nationwide boycott of Farah products, mass employment of strikebreaking labor (some of it from Juárez), and a growing panic among the El Paso business community that events were giving the city a bad reputation in the eyes of potential investors. The threat of plant closure and relocation hung over the whole dispute. The strike was eventually settled and Farah accepted the union, but on the company's terms rather than those of the workers. A union official at Farah clarified the situation: "Once Farah was a union plant, it was in the union's interest to sell pants" (in Coyle et al. 1980:141–142) and not, by implication, to fight for the interests of the workers.[8] These lessons were not lost across the border.

The devaluations of 1976 and 1977 that more than halved the value of the peso, provided relief for most of the industry, but a bonanza for the maquila industry in Juárez. As the peso plunged, more and more U.S. corporations (like Westinghouse, General Motors, Detroit's Essex Group, Chicago's Magnecraft Electrical, and General Electric) either established or expanded maquila activities in Juárez, bringing considerable numbers of what were widely considered to be stable jobs to the city. This belief was reinforced during the second crisis in the early 1980s, when Juárez temporarily lost something over 1,000 maquila jobs between 1981 and 1982, but gained more than 10,000 over the next year when the decline of the peso turned into a collapse. The maquilas of Juárez have continued to register substantial job gains since then, as has El Paso itself. As Ende and Haring (1983) demonstrate in their study of El Paso's manufacturing industry, the late 1970s can be considered to be a period of boom. While they identify the establishment of only 44 new plants in the city between 1971 and 1980, compared with the economic stagnation of the city in the previous decade, this was progress indeed. These plants were largely concentrated in the apparel, electronics, and machinery industries. By 1982, El Paso had reversed the intended practice of the maquila industry by having more "twin plants" on the U.S. side of the border than on the Mexican side. Of the 20 El Paso apparel firms surveyed, 6 had a "twin plant" in Juárez, and of the 12 electronics firms, 4 had a "twin plant" (Ende and Haring 1983:23). Ende and Haring construct a detailed argument to the effect that El Paso and Ciudad Juárez cannot really be considered to be competitors for the same types of industry because there is too much interference by the Mexican government in the running of plants; labor legislation favors the workers; the risks of importing expensive machinery into Mexico are great; utilities, labor productivity, and quality in Juárez are all inferior to El Paso; and red tape along the border inhibits industrial efficiency (Ende and Haring 1983:38). The conclusion that these researchers reach is that the future of high tech industry in El Paso is assured and that Juárez will prosper as long as low skill, low wage, assembly labor is required.

There are many, especially among the Mexican left, who would accept this characterization of the maquila industry not only in Juárez, but all over Mexico. There are others, and I count myself among their number, who see this characterization as historically obsolete and missing important trends of the maquila industry in the late 1980s, particularly as they are manifest in Juárez. In terms of the more general argument being advanced here, the analysis of Ende and Haring is locked into an ideological notion of the new international division of labor which is common to both the proponents of "production sharing" and the analysts of the NIDL. The reformation of capitalism has no particular interest in retaining capital intensive operations in the countries of the capitalist center, certainly not when they hold back the maximization of profits and the accumulation of capital. This does not necessarily mean that any very substantial proportion of the assembly workers in the maquila industry will become skilled technicians overnight, or even over decades. But more on these central issues later.

The physical growth of the maquila industry in Paso del Norte was matched by the growth in number and level of activity of the public and private facilitators on both sides of the border. In 1980 the state of Chihuahua set up its own industrial promotion agency, *Promotora de la Industria Chihuahuense*, which has been instrumental since then in establishing no less than 6 industrial parks for the maquila industry. The Airport industrial park in Ciudad Juárez is one of *Promotora*'s most successful ventures. In these parks the state government offers a variety of industrial facilities and services (Salas-Porras 1986:5). The state has also actively encouraged the growth of the maquila associations which, while not formally part of the state apparatus, clearly enjoy a special relationship with it. In Juárez, the *Asociación de Maquiladoras* (AMAC), is active both politically on behalf of the industry (though it does not consider itself to be involved in direct promotional work), and in a research and information gathering capacity. AMAC, which is legally a private nonprofit organization, is funded by the maquilas themselves, through the affiliation that all registered maquilas must maintain with CANACINTRA. In 1987, AMAC had about 130 members out of the 196 maquilas that were operating in Juárez at the time, but this represented around 95 percent of maquila employment in the city. Since the early 1980s it has been responsible for negotiating an annual "payroll donation" from all the maquilas, which in 1986 amounted to 60,000 pesos per worker (about $60). This money goes to the Ciudad Juárez city council and is used for public works and infrastructure projects. The city, it is carefully noted, gives receipts to AMAC and accounts for the expenditure of this money.

The deficiencies of the infrastructure and social services in Juárez have long been a live issue. For example, in 1984 there was an interesting debate in the local Juárez newspaper, *El Fronterizo*, on the proposition that the infrastructure in the city simply could not support any more maquilas. The official view from central government, represented by SECOFI, was bluntly quoted to the effect that: "Industrial expansion in Cd. Juárez shall be curtailed in order to avoid the rise of a megalopolis" and that this was in line with the National Decentralization Plan (11 February 1984). Arnulfo Castro Munive, the president of AMAC at the time, was identified with the view that neither the physical infrastructure nor the labor force of Juárez could absorb any more maquilas (15 February 1984), but shortly after, the president of the national maquila association argued that such thinking was like "lowering the flags prematurely" and that Juárez, despite short-term infrastructure problems, could still play a major role in the maquila industry (3 March 1984). Castro Munive came back to restate his retrenchement views, which *El Fronterizo* reported under the title: "Cd. Juárez cannot handle any more assembly plants" (26 March 1984). Immediately, César Alarcón Espinoza, the administrative head of AMAC, tried to put the record straight by arguing that although they in no way opposed the establishment of new maquilas in Juárez, AMAC was very conscious of the possibility that infrastructure deficiencies might force the closure of some existing plants (27 March 1984).[9] This debate is by no means resolved, and although the expansionists clearly won the day, the rate of plant growth in Juárez has slowed down in the mid-1980s. Labor shortage, not infrastructure, is most frequently identified as the most serious problem facing the industry there.

AMAC has a battery of committees, one of the most important being its committee for educational institutions. This reflects the view that the time is ripe for Juárez to move into a new and more sophisticated phase of maquila development.[10] AMAC is not alone in this vision of the future. Another maquila promoter, while vice president of Juárez Economic Development, asserted that labor intensive plants were no longer suitable for Juárez, and that they should be redirected to the interior, freeing the border city to go after the high tech capital intensive plants (in *Diario de Juárez*, 7 July 1986). To this end, AMAC has helped corporations such as RCA and General Motors set up training courses for prospective maquila mechanics in technical high schools in Juárez and elsewhere in the state of Chihuahua. While the proportion of production technicians in the total workforce of the maquilas in Juárez was among the lowest in 1975, 6.9 percent to the maquila national average of 8.8 percent, by 1985 it was the next to highest, 12.8 percent to the national average of 11.8 percent (INEGI 1988: table 2). Only Reynosa, with 14.9 percent, had a higher proportion of production technicians.

The image of a high tech maquila industry in Juárez is, of course, something of a two edged sword. It would be almost universally welcomed in Mexico, but the response from the U.S. might be less ecstatic precisely because it would destroy one of the main planks of the maquila defence in the U.S. If the high tech work that the U.S. "twin plants" were supposed to be doing could now be done in Juárez, then the prospects for maquila-induced employment in El Paso would be bleak. The realization that this might one day be the case, has clearly caused some rethinking of the El Paso/Juárez relationship among the facilitators, and the promaquila forces on both sides of the border. On the one hand, there are those who consider that the maquila industry is crucial for the wellbeing of both Juárez and El Paso, and Mexico and the U.S. as a whole. These are invariably people with a personal stake in the industry, which does not invalidate their views but puts them into perspective. On the other hand, there are those whose first commitment is to economic development rather than any particular form of it.

In 1987 there was, officially, practically no unemployment in Juárez, indeed the city newspapers and radio were full of adver-tisements for jobs, inside and outside the maquilas.[11] While we may doubt that the real rate of unemployment and underemployment in Juárez was negligible in 1987, the type of labor required by the maquilas was clearly scarce. El Paso, on the other hand, had an official unemployment rate of 13 percent, and the local labor unions were publicly campaigning against the loss of manufacturing jobs to Mexico. The chairman of the El Paso Central Labor Union (AFL-CIO), Victor Muñoz, in a statement to the USITC hearings on 806/807 in Washington in August 1987, listed specific job losses in El Paso due to U.S. firms establishing maquilas in Juárez. I have already cited the loss of 5,000 jobs at Farah, Billy the Kid Industries accounted for another 3,000, and several firms announced lesser redundancies.[12] Jonathon Rogers, the Mayor of El Paso, when asked how he was going to cope with these problems, responded, "What problems? . . . We're losing low-cost jobs and gaining high-cost. Farah laid off a thousand people at four dollars an hour. But the same day Honeywell came in with a hundred and twenty-five people at an average salary of forty thousand a year" (quoted in Muñoz 1987:10). This is an excellent illustration of the class interests served by the maquila industry along the border.

The benefits that U.S. cities like El Paso derive from the maquila industry may be roughly divided into direct and indirect. Indirect benefits include increased business for airlines, hotels, car rental and dealers, real estate, transportation services, customs brokers, insurance agents, and banks. All of these sectors will do business with the permanent employees of the maquilas, as well as with those who come to do business with the maquilas via El Paso. Direct benefits include the actual twin plants that are established in El Paso and the business generated by the material, component, and service requirements of the maquilas that are not being met, for one reason or another, in Juárez. Over a number of years, William Mitchell of the Grupo Bermúdez had been preparing and circulating "economic impact surveys" of the Juárez maquila industry on El Paso and the rest of the U.S. These "surveys," though of an uncertain methodological status, did provide estimates of the monetary and other benefits that the maquilas in Juárez brought to the U.S. and, latterly, they have begun to trace the sources of supply of materials and components that the maquila industry uses.

In 1986, the El Paso Foreign Trade Association (a group of maquila facilitators), the El Paso IDC, maquila activists in the University of Texas El Paso, and Juárez Economic Development, sponsored a UTEP economist to carry out what they labelled "Project Link." Link was an investigation of employment linkages between Juárez and El Paso, and its basic goal was to demonstrate that the maquiladora industry is a major economic stimulus for employment growth in both cities. No one would deny the impact of the maquilas on Juárez, because maquila employment accounts for about two-thirds of all manufacturing jobs in the city. The impact on El Paso, however, is rather more controversial, as is the method by which Project Link arrived at its conclusions. Link asserts that the maquila industry generates 20 percent of all new jobs in the El Paso economy, 25 percent of new private sector jobs, one-third of real (nonservice) new jobs, and 20 percent of trade and service sector new jobs (Sprinkle 1986:22). These figures, like the Mitchell "surveys" that inspired them, at least in part, have been widely used in maquila industry job creation propaganda by the Border Trade Alliance. I cannot say, and on the basis of the aggregate employment data utilized by Link I do not really think it is possible to say with any degree of certainty, how realistic the maquila job creation effect is, as distinguished from the Juárez job creation effect. It is true that the growth rate of jobs in El Paso has lagged behind those of the state of Texas, the state of Chihuahua, and Ciudad Juárez in recent years, as Link demonstrates, so that any maquila job creation effect might look substantial, but the direct causal connection between Juárez maquilas and El Paso jobs must remain a statistical artifact within the Link methodology.[13]

The last thing that the Link protagonists wished was for El Paso to be seen actually to be losing jobs to Juárez. The loss of low level assembly jobs could be explained away in the familiar argument that these jobs were bound to go to the Third World in any case, and that in the long run existing U.S. jobs would be more likely to be protected by the maquila industry in Mexico in general and Juárez in particular. The loss of high skill jobs to Juárez, however, was a totally different matter and clearly an issue on which the ranks of the promaquila forces could split. Nevertheless, it is important not to lose perspective on this issue, for the vast majority of maquila jobs in Juárez and in the rest of Mexico are still low level, unskilled, minimally trained, and extremely poorly paid, assembly jobs. What is at issue is not the capture of substantial numbers of high level, skilled, maximally trained, and well paid jobs from El Paso and elsewhere in the U.S., but whether there are any trends in the maquila industry that point in this direction. If there are, Juárez would be a sensible place to begin to look for them. In order to understand how the maquila industry in Juárez has been brought to this rather surprising juncture it is necessary to examine the growth of the private facilitators in Paso del Norte, in particular, the Grupo Bermúdez.

## The Facilitators

The major public facilitators at work in the Paso del Norte maquila industry are usually either straightforward arms of local government or nonprofit bodies that are at least partly supported from public funds, and they express the official ideology of the ruling strata on both sides of the border that the maquila industry is essential for the well being of border communities. The borderlands socioeconomic systems both permit and encourage people in such "public" organizations to flit back and forth between the public and the private sectors, and in this they are in no way unique. The private facilitators in the Paso del Norte maquila industry have also been extremely active, and in this section I shall examine the structure and dynamics of the Grupo Bermúdez, which has always been the most important maquila industrial park developers in Mexico.[14]

In 1954 Antonio Bermúdez set up a construction company in Juárez, where he had been a prominent businessman for some time. As we have already seen in chapter 2, Bermúdez was entrusted with the direction of PRONAF, and during the 1960s as he travelled the country and the world propagating the message of the development of the frontera norte, the company prospered. Antonio and his son, Jaime, were quick to see the opportunities that the BIP was creating and following through the PRONAF/BIP strategy on the personal level, Jaime Bermúdez started to build the Antonio J. Bermúdez Industrial Park in the north east part of Juárez. Before long, it became clear that the industrial park business was going to be a very profitable part of the organization's success in Juárez, and later in Chihuahua and the rest of Mexico, and the family restructured its operations under the corporate banner of Grupo Bermúdez.

The recruitment in the late 1960s of William Mitchell, an ex-U.S. army officer, to search out U.S. corporations and persuade them to establish maquilas in the Bermúdez park, was a major move for the company. Mitchell's success in bringing in important corporations in the 1970s is legendary in the maquila industry (recall his pursuit and capture of RCA). In the 1970s, the Bermúdez park grew to over 500 acres and housed so many maquilas that it was said to have a waiting list of companies eager to establish maquilas on its tree-lined avenues. With the opening of the Zaragoza bridge, about 7 miles from the center of Juárez, as an international border crossing, the development of the eastern fringe of Juárez became much more attractive. The Río Bravo Industrial Park, opened in 1978, covers about 250 acres adjoining the Zaragoza bridge, and a second phase of expansion houses a major Japanese color television manufacturer fabricating chassis and sending them across the border to Tennessee for assembly, somewhat reversing the typical maquila process. The Group also has off park industrial sites and industrial locations within other parks in Juárez. For example, Bermúdez has a maquila in the Airport Industrial Park, an area of substantial investment in public housing.

Grupo Bermúdez also set up an industrial park in El Paso, the Pan American Center for Industry, 275 acres in the southeast of the city, about one mile from the Zaragoza bridge and the Río Bravo Park complex.[15] It also has a series of industrial parks outside Juárez, mainly in the state of Chihuahua. These are small parks, ranging from 50 acres in Delicias, housing General Motors and A. C. Nielson plants, to a 5-acre site in Nuevo Casas Grandes with yet another General Motors plant. In addition, Grupo Bermúdez is involved in maquila parks in Coahuila and the Yucatan and actively seeks fresh sites on a continuing basis.[16]

Since 1980, Grupo Bermúdez has been compiling quarterly employment reports, and annual employment totals for Bermúdez plants are available from 1976 to the present. What these figures demonstrate is the dominant position of the Grupo Bermúdez as the single largest private facilitator in the Mexican maquila industry. Since the middle of the 1970s, and particularly since the opening of the Río Bravo Industrial Park, approximately one-half of the total maquila workforce in Juárez was working in a Bermúdez facility. The highpoint occurred around December 1978, when fully 62.6 percent of the Juárez maquila workforce was in Grupo Bermúdez parks' factories. In national terms, it accounted for about 20 percent of the maquila workforce between 1977 and 1985. As more and more maquilas have flooded into Juárez and the rest of Mexico, it is hardly surprising that the Group's share has declined. Whereas in the 1970s it had little competition in the Juárez maquila parks business, today the Bermúdez parks are having to work very hard to attract customers. With several other parks in and around the city, and most rather more convenient than the Río Bravo complex which is in Zaragoza rather than in Ciudad Juárez proper, Grupo Bermúdez has to offer incentives to win the new maquilas. Most of the Industrial Parks in Juárez charge about the same in leases and fees, and Bermúdez provides some of their services and a resident engineer free of charge as an added inducement. In conditions of very high turnover some firms prefer to locate outside the industrial parks so that their labor is less likely to be poached by rival firms on the block. Nevertheless, Grupo Bermúdez is still far and away the most important single player in the maquila industry.[17]

How can this outstanding performance be explained, and can we find an answer to the question of whether Juárez brought success to Bermúdez, or Bermúdez brought success to Juárez? It is important not to forget the global context, namely the reasons why U.S. companies were going offshore in general and to Mexico in particular. The Bermúdez parks were clearly supplying what these U.S. corporations wanted, and in a way that gave them the edge over the many other maquila parks along the border. The industrial parks were a key feature of the success of Juárez in the first decade of the maquila industry, and just as important in the second decade. As early as 1972, the U.S. embassy in Mexico City had pointed out the importance of industrial parks for the progress of the maquila industry, and had highlighted the advantages of Nogales, Matamoros, and Ciudad Juárez in this respect (Department of State "Airgram" 30 June 1972:4). However, neither Nogales nor Matamoros, after strong beginnings, could match the growth of Juárez and the Bermúdez parks. It is the nature of the maquila industry in Juárez that provides the necessary and sufficient explanation. Offering similar and generally efficient services all the parks seemed equally attractive—they are all members of the Washington, D.C. based National Association of Industrial and Office Parks—though all the cities in which they were located did not. The combination of Juárez/El Paso and the excellent Bermúdez parks was bound to succeed.

Nevertheless, Grupo Bermúdez has had its problems in Juárez, and these were largely due to the nature of the Mexican political system. The ruling party, the PRI, was defeated in the election for municipal president (mayor) of Ciudad Juárez in 1983 by the PAN, a center-right party dominated by the progressive business elite and strong in the frontera norte, particularly in the state of Chihuahua. The man who was elected mayor for the PAN was Francisco Barrio, the brother of Federico Barrio, an influential maquila facilitator. Francisco Barrio had served as president of the Juárez employers' organization and was very much in sympathy with the maquila industry. Jaime Bermúdez, at that time the chief executive of the Bermúdez Group, supported the PAN and had contributed to Barrio's campaign. Despite the moves towards decentralization initiated by the de la Madrid administration, the nature of the ultra-centralized Mexican political system, and especially the fiscal relationships between Mexico City and the separate states of the federal Republic, meant that the PRI was able to obstruct Barrio's program in Juárez. Under circumstances that are inevitably a little foggy, the PRI persuaded Jaime Bermúdez to run for them against the PAN in 1986 in the election for mayor of Juárez.[18] Salas-Porras (1987:55) suggests that Bermúdez (and Vallina, another important maquila facilitator who had supported the PAN in 1983) had defected as a warning to the PRI that the government could no longer continue to neglect the interests of that fraction of the regional bourgeoisie that they represented. Having made the protest, and achieved their ends, namely a more positive government stance on the maquila industry, Bermúdez, Vallina, and others felt able to rejoin the PRI.

When the PRI candidates were declared the winners in Juárez in the summer of 1986, the PAN accused the authorities of electoral fraud, an accusation accepted by almost everyone outside, and probably many inside, the PRI, and immediately embarked on a bitter campaign of civil disobedience in order to force the government to deliver a more just verdict. The PAN kept up the pressure and even became involved in a few violent clashes with the authorities, but the result stood. A particular object of attack by the PAN activists were the businesses owned directly and indirectly by Jaime Bermúdez, and in August 1986 the *Panistas* blockaded the international bridge, seriously disrupting maquila traffic. In this they were supported by many people in the maquila industry on both sides of the border, although not by the national maquila council which, indeed, published full page statements in the Mexican press calling on the protestors to desist.[19] Eventually, these protests died down and Jaime Bermúdez, who had originally been prevented from taking up office by a heart attack, recovered and set about the task of governing Juárez.

The pattern was repeated in the presidential elections of 1988 when the PRI candidate, Salinas de Gortari, conceded defeat to the PAN in Juárez (and to Cuauhtemoc Cárdenas in Mexico City), but claimed victory overall. The opposition parties all accused the PRI of electoral fraud, and the PAN embarked on another campaign of civil disobedience. The long term consequences of the political advance of the opposition parties for the maquila industry in Chihuahua, along the border, and in Mexico as a whole, are uncertain.

Juárez/El Paso is widely regarded as representing the leading edge of the Mexican maquila industry not just in quantity but also in quality. If there is in fact a genuine upgrading of the industry in the city and the strategy of the public and private facilitators is working out, we should expect that gradually more and more of the mindnumbing and lowest paid work would be relocated to other sites along the border and in the interior and that the maquila workers of Juárez would be offered more satisfying and interesting work at higher rates of pay, but this does not yet appear to be taking place to any great degree. The very success of Juárez contains the dilemma of the maquila industry as a whole. To put it bluntly, the Mexican government and the U.S. and other foreign corporations are in two minds about what they want out of the maquilas, and about how best to exploit the fact that the industry appears to have reached a more mature phase in Juárez compared with the other main maquila sites. Juárez has acted as a sort of industrial hothouse, where the first frail maquila shoots have grown at an unexpected rate, due largely to the nature of the place and those who have organized the industry in Paso del Norte.

# Notes

1. Which made it relatively easy to close down in 1981–1982 without paying the compensation to which their workers were legally entitled. For the story of the struggle around its closure, see Carillo and Hernández (1985:158–164).

2. The assertion that in 1977 the number of U.S. maquila "twin plant" employees in El Paso was 907 (Mitchell 1977:82), suggests that the 1971 figures were unrealistically inflated, all the more so because the research by Mitchell was an unabashed piece of promotion for the maquila industry (though valuable for the information it provides).

3. Under the name of Bryan, González Vargas, González Baz, Delgado y Rogers, it was said to be the largest law firm in Mexico outside Mexico City (*Oakland Tribune*, 29 September 1982:B-8). Wayne McClintock, in an interview in El Paso in 1987, suggested that they represented about 80 percent of the maquilas in Juárez in the first decade. The firm produces an excellent guide to the BIP (Bryan et al. 1984).

4. The figures are for 31 January 1973, and they are taken from an extremely informative full page advertisement in the (London) *Times* (3 April 1973) placed by the Mexican Institute of Foreign Trade.

5. It is significant that in their excellent review of the crisis, Baird and McCaughan hardly mention Juárez. Where they do, however, it is to report that one maquila did sneak its machinery out of the city in September 1974, leaving its 100 workers without any legal redress (1975:17). This reminds us that there were some hardships for the Juárez workforce, but certainly fewer than elsewhere. Baird and McCaughan offer no explanation for why Juárez escaped the crisis.

6. The Juárez/Rio Grande figures are from House (1982:221) and those from Tijuana are from a list compiled by Homero Reyes in 1978. It is also worth mentioning that there were several small boot making maquilas in Juárez, and this strengthens the point further.

7. This is the plant at which an incident of "massive intoxication or collective psychosis" among the female workforce was reported in *El Fronterizo* (31 January 1980).

8. By 1986, Farah had reduced its El Paso workforce from an historic high of around 7,000 to fewer than 2,000. The Farah Company took an active part in the campaign to protect the maquilas in the mid-1980s, through its involvement with the Border Trade Alliance (see chapter 8 below), and the U.S. Apparel Industry Council, a "production sharing" promotional group operating from Farah's P.O. Box in El Paso, c/o Bobby Ortiz, a Farah executive.

9. These items are conveniently collected and translated in *U.S.-Mexico Report* (1984: numbers 3–7), issued by the New Mexico Border Commission from New Mexico State University at Las Cruces.

10. This view was clearly expressed in an interview with César Alarcón in Cd. Juárez, in December 1986. It is also being discussed in Tijuana, where the idea of a "second wave" of technologically advanced maquilas is gaining ground.

11. In the month of February 1986 the maquilas in Juárez placed about 150 want ads per week, of which one-quarter were for operatives, the rest for managers, technicians, and secretaries (George 1986:25). I conducted a similar exercise in 1988 with similar results.

12. An inventory tax introduced in Texas in 1987 may also have encouraged some companies to relocate in Mexico.

13. It is as well to make clear at this point that Richard Sprinkle, who carried out the research, was not himself among the group of "true believers" and maquila facilitators at UTEP. The leading light in this respect was Don Michie, of the UTEP Business School and the board of directors of the Foreign Trade Association.

14. There are several other significant private facilitators in the Ciudad Juárez/El Paso maquila industry. In the mid-1980s, the most important were Tres Hendrix of the Juárez International Park; José Luis Barraza of Las Americas Industrial Center, already very active in Chihuahua City and now expanding into Juárez; and the Omega Group of Oscar Cantu Murguia. Las Americas and Omega have several maquilas in the Magnaplex Park, which is part of Eloy Vallina's Grupo Chihuahua. The largest shelter

and subcontract firm in Juárez is ELAMEX S.A. run by Charles Dodson with Federico Barrio, whose own company, Constructora Lintel, is also notable.

15. In 1987, there were no less than 17 industrial parks in El Paso, and Pan American was acknowledged to be one of the best and most successful (see El Paso *Commercial-Real Estate Directory*, 1986).

16. That these activities are not always welcomed by the locals is clear from "S.O.S.: Maquiladoras," *Diario de Colima* (21 May 1986).

17. In 1988 Grupo Bermúdez handled around 40 percent of Juárez maquila employment and over 10 percent of the national total.

18. See Cornelius (1986:37–42) on "the electoral debacles of 1985–1986." It is interesting to note that the PRI chose Isela Torres, a maquila worker who had previously been politically active, to run alongside Bermúdez (she was standing for a seat in the state legislature), and the PAN candidate opposing her was a woman lawyer.

19. There have been suggestions of a connection between the growth of the maquila industry and the political advance of the PAN (see, for example, Andonaegui 1985; Salas-Porras 1987), and there is indeed evidence to support this in Chihuahua. For example, it is said that when a PRI official switched on the computers in a new maquila in Chihuahua City in 1986, all the VDUs displayed a *Panista* electoral slogan. While along the border the PAN tends to support the maquila industry, the national party has been more cautious.

# 6

# The Valley

South Texas, and particularly the part of it that is known as the valley, is one of the poorest regions in the U.S., and its border communities are actually at the bottom of the U.S. per capita income tables for Standard Metropolitan Statistical Areas.[1] Apart from some real estate effects, the valley did not share very much in the oil boom years of the Texas economy, though it has suffered from the slump in oil prices and related economic decline. The main border towns in the valley are Brownsville and Matamoros, and McAllen and Reynosa, and there are also several other smaller towns with some industrial and commercial development. Laredo and Nuevo Laredo, to the west of the valley, are also important settlements, but commerce has dwarfed manufacturing there, and the maquila industry in the two Laredos has had an extremely checkered history.

On both the Texas and the Tamaulipas sides, the valley has always been an agricultural area with very little in the way of industrial plants or infrastructure. Like most of the other border communities it was isolated from the centers of capital and industry to the north and to the south. There was little official Mexican federal or local government promotion of the BIP in places like Matamoros and Reynosa when it was introduced in the mid-1960s, although some local Mexican entrepreneurs did become involved with the maquilas at an early stage. The first substantial initiative from Matamoros came in 1970 with the creation of a private industrial park, of which more presently. On the whole, the Tamaulipas public and private economic elites were dimly informed about the potential consequences of the changes in the foreign investment laws but, in any case, they were uninterested because their bases of economic and political power were firmly established without the need for an assembly industry.

The concrete push to create a maquila industry came from the Texas side of the border. The U.S. has for decades had a network of local chambers of commerce stretching down to even quite small towns, and while these have traditionally represented the interests of retailers and the commercial sectors (and the professionals who service them), when the opportunity for industrial development presented itself an organizational framework already existed in many places.[2] In Brownsville and McAllen the preexisting chambers of commerce both set up administrative structures to handle questions of industry shortly after the BIP was announced. In Brownsville, the chamber created an industrial development department, and in McAllen an industrial board was established. Both recruited specific individuals as industrial development managers, and they stayed in the job for a very long time. This meant that an expertise and network of local, crossborder, and, in some cases, global connections were built up, and a methodology of industrial development evolved in parallel with the changing fortunes of the BIP in Tamaulipas.

The maquila industry in the valley can only be understood in terms of the extraordinary condition of economic depression that has existed on the U.S. side of the border for decades. As a local newspaper pointed out in 1985, "While other segments of the valley economy remain stagnant, the maquiladora industry is booming. Consequently, the economic development strategies of Brownsville and McAllen and smaller valley communities have centered around promotion of the maquiladoras" (*Brownsville Herald*, 5 November 1985).

## Matamoros/Brownsville

The eastern end of the valley is basically an area of farmers, ranchers, fisherfolk, their dependents, and those whose livelihoods are bound up with the opportunity to sell them goods and services. Neither Brownsville nor Matamoros had any real manufacturing industrial base in the 1960s. So it was with a measure of hopeful anticipation that the Brownsville chamber of commerce recruited Lindsey Rhodes from Airresearch (Garret) in Los Angeles, a company active in the Californias maquila industry, in the spring of 1966 to design an incentive program that would attract maquila twin plants to the area. Rhodes reasoned that the selling point of the program for the average U.S. corporation would be along the lines of "the Mexican border is your Japan at the back door," and that logistics relative to the Far East rather than the cheapness of labor would be the clinching factor. The first maquila in the area, however, was not a manufacturing plant brought in by the Brownsville chamber of commerce, but a Brownsville shrimping company that had worked out a way to operate in Matamoros as a maquila.

Rhodes sought U.S. companies that were either already producing offshore or might be persuaded to do so. By targeting specific product lines he painstakingly prepared unit cost and market profiles for each of the products of interest to the companies on his lists. If a company did not respond positively at first, he would file it away, and when circumstances changed, return and present all the reasons for the maquila option under the new conditions.

In Matamoros there were also some entrepreneurs who saw the potential of the maquila industry. One such was Sergio Martínez, an accountant who worked with the Brownsville chamber and was involved in the negotiations with some of the earliest maquilas in the city, for example the Electronic Control Corporation, which began by assembling light dimmers, probably the first manufacturing maquila in Matamoros. For the Brownsville chamber of commerce, the point of the exercise was to create a twin plant industry in Brownsville and Matamoros. In the 1960s, Brownsville was an economically depressed area. In 1966 it was in the lowest group of 20 out of over 300 SMSAs in the U.S. in terms of economic growth. By 1977, in a remarkable turnaround in its economic fortunes, it occupied fourth place in the nation, and it reached its high point in 1978 when it was the SMSA with the second fastest economic growth rate in the U.S. While the tourist industry and crossborder retail trade have contributed to this economic growth, the maquila industry has been responsible for a large part of it.

The difficulties of attracting major corporations to places like Brownsville and Matamoros should not be underestimated. Without a tradition of manufacturing industry, there were few industrial support services, engineering shops, parts and material suppliers, and, most importantly, skilled workers available. The one asset that Brownsville had was its deepwater port, which served as an essential conduit for goods for south Texas and northern Mexico. The port of Brownsville operated a Foreign Trade Zone in 40,000 acres of industrial park located in the port, and at another 200-acre site five miles away at the Brownsville/South Padre international airport.

The first years of the maquila industry in Matamoros and Brownsville were rather bleak. By the end of 1968, only five manufacturing and two shrimp processing maquilas were in operation in Matamoros. The manufacturing plants were an auto parts reconstruction operation, local and shortlived, employing only about 40 workers, a paper bag manufacturer, the Duro company from Kentucky,[3] and three other

[119]

out of state (Minnesota, Illinois and Indiana) electronics companies involved mainly in assembly and simple fabrication. This modest beginning, however, was sufficient to stimulate interest in the potential of Matamoros/Brownsville as a maquila site. The breakthrough came with the establishment of the Zenith plant in 1969–1970. Zenith, which is now one of the largest single employers in the whole maquila industry, came to Matamoros to assemble television tuners. The company, as it were, put its stamp of approval on the valley as a maquila site and is certainly one of the success stories of the Matamoros maquila industry, having employed over 5,000 people at one time.[4] Where Zenith went, others followed, particularly in the electronic assembly business. In the early 1970s, a further 17 maquilas were signed up and, of rather more significance, four of these were subsidiaries of Fortune 500 corporations. They were all involved in one way or another with the electronic components industry. More Fortune 500 corporations followed in the mid-1970s, like Parker-Hannifin, DuPont de Nemours, ITT, Quaker Oats (Fisher Price), and the Eaton Corporation. Between 1969 and 1987, 18 Fortune 500 firms established maquilas in Matamoros. In 1988 all these maquilas were still in operation, providing employment for thousands of workers in Matamoros and hundreds in Brownsville—the main reason why Matamoros, with only 4 percent of the maquila plants in Mexico (as of 1987), had about 10 percent of the maquila jobs. Table 6.1 charts the growth of the maquila industry in Matamoros.

Lindsey Rhodes and the Brownsville chamber of commerce had a hand in almost 100 maquilas in all between 1967 and 1983. However, when Rhodes retired from the job in 1983[5] there were fewer than 50 maquilas in Matamoros, and not many of these had genuine twin plants. The maquila facilitators were obviously having to run very hard just to

*Table 6.1*
Matamoros by maquilas and employees, 1970–1988.

| YEAR | NUMBER OF PLANTS | NUMBER OF EMPLOYEES | YEAR | NUMBER OF PLANTS | NUMBER OF EMPLOYEES |
|------|--------|-----------|------|--------|-----------|
| 1970 | 23 | 2,500 | 1980 | 50 | 15,231 |
| 1971 | 34 | 4,000 | 1981 | 46 | 15,607 |
| 1972 | 45 | 6,800 | 1982 | 41 | 14,643 |
| 1973 | 45 | 7,000 | 1983 | 40 | 15,639 |
| 1974 | 45 | 8,000 | 1984 | 39 | 19,454 |
| 1975 | 40 | 9,778 | 1985 | 35 | 20,686 |
| 1976 | 39 | 10,966 | 1986 | 43 | 23,442 |
| 1977 | 37 | 11,357 | 1987 | 68 | 28,730 |
| 1978 | 40 | 13,443 | 1988 (Jan.) | 68 | 29,383 |
| 1979 | 46 | 15,894 | | | |

SOURCES: 1970–1974, my own estimates; 1975–1988, INEGI (1988: table 3), and *Avances*.

maintain their position. Though the numbers of jobs have increased, there was an appreciable decline in plants from the high point of 58 maquilas in operation at one point in 1975, when much of the rest of the maquila industry was just recovering from the first crisis, to 1985 when there were only 35 maquilas in Matamoros. This decline has been reversed and in January 1988, 68 maquilas employing 29,000 people were in operation in Matamoros. While the maquilas of most of the larger companies (and all of the Fortune 500 corporations) were still in business, about 50 maquilas in the city had not survived. The most commonly heard explanations for this involved the failure of the management of some maquilas to control overheads and, in particular, labor costs. To explain why this was so, it is necessary to examine the labor movement in Matamoros.

From the very beginning, the maquila industry on the Mexican side of the valley was almost totally unionized. The huge PEMEX oil refinery in Reynosa was solidly organized by the CTM, and the power of the union extended throughout Tamaulipas. In the Mexican tradition of the "charros," the system of government-backed union bosses, the CTM in Matamoros had been run for as long as anyone can remember by Agapito González Cavazos (see Carrillo and Hernández 1985:149). "Agapito," as he is commonly known, has had a major influence on the development of the maquila industry in Matamoros. The CTM began to organize the maquilas as soon as they started up, and most incoming U.S. companies saw no alternative but to accept this state of affairs. In the early days of the maquilas in Matamoros, each company would negotiate with the union for its annual contract on pay and conditions. Several of the maquilas, however, were not happy to have to deal with the union, and some U.S. companies reputedly affronted them by making difficulties over the implementation of government-imposed wage rises. This was a grave error, no doubt due to lack of specialized knowledge about how the CTM worked in Tamaulipas. The union embarked on a tough campaign for a greater part in the running of the maquilas which lasted off and on throughout the 1970s.

While the CTM may well have succeeded in scaring off some potential U.S. investors,[6] there is no direct evidence that any maquila actually closed down because of the union. The CTM and the maquila industry eventually came to a compromise in 1983 when an historic agreement was negotiated. In return for guarantees of industrial peace, the maquila workers of Matamoros were the first group in Mexico to win a 40-hour week without loss of pay (though incoming maquilas were permitted to operate on a 48-hour week for their first five years). The companies won the cooperation of the union in keeping the production lines moving. With the blessing of the national CTM and the PRI, Agapito and his local colleagues worked out what can be called a "corporatist" solution to the labor question in the maquilas of Matamoros. The CTM handles much of the personnel work of the maquilas, having a say in the hiring and firing of workers,[7] and in some aspects of the organization of production. Instead of each maquila negotiating its own contract, about six of the major companies, always including Zenith and General Motors, negotiated on behalf of all the maquilas in Matamoros. The economic crisis of the early 1980s clearly modified the position of the union, and its main function does appear to be to create the conditions necessary for an expanding maquila labor force for the industry. This is quite clear from statements that Agapito González made to the press in 1983, when he joined the union with efforts of the employers in Matamoros to pull the industry out of the slump that it had been experiencing since 1979. Praising the maquila management for their timely implementation of an emergency inflation related wage rise, he said "Their permanence is guaranteed in Matamoros, since there is no reason for thinking of a withdrawal" (*Mexico City News*, 27 June 1983:14). In other words, shades of Nuevo Laredo were to be banished from Matamoros. This is not to say that there is total labor quiescence in Matamoros, for there were some stoppages in the mid-1980s, and there is the usual anecdotal evidence of low job satisfaction, but no major strike has occurred in the 1980s.

To some extent this is due to the nature of the employers' organization as well as the unions. Matamoros has the distinction of having established the first local maquila association along the border. This was started in the early 1970s by the then Zenith manager. From the beginning the Matamoros maquiladora association was dominated by the managers of the U.S. corporations who personally attended to the business of the association through regular meetings on the premises of the leading maquilas and this, no doubt, has contributed to the generally calm and controlled labor situation in Matamoros and its relatively low turnover rate.[8] These factors are evident in what has become one of the most controversial relocations of a corporation from the U.S. to Mexico in recent years—the Trico case. An analysis of the background of this case and how Trico has entered the maquila industry, teaches us a great deal about the local ramifications of the reformation of capitalism, and how the maquilas fit strategically into the U.S. rustbelt/sunbelt struggle.

"Buffalo, N.Y., has a sister city in Mexico—whether it wants it or not. . . . Matamoros, on the border with Texas, will soon welcome Buffalo's Trico Products Corp., a major manufacturer of windshield wipers" (*Newsweek*, 5 January 1987). Trico had been operating in Buffalo since 1917 and for some years it occupied first place in the manufacture of windshield wiper systems in the U.S. In the 1950s, it had been Buffalo's single largest manufacturing employer, with over 4,500 workers. By

1985 it employed 2,500 people at three facilities in Buffalo, and also had factories in the U.K. and in Australia, and licensees in Japan. Sales totaled $145 million in the U.S. with $28 million abroad. The argument of the management was that it could no longer meet foreign competition, especially from the Far East, and that it was forced to seek to reduce its costs of production. The company had been seriously affected by the recession in the U.S. automobile industry in the early 1980s and had lost a great deal of money. By 1984 it was said to be "on the verge of going broke," but the last straw came in 1985 when Trico's U.S. customers began to tell the company that they were thinking of buying wiper systems made abroad. After unsuccessful attempts to get some relief from local and state agencies, Trico decided that drastic action was imperative. Either it could relocate its manufacturing and assembly operations entirely offshore to somewhere with low labor costs, or it could try to save some jobs in Buffalo and start "production sharing." In November 1985 the corporation decided in principle to reduce its operations in Buffalo. The questions were: by how much? and where to relocate? The *Buffalo News* reported that after a customer suggested the maquila option, Trico president Richard Wolf flew "secretly" to Matamoros and was highly impressed with what he saw there (*Buffalo News*, 10 March 1987:A6). Trico engaged Arthur D. Little to evaluate the various border sites, and some hard bargaining ensued. About four months later, Wolf broke the news that Trico would establish twin plants in Matamoros and Brownsville, employing around 850 and 400 workers respectively, and that about 1,400 jobs would be lost in Buffalo or, as the company preferred to claim, about 1,100 jobs would be saved.[9] Two of Trico's three factories in Buffalo would be closed down over the next few years.

The reaction in Buffalo was one of shock and disbelief. The first half of the 1980s had been traumatic for manufacturing industry in up-state New York. The steel industry, one of the foundations of the city's economy, had already begun to collapse with the closures of the Bethlehem and the Republic Steel plants, and several other large employers had also pulled out or retrenched. The rate of unemployment was rising ominously. The outrage of the concerned citizenry was focused on the "disloyalty" of Trico for abandoning the city in its hour of need. As a local religious leader put it, "The difference with Trico is that it is based and rooted here. . . . We expected better of them" (quoted in the *New York Times*, 17 February 1987:B2). Unions and community groups began to organize to try to persuade the company to change its mind, and two studies were set in motion "to examine the feasibility of retaining some or all of the present Trico operations in Buffalo" (Lazes 1986:1). These studies were carried out by the Program for Employment and Work Place Systems of the prestigious New York

School of Industrial and Labor Relations at Cornell University, and were sponsored by Trico itself, the Urban Development Corporation, and UAW Local 2100, the Trico union. They began in April and May of 1986, that is about six months after the company had made the decision to relocate, and about two months after the choice of Brownsville/Matamoros had been publicly announced. It can, thus, be suggested with a good deal of confidence that these were entirely cosmetic exercises as far as Trico was concerned. If the company had been serious about saving its operations in Buffalo it would have had the studies done before, not after, the decisions were made. This conclusion is confirmed in the *Dallas Morning News* of 21 February 1986: "Wolf said there has been discussion with unions in Buffalo, but the decision to move is final." Though it permitted the study teams to do their research inside the factories, Trico did not go out of its way to help them. Peter Lazes, the head of the Cornell research team, asserts, "The studies were sometimes hampered by lack of access to critical information and Trico personnel. . . . The outside consultants found that information they needed for the new plant study, such as production numbers and estimates of equipment . . . was either incomplete or not available" (Lazes 1986:1). Nevertheless, the studies found that Trico could make sufficient cost savings in several departments to justify most of the company's operations staying in Buffalo. The main exception was the assembly of wiper arms and blades. However, to achieve these cost savings and ensure the continued viability of the company, "Developing an advanced manufacturing facility in Buffalo is seen as critical to the longterm survival of Trico"; and further, moving fabrication operation to Brownsville was declared to be "quite risky." On the maquilas of Matamoros/Brownsville, the Cornell study argues that the area cannot supply sufficient numbers of skilled workers; of the seven "twin manufacturing plants" in the area "none depends on skilled workers in Brownsville" and of the other 37 maquilas that operate in both cities, all "use their Brownsville operations only to manage Mexican operations and to warehouse material" (Lazes 1986:2–3).

In a nutshell, Trico was being accused of taking the easy but possibly the worst option in the face of global competition. Lazes comments that Trico was focusing exclusively on, "cost reduction by lowering wages rather than improving production processes . . . competitors can easily find places where wage rates are low but they do not have the skilled workforce and the resources that we have in New York State to help turn around outdated manufacturing practices and structures" (Lazes 1986:4). Where it should have been thinking of capital investment to make its wiper systems technologically superior and, in the long run, cheaper to produce than those of its competitors, it chose the easy way out by relying on cheap labor, both for assembly and fabrication, to resolve its problems. "The question is, does Trico want to change its present manufacturing and business priorities?" (Lazes 1986:4). The answer was clearly, no! The company ignored the findings of the studies and pressed ahead with the preparations for the Trico twin plants in Matamoros and Brownsville. The company also rejected the proposal to build a new and State Of The Art Factory in Buffalo, "partly because it had already begun construction in Texas and Mexico" (*New York Times*, 17 February 1987:B2). Trico argued that it had been pleading with the city and the unions for years to help with its problems, and that the response of those opposed to the decision of the firm was somewhat belated.[10]

A task force had been set up when it was first announced that Trico was to relocate most of its operations. This was headed by a local minister, the Rev. Robert Beck, who was widely quoted in the press condemning the maquilas as "sweatshops" (*Brownsville Herald*, 7 December 1986:1D; *Buffalo News*, 8 March 1987:A10). The state of New York also became involved with the campaign to save Trico jobs in Buffalo. Vincent Tese, the director of economic development for the state, wrote to *Newsweek* pointing out that it was an oversimplification to explain Trico's move and the moves of other U.S. corporations to low cost offshore locations exclusively in terms of "prohibitively high" domestic labor costs. "The real problem," Tese argued, "is that American manufacturing has failed to retool for the 21st century and now finds its profits impaired by sluggish technology, resulting in poor productivity" (*Newsweek*, 19 January 1987:9). It was clear that a powerful and broadly based coalition was forming against Trico and any other firms contemplating the destruction of jobs in New York in order to take advantage of cheaper labor elsewhere.

The results of the Cornell studies gave some encouragement to those trying to defend Buffalo's manufacturing workforce, but the response of Trico could have come as no surprise to the realists among them. The union and the community groups continued to negotiate with the company, however, and the unions, desperate to save jobs, made a series of commitments to the company to persuade them to retain more of the high-skill jobs in Buffalo. We can only speculate on what would have happened if these commitments had been made before rather than after the relocation decision had been taken. In February 1987, the Trico president announced that the company had agreed to some of the union's requests and that 300 extra jobs would be kept in Buffalo until at least 1990. A regional officer of the United Auto Workers complimented the company on its conciliatory attitude, but the opinions of the actual Trico workers is not recorded.[11]

The Trico decision to relocate in Brownsville and Matamoros was greeted with a mixture of delight and relief in the valley. Press reports suggested that Trico's plant in Brownsville represented an investment of more than $10 million and the maquila in Matamoros represented a further investment of 25 billion pesos, about $38 million at the rate current in mid-1986, though it is unlikely that the Trico maquila actually cost this much to build and equip. These were both very substantial individual investments for the respective cities, and the Trico project will eventually provide Brownsville and Matamoros with their most substantial maquila twin plant.[12] The Brownsville factory, intended to employ about 400 workers, will be engaged in the capital intensive operations and manufacturing of components. The maquila in Matamoros assembles and packages these components and returns them to Brownsville for shipment to U.S. markets. It is not entirely clear why the "labor intensive" maquila in Matamoros, which will employ about 800 workers, has a greater dollar investment than the "capital intensive" plant in Brownsville, which will employ about 400 workers. This might suggest that there are further plans as yet unannounced for the maquila in Matamoros.

This is not a question that has been foremost in the minds of the business community in Brownsville. For materials suppliers, contractors, and builders in and around Brownsville—indeed for the whole construction industry in the valley—the Trico project "has in some cases meant survival, and for others, provided a buffer during tough times."[13] Trico's decision to locate there was widely seen as a substantial vote of confidence in Brownsville and its people, and in the future of the maquila industry across the bridge.

In an informative and evocative series of articles for the *Buffalo News* in March 1987, Michael Beebe gave the people of Buffalo, and the rest of us, an insightful account of what the relocation of Trico has meant for the Mexican workers of Trico Componentes, the new maquila, and those left in Buffalo. Gross pay for the production workers in Buffalo in 1987 was about $8 per hour, and for the maquila workers in Trico Componentes, about 80 cents per hour.[14] Not only did Trico save around 90 percent of its direct labor costs, but the incentives that Brownsville offered the company to locate there, meant that the costs of relocation have been minimal. The city leased the 55-acre site of the new factory at a derisory 1.2 cents per square foot; it waived all property taxes for the first five years, and reduced them for a further ten years; Trico was authorized to use the federally funded Job Training Act which will pay half of the salaries for a quarter of the workers Trico hires in Brownsville; and the city of Brownsville paid the $150,000 to drain the site of the Trico factory (Beebe, 9 March 1987:A-6).

Trico also took advantage of a new scheme introduced by the Mexican government in 1986 to help the country dispose of its massive foreign debt. Labeled the "public debt conversion program" (or the debt equity swap), it permitted companies doing business in Mexico to buy a note for a Mexican public debt from a bank at a discount. The note is redeemed by the Mexican authorities at a higher percentage of face value than what was paid for it, in pesos at the current rate of exchange. For example, the U.S. parent of a maquila could buy a $1 million debt note for $600,000, and receive the equivalent of $750,000 to $900,000 in pesos from the Mexican government to use for certain business expenses in Mexico. Maquilas wishing to expand or purchase Mexican materials and components, were offered the best rates on these transactions, and Trico stated an intention to finance a substantial portion of its Matamoros investment in this manner.[15] Trico, therefore, relocated at a time and to a place that were both extremely favorable for the process of the reformation of capitalism and for the transnational corporation. The prospects for the retention of jobs in Buffalo look bleak. The prospects in Brownsville may look better in the late 1980s, when the depression in the oil industry has released many skilled workers for employment in the valley, but the logic and practice of "production sharing" suggests that pressure on the skilled jobs in Brownsville will inevitably increase to the point at which it will be impossible to retain many of them in the U.S.

It is not incidental that Trico Technologies Corporation is located in Brownsville's airport industrial park, and that Trico Componentes is located in a maquila industrial park in Matamoros. Matamoros, like other maquila locations along the border, saw the advantages of industrial parks, and around 1970 moves. in this direction started in the city. A group of Mexican entrepreneurs formed a company, Empresas Cylsa, in September 1970 to buy land. This was the origin of the Matamoros industrial park. The park was situated in the northeast corner of the city, a few kilometers from the international bridge to Brownsville along a good road. Cylsa's 1,000-acre site was split up into a 400-acre industrial zone to the north of the irrigation canal that bisected the area, and the rest was set aside for housing, some for the workers who would hopefully be required in the maquilas. In its first few years, the park leased factories to Zenith, the Fisher Price toy division of Quaker Oats, and to a wire harness plant of ITT.

The success of the industrial park persuaded other public and private bodies to enter the field. In the mid-1970s, the Mexican government in the shape of *Nacional Financiera* (the industrial development bank controlled by the state but containing some private capital), created the Ciudad Industrial de Matamoros (CIMA). This covered a large area in the southeast of the city, further along the arterial highway that enclosed the Matamoros industrial park to the north, and like it intended to house industrial and residential development. CIMA attracted some local Mexican companies, mostly small metalworking firms, and later began to bring in maquilas of U.S. corporations.[16] Another private park opened in 1979, Fraccionadora Industrial del Norte, S.A. (FINSA), the creation of a local entrepreneur, Sergio Arguelles, and possibly the most important private facilitator in Matamoros/Brownsville. Arguelles accumulated 180 acres of undeveloped land in the industrial zone in the west of the city, about 10 minutes away from the international crossing on the same side of town as the railway bridge. Working through a shelter and subcontract company, Grupo Nova, Arguelles and his associate René González Rascón, pursued a targeted group of U.S. corporations.

FINSA's first coup was to land the Inland Division of General Motors. The negotiations for this were said to have taken 16 months, but it was clearly worth every minute because GM, like Zenith, is a major maquila corporation whose name on a promotional brochure is worth its weight in gold to private and public facilitators alike. By 1988, there were three General Motors plants in the FINSA park employing more than 5,000 people producing many types of automotive components (including, it is said, about 15,000 car radios per day at the Deltronics plant). Another feather in FINSA's cap was to attract the first Japanese maquila to Matamoros, Fabricación Metalica de Matamoros, a subsidiary of the Mitsubishi Corporation. Although a small metal industry plant employing fewer than 100 workers, the symbolic breakthrough that it represented should not be underestimated.[17] A planned expansion of a further 700 adjacent acres is intended to turn the park into the largest maquila park on the border, and sister parks in Nuevo Laredo and Nuevo Progreso will make FINSA the largest private facilitator in the area.

A notable feature of the FINSA park was the construction of a technical school to supply well-trained local skilled workers, mainly men, for the maquilas in the park. General Motors and other maquilas have donated machinery and their technicians give classes for the students.[18] As in other maquila cities, the local provision of skilled labor is widely seen as a problem that needs special attention. The business and engineering facilities at the Matamoros campus of the University of Tamaulipas and at the Matamoros Technological Institute are similarly increasingly geared to the needs of the maquila industry. There is also in the city a technical school sponsored by the government and designed specifically to teach the practical industrial skills that are in daily demand in the maquilas. Courses include automotive, machine shop, mechanics, sewing, engine maintenance, and electrical training. However, many Mexican students speak little English, which is considered to be a serious drawback by maquila management, and the higher level technical and administrative jobs are mainly monopolized by U.S. citizens. The shortage of skilled personnel is certainly connected with the generally low level of the technology of the Matamoros maquilas. It is rare to find any maquila in the city that does much more than simple assembly or fabrication work, and the proportion of technicians in the total labor force in the mid-1980s was the lowest of any of the major maquila locations.

The Brownsville area has three college-level institutions, the Brownsville campus of the Pan American University, Texas Southmost College, and the Texas State Technical Institute (TSTI) at nearby Harlingen. All of these offer business and technical studies, to degree level at Pan American, and many graduates of these colleges have found employment in the maquila industry. TSTI, in particular, has built up a solid reputation for training technicians, many of whom find employment outside the valley.[19] The success that Trico has in recruiting and training sufficient skilled labor to make its twin plant in Brownsville a going concern will be followed with great interest in the valley and in corporate boardrooms in the rustbelt, but with some trepidation in the union halls of Buffalo.

## Reynosa/McAllen

There are three major differences between Reynosa/McAllen and Matamoros/Brownsville. The first, and most obvious, is that whereas one can walk across the international bridge that joins Matamoros and Brownsville from the downtown areas of both cities, McAllen is about ten miles from the Mexican border and is therefore a "twin city" to Reynosa only in the same sense that San Diego is to Tijuana.[20] The actual "twin" is Hidalgo, a very poor, mainly hispanic settlement, like San Ysidro, San Diego's border town. Therefore, the Mexican influence in downtown McAllen appears less marked than it is in downtown Brownsville, just as U.S. influence appears less marked in Reynosa than it is in Matamoros. There is less day-to-day commerce, in both the social and economic senses of the term, between Reynosa and McAllen than there is between Matamoros and Brownsville. The second difference is that Reynosa has a massive PEMEX plant, one of the largest industrial facilities in the valley and in northern Mexico as a whole. The influence of the company, the largest in Mexico and the source of most of the foreign currency that Mexico earns, is to be seen all over the city and across the border.[21] The third difference is that McAllen has one of the most successful Foreign Trade Zones in the U.S., and this zone plays a central part in facilitating the efficient operation of the maquila industry in the area. Given these factors, the latter two of which might be seen as advantages as far as the BIP is concerned, it is surprising that there have always been many more plants and many more maquila jobs in Matamoros than in Reynosa.

The creation of the maquila industry in Reynosa/McAllen was largely a product of the efforts of public facilitators in McAllen and private facilitators in Reynosa, although both public and private facilitators in both cities (and some who straddled both camps) did take part. In Reynosa, two local entrepreneurs, Antonio Villareal and Arturo González, saw the prospects for a maquila industry at an early stage. They were active in setting up a joint industrial team of the Reynosa and McAllen chambers of commerce to promote the industry in the two cities. The McAllen chamber of commerce had an industrial board to handle maquila business, run by Frank Birkhead. He and Wade Terrell, the manager of the chamber, were the main figures on the McAllen side. Noting the steady buildup of maquila plants in other locations along the border, they saw no good reason why Reynosa and McAllen should not have some share. However, it proved to be a difficult task to attract U.S. corporations.

At the beginning of 1968, Reynosa was the only major Mexican border city that did not have a maquila, but in March of that year it was announced that the joint industrial team had notched its first client. Diaper Jeans Inc., a Texas infant wear manufacturer, signaled its intention to open a maquila in Reynosa, and this was front page news in the local paper (*Valley Evening Monitor* 17 March 1968,:1, 3). Unfortunately, Diaper Jeans became entangled in the thicket of U.S. and Mexican textile tariffs and quotas and it did not survive for very long. Two other maquilas came to Reynosa in 1968, a brickmaker from Houston, which like Diaper Jeans, was short-lived, and a local fruit and vegetable packer, Empacadora Calmo, which still provides jobs for over 100 workers, but neither of these plants were the type that would stimulate the industrialization of the region as the proponents of the BIP had hoped. The first real breakthrough came in 1969 when a U.S. company not only decided to establish a maquila in Reynosa, but also to set up a twin plant in McAllen. Rey-Mex Bra, to which I have already made reference, was part of the Form-O-Uth Company which at that time had one factory in Gardena, California and two in the Texas Panhandle making foundation garments. The company phased out the Gardena plant when the Reynosa plant opened at the end of 1969 (and later closed the Texas plants and went even further offshore to El Salvador). The owner of Form-O-Uth, Calvin Fraser, had started out in California and had heard about what was going on in the maquilas of Tijuana and Mexicali, namely high productivity and very low wages. He decided early on to go for the maquila option, but was uncertain as to where the best location for his operation might be. He traveled all along the border looking for a good site and eventually, after over a year of negotiations, chose Reynosa. His reasons offer an excellent insight into the early dynamics of the maquilas of the needle trades.

Fraser was more or less a captive but of course willing supplier to Sears Roebuck, and it was Sears who made the first approach to the McAllen Industrial Board (Birkhead 1984). In fact, Fraser's initial visit to McAllen and Reynosa was arranged by Sears' buyers from Dallas. This visit, like many others, was hosted by the Central Power and Light Company from Corpus Christi, naturally interested in selling energy to industrial users. The people from Sears obviously liked what they saw and heard, but the final decision was up to Calvin Fraser. Fraser chose Reynosa and McAllen because no one else was there (some of the other locations were already looking a little crowded), and because the Industrial Board in McAllen impressed him with its professionalism and commitment. The Bermúdez park had also tried to persuade him to locate in Juárez and had put on a good show, but still he chose Reynosa, preferring the more sedate surroundings and individual attention that it appeared to offer. Fraser acquired land for his factory from Antonio Villareal, a member of the binational team and an engineer by profession. Villareal had been buying up land through his company, Fraccionamiento Reynosa, and now began to plan an industrial park in Reynosa. Villareal built the plant for Rey-Mex Bra, and it was in operation by the end of the year. He had been able to acquire land on the eastern edge of the city near the airport, and in an area adjoining suburban *colonias* which would provide the labor force for the maquilas. Over the next few years, Villareal and his associates developed the Parque Industrial Reynosa, preparing industrial sites, building houses, and organizing bus services. However, Villareal did not offer much in the way of infrastructure or administrative services to the maquilas in the park, nor did he do much in the field of promotion. Rey-Mex Bra (which moved its headquarters to McAllen in 1971), found little help in Reynosa. Fraser had to drill his own well to ensure enough water to keep the plant in operation. It is probably the case that the local authorities in Reynosa, with PEMEX to think about, did not place a very high priority on the development of the maquila industry at that time.[22] Due to the centralization of the maquila industry, a system that is only now being relaxed, and problems over textile quotas, Fraser had to go frequently to Mexico City for permits, and Sears of Mexico often acted as an intermediary to keep the maquila in production.[23] There were problems in the factory too, for Fraser did not wish to have the CTM organizing his workforce. He eventually forced the union's hand by threatening to bring his sewing machines back to the U.S., and this was enough to keep the CTM out. Rey-Mex Bra has one of the few "factory unions" in Reynosa.

The binational team kept up its promotional work, with rather more of an official input from Reynosa as time went on, and each year one or two more companies came in. The number of maquilas crept up to nine in 1972. Then, in 1973 McAllen got on to the front page of the *Wall Street Journal* in an article on the booming maquila industry and the Industrial Board received more than 50 telephone calls in one day from prospective clients. About six of these came to fruition in 1973 alone, the highest one-year total since the start of the BIP, but they were all rather small and decidedly low technology operations. It is not to minimize the achievement of the McAllen/Reynosa promotional effort to note that none of these companies was anywhere near the Fortune 500 range, and although several were solid U.S. firms with several hundred maquila jobs to offer, the area did not manage to attract a core of major U.S. corporations, such as were already in production in places like Tijuana, Juárez and Matamoros. However, McAllen did have the compensation of having genuine twin plants in the town for almost half of the maquilas in Reynosa, providing hundreds of badly needed jobs and, with the crossborder spending of the maquila workers, feeding millions of dollars into the McAllen economy in the 1970s.

The breakthrough for Reynosa/McAllen, as in Matamoros/Brownsville, came with the establishment of a Zenith television components maquila in 1978. By then, several of the Reynosa maquilas had closed down. There were only eight left and employment was in decline, as can be seen from table 6.2. The Zenith plant singlehandedly transformed the situation by doubling the maquila labor force in one year,

*Table 6.2*
Reynosa by maquilas and employees, 1972–1988.

| | NUMBER OF | | | NUMBER OF | |
|---|---|---|---|---|---|
| YEAR | PLANTS | EMPLOYEES | YEAR | PLANTS | EMPLOYEES |
| 1972 | 8 | 600 | 1981 | 17 | 7,848 |
| 1973 | 8 | 600 | 1982 | 17 | 9,259 |
| 1974 | 2 | 180 | 1983 | 19 | 10,660 |
| 1975 | 11 | 1,255 | 1984 | 22 | 13,867 |
| 1976 | 9 | 1,381 | 1985 | 27 | 12,761 |
| 1977 | 8 | 1,258 | 1986 | 29 | 15,887 |
| 1978 | 9 | 2,897 | 1987 | 36 | 17,700 |
| 1979 | 13 | 4,237 | 1988 (Jan.) | 34 | c. 20,000 |
| 1980 | 17 | 5,450 | | | |

SOURCES: 1972–1974, my own estimates; 1975–1988, INEGI (1988: table 3), and *Avances*.

doubling the area of factory floor in use, (the plant covered a massive 250,000 square feet), and giving the seal of approval to the Parque Industrial Reynosa for all in the maquila industry to see. Not only did Zenith transform the maquila industry in Reynosa, but it also transformed it in McAllen because it was the first important client to establish itself in the McAllen Foreign Trade Zone (FTZ).

The FTZ in McAllen embodied innovatory concepts in two respects. In the first place, unlike most other FTZs at the time in the U.S. or elsewhere, it was not a seaport; and second, it was designed as an industrial park very much with the maquila industry in mind rather than simply a warehousing facility. Frank Birkhead and his colleagues at the chamber of commerce, all too conscious of McAllen's drawbacks as an industrial location, were specifically "looking for ways to enhance industry in the area which would make this town unique" (Goodwin 1980:14). After much bureaucratic delay, the McAllen FTZ went through in 1973. The zone works as a sort of geophysical credit card, allowing companies to import goods into the U.S. for purposes of storage or modification without paying any tariffs or duties on them until they leave the confines of the zone for a nonzone destination in the U.S. Where third country trade (transshipment) is involved, tariffs and duties may be avoided altogether. The first maquila to take advantage of the McAllen FTZ was Kimball Piano and Organ from Indiana. They set up their maquila, Kimco S.A., in a good sized plant in the Parque Industrial Reynosa in 1973 assembling piano components and wiring harnesses for their electronic organs, and a twin plant, McAllen American, in the FTZ. Here, British piano components were imported, combined with U.S. components, and shipped over to Reynosa for assembly, free of all tariffs and duties. Only when the maquila in Reynosa was ready to ship its production back to Indiana for final assembly were the requisite duties paid. This represented a considerable cash flow saving for the company and, of course, jobs and revenues in McAllen and Reynosa. Zenith operated in much the same way, but on a far larger scale. It brought a mixture of U.S. and foreign components (mainly from the Far East) tariff and duty free into the FTZ, then shipped them to Reynosa for assembly, paying the duties only when the goods were ready for return to the U.S. Another advantage of the FTZ, particularly relevant for maquilas in the needle trades, is that above-quota goods could be stored there for future quota openings, or even to be transformed into nonquota goods where feasible. The zone could also be used for regular and, compared with most U.S. industrial locations, inexpensive duty free storage, which for a company like Zenith strung out all along the border in the age of "just in time" inventory control, clearly had its possibilities.

Working alongside the public and private maquila facilitators, the McAllen FTZ grew into the largest in the U.S. In its first full year of operation, 1974, it moved just under 4,000 tons of goods valued at about $2.5 million. The effects of the arrival of Zenith in 1978 increased the tonnage fourfold over 1977 (11,000 to 40,000 tons), and the value more than tenfold ($16 million to over $170 million). Between 1978 and 1979, both tonnage and value almost doubled, and the one billion dollar mark was achieved in 1982. The next great leap forward was achieved in the mid-1980s when two more Fortune 500 corporations, General Motors and General Electric, set up twin plants in the Parque Industrial Reynosa and in the McAllen FTZ. Delnosa S.A., the GM maquila, assembled air conditioners for automobiles, and Sociedad de Motores Domésticos S.A., the GE maquila, made fractional horsepower motors. Both employed around 1,000 workers in Reynosa, and though they have created far fewer jobs in McAllen, these tended to be at a higher skill level than the jobs south of the border.[24] The FTZ has certainly been a success, and if the maquila industry of Reynosa/McAllen has not grown to the extent of its neighbor to the east, it is doubtful it would have grown even to the extent it has without the FTZ.

In 1980, rather belatedly, the Mexican authorities began to build their own industrial park in Reynosa. This was a joint venture of national agencies, the state government of Tamaulipas, and CANACINTRA in Reynosa. The original plan was to take a 400-hectare area, about nine kilometers south of Reynosa where housing was already being developed, and design a full service industrial park specifically for the maquila industry (*MN*, June 1980:16). As yet, however, the park has failed to attract a core of maquilas. A more successful though limited step into industrial park development has been taken by an existing Reynosa maquila, Manimex S.A., the Mexican subsidiary of the Wisconsin crane company, Manitowoc. This company, which also manufactures cranes in McAllen, has made a notable commitment to the area. The first phase of its Manimex Industrial Park was under construction in 1987: water pipes had been laid, feeder roads had been built, speculative factory building was in process, and almost 200 acres of good flat land were made available. In addition Lobeira, a major Monterrey construction company, also involved in the FINSA park in Matamoros, has built a small park in Reynosa. Confidence that the maquila industry in Reynosa/McAllen will share fully in the anticipated growth of the industry nationally in the late 1980s was high in local circles.

The maquila association is a major propagator of this confidence. It started in 1981, and as was the case in Matamoros, Zenith dominated at first, but as new large firms began slowly to come in (TRW, General Motors, and General Electric), these began to play a bigger role. The association has for some years been involved in infrastructural improvements in the maquila parks areas of the city, both on its own and in joint projects with the authorities. These have included road-works, electricity supply, communications, waterworks, and sewage (Diamondstein and Torres in Lee, ed., 1988:83–84). Suggestions of wage cartels are vigorously denied by all maquila associations, and this one is no exception. Nevertheless, most plants in Reynosa do pay little more than the minimum wage and have very similar facilities and benefits. This can be explained in part by the fact that almost all of the maquilas are organized by the CTM, which maintain a highly visible presence all over the town.

There have been some serious cases of strike action in the maquilas of Reynosa, most notably in the Zenith plant in 1983,[25] one of the rare cases when Fidel Velázquez, the national leader of the CTM, became embroiled in a maquila dispute. In 1983 Zenith employed over 7,000 workers in what was then the biggest maquila in Mexico, and like all maquilas, the corporation was benefiting considerably from the rapid devaluation of the peso that had begun in the previous year. The workers, battered between the hammer of Mexican inflation and the anvil of their reduced purchasing power in the U.S., put pressure on the union to ask for an emergency wage increase. When the CTM did not respond, the workers, under the unofficial leadership of Daniel López, organized a blockade of the plant in November 1983, and prevented the personnel manager, a U.S. citizen, from leaving for about 24 hours. López was jailed and a local U.S. journalist was abused, but the fact that the Reynosa police did not intervene on any large scale was interpreted by many people to signify that the PRI-controlled city authorities did not wish to provoke a riot so near to election time. The combined efforts of the local people and officials in Mexico City and Washington soon secured the freedom of the personnel manager.

Fidel Velázquez happened to be in the border region at the time, and he came to Reynosa and convinced the strikers, who were on the point of leaving the CTM and establishing an alternative union, to return to work by promising to hold elections for a new local leadership and to help to get the company to review the collective contracts. López was released and he led a "green slate" of candidates to an overwhelming victory in which, for the first time, four women were voted onto the union committee. The CTM declared the elections null and void and they were duly held again, with similar results. This time the union and Zenith forced the ten victorious "green slate" candidates to resign, and four of them began a hunger strike in the central square of Reynosa, a protest that was violently terminated by the police. The company and the CTM compromised over the pay increases and the unofficial union movement declined to the point where it is no longer a force in the Reynosa maquila industry.

Mexican newspapers warned that worker militancy in the maquilas in Reynosa might cause U.S. investors to consider pulling out and closing down their plants,[26] and the message clearly reached those for whom it was intended. The relatively rapid defeat of the unofficial union and the absence of any sustained violence meant that Zenith did not pull out and that other corporations were not excessively scared off. Zenith, in fact, expanded its Reynosa workforce to nearly 8,000 in 1986, and to over 9,000 in 1987, over half of the total maquila employment in Reynosa. As has been already noted, General Motors and General Electric established twin plants in the mid-1980s, and others followed. In March 1987 the McAllen Industrial Board issued a circular to the effect that in the first quarter of the year no fewer than seven Japanese maquila projects were being seriously investigated for Reynosa/McAllen.[27]

The maquilas have also become involved with technical training. For example, the General Electric plant Sociedad de Motores Domésticos is part of a GE global training program; and the Texas State Technical Institute, which has premises in McAllen though its main campus is in Harlingen, in conjunction with the Manimex Park trains welders up to U.S. welding certification level. The main campus of Pan American University at Edinburg, a few miles from McAllen, offers business and technical courses geared to the needs of the maquila industry,[28] and Texas A and I University is establishing an engineering facility in the area specifically for the maquila industry. Reynosa also has some small private colleges and three public technical schools, but it is PEMEX rather than the maquila industry that is the main influence in the city.

That Reynosa/McAllen has a maquila industry at all, let alone a small group of successful Fortune 500 corporations, is a considerable achievement for the two communities. The depressive poverty of south Texas and the industrial dominance of PEMEX, though it employs less workers than it used to, have been formidable obstacles to the maquila industry in McAllen and Reynosa. Through the efforts of a small and dedicated band of public and private facilitators in both cities, some deriving personal enrichment from the maquila industry and others not, a manufacturing base has been established, more than 15,000 jobs have been created, and a range of skills has been transmitted to large numbers of workers who might otherwise never have seen the inside of a modern factory. In these respects, the maquila industry has had a definite transformation effect on these two relatively deprived border communities.

# Notes

1. In the 1980s, the SMSAs from Brownsville-Harlingen, through McAllen, to Laredo occupy the three bottom places, with El Paso not far ahead.

2. By 1965 there were said to be about 200 local industrial development corporations in Texas (Hale, February 1965:3).

3. This is rather an unusual maquila in that, in 1987, it employed 280 workers in Brownsville and about half that number in Matamoros.

4. It is also said locally that RCA was interested in establishing a maquila in Matamoros at this time, but the company was unable to find a suitable plant. When the Bermúdez people discovered this, they built RCA a plant in their industrial park in Juárez.

5. His energetic successor, Jim Ebersole, was the project manager for an electronics maquila in the late 1960s. He went on to run his own subcontract maquila in Matamoros in the 1970s, before joining the chamber as its industrial development specialist.

6. *Business Abroad* (11 December 1967:21) reported that Agapito was trying to get a minimum wage of $4 per *day* for a worker "with a wife [sic] and five children" but that he would probably have to settle for about $2.40. The U.S. minimum was then $1.40 per *hour*.

7. Roger Kennedy, the then chairman of the Matamoros maquila association, is quoted as saying that "the union is the employment agency" for the local maquilas (in a newspaper article reproduced in McAllen Industrial Board 1986, source unknown).

8. The *MN* turnover table (August 1986:9) gives a rate of 5–7 percent for Matamoros, which is the lowest of the major sites along the border but still seems rather high. The local maquiladora association estimated that the turnover rate was 2–3 percent in 1987.

9. "Windshield wiper maker to open plants in Brownsville, Matamoros," (*Dallas Morning News*, 21 Feb. 1986). Trico was persuaded to come to the valley by a combination of public and private facilitators.

10. It can be argued that if Trico had embarked on major automation then many of the jobs in Buffalo would also have been lost. It is also uncertain to what extent the many different types of wiper blades demanded by the market would render automation cost ineffective.

11. This story was headlined "Saving Jobs in Buffalo: Victory and Loss" (*New York Times*, 17 February 1987:B1). Of the original 1,100 jobs that were to remain in Buffalo in 1986, the 550 hourly paid skilled jobs were increased to almost 900 by the 1987 agreement.

12. The ITT wire mill and the Leece Neville plant, both in the Brownsville airport industrial park, are also genuine twin plants insofar as they produce components for assembly in Matamoros.

13. See Daniel Cavazos, "Trico project helps, motivates local businesses" (*Brownsville Herald*, 22 February 1987:1B). Cavazos gives several concrete examples and quotes a small local contractor to the effect that the Trico project "could be a real milestone."

14. This reduced to about $26 take home pay for a 48-hour week, as indicated by the pay slip of a worker reproduced in Beebe's article. As a new maquila, Trico was exempt from the 40-hour week.

15. "Mexico debt swap deal gives Trico a 'nice return,' " (*Brownsville Herald*, 26 October 1986:1D). The scheme was suspended in 1988.

16. Since 1985 several large firms, including AT&T, CTS, and Rohm and Haas, have located in CIMA, and others are following.

17. It was reported in *Business Week* (10 December 1979:46) that Mitsubishi was teaming up with Kawasaki Steel to build a $4.4 million plant in Matamoros, but this arrangement did not work out. The plant became a joint venture between Mitsubishi and a Mexican company.

18. This is a phenomenon that I have also noted in a "maquila" location in the Irish Republic (Sklair 1988:2.2).

19. The Brownsville chamber of commerce reported (industrial committee summary, 27 March 1986) that Texas Southmost and TSTI had offered crash courses for any machine operators and tool and die men [sic] that the new maquila, Trico, might require.

20. The town was built so far from the border because of the danger of flooding from the river. Subsequently, a flood control system has been constructed.

21. As long ago as 1967 Texas was celebrating the fact that PEMEX would be giving its workers the equivalent of $350,000 in Christmas bonuses as over half of this was likely to be spent in the United States (*Journal of Commerce*, 30 November 1967:2).

22. Calvin Fraser reports that Donald Baerreson organized a seminar on the BIP in San Diego in 1971 attended by all the border towns but, in the absence of any official, he represented Reynosa.

23. The problem of textile quotas is one often mentioned today. John Freeland, of Rio Contract Sewing, a facilitator since the 1960s, suggested in an interview in McAllen (March 1987) that this is the major cause of instability in this sector of the maquila industry.

24. Zenith and GE also used the FTZ for testing to avoid payment of duties on rejected units (see *High Technology*, April 1984:70).

25. This account is derived from articles in *MN* (November and December 1983), the first issue of the shortlived radical magazine *Bridge over the Border* (1985), and interviews.

26. See, for example, "Pugnas Obreras Ponen en Riesgo la Operación de Maquiladoras," *Excelsior* (5 November 1984). Cockcroft (1986:191) reports that the strike had been the lead item on CBS evening news on 10 November 1983.

27. In the three years from 1984 to 1987, Nancy Fryer of the McAllen Industrial Board organized 72, 80, and 84 "industrial prospects" visits for potential maquilas in Reynosa (internal document, 1988).

28. The Center for Entrepreneurship and Economic Development at the University is intended to be a "catalyst for economic growth, income and jobs in South Texas"—to quote its own publicity.

# 7

# The Long March to
# the Interior

The fact that the maquilas were a direct consequence of the Border Industrialization Program of the mid-1960s, and that the BIP was a direct consequence of the PRONAF, naturally meant that from the very beginning the maquilas were closely identified with the border. As we have seen in the previous three chapters, the maquila idea was sold to U.S. companies that were going offshore for the first time as well as to experienced TNCs largely on the locational advantages of being situated on the border. It was also a great deal easier to sell the maquila idea to those who appeared to be harmed by it, for example, El Paso garment workers who were seeing their jobs trickling into Juárez, if the spinoffs from the Mexican twin city to the U.S. twin could be directly observed. William Mitchell's "economic impact surveys" for the Grupo Bermúdez, for example, purported to show that the maquilas in Juárez did create jobs in El Paso, though jobs of rather different kinds from those that had been lost.

It will be recalled that the original authorization for the establishment of in-bond plants within the BIP had evolved rather informally between mid-1965, when Campos Salas had introduced the program through PRONAF in Ciudad Juárez, and mid-1966, when the government announced what Villalobos terms "transitory administrative provisions that lacked any of the necessary incentives for investment or the judicial bases which assured the permanence, continuity and suitability of these provisions" (1973:5). The early success of the program—by 1971 over 200 factories employing nearly 30,000 people—had encouraged the Mexican government to give it legal recognition and security through article 321 of the Mexican customs code of March 1971. In June 1971, the U.S. embassy in Mexico City, which was keeping a close watch on the growth of the maquila industry, reported that four established firms in the interior that claimed they could not survive on local markets had been granted maquila status. They were located in Guadalajara, San Luis Potosí, and Torreón. The embassy continued: "Most observers of the program are of the opinion that if a firm can offer sufficient economic advantage to Mexico, it will be permitted to establish a border industry plant almost anywhere in the country" (U.S. Department of State "Airgram", 4 June 1971:3). The customs code was further amended at the end of the following year, removing most of the geographical restrictions on the location of the maquilas and opening up virtually the whole country to maquilization. What was the rationale behind this apparently momentous move?

## The Maquila Industry in the Interior

It is tempting to argue that the rationale behind the Mexican government's decision to permit maquilas in the interior of the country was simply that of capitalizing on success. In 1965, the year in which the BIP was introduced, Mexico's share of U.S. 806/807 imports was a paltry 0.006 percent, but by 1969 it had expanded to 8 percent, and Mexico in that year had outstripped every other Third World country as a source of 806/807 imports. The numbers of factories and jobs were increasing all the time and the impact on the border towns to which the maquilas were going appeared to be both substantial and positive. Industrial development, particularly in modern and attractive industrial parks, was changing the face of the frontera norte and the border was humming with U.S. and Mexican entrepreneurs bringing new ideas for business. It was, therefore, natural for Mexican policymakers to anticipate that what was so obviously happening on the border, even in some quite unlikely places, might be made to happen in the interior of the country with encouragement from the authorities. There was no logical reason, from the Mexican point of view, to restrict the maquilas to the border, for although the BIP had originally been created to build up border industry, the "border connection" had always seemed convenient rather than integral to it. It was the U.S. facilitators, both the shelter/subcontractors and the U.S. border town economic development agencies, much more than the Mexican authorities, who had pushed the proximity arguments.

Nevertheless, the decision of the Mexican government to extend the maquilas into the interior came as much from the perceived weaknesses of the program as from its perceived strengths. The Mexican government began to read a series of warning signals coming from across the border and the response to these signals highlights both the essential ambivalence of Mexico toward U.S. investment and also the dilemmas of the U.S. corporation in its quest for survival, higher profits, or a mixture of both. Mexico was in competition not only with the U.S. for the rapidly expanding numbers of maquila type manufacturing jobs but, of course with the rest of the Third World. Mexico's locational advantage, however, was also its Achilles' heel. The maquilas in Tijuana, Ciudad Juárez, Matamoros and the other twin cities along the border had a high degree of visibility, literally in some cases, from the U.S. side. Unemployed U.S. workers might have had some vague notions about jobs being lost to the Far East or South America, but these were far off and largely unknown places. The worker in San Diego or El Paso or Brownsville knew the towns on the other side of the border, could drive past the industrial parks, and might even know someone working in a maquila. The existence of the maquilas in the border towns and their increasing numbers were a constant reminder of where the jobs had gone, and where the next job losses might go. Mexico, of course, was anxious to hold on to the border maquilas at all cost, but it cannot have escaped the notice of the authorities that the farther away from the border any new maquilas could be situated then the less visible from the U.S. they would be and perhaps the less vulnerable to negative criticism from across the border.[1]

It would be wrong to underestimate the symbolic importance of the border twin cities but, on the other hand, there were clearly other reasons for the Mexican government's decision to extend the BIP to the interior. The most important relates to the single greatest disappointment of the maquila program in its first phase, namely the almost total failure of Mexican domestic industry to sell materials and components to the maquilas. Rather optimistically, it was suggested that the maquilas were not making purchases in Mexico because the potential suppliers were not on the border, but in the interior of the country, particularly around the industrial centers of Mexico City, Monterrey, and Guadalajara. Another factor that was to become increasingly important was the availability of trained managers and technicians. Expatriate staff are always problematic for TNCs, and with the usual exception of chief executive and perhaps some very highly specialized technicians whose role is to protect proprietary knowledge, we may accept that most TNCs genuinely seek to employ local people to run their offshore plants where possible.[2] In the early 1970s there were very few establishments for the training of the types of staff that the maquilas required along the border and even the provision of primary and secondary schools was quite inadequate for the booming youthful populations that stretched the infrastructures of every border maquila town. Though many interior locations were just as lacking in resources, some were better off than others, and the attempt to attract maquilas to them was partly based on the availability of trained people.

The final reason for trying to attract the maquilas to the interior harks back to the original PRONAF rallying cry of Antonio Bermúdez, "Recapture our frontier markets." Despite the low wages that the maquilas paid, the continuing discrepancy between the high prices of some daily necessities on the frontera norte and lower prices for the same goods over the border in the U.S. meant that some of the wages earned by the maquila workers flowed right back across the border. Clearly, the farther away from the border maquilas were established, the less chance of this loss of revenue for Mexico, and the better for Mexican business.

For the foreign investor there were several advantages in locating in the interior. The three main factors that slowly began to push the maquilas off the border and pull them into the interior characterize the three phases of maquila expansion. Up to the mid-1970s, the main attraction of an interior location was that the wages in the interior were even lower than along the border. The changing relationships between the dollar/peso exchange, the minimum wage, and the rate of inflation in Mexico has forced this factor back into the reckoning at various points since the mid-1970s. The second factor is the overstretched infrastructure of the Mexican border cities and, in particular, their declining capacity to absorb more and more maquilas and service more and more industrial workers. During the 1975 to 1982 phase of maquila expansion, the problematic balance of infrastructure and industrial development became increasingly important. The controversy between maquila facilitators in Ciudad Juárez over the future of the industry in that city and in the state of Chihuahua that came to a head in 1984 (discussed in chapter 5 above), serves as an illustration. The third factor is the nature of the labor force available for the maquilas. As the numbers of maquilas on the border continued to grow, for the first time ever there was serious talk of labor shortages in the maquila industry, particularly in Tijuana and Juárez after the explosive growth that followed the devaluations of 1982. Complaints began to be heard of unacceptable levels of turnover and absenteeism, and the phenomenon of "job hopping" appeared.[3]

However, labor shortages were few in the early 1970s when the interior was opened up to the maquila industry. The main reason usually given for the establishment of maquilas in the interior was, as the manager of a Texas-based electronics company bluntly admitted, "the labor; down there [Morelos] we pay 45 cents an hour, here [on the border] it's 72 cents" (Baird and McCaughan 1975:22). The evidence on actual wage rates, however, does not entirely bear out this interpretation.

It is difficult to make meaningful comparisons of actual wages over time and place in the maquila industry due to the variety of minimum wages, above minimum wages, and nonwage benefits. However, we can make some rough estimates of the average differences between wages in the main border maquila sites and those in the interior. Table 7.1 shows the wage differences for maquilas in the interior as against the border, and they are less substantial than we might expect. A saving of around one-quarter on a wage bill that is already low relative to other operating costs would normally be insufficient to outweigh the logistical advantages of the border locations as long as the border locations continued to satisfy the needs of the maquila industry. Thus, we should not be surprised that almost 90 percent of the maquilas were on or near the border in the mid-1980s. No doubt, some corporations had specific reasons for not wanting to establish maquilas on the border or, conversely, for wanting to establish maquilas in particular places in the interior.

The first interior maquilas were located in Chihuahua (which continues to be the leading interior site), Mérida in the Yucatán, and Zaragoza in Coahuila. By 1972, each of these cities had two maquilas, and there were seven more in other interior locations. These 13 plants employed 2,398 people, an average of about 180 per plant, compared with an average of about 140 per plant for the whole industry.[4] Of these, two are not very far from the border. Chihuahua City is about 230 miles from Juárez, while Zaragoza is less than 50 miles from the Texas border town of Eagle Pass.

*Table 7.1*
Maquila industry border and interior average operative wages, 1975, 1980, 1985.

| CITY/AREA | 1975 | 1980 (U.S. CENTS PER HOUR) | 1985 |
|---|---|---|---|
| Tijuana | 94 | 1.12 | 79 |
| Ciudad Juárez | 80 | 1.00 | 75 |
| Reynosa | 66 | 96 | 67 |
| Matamoros | 71 | 1.03 | 84 |
| Border | 79 | 1.03 | 76 |
| Interior | 63 | 84 | 60 |
| National Average | 78 | 1.01 | 74 |

SOURCE: Calculated from INEGI (1988: tables 2 and 3).

By 1974, there were 83 nonborder maquilas employing 12,850 workers (Baird and McCaughan 1975:21). Some of these were established in Guadalajara and around Mexico City itself, in Torreón, Monterrey, and other industrial cities. The crash of 1974 that brought the first phase of maquila expansion to an abrupt end along the border did not spare the interior. In 1975, the base year for the official INEGI maquila statistics, there were only 41 maquilas left in the interior, employing 5,302 people.[5] As table 7.2 shows it took ten years for the number of plants to recover to the 1974 total, though the number of employees had overtaken the 1974 total by 1980, indicating that fewer but larger maquilas were venturing into the interior. The evidence suggests, therefore, that many smaller companies were attracted to the interior, particularly during 1973 and 1974, some of them by the lure of very low wages compared to the merely low wages along the border, that some of these got out when the U.S. recession started to bite, and that they were slowly replaced over the next five to ten years by larger companies tending on average to make more substantial commitments, at least in terms of the numbers of jobs they were offering.

By the late 1970s, the urge for manufactured exports combined with the urge for decentralization, on paper if not on the ground, intensified, and the maquila industry was an obvious mechanism through which to pursue both of these goals. The industrial cities program of 1978 and the industrial development plan of 1979 set out

*Table 7.2*
Maquilas and employees in the interior, 1975–1988.

| YEAR | PLANTS | | | LABOR FORCE | | |
|------|--------|----------|-------------|-------|----------|-------------|
| | TOTAL | INTERIOR | I/T PERCENT | TOTAL | INTERIOR | I/T PERCENT |
| 1975 | 454 | 41 | 9.0 | 67,200 | 5,302 | 7.9 |
| 1976 | 448 | 47 | 10.5 | 74,500 | 7,238 | 9.7 |
| 1977 | 443 | 47 | 10.6 | 78,400 | 7,939 | 10.1 |
| 1978 | 457 | 39 | 8.5 | 90,700 | 8,574 | 9.5 |
| 1979 | 540 | 60 | 11.1 | 111,400 | 10,828 | 9.7 |
| 1980 | 620 | 69 | 11.1 | 119,500 | 12,970 | 10.9 |
| 1981 | 605 | 72 | 11.9 | 131,000 | 14,523 | 11.1 |
| 1982 | 585 | 71 | 12.2 | 127,000 | 13,821 | 10.9 |
| 1983 | 600 | 67 | 11.2 | 151,000 | 15,952 | 10.6 |
| 1984 | 672 | 77 | 11.5 | 199,700 | 22,775 | 11.4 |
| 1985 | 760 | 88 | 11.6 | 212,000 | 25,968 | 12.2 |
| 1986 | 890 | 119 | 13.4 | 249,833 | 39,198 | 15.7 |
| 1987 | 1,125 | 166 | 14.8 | 305,253 | n.a. | n.a. |
| 1988 (Jan.) | 1,279 | 226 | 17.7 | 329,413 | 62,401 | 18.9 |

SOURCE: INEGI (1988: table 1) and *Avances*.

to encourage industrial activity away from Mexico City, Guadalajara, and Monterrey, and establish priority regions for the expansion of infrastructure and industrial investment. Among these priority regions were the main border maquila sites and some less-developed interior places where the government particularly wished to encourage the maquilas, such as the Yucatán and Oaxaca. There was also a hint that interior maquilas might be more likely to be joint ventures of Mexican and foreign companies than those along the border.

The August 1983 decree, as I noted in chapter 3, laid down certain conditions under which the maquilas could gain access to the Mexican domestic market. The man behind this policy, Mauricio de María y Campos of SECOFI, was also an energetic proponent of extending the maquilas to nonborder locations and he built added incentives for maquilas in the interior into the new regulations. Whereas some border maquilas were permitted to sell up to 20 percent of their production in the Mexican market provided the local content levels were achieved, and others in particularly crowded locations might only be allowed 10 percent of local sales, firms that located in nonborder areas where there were few or no maquilas might be permitted to sell 40 percent of their production locally (*Business Mexico*, February 1986:84). Mexican banks also created incentives for interior maquilas. Banamex targeted Hermosillo, Ciudad Obregón, and Chihuahua for new credit lines in excess of $20 million for maquila expansion and discouraged further expansion in Tijuana and Ciudad Juárez "which are saturated and cannot adequately support any more significant growth because of lack of infrastructure" (Scheinman 1987:16).

Clark Reynolds has suggested that for the good of Mexico, the United States should: "Liberalize the U.S. Customs Code, eliminating all U.S. reentry duties for new in-bond plants but focusing particularly on those located outside the border area" (Reynolds in Erb and Ross, eds., 1981:173). For Reynolds, this is the "most reasonable option" because the border dynamic is already more or less unstoppable (and, as I have argued in previous chapters, the transborder coalition of private and pub-lic facilitators is a really powerful force to keep it moving). However, the only real incentive for the U.S. to take this course of action is the hope that interior development might inhibit illegal immigration (Reynolds in Erb and Ross, eds., 1981:165). From the point of view of U.S. border state politicians, there is every reason to keep the maquilas on the border.[6] This is yet another example of the contradictions between regional and national interests as they are intensified by the reformation of capitalism, but with the added complexity that the overall U.S./Mexican national in-terests may, as Reynolds argues, be better served by having the maquila industry grow away from the border, whereas the U.S./Mexico border twin city interests might suffer from such an outcome.

It is a matter of opinion whether the drive by the Mexican government to attract maquilas from the border to the interior has been successful over the years. Certainly, the rate of growth in the numbers of maquilas and jobs between 1975 and 1986 was greater in the interior than on the border, but the proportion of the interior to the national total has only slowly risen from around 10 percent to around 15 percent since the late 1970s. The recent growth of interior maquila plants and employment is probably due to extensive subcontracting under the maquila rules that is being carried out by Mexican manufacturers with excess capacity. As of 1987, Chihuahua City, with around 40 plants employing some 20,000 people—much of the city's industrial labor force—is the only nonborder location where we can properly speak of a maquila industry in contrast to a few, if prestigious, maquila plants, as in places like Guadalajara, or the opportunistic use of Mexican industrial plant. Most commentators see this as, if not exactly failure, a distinct lack of success.

Dillman (1983:47) usefully lists five main reasons why firms have been reluctant to locate maquilas in the interior. These are: (1) difficulty in attracting U.S. personnel; (2) lack of repair services; (3) transport problems; (4) shortages of skilled labor; and (5) customs problems. Each of these is to some extent location specific. There are many Mexican towns and cities that appear to be very popular with U.S. personnel, for example, Guadalajara and Monterrey, or at least as popular as some of the border twin city locations. It is not at all certain that all of the border twin cities do have adequate engineering services for the maquila industry, as the "Trico report" from Cornell indicated (Lazes 1986), nor that some of the interior cities are significantly weaker in this respect. The transport costs of interior maquilas will certainly be higher but, as Dillman himself comments, these may be compensated for by lower labor and other costs. Since the time that Dillman wrote, shortages of skilled labor have appeared on the border as well. The fact that turnover in the interior is said to be very much lower than along the border, may encourage maquilas in the interior to invest in training more seriously in these nonborder locations than hitherto.[7] Finally, the problems of customs clearance between the interior and the border were probably more serious in 1975, the date of the reference for the problem in Dillman's article, than they are today, but this is not a problem specific to the interior maquilas any more.

An assessment of some of the developments in the main interior location, Chihuahua City, and in the "deep" interior (in particular, Guadalajara, a major industrial center in its own right), will illustrate the trend of maquila development beyond the frontera norte and will provide a more systematic picture of the attractions and drawbacks of venturing beyond the border.

## The Maquilas of Chihuahua City

Ciudad Chihuahua is a city with a great revolutionary tradition as is illustrated by the *Museo Francisco Villa* (Pancho Villa's Museum of the Revolution) that lurks inconspicuously in a quiet suburb. The city has traditionally been a cattle and mining center with a small manufacturing base. It is about five hours' to drive from Ciudad Juárez and the U.S. border on the Pan American Highway which connects with Mexico City and other main centers.[8] Chihuahua is also on a main railway line, and has an airport. The population is in excess of half a million and is relatively well endowed for higher education, having campuses of the *Universidad Autonomia de Chihuahua*, the *Instituto Tecnológico de Chihuahua* (specializing in industrial relations and engineering), and the *Instituto Tecnológico y de Estudios Superiores de Monterrey* (law, business studies and computer science). Since the early 1980s, there has been a small industrial revolution, due mainly to the entry of the maquila industry.

The first genuine foreign maquila to open its doors in Chihuahua was probably Electrocomponentes de México, one of the several General Electric subsidiaries in Mexico. This plant has been engaged in the fabrication of wire harnesses for white goods and the assembly of heating apparatuses since August 1971, anticipating the regulations a little. Then as now, in Mexico as elsewhere in the job-hungry Third World, and with very few exceptions, the prospect of a prestigious Fortune 500 corporate investment far outweighed the legal niceties. In any case, the authorities in Mexico City and in Chihuahua would surely have known in 1971 of the changes that were about to be announced in the rules of location for the BIP.

Having seen what was happening all along the border, particularly the success of Jaime Bermúdez in Ciudad Juárez, and realizing the potential of the maquila industry for Chihuahua City, a group of Mexican developers created an industrial park just outside the city and began to build factories. Parque Industrial las Américas (American Industrial Parks) opened its gates in 1975 and now accommodates the largest concentration of maquilas outside the border area. 1975, on the surface, would seem to have been an inauspicious year for such an initiative but, as I argued in chapter 3, the "collapse" of the maquila industry in 1974 was a very shortlived phenomenon, and these developers were a farsighted group of entrepreneurs with good nerves. The U.S. electronics corporation Honeywell used the las Américas park for the first of what were to be several maquila sites in Mexico. Beginning assembly of various electronic components in February 1976, Honeywell is still in Chihuahua City and has employed between 500 and 1,000 people for some years. Honeywell was followed into las Américas park by other wire harness and electronic assemblers.[9]

The economic development authorities of the state of Chihuahua, the city being the state capital, thought it both appropriate and profitable to enter the industrial park business on their own account. As noted in chapter 5, the state established its own industrial promotion agency—the *Promotora*—in 1980. Under the energetic leadership of Governor Ornelas Kuchle, the state government developed the Complejo Industrial Chihuahua (Chihuahua Industrial Complex) in the early 1980s, and soon garnered a group of small Mexican light industrial and service companies. The main coups of the Complejo were to attract the Ford Motor Company to build an engine plant, which employs about 1,000 workers and makes a major contribution to the industrial profile of Chihuahua, though this does not operate under the maquila rules; and Productos Magnéticos, a subsidiary of the Zenith Corporation.

Many of the maquilas in Chihuahua City operate under shelter or subcontracting plans run by what I have termed the private facilitators. The major private facilitator in the city is American Industries Inc., also active in Ciudad Juárez, which have their headquarters in las Américas park. The founder and chief executive of American Industries, Luis Lara, was the manager of the las Américas park when it first opened, but the slow rate of growth in the early years did not satisfy the shareholders and in 1982 Lara bought some of them out and began to operate on his own account. Through a creative use of shelter and subcontracting arrangements and by skillful marketing of Chihuahua as a maquila center, Lara was able to build up American Industries from a small operation managing the labor of about 100 people to its present position as the employer of over 2,000 maquila workers and staff.

The business philosophy of American Industries deserves some attention in this context. The experience of what many people saw as the too rapid growth of the maquila industry in Juárez had convinced Lara and his associates that the future of the industry lay in the interior. "Ciudad Juárez," in the words of the director of business development for American Industries, "is becoming another Mexico City."[10] The only way to overcome the potentially crippling problems of labor shortages, turnover, and absenteeism, without resorting to the self-destruction of decent wages, is to move away from the border where the available labor is scarce to the interior where the available labor is abundant and also cheaper. The key, therefore, is to bring the jobs to the workers and not to try to get the workers to come to the jobs. American Industries still operates out of Ciudad Juárez and still has some contracts for maquilas there, but increasingly the strategy of the company is to persuade potential clients to locate in the interior.

An interesting illustration of this strategy in action involves the locational decision of a relatively small private company from South Bend, Indiana, a subsidiary of the Bristol Corporation and going offshore for the first time. The company approached American Industries for help in setting up a maquila to assemble electronic heating pads, and were sold the shelter plan idea. The company representatives were shown around Juárez, where they were advised of the industrial over-crowding and labor shortages, and Nogales, where they were advised of the history of union troubles. They were then taken to the wide open spaces of the Complejo Industrial Chihuahua, and advised of the ample labor pool and the absence of the unions. They chose Chihuahua, and a very rapid and successful start-up phase with a team from Indiana, who were able to train local supervisors and hand over to them, a willing and able workforce, left them well satisfied with their decision. It is probable that this company was comforted both by the expert attention that the American Industries shelter operation provided, and by the proximity of U.S. industrial giants like Ford, Westinghouse, and General Electric. Further, as I have indicated, in fact and symbolically, Chihuahua City, while not on the border, is not exactly deep in the interior either. It seems, therefore, a sensible place to locate a maquila, avoiding the problems besetting many of the popular border locations and the isolation of some of the deep interior sites.

One of the established maquilas whose presence no doubt encour-aged the decision of the heating pad company to locate in Chihuahua was the Westinghouse subsidiary, Sistemas Electrónicos de Man-ufactura, which makes cable assemblies and printed circuit boards. Sistemas came to Chihuahua in 1982 and moved into a 67,000-square-foot factory in las Américas park under a shelter arrangement with American Industries. The maquila began with 30 employees, and gradu-ally worked up to several hundred, reaching a peak of around 550. It set up an "information service bureau" (ISB) for transforming hard copy onto discs and for developing business software and computer-aided design systems. ISB recruits graduates from all three of the city's higher education establishments, in particular from the Monterrey Technology College (Chihuahua campus), which provides most of the technicians for the local maquilas. Part of the degree work of the engineering students consists of "professional practice" of two months in local maquilas. The maquila managers report on the students, and in this way much technical recruiting is conveniently achieved.[11] Sistemas em-ploys several of these students, both in this plant and elsewhere in the Westinghouse maquila network. This plant has an unusually high ratio of technicians to operatives: 350 operatives, 95 percent of whom are women, work on the assembly line, to 200 technicians and staff. In ISB, 40 percent of the employees are women, many of whom are technicians.

Although most of the maquilas in the city are unionized by the CTM, none of the American Industries plants has a union. Instead, American Industries have developed an alternative to both the labor union and the company union, which they call the system of "communications specialists" (*especialistas de comunicación*). Communications specialists are neither part of the management structure nor operatives, but occupy an intermediate position on the shop floor, which permits them to liaise with workers, represent the wishes of the workers to the management, and transmit company policy back to the shop floor. This work includes home visits one day each week to try to sort out the domestic and work-related problems of the operatives, most of whom are young women. Although Sistemas did have this system in operation, it was most highly developed in another American Industries plant, a subcontracting operation for Packard Electrical, the wire harness division of General Motors.

The Packard plant, Alambrados y Circuitos Eléctricos, was one of the first group of maquilas in las Américas park, and now shares a building with the headquarters staff of American Industries. Packard has eight wire harness maquilas in Mexico and operates on a system of competitive performance ratings, with premiums for delivery and quality indexes for intermediate and final assembly products. So worker satisfaction that translates into accurate and efficient production is the number one priority in the plant. Most of the maquilas do very well on these tests—presumably any facilitator who let standards slip for too long would lose the contract. This American Industries plant has been achieving almost perfect results for some time. The management attributed this success at least in part to the work of the two communications specialists who liaise closely with the workers.[12]

The underlying philosophy of the communications specialists system is to forge links between the plant and the home, between the individual as worker and the individual as a member of a family. To this end the maquila invites the families of the workers to tour the factory, and no opportunity is lost of including the family in the life of the factory. Therefore, the method of home visits is an integral part of this philosophy to show the worker and (usually) her family that the company cares about that part of the life of its employees that takes place outside the factory.

In mid-1987 the two communications specialists in Alambrados were young women, not much older than most of the operatives. They were housed in a rather tacky office on the shop-floor, which would suggest that they were not, in fact, actually in the management even if they were seen as part of it.[13] The workforce was on a two-shift system, so the two specialists had one shift each in order to cover the whole of the working day. They defined their jobs as coping with the family and personal problems of the workers, and organizing social activities that would bring the families of the workers into contact with the plant. Good attendance at these social events was considered to be very important. Their door was always open and the workers were encouraged to come and see them at all times. They also toured the plant daily to seek out problems. The backgrounds of the communications specialists were also interesting. One had worked for two years as personnel officer in a local minerals company after she had completed her training as a social worker; the other had studied industrial relations in Chihuahua. Her course had been introduced in the early 1980s in the *Instituto Tecnológico,* clearly as a response to a perceived demand from the growing maquila industry.

These communications specialists have a difficult and ambiguous job. It is tempting to suggest that they are always on the side of the management, and are paid to convince the workers to accept company policies.[14] This seems much too simplistic a view of what is actually going on. If the workers saw the specialists entirely in these terms, then they would certainly lose most of their effectiveness. No one is in any doubt about who pays the wages of the workers and of the specialists. However, when it comes to decision making, the specialists do have some degrees of freedom which connect fundamentally with their true function, namely to ensure uninterrupted accurate production.

One of the tasks of the specialists on their daily rounds is to look out for workers who show a sufficient degree of competence and a satisfactory attitude that would make them candidates for promotion. Many women are promoted from the ranks of the operatives to quality control inspectors and supervisors precisely because they know the problems of the line first hand. The communications specialists advise on these promotions, although the personnel department has the final word. The specialists, therefore, can keep a foot in both camps and are permitted degrees of freedom to disagree with management on behalf of the workers, or some section of them. Indeed, their credibility is bound up as much with being able to disagree with management and survive to fight another issue, as it is with actually winning concessions from management for the workers. The promotions issue is one key area of potential conflict, and others are holidays, time off, and workplace conditions. Wages are excluded from the brief of the specialists.

All of this is enough to make most supporters of the labor movement and the rights of workers cringe. This is an understandable if subjective response. It is more fruitful to compare the communications specialists with the other available alternative expressions of the interests of the workers. The reason why this system appears to have had some success where it has been applied, and why there appears to have been little independent worker demand for the establishment of an official union in these maquilas, is that the official unions are widely considered to be thoroughly corrupt, particularly where women are concerned. From the point of view of women who work in the maquilas, a female communications specialist is not necessarily worse than a male union official to represent your interests. For those who have certain knowledge that the local union bosses sexually abuse women workers, having to deal with a female communications specialist may be a great deal easier and less threatening. This is a problem that the official unions along the border as well as in the interior have yet to solve.

## The "Deep" Interior

As of December 1987, there were 120 maquilas in the "deep" interior, employing more than 20,000 people.[15] The largest single contingent was in the city of Guadalajara, which has had a few electronics maquilas since the late 1970s. The veteran companies are Burroughs de México and Semiconductores Motorola, both plants that have employed in excess of 1,000 workers. By 1984, there were eight maquilas in and around the city, amongst which was Mexicana de Zapato, the Mexican licensee of Dr. Scholls sandals and one of the biggest exporters of footwear in the country. Of these eight maquilas, with the exception of Motorola, all were unionized by the CTM, and it is interesting to note that the Jalisco Maquila Association advised any new maquilas to accept the union "to begin on a strong foothold with local authorities, especially since unions in Guadalajara tend to facilitate rather than impede internal plant relations" (*MN*, June 1984:14).

The main maquila development in Guadalajara in recent years has been the arrival of Hewlett-Packard in the city, not so much for the numbers of jobs (about 200 in a city of 4 million people), but for the type of production that the company has brought. There are two HP maquilas, one producing the HP 300 computer, and the other PC disc drives. The strategy of the company is to use the interior of Mexico as a jumping-off point to attack the Latin American computer market. In order to do this more effectively, and also to be able to sell in Mexico itself, Hewlett-Packard "has an active program to use local resources, develop suppliers and buy materials locally" (Reifenberg 1986:115).

It is not entirely clear why the maquila industry has not taken off into self-sustaining growth in Guadalajara. The only obvious disadvantage of the city compared with, say, Chihuahua is the distance from the U.S. border—about 1,000 miles—and therefore a definite disincentive for any manufacturer whose prime objective is to assemble and return the products to the U.S. under GSP or 806/807. However, for those maquilas like Hewlett-Packard, the nontraditional type, who are looking south rather than north for markets, Guadalajara might be a workable location.

The same can be said for Yucatán, where there has been a substantial industrial park development in the last few years. Mérida's port, Progreso, is actually only about 500 miles across the Gulf of Mexico from Brownsville, and this offers possibilities for maquilas that could operate on the basis of sea freight. The first and for several years the only maquila in the Yucatán was Ormex, a subsidiary of the Ormco Corporation of California, who started to manufacture orthodontic supplies in Mérida in 1981. Ormex, however, relies on air transport.

The state government and the Grupo Bermúdez jointly began to develop an infrastructure for the maquila industry and two industrial parks have recently been opened, the Yucatán Industrial Park in Mérida, and the Poligono Industrial Park on the road to Progreso. The secretary of economic development for Yucatán, Adolfo Peniche Pérez, was reported to have budgeted half a million dollars to promote the state as a desirable location for foreign investment, particularly in the U.S. (Horowitz 1986:1A, 3A). His efforts have to date been rewarded, if modestly. At the end of 1986 the U.S. company, Maidenform, became the first U.S. maquila in the Yucatán Industrial Park, and a Mexican-Korean clothing joint venture, and several other substantial U.S. corporations are to follow. The attractions of cheaper and less mobile labor than at the border, a pool of technical graduates, and the physical beauty and amenities of the Yucatán, may well be sufficient incentives for certain types of maquila operation. *Frontier Business* (June–July 1987:A2) reported that eight U.S. maquilas were actually in operation in the Yucatán, another eight were just about to begin operation, and a further 20 were conducting feasibility studies. The general manager of Ormex is quoted here pointedly as saying, "Eighty-seven percent of our workers are from the State of Yucatán. They are stable, industrious, and not preoccupied with emigrating." As with Jalisco there is, however, little likelihood that the Yucatán will host large numbers of maquilas in the foreseeable future.

The conclusion seems unavoidable that those obstacles that were identified as inhibiting the growth of the maquilas in Chihuahua City and other barely interior locations, operate even more strongly in the "deep" interior. The logic of maquila establishment that drives the average U.S. corporation appears to become more and more dilute as we move away from the border. It seems to be the case that most U.S. companies would rather put up with the inconvenience and expense of locating along the border than risk the different types of inconvenience and expense of locating in the interior. The wage differences, for most maquilas, will be relatively insignificant as long as the dollar wage stays more or less where it is. The continuing problem of labor shortages and turnover in the central and western half of the border will be managed by a combination of the carrot (better benefits, particularly attendance-related ones) and the stick (more intense exploitation of labor as long as it is around). Where capital intensive production is slowly replacing labor intensive production, the problems due to the labor force will, of course, diminish, though other problems like the demand by Mexican managers and technicians for higher salaries, may arise.

From the point of view of the U.S. corporations that presently dominate the maquila industry, the interior represents, in most cases, a negation of the rationale that encouraged them to establish maquilas in the first place. To the extent that it is fruitful to analyze the recent expansion of the maquilas as a consequence of the transfer of U.S. manufacturing from the rustbelt to the sunbelt—my own view is that this argument is quite fruitful as part of a more general analysis in terms of "production sharing"—the farther away from the border the plant is located the greater the loss of "sunbelt comparative advantage." This reasoning is particularly salient for those promoting the interests of the U.S. border communities, as the view of Texas Senator Lloyd Bentsen makes clear.

This is not to say that attempts to introduce maquilas into the interior are bound to fail. As we have seen, there are already many maquilas doing well in these places, but the prospects for explosive growth as has been experienced on the border are dim. Much of the present expansion of maquila activity in the interior appears to be in the form of U.S. firms subcontracting work to Mexican companies whose plant is idle due to the reduction in domestic demand that the Mexican economic crisis has produced. The maquila strategy, as it is presently conceived, cannot work for the interior of Mexico. The question that must now be posed is: can the maquila strategy as it is presently conceived work for the frontera norte?

## Notes

1. Much of the negative publicity on the maquilas in the 1980s dwells on the themes of poverty and squalor in the living conditions of maquila workers just across the border, as the media section of my annotated bibliography amply demonstrates (1988: part 3).

2. In addition to the sociopsychological costs of relocation for the expatriates and the TNCs, it is also true that local managers and technical staff are much cheaper to employ. See chapter 9, below, for further discussion of this point.

3. There are stories of gifts to retain workers, poaching the workers of other maquilas outside the factory door, and rewards for workers who brought their friends in for jobs. George speaks of "musical chairs among maquilas" in Juárez (1986:21).

4. See *El Mercado de Valores* (29 Oct. 1973), summarized in Peña (1981:A–23, 24). As I noted at the beginning of this chapter, some already operating interior firms gained maquila status in 1971.

5. The 1974 figures are probably inflated. The INEGI category "*Otras Entidades Federativas y Municipios*" includes some small border locations as well as those in the interior.

6. Senator Lloyd Bentsen of Texas made it quite clear that his support for the maquila industry, which has been very influential, would evaporate if they were to be forced off the border (see *San Antonio Express-News*, 27 November 1986).

7. When Zenith decided on Chihuahua City for a new high-tech facility in 1984, *El Fronterizo* explained: "Cd. Chihuahua was chosen for the site of the Zenith project because of its highly qualified workforce and the training facilities offered by the Chihuahua Job Training [schemes]" (27 March 1984, in *U.S.-Mexico Report*, 1 June 1984:1).

8. All data on Chihuahua City refer to the mid-1980s, unless otherwise identified, and derive from a mimeo brochure "Chihuahua Community Profile," distributed by the maquila association.

9. Las Américas Industrial Park is owned by one of Mexico's largest privately owned conglomerates, the Grupo Chihuahua, which also has interests in steel, cement, forestry, mining, chemicals, oil equipment, real estate, and insurance.

10. Interview with Rex Maingot, Cd. Juárez, December 1986.

11. For similar relations between the foreign-owned export-oriented assembly firms in the midwest of Ireland and the local technological university, see my earlier study (1988a:170).

12. The structure of the labor force in this plant, relevant for what follows, was (in April 1987) approximately 390 direct laborers (overwhelmingly young female operatives), 100 indirect laborers (including supervisors and quality control inspectors, warehouse staff, and lower level technicians, 70 percent female), and 50 administrative and clerical staff.

13. The office of the personnel manager, to whom the communications specialists were responsible, located off the shop floor in the suite of administrative offices, was quite luxurious in comparison.

14. These were almost the exact words of one young male technician present during my interview with the communications specialists at the Alambrados maquila (Chihuahua City, April 1987).

15. The "deep" interior is usually defined as the nonborder states. The figures are from INEGI's *Avance* of May 1988.

# 8

# Labor, Gender, and Politics

The arguments in favor of the maquila industry have always been simple. Mexico needs the jobs that it brings, particularly along the border where rates of unemployment are high. The difficulties of creating an indigenous base of manufacturing industries meant that the types of jobs that the maquilas brought were particularly welcome. Mexico also needed hard currency, and this became a matter of desperation rather than convenience in the 1980s when the price of oil dropped and the interest payments on Mexico's foreign debt began to rise at an alarming rate. The arguments in favor of the maquila industry from Mexico's point of view, therefore, can be summed up as "jobs, skills, and dollars."

From the perspective of the U.S., the arguments in favor of the maquila industry are equally simple. The U.S. border towns also need jobs. However, the cost of labor in the U.S. has increasingly meant that foreign, and particularly Third World, competition has been undercutting U.S. products, forcing changes in production processes to take advantage of cheap labor abroad. This "production sharing" aims to export the low skill, low value jobs and retain the high skill, high value jobs within the U.S. The proximity of the Mexican border made it much more feasible to use components and services from the U.S. than in, say, the Far East. This allows more of the business and more of the profits to stay within the U.S. corporation. The arguments in favor of the maquila industry from the point of view of the U.S., therefore, can also be summed up as "jobs, skills, and dollars."

In chapter 1 it was argued that "production sharing" is an ideological concept that fulfills economic and political functions in the struggle between capital and labor in the U.S. and the struggle between the transnational corporations and economic nationalists in the Third World. This was located within a shift in the relations between the core countries of global capitalism and the countries of the Third World within their orbits—the reformation of capitalism. The following chapters traced the concrete manifestations of these processes over time and space. This chapter will concentrate on three specific issues that have become central to the understanding of the place that the border, north and south, occupies in the reformation of capitalism through the maquila industry, and the connection between these border specific trajectories and their implications at the global level. The issues are: (1) the border labor market; (2) the sexual division of labor in the maquila industry; and (3) the Border Trade Alliance, a campaign to defend the maquila industry as an essential support of U.S. global economic power. The uneven balance of power between an underprivileged region, the frontera norte, and the forces of global capitalism, led as they are in this case by a group of U.S. TNCs, structures this localized regional analysis. The sometimes complementary and sometimes competing intranational and international interests of those involved in both the U.S. and Mexico will be on the agenda, and sets the scene for the task of the next chapter, which is to assess the significance of the maquila industry as a developmental strategy for Mexico as a whole.

## The Labor Market: Beyond Borders but Within Systems[1]

The orthodox view of the U.S.-Mexico border is that it works well. In the words of Whittemore Boggs, in his classic text on *International Boundaries*, "Few boundaries anywhere in the world operate with less friction and with greater adaptation to the needs and interests of the peoples concerned than the frontiers of the United States with both Canada and Mexico" (1940:73). Those who support this conception cite the long period of peace that has prevailed along the border, the considerable level of binational cooperation on a variety of issues, and the relative openness of the border. The settling of the Chamizal dispute over the exact location of the border between Ciudad Juárez and El Paso which had been based on a constantly changing river, and the boundary treaty of 1970, appeared to confirm this impression (House 1982). With the exceptions of periodic interventions to arrest the illegal passage of people and narcotics across the border, the U.S. government at the federal level has generally stood back from the border and acknowledged its somewhat special status, more or less by default.

There is, unsurprisingly, an unorthodox view. Raúl Fernández (1977) has argued powerfully that the border is a line that has bred hostility rather than friendly relations, ever since the treaty of Guadalupe-Hidalgo ceded California to the United States in 1848 and secured the process of capitalist penetration in the southwest. Hostility is expressed in a variety of forms, for example, over environmental issues, and when Mexico refuses U.S. agents permission to pursue drug smugglers across the border on the grounds that this would violate national sovereignty.[2]

Successive Mexican governments have busied themselves by legislating a continuous stream of policies, administrative bodies, and fiscal incentives in order to promote the development of the frontera norte. The most visible result of all this activity has been, of course, the remarkable transformation that has taken place in the urban landscape of the Mexican border cities over the last two or three decades. Roads, civic centers, parks, universities, shopping malls, and tourist attractions have brought what were not very long ago dusty and primitive towns into the late twentieth century. The maquila industry is one facet of this transformation, and the contradictions between north and south are nowhere more clearly seen than in the effects that the industry has had on the borderlands labor market.

## The View from the North

The relative inactivity of the U.S. government and the relative activity of the Mexican government were both taking place "beyond borders but within systems." Implicitly, the unwillingness of the U.S. government to seriously tackle the problems of illegal immigration and undocumented Mexican labor in the border states was a clear statement of the fact that the borderlands system did operate across the border and to the advantage of the employing class in the U.S. The incredible anomaly that it was illegal for someone to work without the proper documents but that the employer was doing nothing illegal by employing such a person demonstrates more clearly than any statistic just whose interests the U.S. government was serving.[3] Successive U.S. governments used the border as a source of cheap labor, both explicitly as in the bracero program and the "green card" work permit system (see below), and implicitly in that the employer took no risks in hiring undocumented labor. The effects of this policy on the indigenous working class of the border states were predictable, and it would be a mistake to think that this is a post-World War II phenomenon. When U.S. employers found some of their traditional nineteenth-century sources of cheap labor (Japan and China, for example) cut off in the early years of the twentieth century, substitutes had to be found. While the 1924 National Origins Act put a stop to mass immigration from Europe and elsewhere, Mexicans were excluded from its provisions. This facilitated the flow of workers across the border to compensate for the shortage of labor in the 1920s. Mexican workers tended to be cheap, but unlike immigrants from farther afield, they were less likely to become permanent residents in the U.S. Although large numbers of Mexicans have settled legally or illegally in the U.S. since the turn of the century, the evidence suggests that, "the vast majority of the migratory workers who cross the border into the United States do so for a certain length of time that terminates in their return to Mexico. This is not a recent practice" (Bustamante and Martínez 1979:268, see also 271, and note 10).

That these workers were considered entirely expendable by the U.S. government is evident from their treatment during the depression of the 1930s when forced repatriation of many Mexicans took place. There was, at that time, no shortage of dispossessed Anglo farmers willing to work for next to nothing at the jobs that the Mexicans they were displacing had done. As global events dramatically changed labor market conditions during the war, Mexicans were once again encouraged to come to the U.S. to find jobs, this time under the bracero program for migrant workers which brought hundreds of thousands of Mexicans across the border every year between 1942 and 1964 (Galarza 1964). Cockcroft (1986) evocatively describes this as "the revolving door"—a constant cycle of importation and deportation of Mexican workers to satisfy the changing needs of U.S. capital.

Parallel with the bracero program, and surviving it up to the present, the systems of "green card" commuter workers and "white card" visitors also attest to the ambiguities of the labor and immigration policies of the U.S. government. Green cards were issued for daily commuter workers as well as seasonal migrant workers. As Corwin and McCain argue (in Corwin, ed., 1978: chapter 4), by the 1960s the rise of the Chicano barrios in many nonborder U.S. cities transformed the employment opportunities of Mexican migrant workers, supplementing traditional stoop labor with a variety of jobs in the urban centers. It was not only the U.S. farm laborer whose job was seen to be at risk from the migrant worker, but the wages and jobs of the whole of the working class in many parts of the U.S. appeared threatened by two groups of Mexican workers, namely undocumented, illegal workers and the legal green card commuter workers. The issues of whether or not the presence of Mexican workers depressed wages for the categories of jobs that they were commonly employed to do, and whether such workers were actually in competition with the indigenous working class for the same types of jobs, are still highly controversial matters.

The shortage of Immigration and Naturalization Service (INS) staff along the border, dependent on Washington for funding, meant that the strict rules governing what these card holders could and could not do went largely unenforced. Green card holders would officially lose their cards and thus their right to seek work if they were unemployed for more than six months. Also, they could not be used as strikebreakers, and since 1965 they have been required to obtain certification to the effect that the category of job in which they seek employment is one in which there is a labor shortage. None of these regulations was tightly enforced in the 1960s (Briggs 1973:10–17) or since then (Briggs 1984). The infamous raids by the Migra (as the INS is commonly known) on sweatshops, restaurants, etc. that were suspected of employing undocumented workers all along the border and as far afield as Los Angeles, New York and Chicago caused much individual fear and suffering, but they hardly disrupted the low paid end of the U.S. labor market in any substantial manner.[4]

The system of white card visitor visas for Mexicans is similarly open to abuse. The white card entitles the holder to stay in the U.S. for 72 hours within 25 miles of the border, but he or she is not permitted to seek employment. Many commentators report that it is common practice for Mexicans to mail their white cards back home to Mexico, search for employment within or beyond the 25-mile limit, which is not intensively policed,[5] and if they are caught, declare themselves to be illegal and opt for voluntary repatriation to Mexico, which is unrecorded. As Briggs comments, citing U.S. government hearings on illegal aliens, "When he [sic] returns to Mexico, his white card is waiting for him so that the entire cycle may then be repeated" (1973:13; see also Martínez in Young, ed., 1986:147).

While not everyone accepts the view that undocumented workers, green card commuter workers, and white card visitors have always had the effect of depressing wage levels and shifting the balance of power away from labor to capital in the Southwest of the United States, it is difficult to escape the conclusion that Mexican migrant labor has been used in these ways by employers in the U.S. and perceived in these ways by the working class north of the border. Even the legislation enacted in the 1960s, purportedly to ensure that foreign workers were only permitted to seek employment in areas of labor shortages, was seriously flawed in practice. Certification was carried out for only a small minority of green card holders, and in any case it was done only at the first application and took no account of changes in the domestic labor supply or the fact that holders of green cards did not always stay in the same job.

The U.S. Southwest does not look the same from the northeast rustbelt as it does from the south, across the Mexican border. From the point of view of the U.S. border working class, the benefits of industrial relocation from the rustbelt are often wiped out by the costs of legal and illegal Mexican workers competing in the labor market. With the establishment of the maquila industry, this became even more marked, as the process literally moved beyond borders but within systems, namely the systems established by the transnational corporations, be they gigantic, large, medium, or small. The threat of the maquila was one factor that kept wages low along the border, particularly for the unskilled worker, and also contributed in no small measure to the ease with which capital exerted its control over labor in the workplace. The working class on the U.S. side of the border, and particularly the unskilled part of it that is overwhelmingly Chicano, pays for the policies of the government in far-off Washington. It is not really relevant for those who suffer as a result of these policies whether they are primarily intended to help Mexico feed its population or to help employers in the Southwest reap ever greater profits, or both. One passionate attack on the system of Mexican migrant labor, leaves no doubt as to the remedy:

> Illegal entry must be stopped by expanded enforcement, prosecution of offenders, and a sweep of the labor markets to return those already here; criminal penalties should be adopted for U.S. employers who hire illegal entrants; the commuter system must be terminated forthwith; and the tariff provisions that encourage the "twin plants" arrangements repealed. . . . the foundation of the existing policies is the impoverishment of hundreds and thousands of Chicanos (Briggs 1973:22).[6]

Is this a realistic strategy? In the first place, it is not only undocumented Mexican workers that are said to threaten the welfare of the working class north of the border, but Mexicans who are legally entitled to work in the U.S., namely those who have green cards, and their impact can be quantified to some extent as they operate within the confines of a bureaucratically controlled framework, though the INS has neither the resources nor, one suspects, the motivation to impose it stringently. Accurate information about illegal aliens and undocumented workers, on the other hand, is almost impossible to collect. The nature of the case defies rigorous methodology and encourages more or less sophisticated "guestimation."[7] There have been, however, a good number of studies that have tried to quantify the presence of undocumented workers in the labor markets of the southwest. In a survey of 100 illegal aliens in San Antonio, Texas, Cárdenas (1979) found that the vast majority worked in unskilled laboring or service jobs, and that while their average wage was $2.15 per hour, about half were earning less than the minimum wage of $2.10 per hour. However, and this is just as significant for the point I am making, average hourly earnings for Mexican-American workers in San Antonio were only $2.55, and for blacks only $2.68, compared with $3.71 per hour for white workers. More speculatively, another evaluation of impacts on the Texas economy of a curtailment of illegal immigration from Mexico asserts that the occupations that Texans who speak little English (presumably Chicanos) tend to enter, are those in which the illegal workers are most likely to be found, and that reduced immigration would also affect wages in a further group of occupations, namely those that attract Texans who might speak English but have not finished high school. The argument is that if restricted immigration produced higher wages in the principal occupations for non-English speakers, "those occupations might begin to attract people who other- wise would have found employment in the occupations [for high school dropouts]. This competition would then exert upward pressure on wages in the occupations [for high school dropouts]" (Pearce and Gunther 1985:11). One cannot fail to perceive the message that keeping out illegal immigrant workers might lead not only to their substitution by Chicano workers (who are not much more expensive), but could have further consequences for working-class wages in general.

Texas, however, has only about 15 percent of the undocumented Mexican immigrants thought to reside in the U.S. About two-thirds of the total are said to be in California (Passel and Woodrow 1984). The introduction of the Simpson-Rodino Immigration Act has stimulated attempts to assess its effects on the Californian labor market. For example, Cornelius and colleagues at UCSD have begun to demonstrate that if California expelled all its illegal workers, not exclusively but largely Mexican, then some businesses dependent on low wage labor in Los Angeles and other parts of southern California, would be forced to close or restrict their activities.[8] It is entirely unrealistic to expect that local workers would automatically step into the jobs filled by undocumented workers because such workers might not be available and/or the jobs might disappear.

In the informal sector, families in the U.S. are not alone in the First World (and Second and Third Worlds for that matter) in relying on undocumented workers employed as maids, cleaners, and child carers who, under the prevailing rules of patriarchal sexism, release women for more or less well-paid jobs. Miller makes the interesting point that the extremely low cost of employing home help from Mexico means that in Brownsville "their employment enables many families who could not afford the cost of conventional child care and homemaking services to augment their incomes by freeing wives to work outside the home—thus rendering the local job market even more competitive" (Miller 1982:35).

All the way from Brownsville to San Diego, live-in maids, who return to their homes in Mexico on weekends, or even less frequently, can only survive on the wages they receive because they do not have to pay the full costs of living in the U.S. Indeed, some U.S. citizens along the border choose to live in Mexico rather than in the U.S. because even a rather modest regular dollar income ensures a good standard of living in Mexico. Workers who live permanently in the U.S., therefore, have always considered green card commuters and particularly undocumented Mexicans to represent unfair competition, and U.S. border communities have often complained that Mexicans use far more local services than they pay for in taxes, though some argue that illegal aliens pay more in taxes than they use in public services. McCarthey and Valdéz make the telling point that the federal government receives most of the immigrant tax revenue, but local and state governments pay for most of the public services that the immigrants use, namely health care and education.[9] Nevertheless, such views are not commonly held or broadcast, and there has always been pressure to tighten up immigration controls along the border with Mexico. These pressures culminated in a new immigration law in late 1986 which made it an offense for an employer to hire any worker who failed to produce documents showing an entitlement to work legally in the U.S., but sought to balance this out by formalizing the procedure whereby aliens who had moved to the U.S. before 1982 and could prove continuous residence might apply for legalized status. It is beyond the scope of this work to search out the reasons why the Simpson-Rodino Act was passed when it was, and in the form that it was (see Cockcroft 1986: chapter 8). What can be said is that the law has been framed in such a way that it is unlikely that large numbers of Mexican workers will be deported, short of the most draconian measures which the INS, in any case, does not have the personnel to enforce on an appreciable scale. The INS has gone on record to this effect.[10] It is as yet unclear whether this new legislation will bring much benefit to the working class on the U.S. side of the border, though it may force some Mexicans to seek maquila work in the absence of U.S. job openings.

## The View from the South

The borderlands labor market has always brought mixed blessings to Mexico. However poor the wage and however miserable the job, there has never been a shortage of Mexicans willing to cross the border, legally or illegally, to search for work. All the evidence, with only minor exceptions, demonstrates that it is economic necessity due to the inability of Mexico to provide decent jobs in sufficient numbers that forces its citizens to uproot themselves in this manner. Studies of migrant workers have documented the importance of the remittances that they send back home to Mexico, and their impact on the socioeconomic development of the sending communities (see Cornelius 1982; Cockcroft 1986). There are several views from the south reflecting a variety of interests, and the material circumstances from which they are derived differ quite dramatically.

The U.S. has acted as a safety valve for Mexico during the twentieth century. As the manufactured goods of the United States flowed south, the people of Mexico flowed north, and it is important to be continually reminded of the fact, many Mexicans who crossed the border in search of work have done so as a temporary expedient, returning to Mexico when circumstances permitted. Research on sending communities shows a consistent pattern of remittances and purchase of land and other capital goods which signals, even if it does not conclusively prove, that migrant workers who can save money do send it back to the place they consider as "home" in order to have a more secure stake when they return than they did when they left.[11]

Research on Mexican *indocumentados* indicates that, "the kinship/friendship network is central to their decision to migrate as well as their post-migration situation in the United States" (Cornelius 1982:392). These networks act as channels of communication along which information about jobs and pay flow quickly and accurately, as well as providing housing and subsistence to new migrants while they are looking for work. For some illegal entrants it is clearly extraordinarily difficult, dangerous, and expensive to cross the border and find work,[12] but for those with family or friends in the U.S. to help them, the process may well be less harrowing.

One rationale for the maquila industry, often acknowledged in Mexico and the U.S., is precisely that it tends to keep Mexicans in Mexico and dissuades them from crossing the border to seek work. The fact that the Mexican border towns and cities act like magnets drawing people north in search of a better life across the border is universally accepted, and the maquilas are often seen as alternative poles of attraction helping to retain population on the Mexican side and therefore giving the Mexican border communities a more dignified status than simply watering holes on the journey to *el norte*, the promised land. Some of the major cities of the frontera norte, are attracting people from Mexico City and elsewhere in their own right because of their apparent prosperity in a time of economic crisis, and the maquila industry is part of this process.

A good deal of research has been done on patterns of northward migration in Mexico, some of it focusing on who the maquila workers are and where they come from. In the mid-1970s, the Mexican researcher Wolfgang Konig carried out a major study of the maquila industry in several major border locations and some interior sites.[13] The fact that Konig's survey population was 31 plants with about 15,000 workers tells us that the sample was very heavily weighted toward the large U.S.-owned maquilas. The main purpose of Konig's research was to evaluate the effects of the maquila industry on Mexican society, and he provides some useful information on the origins of the maquila workers. With the exception of Nogales, where 87.4 percent of the workforce was migratory (no doubt because of the presence of a large maquila park in a very small town), most of the maquila workers had not migrated to the border in search of maquila jobs. Of the 270 operatives out of Konig's sample of 502 who had migrated to the border, only 41 percent had migrated specifically to find a maquila job, and about one-quarter of the total sample knew of family or a friend who had come to the border in search of employment in the maquila industry. Interestingly, Konig suggests that maquila management preferred to hire local women or those who had lived in the place for several years over migrant women, but despite the apparent discrimination, almost two-thirds of the migrants to the border who sought maquila jobs got them, with 19 percent remaining unemployed. This compared with a rate of about 80 percent unemployment among those in the interior seeking maquila jobs, and 14 percent getting maquila jobs. This is not very surprising for, as was pointed out in the previous chapter, the drive to attract maquilas to the interior has been largely unsuccessful.

In their *Maquiladoras and Migration*, Seligson and Williams (1981), with a sample of 739 maquila workers, contrast the "buffer zone" thesis with the "magnet thesis" of migration. Both of these theses are related to what is commonly known as the "two-stage migratory hypothesis," namely that the process takes place in two stages, first the migration from the interior of Mexico to the border, and second the migration across the border. The "buffer zone" thesis is that the maquila industry absorbs potential migrants by offering them alternative prospects of employment. The "magnet thesis" is that the maquilas attract migrants from the Mexican interior to the border, but cannot absorb them and therefore border crossings and the numbers of green card and undocumented workers increase.

Their findings were very much in line with the accepted orthodoxy in the late 1970s. Maquila workers in the sample were predominantly female, 72.3 percent female compared with 48.1 percent female in the labor force of the border cities as a whole, and 23 percent in Mexican industry as a whole. Maquila workers also tended to be younger and better educated than nonmaquila workers, and those in the interior were even younger and better educated than those on the border. Between one- and two-thirds of the maquila workers had "migrated" to the border from some point either in their home state or elsewhere in Mexico, but Seligson and Williams found little evidence that many of them had come to the border specifically to seek jobs in the maquilas: "At most, approximately 4 percent of *all workers* in the industry were interstate migrants motivated to move to the border in search of BIP employment, strictly defined" (1981:162).[14] More of the young women had come to the border to join their families than to look for maquila work and, significantly, few were the typical landless peasants that had provided the bulk of undocumented Mexican laborers heading north across the border. Although about one-third of the maquila workers were state to state migrants (compared with one-fifth of the general population), this is more likely to be a result of the general pull effect of the border than any specific maquila effect. Once in maquila jobs, women tended to remain there. Only 10 percent of the female workers in the sample had ever migrated to the United States for any length of time.

The men who worked in the maquilas, however, displayed different patterns of behavior. About 30 percent of the male sample had crossed the border to work, and almost 20 percent intended to do so at some future time. However, maquila workers who had crossed the border and found work were much more likely to want to return to the U.S. than those who had never crossed for work. Almost two-thirds of all the maquila workers in the sample expressed a desire to emigrate to the U.S. if they could do it legally, while 17 percent had thought of crossing the border illegally. Seligson and Williams conclude that the "two step migratory hypothesis" is not confirmed in this case, because those who have come to the border from the interior are no more likely to want to cross the border than those who were born in border towns. Those most likely to migrate to the U.S., were young "males with anomic tendencies who demonstrate a higher degree of political alienation and vocational dissatisfaction than their fellow workers" (1981:165) wherever they were born, though those from the interior were rather more disposed to return to their places of birth if and when jobs became available. This suggests that the hiring policies of the maquilas in the late 1970s that effectively inhibited the employment prospects of young and unskilled Mexican men, combined with the absolute dearth of employment in Mexico, may indeed have had the effect of propelling those young Mexican men, who had come north to look for work and not found it, across the border. So the sexual division of labor in the maquila industry, both in its wide sense of the disproportionate number of women employed, and in its more precise sense of the jobs that men do and the jobs that women do in maquila plants, is the nettle that now has to be grasped.

## The Sexual Division of Labor

The facts as set out in table 8.1 are clear enough on the numbers of women and men employed in the maquilas. Although the proportion of men in the industry has been steadily rising in the 1980s, there are still many more women on the maquila shop floor than men.

There is no single topic within the field of maquila studies that has caused as much controversy as the "women in the maquilas" question. This is partly due to the fact that there has been a good deal of research carried out from an anti-TNC perspective on the central role that women workers play in the new international division of labor. All over the world, particularly but not exclusively in the Third World, women have been recruited by the export processing and assembly industries, which have been driven by the demands of the TNCs (see Lim 1985). There is a theoretical and a practical dilemma at the heart of

*Table 8.1*
Female and male operatives in the maquilas, 1975–1988.

| YEAR | TOTAL OPERATIVES | OF WHICH | | PERCENT FEMALE OPERATIVES |
|------|------------------|----------|--------|---------------------------|
| | | MALE | FEMALE | |
| 1975 | 57,850 | 12,575 | 45,275 | 78.3 |
| 1976 | 64,670 | 13,686 | 50,984 | 78.8 |
| 1977 | 68,187 | 14,999 | 53,188 | 78.0 |
| 1978 | 78,570 | 18,205 | 60,365 | 76.8 |
| 1979 | 95,818 | 21,981 | 73,837 | 77.1 |
| 1980 | 102,020 | 23,140 | 78,880 | 77.3 |
| 1981 | 110,684 | 24,993 | 85,691 | 77.4 |
| 1982 | 105,383 | 23,990 | 81,393 | 77.2 |
| 1983 | 125,278 | 32,004 | 93,274 | 74.5 |
| 1984 | 165,505 | 48,215 | 117,290 | 70.9 |
| 1985 | 173,874 | 53,832 | 120,042 | 69.0 |
| 1986 | 203,894 | 64,812 | 139,082 | 68.2 |
| 1987 | 248,625 | 84,525 | 164,100 | 66.0 |
| 1988 (Jan.) | 267,127 | 95,524 | 171,603 | 64.2 |

SOURCE: INEGI (1988: table 2) and *Avances*.

this phenomenon (Sklair 1988:702–707). Theoretically, for the feminists who have been responsible for the bulk of the research on women in the assembly industries, the Engels thesis has provided a central focus, arguing that the liberation of women can only be achieved when women are brought fully into the occupational structure and when they have equality of opportunity with men, particularly in industrial employment. Thus, one might expect that most feminists would welcome any industrial development that does not systematically exclude women.[15] However, in most societies there is a marked sexual division of labor in most occupations, especially in manufacturing industry. For example, metalworking employs very few women, and the needle trades employ very few men. The export processing and assembly industries have largely reproduced this pattern, and some extreme cases of this are to be found in the maquilas.

The practical dilemma is (to put it bluntly) whether girls and women are actually better off inside or outside the factories that offer them employment. It is important to ascertain what alternatives are available for these women in other forms of paid employment or in unpaid work of one type or another. Evidence from around the world strongly leads to the conclusion that most of the young women who work in the assembly industries do so as their first experience of paid employment, and that there are practically no other jobs in manufacturing industry open to them. Such jobs, therefore, however low or high they may rate in terms of absolute job satisfaction, do tend to expand the available job opportunities for women. These jobs are quickly taken up and the demand for them usually far exceeds the supply, yet the obvious wish of women to do them is in apparent contradiction to much of the research on how unpleasant, tedious, dangerous, sexually threatening, and physically demanding many of these jobs actually are (Fernández-Kelly 1983: chapter 6 and passim). This is the context in which specific questions of the experience of women in the maquila industry must be posed.

Much of the literature on "women in the maquilas" is predicated on the unspoken assumption that somehow in Mexico jobs for young women are less valuable than jobs for men, and that the fact that the maquila industry employs mostly women is in itself a valid criticism of the industry. These are, of course, thoroughly sexist assumptions that ignore the longstanding industrial participation of women established in many countries, including Mexico.[16] In a study of the participation of women in the labor force in Baja California in the 1960s, Noriega Verdugo vividly demonstrates the effect of the maquila industry in a way that is instantly recognizable to those who have studied export oriented assembly industries in other and widely dispersed parts of the world. In 1960, women made up 7.6 percent of the Baja California economically active population, or EAP (that is in paid employment or actively seeking it) in the primary sector, mainly agriculture; 10.1 percent in the secondary sector, manufacturing industry; and 27.8 percent in the tertiary sector, services. By 1969, women in agriculture had dropped slightly to 7.2 percent, women in the service sector had remained about the same at 27.7 percent, but women's participation in the secondary sector had more than doubled to 23.3 percent. Noriega breaks this down to its constituent parts. Between 1960 and 1969, the number of women employed in the extractive industries rose from 97 to 158, in construction from 199 to 402, in the electrical industry from 121 to 138, and in the transformation industry (mostly maquilas) from 2,801 to 12,143 (1982:14–15). The data show that the maquila industry did not in fact take many workers from other sectors but, as it were, created its own workforce by recruiting large numbers of young women, from age 15 upward, most of whom had not previously been in the EAP. In fact, between 1960 and 1969, the total number of women in the EAP expanded from 26,649 to 48,693. Women who had not previously sought paid employment had done unpaid domestic work in their own homes, and probably many of them helped out without pay in family farms or small businesses as well. Most of these women no doubt welcomed the opportunity to earn wages working in the maquilas, bearing in mind that at this time the minimum wage, which most of them were earning as maquila employees, was higher in Baja California than elsewhere in Mexico. Starvation wages in the U.S. were, for previously unwaged young women, pesos and dollars in their pockets that permitted them an independent purchasing power that most had never before enjoyed. This is exemplified by the many reports of young maquila women workers from Tijuana coming to San Diego to buy the fashionable clothes and cosmetics which were unavailable in Tijuana (see, for example, *New York Times*, 31 January 1971:1, 14). Not all of these stories can be the inventions of maquila propagandists, though the ubiquity of the phenomenon may be exaggerated as there is also evidence that many of the maquila women were the sole wage earners in their families and would therefore have little discretionary income for such expenditures. Baerreson reports that INS officers often required proof of regular employment before they would issue the "white cards" that entitled Mexican workers to spend their wages in the U.S. (1971:34–35).

The evidence from Baja California, therefore, suggests that women held about 10 percent of jobs in the transformation industries in 1960, increasing to 25 percent by 1969. Susan Tiano, in a creative analysis of the 1979 Mexican employment survey (in Ruiz and Tiano, eds., 1987: chapter 1), interprets these figures in a potentially highly revisionist way. The current orthodoxy is that unemployment along the frontera norte affects mainly male workers and that the maquila industry has exacerbated the problem by recruiting young women who would otherwise not be in the labor force at all. The imputed blow to male employment prospects is therefore twofold. The maquilas tend not to offer many jobs to men, and the women who get most of the maquila jobs do not generally vacate other jobs in the process. Tiano shows that this argument is suspect on empirical grounds. On the basis of the 1979 employment census, Tiano argues that there is:

> no evidence that the maquiladora program has enhanced northern Mexican women's position in the labor market, relative to men in the region or to women in Mexico generally. Nor . . . the related claim that the program contributes to male unemployment through the large-scale mobilization of young women out of the household and into the labor force. Women in the north do not have higher labor force participation rates or lower unemployment rates than the average for the nation as a whole. The highest unemployment is found among women from the younger age categories, the sector from which the bulk of the maquiladora labor force is recruited. Similarly, northern Mexican men are no more likely to be unemployed than their counterparts in other parts of Mexico. Finally, unemployment rates for northern Mexican women, like those for women in the rest of the country, are generally twice as high as comparable rates for men (in Ruiz and Tiano 1987:35).[17]

The logic of Tiano's argument is that the maquila industry does not create male unemployment by its preference for hiring females, but on the contrary, the existence of a large pool of unsupported unemployed women, many with dependents of their own, has encouraged large-scale maquila investment along the border. The strength of this argument is that it simultaneously disarms two ideological counterarguments, one sexist and the other economistic. The sexist argument is that women who do not really need proper jobs and would be otherwise adequately occupied in their homes, are depriving male breadwinners of employment. The generally higher rates of unemployment among women than among men (despite the maquila jobs), the incidence of women whose maquila wage is the sole monetary support of households, and the rapidly growing labor force participation rates of women throughout Mexico, will not convince anyone who believes that only men should have industrial jobs, but they will help to persuade those who wish to understand how the maquila labor force has evolved. The other ideological counterargument, the economistic, concerns the imputation that by employing women the maquilas are able to get away with paying lower wages and imposing tougher conditions of work. Mexico had formal wage and labor law equality for men and women long before the establishment of the maquilas, and though as in many other countries women at work are still discriminated against, there is no evidence to suggest that female and male operatives in the maquilas are paid differently for the same categories of work, or that, for example, men work fewer hours or with more perks than women. The economistic argument that women are cheaper to employ than men is often true, but for the maquila industry it is not. The maquilas have had no reason or compulsion to pay men more than they pay women.

Why, then, were about 80 out of every 100 maquila workers recruited into the industry up to the late 1970s women? Tiano's explanation, that there were plenty of unemployed women around at the time, is true but not entirely convincing for the simple reason that there were also plenty of unemployed men around. The answer lies more in a combination of the employment situation and the peculiar nature of the work that most maquilas were doing. In the first place, the fact that many Mexican women were employed (rather than unemployed) in manufacturing industry in the 1960s was significant. Female employment in factories was not entirely unknown in Mexico before the maquilas. In Mexico as a whole the number of women in paid employment in 1969 was about 2.5 million, and there was even a higher proportion of employed women in manufacturing industry (about 450,000, or 18.2 percent of the female EAP) than employed men (about 1.75 million, or 16.4 percent of male EAP). These women tended to work in the food industry, and in clothing and shoe factories (see Gloria González Salazar in Nash and Safa, eds., 1980: chapter 10). Thus, whether or not most maquila workers were enticed out of their homes to enter factories for the first time, and no doubt many were, there must have been enough women working in factories, even along the border, for it not to have seemed particularly unusual. Further, as already noted, many of the first tranche of maquilas were sewing shops of one kind or another that would have traditionally recruited women in any case.

When the Fortune 500 corporations and other U.S. companies moved in with auto parts and electronic assembly operations, they were bringing industries that were new to the frontera norte and for which there was no traditional labor force, female or male. That these maquilas overwhelmingly employed women in preference to men has little to do with the particularities of the Mexican labor market. Assembly work of these types is done by women in First World, Third World and increasingly Second World global production factories for reasons that are now well documented and widely accepted (Elson and Pearson 1981; Nash and Fernández-Kelly, eds., 1983). From various countries and over various "feminized" occupations in the assembly industries has come a litany of docile, undemanding, "nimble-fingered" women

[171]

workers uninterested in joining unions or standing up for their rights. This is not entirely mythical but it does need unpacking. The maquila industry is a good place to begin the unpacking.

The litany, as I chose to call it, operates at two levels. First, it serves as an ideological rationale for a course of action; and second, it purports to provide a correct description of a state of affairs in the real world. As an ideological rationale for the employment of women workers, it is accepted by friends and foes of the maquila industry alike, for the very good reason that it gives an explanation of the preference of the maquila for women over men. For the maquila employer, the image of the docile (and so on) woman worker is a positive one, for most of the critics of the maquilas it is a negative one, but for both it serves a purpose in the debate over the maquilas. It is when the litany is offered as a correct description of the predominantly female maquila labor force that its most powerful ideological manifestation appears. In this sense, it becomes a weapon in the struggle to impose the reformation of global capitalism on men as well as women in the working class, in this case on the Mexico-U.S. border, but radiating throughout a world in which the TNCs are themselves engaged in the struggle for dominance.

This image of the woman worker makes no sense unless it is used comparatively. As an ideology, the docile female worker is used against its opposite, the aggressive male worker. Woman's docility is contrasted with man's aggression, the undemanding woman with the demanding man, the nimble-fingered woman with the clumsy (but strong) man, the nonunion woman with the union man, and the woman who does not stand up for her rights with the militant man. These are all complexes rather than unidimensional attributes and they cannot really be abstracted from the structures and dynamics of a patriarchal society and applied in isolation in the workplace. The image of the "ideal" woman worker for the maquilas and for TNC employment around the world is the image that the transnational capitalist class is gradually developing of the "ideal" worker, per se, for the epoch of the capitalist reformation. The technological transformation of the workplace and the de–skilling that accompanies it may not have gone as far as some suggest, but it is clearly the trend of the future. Docile, undemanding, nimble-fingered, nonunion, and unmilitant workers will be offered the jobs on the global assembly lines, while aggressive, demanding, clumsy, union, and militant workers will not. In the last resort it does not matter to capital whether it is employing men or women—capital is not sexist (nor racist, for that matter), though it does use sexism (and racism) to suit its purposes, which are the production of profits and the accumulation of private wealth. The maquila industry did not set out to employ women because they were docile, undemanding, nimble-fingered, nonunion, and unmilitant. They employed women because it was quite naturally assumed, in terms of sexual stereotypes in both the U.S. and Mexico, that women could be constrained within the workplace to adapt themselves to the image of the "ideal" worker that the industry wished to create, better and faster than men. Once the image of the "ideal" maquila worker is institutionalized and accepted by the working class along the border, the need to employ women in preference to men diminishes, and job opportunities for docile, undemanding, nimble-fingered, nonunion, and unmilitant men open up.

Along the border the experience of the maquila industry gives rather contradictory signals about the closeness of fit between the ideology and the reality of the docile woman worker image. Jorge Carrillo (1985), in his path-breaking research on labor conflicts in the maquilas, provides information that would contribute to one measure of docility by tracing the numbers and types of complaints (*demandas*) registered with the Labor Tribunals for maquila workers along the border. He demonstrates that there are regional and sex differences in the frequency of these demandas, for example, more women make official protests in the maquilas of Tijuana, where there are few union members, than in Matamoros, where there are many. Carrillo's evidence suggests that the maquila workers are not particularly docile as they are prepared to take their complaints in substantial numbers, and presumably at some risk to themselves, to the authorities.

Whether the maquila worker is "undemanding" is difficult to answer because, in relation to what women and men working in domestic industry have to put up with, conditions of work in the maquila industry may well be superior. It is important to distinguish between Fortune 500-type firms—those with a corporate image they wish to protect, at least on the surface—and the mass of reasonably well-run small- to medium-sized maquilas, on the one hand, and the limited group of atrocious factories that would be a scandal anywhere in the world, on the other. Of the latter group, most tend to be short term, superexploitative operations that give the industry a bad name and are as much an embarrassment to the public and private facilitators as they are a gift to antimaquila elements in Mexico and the AFL-CIO. Further, as the Mexican government legislates the minimum wage (increases are frequent though rarely satisfactory), there is less pressure on the maquila employers for wage rises than might otherwise be the case. Nevertheless, when discretionary or emergency wage rises come up, as they sometimes do, maquila workers make their own demands. When these come from the shop floor, women workers are often involved (see Iglesias: chapter 7).

The ideology of female "nimble fingers" is, to put a finer point on it, a piece of blatant sexist nonsense that has served both the most traditional and the most modern flagship industries of transnational capital (namely, sewing and electronic assembly) very well. Men have no monopoly on fat and clumsy fingers, nor are they unable to play the piano or the violin or perform brain surgery, and not all societies exclude them from basket weaving and other intricate crafts. However, the ideology does point to the important social rather than biological fact that in most societies girls are much more likely than boys to be trained to sew, and they are much more likely to be kept in or around the home to work at domestic tasks. This might, conceivably, teach girls to work better with their hands, though this is rather doubtful as in many societies boys are encouraged to make models, work with wood and metal, and so on. Some have interpreted the "nimble-fingered" question as a proxy for the more general idea that girls are trained to be patient and stick to tasks while boys are encouraged to seek adventure and be active. Be this as it may, the gradual introduction of men on to the production lines of the assembly plants to make up for the shortage of female labor (which I shall look at in more detail below) gives the lie to the sexist "nimble-fingered" image more effectively than any cross-cultural study of child-rearing practices could do. It also supports the explanation of the ideology of the "ideal worker" in the reformation of capitalism that I am proposing.

The question of trade unionism in Mexico is complicated by the fact that the CTM (and other official unions) act more as an arm of government, an increasingly more junior partner in the ruling coalition in Mexico, than an independent labor movement whose prime task is to fight for the rights of its members. These unions are almost entirely male dominated, even where they operate in plants in which 80 percent or 90 percent of the workforce are women. They are also said to be thoroughly corrupt and to tolerate, if not actually encourage, officials who use their considerable powers on the shop floor to sexually exploit their women members. Despite this, the incidence of union membership and support varies geographically and to some extent historically along the border, but not in terms of the sexual composition of the workforce. Unionization declines rapidly from the almost totally unionized east to the almost totally nonunion west. In the maquila industry, as in most of the rest of Mexico, whether a new plant has a union is not so much a matter for the workforce to decide by democratic processes, but more the result of deals worked out between management, unions, and sometimes the local authorities. It is, therefore, not strictly true to say that maquila women have been less likely to favor the union than maquila men.

Neither is there very much evidence to suggest that women have been less militant than men during the major labor struggles that have wracked the maquila industry (Baird and McCaughan 1975; Carrillo and

Hernández 1985), nor that women working in the maquilas are any less liable than men to resist management on the shop floor (see Peña in Ruiz and Tiano, eds., 1987: chapter 6). Women played major roles in the most important labor struggles that took place in the maquila industry in the 1970s, namely, the protracted disputes between the workers and the employers, often helped by the official union, in Mexicali and Nuevo Laredo. It is not accidental that these struggles, like the one against Acapulco Fashions in Juárez, ended with the closures of the plants involved. The maquila employers were able to tolerate the prospect of living with the union, even where it has phases of militancy, but not the prospect of living with militant workers when they are no longer under the control of the union.

Since the flood of new maquilas and new jobs that resulted from the devaluations of 1982, particularly in Ciudad Juárez, there has been an increasing tendency for the industry to recruit more men. This trend was, as it were, "officially" announced as a finding from a maquila survey carried out in Chihuahua in 1983, showing that for new hirings during the first six months of 1983 the ratio of women to men in the maquilas of Juárez was about two to one, compared with the original ratio when the maquilas first came to the city in the 1960s of about ten to one.[18] A maquila association spokesman was quoted to the effect that all the maquilas in Juárez were willing to employ personnel of both sexes, and that "it has been clearly shown that men are able to produce as well as women" (in *U.S.-Mexico Report*, Nov.2–Dec.4 1983:5). This formulation is a cipher for the new docile, undemanding, nimble-fingered, nonunion, and unmilitant male worker. Maquila management is not very likely to state publicly that those men who are prepared to behave like the "ideal" woman worker—docile and so on—will have more opportunity for maquila employment. Information about recruitment spreads quickly in a system like the maquila industry, concentrated as it is in particular cities and particular industrial parks. Messages from management via current employees or unions to prospective employees as to the qualities required are passed speedily and accurately in such a system. One of these messages has been that men are increasingly welcome to apply for shop floor jobs.

Between 1982 and 1986, female operatives in the maquilas of Juárez increased by 16,893, while male operatives increased by 16,975 (INEGI 1988:6). The ratio of male to female operatives has been rising steadily over the last few years, but the figures are often confused by the failure to distinguish direct and indirect employees. The INEGI data give a sex breakdown for direct labor, *obreros* (sic), but does not do so for production technicians (*técnicos de producción*), and administrative staff (*empleados*), although we are probably safe in assuming that most of the technicians are male and half the staff are female.[19] The rate of expansion of technical and staff employment in the maquilas since the mid-1970s has been substantially higher than that of direct employment (which suggests a general upgrading of the industry, a topic to be taken up in the next chapter). Comparing 1980 with 1975, total direct employment increased by 76 percent (with 84 percent more men and 74 percent more women workers), while there were 83 percent more technicians and 95 percent more staff. By 1985 total direct labor had increased by over 200 percent compared to 1975 (328 percent more men and 165 percent more women), while there were 323 percent more technicians and 279 percent more staff (calculated from INEGI 1988:5). Thus, rates of increase in employment were highest among male operatives and the technicians. According to these official figures, in 1985 the proportion of direct workers who were men was 30.4 percent compared to 21.7 percent in 1975. If we assume that two-thirds of the combined total of technicians and administrative staff are male (an arbitrary but not outrageous assumption) then this would give rough estimates of the ratio of men to women in the maquila industry as a whole. These estimates suggest that about 28 percent of total employees in the industry in 1975 were men, around 37 percent in 1985, and probably 40 percent by 1988. If we look at Ciudad Juárez alone, then we find that the number of male direct workers increased far more quickly than the national average from 1975 to 1985 (by 460 percent), but that technicians increased even more, by an unprecedented 627 percent in this period (staff also increased by 378 percent). Using the same formula as before, we arrive at the rough estimate that in 1975 about 27 percent of the maquila employees in Juárez were men, and by 1986 about 42 percent were men.[20]

Two trends are apparent in the 1980s that have consequences for the sexual division of labor in the maquilas. The first is the greater rate of increase of male direct labor compared with female direct labor. The second is the greater rate of increase of the technical and staff workers than direct workers. The second trend, the increase in the proportion of indirect workers, and particularly production technicians, says a great deal about the evolution of the industry, and I shall discuss it further in the next chapter. The first trend, the rising proportion of men in the direct labor force, has been marked all along the border (though curiously not in the interior where the numbers of women in the direct labor force have risen faster than those of men since 1975). There are at least two reasons usually given for the employment of more men on the maquila shop floor. First, it is said that the expansion of the metal products industries has created more job opportunities for male workers (see, for example, Sanders 1986:4) and there is clearly some truth in this. As indicated earlier in table 3.4, for statistical purposes the maquila industry is usually divided into twelve sectors, and of these only two, "furniture and fixtures and other wood/metal products" and "nonelectrical equipment parts and apparatus," had a majority of male workers in 1986 (INEGI 1988: table 9). Together these two sectors had employed fewer than 5,000 workers in 1980 and something over 9,000 workers in 1986, so their growth accounted for only a small part of the total increase of over 38,000 male direct workers between 1980 and 1986. Of the large employment sectors, in "transportation equipment and accessories" men were over 42 percent of the direct labor force, some 30,000 new jobs being created between 1980 and 1986, and the electrical and electronic equipment and parts industries had created about 10,000 and 15,000 new jobs respectively, though men occupied only about one-quarter of the jobs in these two sectors. It is therefore unlikely that the increase in male direct labor was primarily due to the increase in the "metal products industries" if the implication is that these industries were responsible for the introduction of large numbers of "male" jobs, in terms of the traditional sexual stereotypes that characterize the occupational structure in both the U.S. and Mexico.

The second explanation, even more common than the first in places like Juárez and Tijuana, is that the female labor pool is drying up and that the maquilas have been forced to employ men. Again, there is clearly some truth in this, perhaps more than the maquila industry has been willing to admit. In a talk to the AmCham annual maquila seminar in 1984, J. Chris Dobken, a prominent facilitator, distinguished between "job creation" and "workforce creation." Having listened to some labor recruitment commercials on Tijuana radio, he consulted the Mexican census and found that, "Tijuana maquiladoras were already employing over 80 percent of the 'maquiladora-grade' females. Even if these census data were off by 50 percent, which in fact they were, my conclusion is just as valid—how much more than 40 percent of any eligible population segment can one attract to any one industry?" (1984:5). For cities like Tijuana and Juárez, where San Diego and El Paso drain off many workers, Dobken suggests three measures: "a more positive compensation policy" (higher wages); "job restructuring and changes in benefits to attract older segments of the local labor force and male workers"; and (an imaginative if somewhat suspect proposal) to combine employment in maquilas and construction companies for whole families.

The main problem with this approach, perhaps its fatal flaw, is the ambiguity of its central idea, "maquiladora-grade" females. Formulations like this are a shorthand for young, well-educated, female workers with all the "ideal" characteristics that were discussed above, and an essential attribute of such females is that they are prepared to work for the going wage which is usually not a great deal more than the current minimum wage. The suggestion that if the maquilas wish to attract and hold on to more workers they need to begin to pay higher wages, is open to several interpretations. A good deal of research has indicated that the high turnover that the maquilas are experiencing, particularly in Juárez and in Tijuana, is due to the fact that many women who would like to work in the maquilas and who are "maquila-grade" simply cannot survive on the wages they take home to support children and other dependents. Some of these women are forced to turn to prostitution and/or to become undocumented workers in the U.S.[21] A second group is, for various reasons, outside the formal labor force. They would be attracted into the maquilas if the money was sufficient to make it worth their while. The mystery is why wages did not rise dramatically as they are supposed to do in conditions of acknowledged labor shortages, in Tijuana and Ciudad Juárez in the mid-1980s. At this point, the border labor market and the sexual division of labor interact in complex ways.

In one sense, of course, wages did rise dramatically along the border in the 1980s. This was because the Mexican government increased minimum wages in a despairing attempt to compensate for inflation and devaluation and retrieve the living standards of the workers, in particular for the main maquila sites which were included in the top wage zone. This had nothing to do with the maquila employers offering higher wages to attract workers, and the official figures on wages, salaries, and benefits in the industry offer very little evidence that the employers were raising wages in the places where there were the highest rates of turnover and labor shortages. Comparing the average maquila wage in 1985 for direct workers at the national level, and in major maquila sites, we find some quite surprising differences. The national average was 480,000 pesos, and was about 6 percent higher in Tijuana, at 508,000 pesos, but it was also over 4 percent higher in Mexicali, which was not reporting any substantial problems of turnover or labor shortage. It is also interesting to note that the premium on these actual maquila wages in Tijuana was somewhat lower than the premium on minimum wages between Baja California and the next wage zone, and very much lower than the difference between Baja California and the lowest wage zone. The fact that most of the maquilas are in the top wage zone somewhat dulls this effect, but it is still worth mentioning. As we move east to Ciudad Juárez where the highest turnover rates and the most severe labor shortages were to be found in the mid-1980s, it is baffling to discover that the average maquila wage in 1985 was actually less than the national average—479,000 pesos. Finally, the average wage in Reynosa was only 433,000 pesos, but in Matamoros it was 541,000 pesos (calculated from INEGI 1988: tables 2, 3). The very high wage in Matamoros was no doubt due to the 40-hour week won by the CTM and the low wage in Reynosa, no doubt reflected the fact that there were plenty of "maquila-grade" females in the town competing for relatively few maquila jobs.

What, however, was going on in Juárez and Tijuana? If one asks a private or public maquila facilitator in Juárez or in Tijuana why wages have not risen fast enough to preempt labor shortages the usual response is that because Mexican workers have to pay income tax on that part of their wage that exceeds the minimum, the employers and the workers prefer to improve benefits rather than raise wages. This is unconvincing for two reasons. First, in most places along the border, wages are already above the minimum, but not by much; and second, the rate of income tax is low at this level of wages and it would be surprising if workers were to turn down raises because they had to pay a small percentage back in tax.[22] There is no evidence that workers do prefer savings plans, cafeterias, better retirement schemes, and sports facilities—the most common benefits—over pay increases. The most likely explanation, though one that is impossible to prove with the sources at our disposal, is that a maquila employers cartel has been able to impose a discipline on the maquilas in places like Tijuana and Juárez to keep wages down and to prevent the outbreak of unrestricted competition for labor, bidding up of wages, and an inevitable decline in profits.[23] Workers who do not like this are welcome to leave, and perhaps to return once or twice for another chance. The costs of turnover, apparently, are easier to bear than the costs of increasing wages to the level of the "marketplace." This is the implication of the most systematic research to date on the question of turnover in the maquila industry (Lucker 1987). My conclusion, therefore, is that there is no real labor shortage in Juárez, or Tijuana, or anywhere else along the frontera norte, but that an artificial labor shortage has been unintentionally created by the maquila industry being reluctant to pay decent wages, caring little about excessive labor turnover, and its gradually changing attitudes to the employment of men. It has to be understood that "labor shortages" in the maquila industry refer more often than not (vide Dobken) to shortages of "maquila-grade" females, rather than to a shortage of labor as such. As Tiano has shown, and no one denies this, unemployment and underemployment are high all along the border, and this includes all the maquila cities. "Labor shortages" in the maquila industry, therefore, can be seen as an encouragement to men to apply for maquila jobs with the expectation that they will get them. The closer the male applicant resembles the "ideal" maquila worker, the greater his chances of securing a job. The reformation of global capitalism entails the reformation of the working class, and this is the fundamental significance of the growth of male employment in the maquila industry along the border.

"Production sharing" is as yet a small (but rapidly growing) part of global production and some might consider this attempt to push them into the vanguard of the reformation of capitalism as highly speculative, even fanciful. However, the same tendencies can be observed in some of the more traditional industries, in the decline of union power in many countries, in the rise of part time and less secure employment, in large-scale regional shifts like the movement from the rustbelt to the sunbelt in the U.S., and similar phenomena elsewhere. A common feature is the increase in less than whole jobs for women and vulnerable minority groups and the decrease in whole jobs for men, in traditional terms (Bluestone and Harrison 1982). In the advanced industrial countries these trends are promoted by some as an opening up of the labor market and some workers might find that the increased flexibility that such a regime offers in terms of work sharing and "flexitime" fits in well with the ways in which they want to live their lives. For the majority of affected workers even in rich countries, however, these welcome prospects are quite irrelevent. For maquila workers, men or women, jobs are less than whole if they cannot support themselves and their families at a reasonable standard of living on the wages that they earn. As the peso buys fewer and fewer dollars, and as inflation steadily reduces the purchasing power of the peso, the claim of the maquila industry to be providing Mexico with whole jobs becomes increasingly less plausible. The dilemma for Mexico and its people is poignantly summed up in the words of Rosa Ramírez, a mother of three working in an electronics maquila in Juárez, "It is low pay, but at the point I'm at now I would accept it even if it were lower because I need the money to eat" (*San Francisco Chronicle*, 29 February 1988:A6).

## The Border Trade Alliance: Maquilas for Mexico and Maquilas for the U.S.

In December 1986 something unusual happened. The U.S. Department of Commerce was forced, clearly against its will, to withdraw its sponsorship of Expo Maquila 1986, a trade show designed to exhibit the advantages of the maquilas for U.S. manufacturers (see Mendelowitz 1986). The opposition came mainly from rustbelt politicians worried about the loss of manufacturing jobs being suffered by their constituents, encouraged by the AFL-CIO, which had been campaigning against the maquilas since the 1960s when the BIP was first introduced.

While it has never officially recognized the maquila program, the attitude of the U.S. government has varied from neutrality to implicit support. In its issue of March–April 1986, the *Boletín Comercial* of the U.S. embassy in Mexico City announced that it would be holding an Expo Maquila '86 in December at Acapulco. It did not take the AFL-CIO long to catch on to what was happening. A spokesman was quoted as saying, "When we heard about the fair we went out shopping for someone who would put a stop to it" (*San Diego Union*, 23 October 1986:C2). They found a group of congressmen, divided by party but united by their rustbelt constituencies, to spearhead an effective legislative campaign against Expo, which culminated in October when the wording of the instrument of appropriation of the funds for the Department of Commerce International Trade Administration, from which the money for Expo was coming, was invoked against it. The restriction read, "None of the funds appropriated herein may be used for activities associated with conferences, trade shows, expositions, and/or seminars which feature or convey the advantages of relocating U.S. industries, manufacturing and/or assembly plants, or companies, in a foreign country" (Mendelowitz 1986:10). In tandem with the legislative campaign, the AFL-CIO attempted to rouse public opinion on the issue of the effect of the maquila industry on U.S. employment. The United Auto Workers inserted full-page advertisements in newspapers in the Midwest asking President Reagan, "Why are you moving our jobs to Mexico?" (see, for example, the *Evansville Courier*, 28 October 1986).[24]

On 29 October the commerce department announced that it was withdrawing from Expo, though the show would go on without official U.S. involvement under the wing of the Mexican advertising agency, one of the original organizers. Commerce was clearly unhappy about being forced to withdraw its sponsorship, and secretary Balridge, in a letter to Congress confirming the withdrawal, reaffirmed his support of the maquila program. Other officials did the same, including a spokesman at the U.S. embassy in Mexico City who called the decision to withdraw "unfortunate" (*San Diego Union*, 30 October 1986). These unrepentant attitudes unleashed a flood of congressional activity by the opponents of the maquila industry into the exact role of the government and its agencies, specifically the Department of Commerce, in the imputed export of U.S. jobs. The General Accounting Office was brought in to probe whether Commerce had breached the law by financing other activities like Expo. The GAO reported on 10 December and found that Commerce had been sailing very close to the wind in its participation in a conference on the Caribbean Basin Initiative (a maquila-like program created by the U.S.).

The House economic stabilization subcommittee (LaFalce) hearings gave supporters and opponents of the maquilas in Congress a public platform to air their views and to bandy about entirely contradictory statistics. LaFalce claimed that for every two and a half maquila jobs created, one U.S. job was lost, while Jim Kolbe, a Republican from Arizona deeply immersed in the campaign to defend the maquilas, claimed that two and a half U.S. jobs were saved or created for every one maquila job. As Kolbe argued, "Here we have a perfect example of the kind of bilateral, mutually cooperative effort that works to the ultimate advantage of both nations." LaFalce countered, "To people doing business in the depressed sections of the Midwestern and Northeastern United States, this promotion of offshore production comes as a cruel joke" (*El Paso Times*, 26 November 1986:1A). The battle was well and truly joined! (United States Congress 1986). The Florio hearings, held after Expo Maquila had taken place, intensified the argument. The United Auto Workers, the Communications Workers, and the International Union of Electronic, Electrical, Technical, Salaried and Machine Workers—all of whom claimed to have lost members and jobs because of the maquila program—turned up to rebut what was increasingly being seen as a promaquila lobby from the commerce department.[25]

Into the fray at the beginning of December 1986 came Senator Lloyd Bentsen, from McAllen, Texas, and a seasoned politician who was about to become the chairman of the influential Senate Finance Committee. Bentsen had been instrumental in the production of a massive U.S. International Trade Commission report on U.S.-Mexico border trade, which turned out to be a significant piece of ammunition for the maquila industry arsenal. The report concluded that the numerous U.S. programs to improve life along the border were not showing much in the way of benefits for the southwest, and that the only real prospect for substantial socioeconomic development lay in the maquila industry (USITC: 1986). Bentsen was quite clear about the extent to which he personally was prepared to support the maquila industry and the distribution of costs and benefits it had brought to the southwest. He is reported as explaining that, "most of the blue-collar work has been transferred to Mexico while the United States has retained mainly the executive jobs. . . . The [maquila] program benefits retailers in the U.S. border towns because the Mexican laborers spend 40 percent of their wages in the United States" (in *San Antonio Express-News*, 27 November 1986).[26]

Expo Maquila duly went ahead under private sponsorship and was by all accounts fairly successful in promotional terms. There were almost 100 exhibits mounted by public and private facilitators, and 450 participants. Congressmen, from both the promaquila and the antimaquila camps, were also in attendance. Jim Kolbe gave a rousing speech which contained proposals for border regeneration (a Mexican-American development initiative) and exhorted the U.S. and the Mexican business communities to stand together on the maquilas.[27]

Kolbe did not have long to wait for a response to his challenge. Maquila influentials met in El Paso at the end of December to plan for what they perceived to be the upcoming struggle over tariff and trade legislation that could effectively stifle the maquila industry. Of the 150 who attended the meeting, there were about 50 delegates from border cities all the way from San Diego/Tijuana in the west to Brownsville/Matamoros in the east. The campaign to defend the maquilas was masterminded by a combination of local and national activists. Along the border, the initiative came from people involved in the El Paso Foreign Trade Association and the chamber of commerce. From Mexico City came representatives from the maquila section of AmCham, and from Washington came Don Hagans, an El Paso lawyer who, with others, was organizing a promaquila lobby in Congress.

Though the maquila managers themselves soon became involved, they did not initiate the campaign. This can be explained by the fact that the maquila industry has usually avoided publicity, the exceptions being the commercially involved promoters, the private "facilitators." By early 1987, the campaign had developed an organizational form as the Border Trade Alliance (BTA) and lobbyists were traveling the U.S. border cities and towns trying to mobilize the maquila industry (a task that was easier in some places than others) to fight attacks that were gradually gaining momentum. By March, when the BTA put together a major lobbying effort in Washington on behalf of the maquila industry, several of the U.S. border cities and towns had prepared position papers purporting to demonstrate that the maquilas meant jobs, income, and business not only in Mexico but also in the United States. It is, therefore, a curious irony that the U.S. interest in the maquila industry itself should provide some of the evidence that permits us to assess the distribution of costs and benefits of the industry.

The main thrust of the BTA argument is that far from causing job losses in the U.S., the maquilas actually save jobs, and sometimes even create jobs, in the U.S. The reasoning behind these claims is based on the ideological notion of "production sharing"—the concentration of labor intensive operations in low wage locations in the Third World and the capital/knowledge intensive operations in the First World. On these premises, maquilas help to keep manufacturing industry competitive and thus save U.S. jobs. Moreover, the Mexican maquilas use mainly U.S. components, saving even more jobs that tend to be lost when U.S. manufacturers go to the Far East. Finally, Mexican border residents do a great deal of their shopping in the U.S., so a large proportion of maquila wages comes back across the border.

It would be absurd to expect the BTA to produce a political economy analysis of the maquila industry, so I shall have to try to do it for them. It is by no means certain that any given example of "production sharing" is inevitable, even if it can be proved globally that it is an irreversible process (a question on which I shall plead agnosticism). The Trico case, discussed in chapter 6, showed just how complex this issue is. Cornell's School of Industrial and Labor Relations argued that if Trico had reinvested more capital to improve the technology of its Buffalo plant it could have stayed competitive and saved jobs in Buffalo (Lazes 1986). There are still many U.S. manufacturing workers competing quite successfully with foreign imports assembled or produced by workers earning far less than they do. This has led some to argue that the maquilas are a prop to inefficient industries, particularly those in high wage, highly unionized, rustbelt areas, and that the maquilas are most accurately conceptualized as an extension of the U.S. sunbelt that happens to be located across the border in Mexico.[28]

It is important to distinguish those who lose and those who gain in the U.S. from the maquilas. Clearly, the manual working class in the rustbelt loses jobs that are hard, if not impossible, to replace. Job creation due to the maquilas, even in the rustbelt, will tend to be technology intensive, and while a few of their children may benefit, the unemployed rustbelt workers are likely to constitute a lost generation. Similarly, there is little evidence that many manufacturing jobs are created by the maquilas in U.S. border cities. Business consultants, lawyers, brokers, real estate firms, retailers, hotels, car hire firms, and even some academics, particularly in El Paso and San Diego, are doing well out of the maquilas, but actual manufacturing "twin plants" on the U.S. side are very rare. As George asserts, "the term twin plant is an exaggerated misnomer" (1986:23).

The BTA amasses some powerful arguments and data to demonstrate that the maquilas do a great deal for the U.S., particularly for specific groups along the border. Ever since the 1970s when William Mitchell of Grupo Bermúdez began to collect information about the economic impact of the Juárez maquila industry on El Paso and the rest of the U.S., maquila activists had been trying to show that the industry did have substantial economic benefits for the United States. It is as well to remember that since 1985 the U.S. balance of trade (imports over exports) has been running an annual deficit of more than $100 billion, and that this has been intensifying the protectionist shock waves that are never entirely absent from U.S. politics, which a basically free trade administration was finding difficult to control. In 1986 the group that was to create the BTA decided to extend the Mitchell study in scope and to tighten its methodology to give it more credence in the tougher atmosphere that was closing in on the maquila industry. Under the direction of Donald Michie at UTEP a "maquiladora industry impact survey" was circulated through the local maquila associations to maquilas all along the border. The results of this survey have been widely used in the battle to defend the maquilas.[29]

Although only 163 out of a population of about 900 maquilas replied, it is safe to assume that a substantial group of large and important maquilas was among the respondents. The maquilas that responded were estimated to account for about half of the total maquila employment and production, and were said to support over 1,750 related facilities in 49 states (counting parent plants, direct customers, and major suppliers). They were also said to be responsible for more than 1.2 million "direct jobs" in the U.S. These facilities and these jobs were not, as one might have expected, largely concentrated in the border states. Of the ten states with more than 20,000 "direct jobs," five out of the top six (Illinois, Michigan, Indiana, Iowa, and Ohio) are more rustbelt than sunbelt states. The only sunbelt state in this group is California, in third place. Texas is just squeezed out, its 18,646 jobs giving it eleventh place (El Paso Chamber of Commerce 1987).[30] The survey also collected information on maquila shipments for 1985 through four border ports of entry, Brownsville, El Paso, Nogales, and San Ysidro (San Diego) by means of a convenience sample. It was calculated that a total of more than 50,000 shipments from the maquilas entered the U.S. through these four points in 1985. The distribution of shipments, facilities and jobs in the top 20 states of the U.S., what the BTA calls the "maquiladora production sharing system," leaves no doubt that the economic impact of the maquila industry is not restricted to the border.

All these data are intrinsically very interesting but, it must be said, they prove little about the differential distribution of costs and benefits of the maquila industry for the U.S. In the absence of details about the origins of the sample population it is impossible to say whether, for example, Texas does better or worse than, say, Michigan or California, in terms of job losses and job savings. Although the U.S. companies "supported" by the maquila industry are divided into parent plants, direct customers, and major suppliers, without details of how the "supported" facilities relate to the maquilas, it is impossible to say how many of these facilities and/or these jobs would survive without the maquilas.[31] It would be useful to know if, for example, all the jobs in Sears Roebuck were counted as "saved" by the maquila industry because many of Sears' captive suppliers operate through maquilas. The shipments data are also suspect. Almost two-thirds of the shipments, and 58 percent of the total tonnage recorded, were bound for only two states, California and Texas, and only two other states, Ohio and Mississippi, have more than 2,000 shipments and 25,000 tons of freight. It is difficult to reconcile these figures with the figures on facilities and jobs and, in particular, to judge the *significance* of maquila business for the individual firms that the maquila industry is said to "support." Further, one must conclude that there is a considerable propagandist and ideological element in the public use to which the BTA "research data" have been put. Two examples will suffice to illustrate this point.

The first concerns an article in the magazine *Global Trade* (June 1987:34–35) which discusses the economic ties between a maquila in Juárez, Outboard Marine, and its U.S. suppliers, numbering 189 different companies in 124 cities in 28 U.S. states. What is not made clear is that Outboard Marine employed only about 400 workers, and therefore many of its U.S. suppliers must be responsible for relatively small amounts of supplies. Any implicit suggestion that Outboard Marine "sustains" 189 companies in 124 U.S. cities is highly misleading as is any suggestion that the maquila industry is responsible for the jobs of the workers in these 189 companies. There are, no doubt, some U.S. companies that are substantially dependent on the maquila industry, and some suppliers of Outboard Marine may be among their number, but this is a matter on which the BTA gives little information.

The second example is an interview with Donald Michie quoted in a *San Francisco Chronicle* article (29 February 1988:A6). Commenting on the BTA study that identified 1,800 U.S. companies which employ 1.5 million workers supplying the maquilas, the writer adds that Michie "thinks the study uncovered only about 50 percent of the companies, so the total is upward of 3,000 companies and 3 million U.S. workers dependent on the maquiladora industry, plus an additional 15,000 suppliers of raw materials to the Mexican plants." These are, indeed, the impressions given by the BTA study. However, it is pure speculation to suggest that the hundreds of small maquilas that did not respond to the BTA survey share the economic impact characteristics of the group of large companies that did. It is also quite likely that many maquilas that did not respond declined to do so because they use foreign rather than U.S. materials and components. Subtracting the 807 duty-free amounts from the total imported inputs in the maquila industry shows clearly that a substantial proportion of maquila inputs (perhaps as much as 25 percent) does in fact come from non-U.S. sources, mainly Asia. These factors suggest that the hard evidence provided by the BTA survey has long since parted company with the claims that are appearing in newspapers and magazines all over the U.S.[32] In this way, those who are in the local vanguards of the reformation of capitalism create their ideological visions of reality and seek to persuade the worker who has lost her or his job to company relocation in Mexico (or elsewhere in the Third World) that the maquilas and "production sharing" protect and create jobs in the U.S.

1987 witnessed a well organized and intensive BTA campaign along the border and in Washington to outflank the critics of the maquila industry. Texas Republican Senator Phil Gramm publicly went on record to chide the major U.S. companies involved in the maquila industry for not coming out more openly in defense of the industry (see *Brownsville Herald*, 23 January 1987:1B), and the BTA embarked on a variety of activities to bring the big companies into the campaign in a more active fashion. Don Hagans and others travelled the length of the border, working through chambers of commerce and the local maquila associations, exhorting the U.S. border public and private maquila facilitators to provide information for the national campaign and to become politically active on behalf of the maquilas at the local level. Maquila activists in all the major locations were urged to contact the political and business notables in their respective cities to solicit messages of support for the industry, and to compile information packs detailing the benefits of the maquilas in Mexican twin cities for their U.S. counterparts.

In San Diego, a Border Strategy Task Force was set up in December 1986, and by the new year was arranging for draft resolutions to be placed before city and county councils in San Diego, Orange County, and Los Angeles, with a good deal of success.[33] The San Diego task force was rather less successful in gathering information than it was in garnering local political support, no doubt due to the fragmented nature of the maquila industry in Tijuana compared with other major sites in the border, to which I drew attention in chapter 4. Here, the U.S.-based Western Maquila Trade Association rather than the maquila association in Tijuana was the vehicle for the campaign, in contrast to most of the other cities where the maquila associations, by virtue of their binational existence, were more effective in mobilizing the maquilas themselves as opposed to the maquila facilitators.

Under the auspices of the Committee for Production Sharing,[34] the BTA organized a series of meetings in Washington in March with government officials, senators from the border caucus, and congressmen. In three days the BTA met with 8 senators and more than 30 members of Congress, and consulted with officials from the departments of State, Commerce, and the Treasury (see *Paso del Norte Trade News*, June 1987:4). While most of the border caucus supported the maquilas, the BTA also made sure that its message reached politicians who were hostile. For example, Congressman Torres and Senator Cranston, both from California, told the BTA that the loss of U.S. jobs was still a serious issue that had to be resolved. The BTA came away from Washington with the conviction that a real political opposition was building up against the maquila industry and, more seriously, that the antimaquila forces were winning the propaganda battle. It was the

U.S. job loss figures that were sticking in the minds of the legislators, not the figures on the jobs that the maquila industry was said to create and protect in the U.S.[35] The focus of the debate was U.S. tariff items 806/807.

A question that is, curiously, rarely asked is the real as opposed to the symbolic significance of 806/807. In 1981, the Banamex maquila expert, León Opalin, caused a stir at an AmCham maquila seminar by claiming that Banamex surveys pointed to the conclusion that many maquilas could operate successfully without 806/807. Two U.S. officials present at the meeting, the staff director of the House Ways and Means Committee and a U.S. customs counsel, immediately leapt in to rebut Opalin. The counsel argued, "in a very real sense, there would be no maquiladora program without the U.S. tariff laws" and that 806/807 "has allowed it to flourish" (*Mexican-American Review*, May 1981:35). The U.S. officials supported their argument on the salience of 806/807 for the maquila industry with reference not to the actual benefits of the items, but to the sustained efforts of U.S. labor and their congressional allies to have them repealed. The Border Trade Alliance, the new defenders of the maquila industry since 1986, pay the same compliment to the U.S. labor movement by agreeing to fight the battle for the maquilas over 806/807. It is, therefore, important to ask what the effects of the repeal of 806/807 would be.

The first, and by far the most important, effect would be symbolic. It would signal to the Third World that, in the political climate of the late 1980s, the U.S. was serious about protecting itself from the ravages of "unfair" foreign competition. It would signal to U.S. corporations that the legislature was prepared to act to prevent further massive manufacturing job losses to cheap labor locations. None of these conclusions actually follows necessarily from the repeal of 806/807, though most supporters and most opponents of the maquilas appear to believe that they would.

The actual practical effect would be that some maquilas would close down and some maquilas would be quite unaffected. The majority would be forced to pay more duty on reimportation of their products to the U.S. This would put pressure on some maquilas, probably a large number, to seek to purchase cheaper foreign materials and components to offset these higher duties, as there would no longer be any fiscal advantage in using U.S. materials and components. It might also encourage U.S. suppliers to cut their costs. Another effect would be to dissuade some U.S. corporations from establishing maquilas, but they would not necessarily look to other Third World sites, for in the absence of 806/807 it might pay to take more seriously the option of technological innovation at home rather than seek to remain competitive by finding cheaper labor. In short, though the symbolic significance of a repeal of 806/807 would be a "victory" for labor and a "defeat" for the maquila industry, the actual concrete effects would be bound to be mixed. Mexico would certainly lose some maquilas, but it might gain from the sale of materials and components to the remaining maquilas. In these cases, those U.S. workers at present producing inputs for the maquilas would lose their jobs, but other jobs might be saved. It is difficult to see how the repeal of 806/807 could actually create more jobs in the U.S. than it would destroy. What 806/807 does at present is to encourage some U.S. corporations who have relocated in the past to Asia to consider moving closer to home, namely Mexico or perhaps the Caribbean.[36] If my analysis is correct, and there are definite costs and benefits for the maquilas and for the U.S. labor movement in both the retention and the repeal of 806/807, it would be necessary to explain why both sides have chosen it as their agreed field of battle. The answer to this question takes us deeply into the social and political structures of the maquila movement and its opponents. The AFL-CIO campaigns for the repeal of 806/807 because of its symbolic significance and because it appears to be true that these items actually do encourage U.S. corporations to assemble their domestically manufactured components abroad, particularly in Mexico. The reasons why the defenders of the industry oppose the repeal are twofold, corresponding to main interest groups. For the subcontractors, whose livelihood resides in their ability to persuade U.S. manufacturers to assemble in Mexico, the answer is obvious. However, for the independent maquilas, either U.S. and/or Mexican owned, the situation may be quite different. For many of these, 806/807 may make very little difference. However, they are happy to defend it, and permit it to take center stage, in order to detract attention from the other facets of the maquila industry which are not so visible, but whose exposure might be damaging to their interests.

As I have argued, the largely Chicano working class all along the border, and the absolutely poor regions of the U.S. borderlands—virtually the whole area except parts of San Diego—will be fortunate if the benefits within the present structure of the maquila industry more than balance the burden of costs that tends to fall disproportionately upon them.

The costs and benefits for Mexico, apart from the very real value of more than 300,000 industrial jobs and some operating income to the state and private developers, are rarely discussed by the BTA and other maquila facilitators in the U.S. for the simple reason that the costs (and absence of benefits) for Mexico are the mirror image of the benefits (and absence of costs) for the U.S. This parallels the argument around the six criteria of the creation of development zones introduced in chapter 1. That the Border Trade Alliance has mounted such a powerful defense of the maquilas shows that the present distribution of costs and benefits are not carved in stone. As the debate intensifies, so the evaluation of the maquila strategy for the development of Mexico is inevitably pushed onto the agenda.

## Notes

1. This excellent formulation which exactly characterizes what this section, and to some extent, the whole book is about is borrowed from Bustamante and Martínez (1979).

2. See Herzog (1989: chapter 7) for a subtle discussion of these issues.

3. See Cockcroft (1986). This anomaly was removed in the 1986 immigration legislation which has, unsurprisingly, created a whole host of new anomalies and uncertainties.

4. Miller (1982:54) reports that, "According to informal work rules, the [border] patrol does not apprehend suspected undocumented aliens working on farms located between the Rio Grande and the Military Highway" outside Brownsville. There is every reason to believe that similar informal work rules operate elsewhere, in cities as well as in the countryside.

5. The freeway from San Diego to Los Angeles has a checkpoint on the northbound lanes, but an illegal immigrant would have to be both naive and unlucky to be caught.

6. Updated in his subsequent book on immigration and labor which specifically cites the maquila industry and 806/807 as part of the explanation for the continuing excessive poverty of the southwest (Briggs 1984:241–242, and chapter 7, passim).

7. Corwin (1983) entitles his chapter on the statistics of labor migration from Mexico "*¿Quien Sabe?*" (Who Knows?).

8. From seminar presentations by Wayne Cornelius, Kitty Calavita, and Anna García at the Center for U.S.-Mexican Studies.

9. Cited in USITC (1986:32–33). The whole section on "Labor market effects of Mexican immigration to the United States" (25–36) is very instructive.

10. "Alan C. Nelson, commissioner of the Immigration and Naturalization Service, met President de la Madrid last month to assure him that the United States planned no massive deportation of Mexican workers" (*San Diego Union*, 26 January 1987:6 [border section]).

11. Cockcroft (1986:83) makes the interesting point that, where a male migrant worker is married, his "dollar remittances normally go directly to the father-in-law." This has obvious implications for wives who are thinking of the possibility of maquila work.

12. The "coyote" who smuggles people across the border, often swindling them in the process, is part of migratory folklore (Cockcroft 1986). However, Cárdenas (1979:188) comments that only 6 percent of his sample used a "coyote" while Seligson and Williams (1981:111–112) report findings of 12 percent to 40 percent in various studies of illegal migrants using "coyotes."

13. See Konig (1981) and further details in the lengthy summary of the original research report in Peña (1981:A66–67)

14. Fernández-Kelly's study of 510 maquila workers in Juárez in 1978–1979 found a much higher proportion of migrants, but this may have been a function of her sample (1983: chapter 3). Seligson and Williams predicted that the proportion would rise as news of the demand for labor in the maquilas spread and economic conditions in the interior worsen, and this is confirmed by the more recent research of Brannon and Lucker (1988:12–13) in Juárez.

15. Few feminists actually subscribe to the Engels thesis in its entirety, though it has been influential in structuring the debate on the employment of women. See Tiano

(1986) for an informative discussion of this, enlivened by the fact that she has herself made notable contributions to research on the maquilas.

16. However, many scholars do argue that there has been systematic discrimination against women in industrial employment, particularly in the Third World (see Anker and Hein, eds., 1986).

17. It is worth mentioning, in light of the Noriega study discussed above, that the 1979 rate for "open" unemployment among women in the northwest (which includes Baja California) is higher than for men on average, but in two age groups, 12 to 19, and 20 to 24, the rate is lower (see Tiano in Ruiz and Tiano, eds., 1987:31). This may be related to the finding that the average age of women in electronics tends to be lower than in apparel maquilas.

18. See Alderete (1983:III:2, 5); reported in *El Fronterizo* (4 November 1983); *MN* (Dec. 1983:4); and eventually in "Mexican Border Plants Beginning to Hire Men," *New York Times* (19 March 1984).

19. Despite the fact that the Chihuahua survey of 1983 shows 91 percent of the technicians in Juárez to be women, surely an error. (Compare Alderete 1983:IV:4, 2; and 1985:IV:4, 2.)

20. Data from various INEGI sources. See table 9.1 and the discussion on the technical upgrading of the maquila workforce around it. Different companies have different employee categories, for example, "direct operators" and "support employees"; and many maquilas distinguish between what are termed "confidential" and "nonconfidential" employees, namely nonunion and union labor. There are also several types of supervisors.

21. Research by Ofelia Woo Morales (reported in "Incremento en la Deserción de Mano de Obra. Las Obreras Prefieren Ganar Dolares en EU," *Diario de Juárez*, 20 April, 1988:1–B), demonstrates that one key reason for labor shortages in the maquila industry is that increasing numbers of female workers are crossing the border to find better paying jobs in the United States.

22. Mexico is not the only country where employers prefer to improve fringe benefits rather than increase basic wages.

23. It is interesting to note that though it had been conducting surveys of salaries and benefits in the maquila industry for some years, AmCham only began its own survey of wages in 1986.

24. The union campaign was widely criticized in Mexico and led one newspaper, *Últimas Noticias*, to describe the UAW advertisement as a "low blow" and signaling a "U.S. union offensive against Mexico" (cited in *San Diego Union*, 30 October. 1986:E–1,2).

25. These "Hearings" are to be found in U.S. Congress (1987), which includes statements opposing the maquila industry from unions and AFL-CIO headquarters staff. I have been able to locate only one union leader, Henry Schickling of the International Tool, Dye and Mold Makers (1,800 members), who has publicly supported the maquila industry, on the grounds that "twin plants save U.S. jobs" (see *Frontier Business* (June–July 1987:A–13).

26. See Bentsen's threat that if the maquilas were to move off the border then they would lose his support (Chapter 7, note 6 above).

27. For comment on Expo Maquila see Lindquist (1986); Vrazo (1986).

28. Susan Sanderson (1987) argues that U.S. manufacturing industry is now totally dependent either on foreign assembly or components from cheap labor sources, but that increasing automation will soon destroy maquila-type industries in Third World countries. I shall return to this in my concluding chapter.

29. First results, based on a sample of 140, are in El Paso Chamber of Commerce (1987). A second set, based on 163 responses, is in BTA (1987), bound together with two papers by Michie on the benefits of the maquilas for the U.S.

30. Oddly, in this early presentation of results, an introductory graphic neatly included Texas in the top ten by the simple device of leaving out Ohio. This is a good example of the pride of localism obscuring clear vision. By the time all the responses were in, Texas had, indeed, made tenth place (BTA 1987).

31. See chapter 5, where I raise similar doubts about the value of an earlier attempt to connect the maquilas in Ciudad Juárez and job creation in El Paso. BTA

(1987:4) specifically admits: "The data cannot account for job dislocations that are attributable to the maquiladora industry."

32. BTA "data" on maquila related jobs were widely circulated along the border and elsewhere in the form of information books on the maquila industry. For examples of how they have been picked up by newspapers and magazines, see many 1987 and 1988 items in my annotated bibliography (1988: Part 3).

33. For an interesting account of the passing of such a resolution in the San Diego city council, see *Los Angeles Times* (18 February 1987: Part II,4). For similar resolutions in the lower Rio Grande valley see *Brownsville Briefing Book* (1987: Part V).

34. A lobbying organization established as the "Committee for 806.30 and 807" in 1976, whose "mission" (according to its publicity material) "is to foster the improvement of U.S. competitiveness by combining technology and U.S. content in partnership with developing country labor and skill." It is credited with helping to organize the BTA, in the *El Paso Times* (29 March 1987).

35. The headline on a *New York Times* front page story on the maquilas "U.S. Goods Made in Mexico Stir Concern on Jobs" (29 December 1986) could not have pleased the BTA, though the editorials in the *Times* in the following week "Hecho en México" (5 January 1987) and in *Business Week*, "Keeping Jobs in Mexico Benefits the U.S." (19 January 1987), were both highly supportive of the maquilas. I do not know if the BTA provided material for these editorials, but it is certainly possible.

36. Many maquilas, of course, already use foreign, mainly Asian components, and the expected rapid rise in Asian- and European-owned maquilas may well increase this tendency.

# 9

# *The Maquila Strategy*

The maquila industry began as a territorial device to stimulate the economic and social development of the frontera norte, but by the end of 1972 the Mexican government had decided to permit maquilas to be established more or less all over the country. Thus, at an early stage, the maquila became a functional rather than a territorial development concept. While the concept has become functional, the reality has remained largely territorial. There are few maquilas located very far from the northern border. The belief of President Echeverría that the maquila industry was a temporary expedient to help Mexico through a difficult economic phase has proved illusory, and as long as Mexico is locked into the global system of trade and finance, and to the extent that the dominant forces that direct the Mexican economy and society are outwardly rather than inwardly oriented, the maquila industry will continue to occupy an important place in Mexico's development strategy. It is to this end that those responsible for the reformation of capitalism have been working in Mexico.

From the point of view of the ruling strata in Mexico this has come about in a rather accidental manner, partly because of the marginality of the frontera norte and partly because of the relative strengths and absolute weaknesses of the Mexican economy. The relative strengths are reflected in its status as one among that select group that has been designated by the honorific title "newly industrializing country" (NIC). Mexico, like the other NICs, has a formidable industrial base, a declining proportion of the labor force engaged in agriculture, has long since replaced agriculture as the main component of GNP (oil is the most valuable economic sector), and a rapidly expanding manufactured exports sector. In the global league table of the World Bank

*Development Report*, Mexico actually improved its relative per capita income position in the last decade, climbing from 76th place in 1978 to 82nd place out of 119 in 1985—119th being the wealthiest—though it slipped back to 77th place out of 120 countries in 1986. In the 1970s, the Mexican economy was considered far too substantial to rest on "gimmicks" like the maquila industry, but in the early 1980s, this began to change.

At least since 1982, most commentators have argued that Mexico's relative strengths have been overwhelmed by its absolute weaknesses. Devaluation and domestic inflation did not occur for the first time in 1982, but a devaluation-inflation spiral set in at that time, bringing on a crisis from which the country is yet to emerge.[1] Successive devaluations of the peso have reduced the cost of Mexican labor and utilities for those who are buying them in dollars, thus creating the conditions for rapid growth in the maquila industry. The deeper the crisis the more favorable the climate appeared to be for the U.S. investor.

Thus, in the 1980s the theme that the maquila industry was "the one bright spot" in a dismal Mexican economy became commonplace in both the U.S. and Mexico.[2] As oil revenues declined, Mexican policymakers were forced to pay more attention to "the one bright spot" in the economy almost by default. Those who had always been opposed to the maquilas could not now risk damaging them for fear of being seen to worsen the crisis, while those who had always supported the maquilas took the opportunity to push forward changes that clearly served the interests of the industry. Those who had always been more or less neutral in the debate could not fail to be impressed by the apparent growth of the industry. Slowly but surely the maquila industry began to move toward center stage.

The maquila industry occupies a small though significant place in Mexican industry as a whole. The proportion of workers in Mexican manufacturing industry that the maquilas employed rose from 1 percent (about 20,000 out of 1.7 million) to over 11 percent (268,000 out of 2.3 million) between 1970 and 1986, and the maquila employment growth rate (17.6 percent between 1966 and 1985) exceeds by far manufacturing industry as a whole (2.3 percent). The value of the maquila contribution to Mexico's total manufactured exports, however, declined from about 30 percent in 1980–1982 to about 20 percent in 1986, reflecting a rapid rise in nonmaquila exports (in Lee, ed., 1988: first endtable). The growth of the maquilas and the adoption of a program increasingly characterized by the tenets of the capitalist reformation, operationalized in terms of the ELIFFIT strategy, made some options less and others more possible for those responsible for steering Mexico's economic and political course. For the Mexican policymakers, the increasing importance of the maquila industry was incidental to some painful decisions that had to be made on the economy as a whole, principally over devaluation and the control of inflation. From their point of view, the rise of the maquila industry to the position it presently occupies in the Mexican economy was accidental. From the point of view of global capitalism, if I may be permitted a fleeting reification, was no accident.

This line of reasoning raises several theoretical and substantive issues. The forces of capitalist reformation did not deliberately organize the massive bank loans to Mexico in the 1970s, nor did they organize the reductions in oil prices that have seriously interfered with Mexico's capacity to repay them. Neither did they engineer the devaluation of the peso, nor the worsening of domestic inflation in Mexico. What the forces of capitalist reformation did do through the medium of the TNCs was to provide the beleaguered Mexican economy with a possibility of relief. The maquila industry not only offered jobs, always welcome in Mexico, but precious dollars with which to purchase the imports necessary to keep the economy going and to repay at least the interest on the foreign debt. If we see the debt problem as part of a spider's web in which the spider (the banks) and the victim (Mexico) are both entangled, then the maquila industry, in part promoted by the consequences of the debt problem, is but a more complex spider and a more complex victim entangled in the same web. The question that has been posed, and that now must be answered, is whether all the spiders and all the victims must inevitably perish, or whether some spiders or some victims can ever escape. In less metaphorical terms, what does the maquila industry in Mexico tell us about the developmental prospects for Mexico under the conditions dictated by the reformation of capitalism? And, to what extent can this particular set of dependencies be reversed?

One can hardly argue with those in the maquila industry who claim that the maquilas have made a positive contribution to the Mexican economy in terms of jobs and foreign exchange earnings. In this sense, the main maquila locations can be justly described as successful "economic zones" in a rather vague and mechanistic usage of the term. In chapter 1 the framework of a methodology for the evaluation of such "success" was presented, and this was worked into a concept of "development zones" that was intended to signal the transition from mere economic growth to a state of relatively self-sustaining development on a local basis. While the success or failure of the maquila strategy is not simply the sum of the successes and failures in each border city, there are clearly connections between the one and the other. The socioeconomic goals of the various strata in these cities are not necessarily the goals of Mexico as a whole, or rather the various strata of which it is composed. To evaluate the successes or failures of the maquila strategy, it is as well to recall the developmental criteria, elaborated in chapter 1:

(1) *Concrete linkages*, the share of imports (backward) of a firm's inputs and the share of exports (forward) of a firm's products that come from and go to the host economy. The greater the extent of backward (raw materials, components, services) and of forward (intermediate goods) linkages achieved with the host economy, the more likely is the creation of a development zone.
(2) The higher the proportion of *foreign currency retained* to value added produced in the host economy then the more likely is the creation of a development zone.
(3) *Upgrading of personnel*, the higher the proportion of indigenous to expatriate managers, technicians and highly trained personnel, the more likely is the creation of a development zone.
(4) The greater the degree of *genuine technology transfer*, the more likely is the creation of a development zone.
(5) The more favorable the *conditions of work* are for the labor force in relation to conditions in the rest of the host society, the more likely is the creation of a development zone.
(6) The more equitable the *distribution* of costs and benefits between the foreign investors, the competing strata among the local populations, and the authorities inside and outside the zone, the more likely is the creation of a development zone.

These criteria rest on a notion of the dependency of a much weaker economy and society on a much stronger economy and society, though the weaker does have its strengths and the stronger does have its weaknesses. This analysis implies the potential for the achievement of limited dependency reversal within the context of an ongoing reformation of capitalism.

In 1988, Mexico had about 1,200 maquilas, employing over 300,000 workers, and export earnings from the maquila industry were in the region of $1.5 billion. This is a genuine success story and it is not an exaggeration to describe the maquiladora industry as "booming." However, in terms of these six criteria, can we argue that the major maquila sites were truly being turned into development zones? This analysis focuses on the maquilas in Tijuana, Mexicali, Juárez, Reynosa, Matamoros, and Chihuahua City, which together account for around three-quarters of the plants and maquila employees in Mexico. Each of the criteria for all these sites will be assessed, drawing attention to particular cities where they are significantly different from the border as a whole on one or other of the criteria.

## Linkages

The maquilas have never made substantial purchases in Mexico, in aggregate terms. The original intention of the maquila program left the question of backward linkages rather ambivalent. On the one hand, the very fact that the industry was often called "in-bond" by Mexican officials and U.S. corporations alike, suggested that the inputs as well as the equipment used in the production processes would come from abroad. The official English language publication from the office of the president, in a statement about the maquilas in 1971, is quite clear about this: "The assembly system also stimulates employment in the investor country where the lesser cost and price of processed articles created greater demand and, in consequence, increased local production of parts and other inputs" (*Mexican Newsletter*, 30 May 1971:6). On the other hand, there was no prohibition on the maquilas purchasing Mexican materials and components, and by the mid-1970s the Mexican authorities started to exhort the maquilas to buy more of what they needed in Mexico. Thus, in 1975 Baird and McCaughan could write, "Despite Mexican government efforts to encourage the use of national resources, very few of the raw materials and components used in the assembly operations come from Mexico" (1975:10), and go on to show that, interestingly, the Warwick television maquila in Tijuana (a captive supplier of Sears), used mainly Japanese parts. Nonmaquila foreign investment, particularly the TNC-dominated automobile industry, had long been operating under a "domestic content" regulation whereby all the finished products of the industry had to contain a certain proportion by value of Mexican parts.[3] At various points in time rumors that the government was about to impose minimum domestic content requirements on the maquila industry circulated in Mexico, but they remained rumors. However, from the mid-1970s onward the federal government, the state governments, and various public and private bodies took up the challenge of selling to the maquilas, but with very little success.

The first major maquila inputs exhibition took place in Mexico City in June 1976. The date is not accidental. It will be recalled that the first maquila crisis occurred during 1974 and 1975, and that a partial resolution of it had been achieved by the devaluations of the peso in 1976. These devaluations meant that Mexico had to work harder for every dollar it earned. Although the value added in pesos of the maquila industry for Mexico increased by nearly 25 percent from 1975 to 1976, the dollar value declined by about the same proportion. The lesson was clear. To recoup some of the dollar losses it was necessary to try to sell more to the maquilas. Indeed, this was the point of the maquila inputs exhibition. The exhibition brought together foreign enterprises, Mexican maquila contractors, the maquilas themselves, national manufacturers, and officials of the government agencies.[4] The questionable wisdom of holding such exhibitions in Mexico City was increasingly recognized and in 1984 *Desarrollo Económico* (a private promotional agency in Chihuahua), established a national exposition of inputs for the maquila industry, which has been held regularly since then in Ciudad Juárez.[5]

The experience of trying to bring maquila buyers and Mexican sellers together showed that it was not always the buyers that were reluctant. The sellers were often unwilling or unable to offer what the buyers required. One of the stalwarts of the Tijuana maquila industry, Mier y Teran (1984), points out that both SECOFI and Mexican Customs maintain precise computerized records of everything that the maquilas import, so it should be relatively easy to identify the requirements of the industry. However, the philosophy of business traditionally practiced in Mexico is very different to what is required by those types of companies, many of them substantial transnational corporations, involved in the maquila industry. For example, international subcontracting involves a level of information sharing, especially on costs, that would be unthinkable in the domestic market.

It is easy to sympathize with a Mexican manufacturer who seems reluctant to supply a maquila demand. Though the industry as a whole has more or less cast off the image it once had as a temporary and unpredictable phenomenon on the Mexican industrial scene,[6] it is still widely regarded as unstable, an impression fortified by the maquilas themselves through veiled threats of relocation to cheaper locations at times of increases in minimum wages and labor unrest. Even where a Mexican manufacturer wishes to start a new product line or increase volume to supply the maquilas, it is often extremely difficult to obtain loans for this purpose, and even then interest rates are prohibitively high.[7] Nevertheless, much of the growth of the maquila industry in the mid-1980s is due to the use by U.S. and Mexican maquila operators of production capacity "released" by the virtual collapse of domestic demand induced by the crisis. The Mexican government, through fiscal policy and through the banks, has only recently begun to act on this, for example, in the temporary importation program for Mexican importers who supply the maquilas.

The reasons why so little has been done to facilitate linkages reflect as much on the conflicting interests of the domestic and export sectors of the Mexican bourgeoisie and their respective allies in government departments, and the parastatals that provide the scaffolding for the Mexican economy, as they do on attitudes to the maquila industry per se. The maquilas have forced themselves more and more into a center stage position in the Mexican economy by their tremendous growth in the 1980s, and Mexico's decision to join the GATT in 1986 has also concentrated the minds of Mexican industrialists on Mexico's future in the global economy and society. Carlos Pérez Iglesias, the head of the maquila division at CANACINTRA, expressed this when he asserted, "Our attitude has changed. We have found that it is beneficial to collaborate with the maquiladoras. . . . Selling to the maquiladoras . . . is exporting within our own country and helps us generate the capacity to compete within the international market" (*Brownsville Herald*, 16 November 1986:1D, 10D).

The strategy adopted by the Mexican authorities to persuade Mexican manufacturers to supply the maquilas is encapsulated in the slogan "Export to Mexico," that is, sales to the maquila industry by domestic suppliers count as Mexican exports. There are now various incentives for exporters that also apply to maquila suppliers, but these have not as yet made any dramatic difference to the outcome, namely that the maquilas actually purchase only one or two percent of their materials and components in Mexico.

There is no given level of linkages that distinguishes a successful from an unsuccessful maquila program. The criterion of backward linkages simply stipulates that the proportion of domestic to foreign inputs should be increasing. The maquila factories have almost no concrete linkages with local industry along the border, or indeed industry elsewhere in Mexico and the proportion of national inputs actually decreased from 1.7 percent in 1980 to 0.9 percent in 1985, though it recovered to 1.5 percent in 1987. The logic of transnational production either encourages, permits, or forbids backward linkages. Where a product is vertically integrated within the TNC or its captive suppliers' networks, or where the intermediate components or materials are so specialized that there are no available suppliers outside the existing TNC network, then backward linkages are literally forbidden by the logic of global production. In Ireland, where there are many highly specialized TNCs producing for the world market, there are several examples of this (Sklair 1988a:3, 6).

Ireland, though hardly an advanced industrial society, is not a Third World country either, and its complement of TNCs reflects this fact. Most TNCs operating in low cost locations, like Mexico, tend to be involved in more traditional and non-state-of-the-art product lines where materials and components tend to be more readily available. This is the case where, on the surface at least, the logic of TNC production appears to permit backward linkages, for example, in Mexico where many U.S.-owned maquilas claim to be actively seeking local materials and components. In addition, the Mexican authorities at the federal, local, and parastatal levels have for some years been trying to organize Mexican industry to supply the maquilas with what they need. This is considered by many to be a potential gold mine for Mexican industry. The reasons why it has not happened are usually that Mexican production is not of the quality required by the world market, that prices are too high, and that delivery is unreliable (Alderete 1983:III:9, 2; Dillman 1983:48). No one familiar with the performance of Mexican domestic industry would be amazed by any of this, but one might wonder why the level of local sourcing remains so low. This suggests that the logic of global production is again operating, but through transfer pricing and captive suppliers. By the very nature of the case this is almost impossible to research at the present time in Mexico. Only when Mexican factories actually begin to produce what the maquilas need at competitive prices, quality, and delivery, will Mexico be able to challenge the TNCs and will we be able to answer these questions.[8]

Industrial parks often actively seek backward linkages for the maquilas they service. The main problem appears to be volume. One maquila that has been producing audio cassettes in PIMSA in Mexicali for many years looked for a Mexican company to supply 280,000 small screws daily, but a search as far afield as Mexico City failed to find a supplier to guarantee delivery. Grupo Bermúdez has also made great efforts to persuade Mexican manufacturers to supply the maquilas, (the maquila demand is taken for granted), but it too reports a general unwillingness of Mexican industry to risk retooling and/or increased production when the maquilas could disappear at any time. It is possible that the great increase in the installed capacity of Mexican domestic industry that is lying idle might make the difference to some manufacturers who are desperate to resume production and who might therefore be prepared to take the risk of supplying the maquila industry. In addition, amendments to the foreign direct investment laws that make joint ventures between Mexican and foreign partners more attractive could encourage certain forms of subcontracting to the maquila industry and increase backward linkages.

It would be wrong, however, to give the impression that no Mexican companies have taken bold steps to capitalize on the maquila opportunity. For example, a San Luis Potosí plastics molder, a specialty that is in scarce supply but substantial demand in Mexico, sent a worker to a company in Chicago to improve his technical skills and paid his wages for the three years that he stayed in the U.S. Fortunately, the man came back and passed on what he had learned. The firm now supplies mirror casings and plastic lenses to various maquila and nonmaquila manufacturers in Mexico.[9]

The evidence suggests that most maquilas would purchase more materials and components locally if they were available. They do buy packaging materials locally, but these are items of low value. The problem for Mexico is that in this context "local" usually means both sides of the border, and in some areas it is small U.S. rather than Mexican firms that are taking advantage of the opportunities opening up for local suppliers. For example, the New Mexico Minority Supplier Development Council, one among 50 such councils that operate throughout the U.S., established a satellite office in 1986 specifically to serve the maquilas in the Las Cruces/El Paso/Ciudad Juárez area (see *TPN*, September 1986:18–19, and November 1986:16). In the lower Rio Grande valley, studies indicate that the job creation potential of an indigenous maquila suppliers industry for the depressed communities from Laredo to the Gulf of Mexico would be substantial, and that such a development is already underway. Patrick and Arriola report that local maquilas have been instrumental in the relocation of three supply firms from the midwest to the Rio Grande valley and in the establishment of two new suppliers locally (1987:13).[10] Although many Mexican-Americans benefit from these linkage creation efforts in New Mexico, west Texas, and the valley, few of the benefits return to Mexico. Such initiatives from the U.S. side must be counted as lost linkage opportunities for Mexico. Why, for example, does the TRW maquila, which brings a million components per day into its plant in Reynosa, the home of PEMEX in Tamaulipas, look to south Texas and not to Mexico?

Thus, though neither the frontera norte nor the rest of Mexico appears at this point in time to be picking up much in the way of backward linkages, the southwest of the U.S. looks to be in a better position to do so. This is consistent with the logic of "production sharing" and is very much connected with the struggle to secure the maquila industry from the attacks of its enemies in the U.S. Labor in U.S. border towns tends to be cheap and nonunion, conditions the reformation of capitalism seeks, so the opportunities that do arise for local sourcing are likely to be snapped up by U.S. rather than Mexican companies.

In an exclusively export oriented maquila industry, forward linkages with the host economy would not arise. However, it is apparent that the days of pure export processing are numbered precisely because of the way in which the global economy is evolving. In Mexico, the decisions to permit maquilas to sell to each other, and to allow access to the domestic market as a reward for local content (actually originating in the late 1970s but hardly put into practice), while not producing an immediate flood of activity, are signs that export orientation excludes neither forward nor backward linkages with the local domestic economy. Maquilas could supply intermediate goods to Mexican producers with profit for both parties. In Juárez, for example, a U.S. maquila sells electronic filters in the Mexican market (see Stockton 1986).[11] However, the capacity of the host economy to buy is conditioned by the logic of global production that permits or forbids TNCs to sell. Prestigious international companies avoid forward linkages when their need to maintain a reputation for quality clashes with their inability to control the end products which contain their components.

The level of backward and forward linkages is so low that there is no point in looking for the places where there are more linkages than in other places. However, maquilas in the interior have always tended to purchase more local inputs than those along the border (González-Arechiga et al. 1987:34, 48). In 1987, national inputs for maquilas in the interior were 17.5 percent, compared to 1.0 percent for those on the border (INEGI 1988: table 4). Dillman reasons, "Maquiladoras in the interior are more accessible to Mexican firms who are thus better able to meet delivery schedules" (1983:55), but this is only part of the cause and, in my view, the less important part. It is not so much the physical distance involved that precludes linkages where the maquila genuinely wishes to purchase, but a combination of the lack of productive capacity in Mexico and the unwillingness of the Mexican manufacturer to produce the goods when the capacity is available. Distance is a factor because the farther the maquila is from the border the more expensive its supply lines from the U.S. (assuming it is sourced from the U.S.). This clearly predisposes management to look harder for local suppliers, and even on occasion to create them, than would normally be the case along the border. This can lead to joint ventures.[12] The growth of the maquila industry in the interior, if it takes place on a substantial scale, therefore, may lead to the proliferation of joint ventures between U.S. corporations and Mexican subcontractors, and between the subsidiary maquilas and independent Mexican firms. Such arrangements may be positive or negative for the Mexican developmental effort, but it is unlikely that the border will benefit very much from them. The locational advantage of the frontera norte becomes a disadvantage where the creation of backward linkages is concerned.[13]

## Foreign Currency: Earnings and Retention

There are two dimensions to maquila foreign currency earnings: value added dollars from the exports of maquila products and the retention of these dollars in Mexico. The arithmetic of value added is complicated by the imports required to produce the exports and the relative values of the currencies. Value added can be divided into four parts, and over the last decade (a) wages and salaries have accounted for something over half, (b) diverse expenses (*gastos diversos*) about one–quarter, (c) utility costs something less than one-quarter, and (d) national inputs one or two percent. While the utility and diverse costs increased more than 100 times between 1975 and 1985, the rate of increase of wages has been less, and of local inputs much less. Indeed, Mexican inputs has been the only item of the four to have experienced actual drops in peso revenues in some years.

Table 9.1 details value added in both pesos and dollars for the maquila industry from 1975 to 1988 along with the ratio of value added to imported inputs, which can be taken as a proxy for Mexico's share of the maquila industry. In considering these figures it is important to note that at the end of 1980 the Banco de México tightened up its methodology to exclude exports and reexports that were not genuinely Mexican, and made other more marginal adjustments. The major effect of these changes on maquila statistics was to exclude the value added on parts and components that were neither U.S. nor Mexican in origin (usually Japanese), but that were being incorporated into the maquila value added totals (see *MN*, November 1980:1–3).[14]

The trend of value added revenue in pesos is permanently and substantially on the increase, while the trend in dollars is quite uneven, though generally positive. There can be no doubt that Mexico has

*Table 9.1*
Mexico's share of the maquila industry, 1975–1988.

| YEAR | VALUE ADDED | IMPORTED INPUTS | VALUE ADDED AS PERCENT OF IMPORTED INPUTS |
|---|---|---|---|
| 1975 | 4.01 | 8.69 | 46.1 |
| 1976 | 5.43 | 11.83 | 45.9 |
| 1977 | 7.12 | 18.25 | 39.0 |
| 1978 | 10.00 | 25.46 | 39.3 |
| 1979 | 14.54 | 35.90 | 40.5 |
| 1980 | 17.73 | 40.10 | 44.2 |
| 1981 | 23.96 | 54.68 | 43.8 |
| 1982 | 46.59 | 108.93 | 42.8 |
| 1983 | 99.52 | 344.78 | 28.9 |
| 1984 | 194.76 | 629.30 | 31.0 |
| 1985 | 325.25 | 980.55 | 33.2 |
| 1986 | 792.02 | 2,653.20 | 29.9 |
| 1987 | 2,235.15 | 7,588.32 | 29.5 |
| 1988 (Jan.) | 305.01 | 1,063.75 | 28.7 |

SOURCE: INEGI (1988: table 1) and *Avances*.
NOTE: figures are in billions of pesos.

derived substantial dollar earnings from the maquila industry.[15] The contribution of the maquilas to Mexico's total foreign earnings has been masked by the rapid rise in the dollar value of petroleum exports between 1980 when they first overtook nonoil exports, and 1985 when they were about double nonoil exports, despite the fall in the price of oil. During this period the value of maquila exports was about one-quarter of total manufactured exports. It is by any standards an important industrial category in its own right.

Between 1975 and 1987, the ratio of value added to imported inputs declined from 46 percent to 29 percent. As the total value of the industry has increased, both the Mexican workers and the Mexican state were receiving a diminishing share of the proceeds, and the maquila owners and/or the maquila facilitators were reaping higher profits. Profits as a percentage of value added did indeed rise from 17.7 percent in 1984 to 22.5 percent in 1986, while wages fell from 39.9 percent to 34.7 percent (in Lee, ed., 1988: sixth endtable). Though Mexico earned more dollars in this period its share of the total maquila cake was decreasing. This will continue to be the case as long as the dollar value of wages remains low, and as long as the purchase of national inputs, backward linkages, stagnates.

The second dimension of the question is how much foreign currency is retained within Mexico, and this varies dramatically with the value of the peso and the spending patterns of the workforce. Various studies have suggested that prior to the devaluations of 1982, maquila workers were spending more than half of their wages in the U.S. This has always been a very political issue. The claims of the Border Trade Alliance that maquila workers spent heavily in the U.S. border cities was an intervention in a commercial struggle that had been going on for over a century between Mexican and U.S. merchants to capture the frontera norte consumer. Since 1982, the Mexican border merchant has had a historic opportunity to reclaim the local consumer as most local consumers could no longer afford to shop in dollars. Nevertheless, some maquila promoters along the border still claimed that half of maquila wages were spent in the U.S.[16] though the consensus of opinion is that this cannot be the case. One report on maquila households in Matamoros suggests that shopping in Brownsville is rare, and on a weekly maquila wage equivalent to $25.64 this is not surprising (Beebe, 8 March 1987:A10). This confirms the results of a study, based on a small sample of maquila workers in Juárez in 1985:

> It is difficult to imagine how a maquila worker who makes less than $4 per day will be able to feed his/her family in Cd. Juárez, and still find a surplus for discretionary spending in El Paso. Actually, our survey found that workers spend very little on anything beyond subsistence necessities

in Cd. Juárez, where costs keep rising. However, administrative and technical personnel interviewed boasted about their ability to shop more or less regularly in El Paso for several items that, paradoxically, are cheaper in El Paso than in Cd. Juárez (George 1986:17).

There is a real paradox about the border and an ideologically manufactured paradox about the maquila industry. The real paradox about the border is that some items are indeed cheaper in the U.S. than in Mexico. Commenting on this in 1984, *El Fronterizo* explained that the propensity of *Juarenses* to shop in El Paso meant reduced sales volumes and therefore higher prices in Ciudad Juárez for some items of food and clothing (in *U.S.-Mexico Report*, 30 June 1984:5). The saturation advertising of El Paso supermarkets on the public of Juárez that Martínez (1978: chapter 7) vividly described for the 1960s and 1970s, continues in the 1980s and captures such retail business that is to be captured from Juárez. The ideologically manufactured paradox is the lack of coherence between the known facts about maquila wages and the claims that maquila workers are spending large amounts of dollars on a regular basis in the U.S. It is clear from data on border transactions that some Mexicans are certainly spending large amounts of dollars in the shopping malls of U.S. border cities but, since 1982, the suspicion is that there are not many maquila workers among them. González-Arechiga (1985) argues that most Mexicans along the border, and in Mexico City, have been forced out of the market for many commodities due to the devaluations and Mexican inflation. Although his study does not single out maquila workers, we can safely extrapolate that the great majority of maquila workers who can no longer afford to shop in the U.S., and the additions to the labor force since 1982 who have never been able to make substantial dollar purchases, have either found cheaper Mexican substitutes or have stopped buying certain commodities altogether. Half of George's small sample of maquila workers in Juárez spent nothing in El Paso, and the rest spent less than $10 per week (1986:22). Dollars are flowing back to the U.S. from the maquila industry, but it is extremely unlikely that it is the workers who are responsible for spending the bulk of them. The leakage from the maquila industry must be mainly from the salaried personnel.

This means, of course, that the retention of dollars within the Mexican economy is less than the value added because of the maquila industry, though since 1982 a larger proportion of the wages paid to the workers is probably finding its way into the shops and markets on the Mexican side of the border than was previously the case. As I pointed out in chapter 2, there has been a boom in Mexican retail property development along the border since 1982, and growing numbers of U.S. consumers are changing dollars into pesos and shopping in Mexican border cities for some staple items. Some of these pesos no doubt become dollars once again that are spent by Mexican merchants and their families in the U.S. It is probable that as maquila wages become less and less able to afford the maquila working class a decent standard of living, a smaller and smaller proportion of them leaves Mexico in the direct form of dollars spent in U.S. border cities.

In this simple sense, therefore, the criterion of foreign exchange earning cannot be said to be fulfilled to the extent that the creation of development zones is certain. This has both a national and a local dimension. Most of the wages and salaries that the maquilas pay to their Mexican employees will stay in the local economy, mostly on the Mexican side. National inputs are very meagre and are divided between local suppliers and out-of-state suppliers, some of whom will be agents for foreign goods rather than manufacturers. Utility and diverse costs, including power, communications, freight charges, rents, and administrative fees, will be divided between local and federal recipients. Federal taxes on the maquila industry are not heavy, and changes to Mexican business tax law in 1987 giving a measure of inflation indexing promised even lower taxes for U.S.-owned maquilas (*MN*, November 1986:5). Given this structure of costs and benefits, it is likely that the Mexican government is clawing back a substantial proportion of the benefits from the maquila industry from the border cities in which they are mainly generated. On the other hand, the federal government has not exactly poured funds into these border cities for the infrastructural support that the maquila industry has called for. The housing subsidy that is collected by the government as part of the burdened wage of maquila workers rarely finds its way back to the border cities. While the absolute value added earnings of the maquilas may have proved to be satisfactory to the Mexican government in terms of its goals for the industry, they have been disappointing because of the reduced dollar earnings due to the very rapid devaluation of the peso. The retention of more of the wage element of these dollars due to the inability of most Mexican consumers to buy as much across the border as they used to, has been counterbalanced by increased dollar spending by maquila salaried personnel.

## Upgrading of Personnel

There is a good deal of information on the upgrading of Mexican personnel. Field research confirms industry claims that Mexican nationals routinely hold positions of managerial and technical responsibility in the maquilas. As table 9.2 shows, the numbers of production

Table 9.2
Production technicians and administrative staff in the maquilas, 1975–1988.

| YEAR | PRODUCTION TECHNICIANS | STAFF | PERCENT OF TOTAL LABOR FORCE |
|------|------------------------|-------|------------------------------|
| 1975 | 5,924 | 3,440 | 13.9 |
| 1976 | 6,165 | 3,661 | 13.2 |
| 1977 | 6,348 | 3,898 | 13.1 |
| 1978 | 7,543 | 4,591 | 13.4 |
| 1979 | 9,569 | 5,978 | 14.0 |
| 1980 | 10,828 | 6,698 | 14.7 |
| 1981 | 12,545 | 7,744 | 15.5 |
| 1982 | 13,377 | 8,288 | 17.0 |
| 1983 | 16,322 | 9,267 | 16.9 |
| 1984 | 22,381 | 11,798 | 17.1 |
| 1985 | 25,042 | 13,052 | 18.0 |
| 1986 | 30,367 | 15,572 | 18.4 |
| 1987 | 39,952 | 21,414 | 19.0 |
| 1988 (Jan.) | 40,449 | 21,837 | 18.9 |

SOURCE: INEGI (1988: table 2) and *Avances.*

technicians and staff have grown rapidly over the last decade as has the proportion of total maquila employees in these categories. Not everyone classed under the rubrics of "technicians" or "staff" is necessarily carrying out technical or administrative functions. Some "technicians" or "engineers" employed in the maquila industry are, like their counterparts in other countries, little more than supervisors and perform work whose technical content is very low. Similarly, many of the "staff" in the maquilas will be clerks, typists, and receptionists, for whom upgrading of skills may be minimal. Nevertheless, there are many Mexicans for whom the advent of the maquilas has meant significant opportunities.[17] Transnational styles of management and technique are being transmitted through the maquilas to Mexican industry as a whole (Kras 1987). Given the complaint that Mexican domestic industry has been protected for so long that it is unable to face up to global competition, the significance of this fact should not be underestimated.

Foreign-owned maquilas have great incentives to employ Mexican managers and technicians. They speak Spanish, they are probably "streetwise" to some extent, and they are much cheaper than equivalent personnel from the home country. Many maquilas have close contacts with Mexican universities and technical colleges, particularly in Juárez where the Instituto Tecnológico Regional has supplied professionals to the maquilas over the years. It has been a definite policy of most of the maquilas at the higher end of the technology spectrum to become involved with their local colleges and to provide facilities for on-the-job training for students in the technical and administrative fields. This is not, of course, an entirely disinterested policy as there is a general shortage of qualified personnel in Mexico, as in most Third World countries, and Mexico has the added disadvantage that it is contiguous with the U.S. and therefore more vulnerable than most to the ravages of the "brain drain."

There is also job mobility for Mexican professional staff, both between maquilas and between the domestic sector and the maquila sector. Some maquilas have actively recruited executives from Mexico City, Monterrey, and other industrial centers, and salaries along the border for top positions in the maquilas are among the best in Mexico. In order to attract such people and to retain those they already have, border maquilas have begun to match the perks offered by domestic industry in the interior. For example, one survey discovered that in 96 percent of major companies in Mexico City, those who report to the chief executive had traditionally been given company cars. This was not a practice of the maquila industry in its early days, but by the mid-1980s, almost half of the major border maquilas had started to assign company cars to their top executives, both Mexican and U.S. citizens. Country club memberships, stock options, and performance bonuses are all becoming common along the border (Ibarra and Sander in Lee, ed., 1988:59–68). Mobility within the maquilas has also been on the increase in recent years. The rapid increase in the numbers of maquila plants has resulted in many maquila workers being promoted to supervisory positions and many junior staff to senior staff positions. The demand for Mexican professional staff has always outstripped the supply.

The maquila industry has certainly been responsible for the up-grading and encouragement of professional skills all along the border. Since the 1960s it has provided educated youth with tens of thousands of technical and managerial posts, has introduced to these once quite backward areas new occupational categories, and has stimulated numbers of enterprising Mexicans to leave their maquila employment and to establish businesses of their own (Stockton 1986). In these respects the maquila industry can justly claim to have played a key role in the socioeconomic development of the frontera norte.[18] Nevertheless, one cannot assume that all these Mexican managers and technicians will identify more readily with Mexican national interests and goals where they conflict with the interests and goals of the corporations that employ them than foreign managers and technicians would. The creation of such a comprador bourgeoisie, as I have argued, can have contradictory consequences for development.

The image of maquila work that is projected by the critics of the industry is of low level assembly and mind numbing boredom, tempered from time to time by tasks that are injurious to health and dangerous to life and limb (Fernández-Kelly 1983; Iglesias 1985). Field work in the maquilas cannot simply be rejected out of hand on the basis of the soothing images of the maquila promoters' glossy brochures. Two specific questions need to be posed. First, have the jobs that maquila operatives do changed over the last 20 years? The simple answer to this question is yes. Second, do these changes represent a genuine upgrading for the workforce in terms of transferable skills? This is a much more complex issue.

The main indicator of the changing nature of maquila jobs is the proportion of the workforce in the various industrial sectors into which the Mexican authorities have divided the industry. These are 12 in number and table 3.4 provides the necessary data. The main changes have been the relative decline of the apparel/needle trades and the rapid growth of transport equipment and electrical and electronic parts and accessories. Electrical and electronic equipment, one of the major employers, has grown, but at less than the average for the maquilas as a whole. Many entirely new branches of industry have been introduced into the frontera norte by the maquila industry, like printed circuit boards and electronic devices for consumer and capital goods, some embodying technology that did not exist in the 1960s.

So the products that maquila workers produce have changed over the last 20 years, and many of these products are new to the border and, in some cases, new to Mexico. The exposure of the workforce to the techniques, the materials, and the components used in these new industries obviously does have some consequences for the transfer of industrial skills and attitudes, though it is not at all obvious exactly what these consequences are. The work of an unusual research team under the direction of Valdés in Ciudad Juárez has made an important contribution to answering this question. The team was unusual in that the investigators were women who had worked on the maquila production line. They carried out an intensive program of research to discover if technical skills really were transmitted on the maquila shop floor and how the workers reacted.[19]

The COMO team discovered that many of the 182 maquila workers interviewed for the project had learned an informal technology of "manufacturing engineering" that involved processes that would normally be considered technical in nature. For example, almost 90 percent of the workers routinely performed maintenance work on their machines and tools, about half had made innovations to machines or products that had increased production, and about one-third had modified an established system of production. Many women were reluctant to share their innovations with either management or coworkers because they felt that this might result in further pressure to increase production and, in any case, they were not rewarded for anything they did beyond the narrow specifications of their jobs. Having improved their own productivity by their own efforts, they kept these techniques to themselves in order to meet the official production standards more easily. Devon Peña, who was also connected with COMO, came up with roughly similar results from a survey of 223 maquila workers in electronics and garment plants. Peña argues that, "maquiladora workers engage in a variety of skilled job tasks for which they are neither trained or paid. Management has acknowledged the existence of skilled activity but has resisted official recognition which might involve imposition of a higher wage regime" (Peña 1984:190).[20] Peña catches the double bind in which the maquilas find themselves over the upgrading of workers' skills. In a nutshell, the idea of the skilled worker is good for morale, but bad for corporate profits if taken too far. In one survey most of the maquila workers, "avoided the term assembly work . . . while most managers stated that there are no skill requirements for the assembly workers they hire, fully two-thirds of the workers interviewed classified their jobs as semi-skilled, and 21 percent of them maintained that theirs were skilled jobs" (George 1986:20–21).

This raises the controversial question of training. By law, all maquila workers must be offered a minimum of training,[21] though most scholars argue that actual training is more often minimal than minimum (for example, Carrillo and Hernández 1985:III). In the 1970s, when such a large proportion of the maquila workforce was composed of young women in their first industrial jobs, the need was for a general orientation to factory life as much as for specific job training. By the 1980s, when a factory culture had been established in all of the border cities, and most families either had a maquila worker among their number or knew of one, the border working class had reached a level of "sophistication" similar to that of the main industrial cities in the Mexican interior. The concentration of Fortune 500-type U.S. and Japanese corporations along the border also contributed to this industrial ethos. The maquila industry has long been conscious of its reputation as a low wage employer, and it has striven to counter this reputation not only by offering an array of nonwage benefits, but also by holding out the promise of promotion within the context of the glamourous high technology fields in which many of the maquilas operate.[22] It is true that, on average, there are many more supervisory positions in the maquilas than there would be in equivalent plants in the U.S., but it is also true that the wage differentials between the operatives and line chiefs or group leaders, and between them and the quality control supervisors, are much smaller than would be the case elsewhere. Ambitious workers who study on their own time can also take advantage of in-house training provided by some maquilas. So, while there may be opportunities for promotion in the maquilas, the material benefits are often small.

Compared with the absolute shortage of technical and managerial opportunities along the border in the 1960s, it is undeniable that by the 1980s some upgrading of Mexican personnel, professional, supervisory, and production workers, has taken place. To this extent, the major maquila sites satisfy this criterion for the transition from economic to development zones.

## Technology: Relocation and Transfer

Technology transfer, according to the maquila promoters, is taking place everywhere in Mexico that the maquilas have penetrated. León Opalín, long the maquila specialist at Banamex, in a *Wall Street Journal* Mexico supplement (23 December 1985) specifically asserts that the maquila program "acts as a vehicle for accomplishing technology transfers." This was very much in line with the intention of the de la Madrid government policy on the maquilas. It is generally acknowledged that the 1983 Maquila Industry Decree set a new tone for the development of the industry, emphasizing some specific aims for the expansion of the maquilas in the direction of higher technology. Article 16 of the Decree committed the authorities, among other things, to "Promote investment in advanced technology sectors, and incorporate new technology which modernizes production processes" (as translated in Bryan et al. 1984: sec.8, 8).

Lists of transnational corporations that are identified with advanced research and high technology products are routinely used as a surrogate for technology transfer itself.[23] Technology relocation must not be confused with technology transfer. It is important to distinguish between, for example, General Motors producing auto parts in a General Motors plant (whether in Detroit or in Matamoros) and General Motors producing auto parts in a U.S. plant or in a Mexican maquila. This rather convoluted expression is my way of arguing that there is a difference between GM producing parts totally under GM control in any GM plant wherever located and a Mexican plant genuinely producing auto parts whether for GM or anyone else. The former is technology relocation (often misnamed technology transfer), the latter is *genuine* technology transfer, or anchorage.

There is plenty of evidence of technology relocation in the maquilas, but very little of technology anchorage. The reasons are not hard to find. All high tech companies protect their advanced knowledge jealously and demand a premium for it in the marketplace. The ideology of production sharing is based on the premise that the capital and knowledge intensive parts of production are carried out in the capitalist heartlands where expertise is available, while the labor intensive parts are carried out in the Third World where labor is cheap. It would therefore make no sense for a transnational corporation to gift its technology to Third World countries and risk losing its "share" of the production.

Each main maquila center has its own examples of state-of-the-art technology where some genuine technology transfer appears to be taking place. The Matsushita TV maquila in Tijuana is said to be one of the most modern assembly facilities in the world, incorporating the most advanced techniques and processes. Emermex in Mexicali produces what are probably the most sophisticated transformers and uninterruptible power supply assemblies in Mexico. Elamex Printed Circuits has "UL" and "Milspec" approval, and with the introduction of surface mount technology, claims to be competitive for quality with any P.C. board manufacturer in the world. The Allied Bendix maquila, Aerotech Matamoros, assembles and fabricates rotating aircraft components to the most exacting standards. And in Chihuahua City, the Westinghouse maquila, Sistemas Electrónicos, works to a complete system of military specifications.[24] The difficult questions are: how representative are these maquilas and do they actually entail genuine technology transfer?

A comparison of labor intensive border maquilas with maquilas in the interior suggests an answer to this question: "High-tech U.S. firms such as Unisys Corp. and Eastman Kodak Co. and traditional U.S. manufacturers such as Ford Motor Co. have started combining some of the most automated manufacturing technologies and the latest management techniques with some of the world's lowest-paid workers" (Stokes 1987:1572). The apparent paradox lies at the heart of the ideology of production sharing and the technological core of the reformation of capitalism. Given the capacity to break down the production of practically anything into its component parts and to assemble these parts more or less anywhere it chooses, the TNC can now unite capital, technology, and labor in an historically unique fashion. The level of technology has generally varied with the wages paid to labor, high technology tending to be found in high wage areas, and low technology in low wage areas. Those workers in the advanced economies, in more capital intensive enterprises, therefore, tend to earn more than workers in more primitive economies, working in more labor intensive enterprises. Production sharing means that in some major industries, particularly those that are based on electronic control systems, the high technology processes can travel in the form of components to low wage areas for further processing. Thus, the technology has been relocated, not anchored in production processes within the low wage areas where the further processing is taking place. Production sharing allows for almost limitless experimentation with the division of labor, and the maquila industry, perhaps more than any other assembly industry in the world, has capitalized on the possibilities of cost saving by manipulation of systems of production, fabrication, assembly, and subassembly.[25] So, for the most part, high technology is contained in the components which are assembled in a standardized and simplified fashion by low-paid maquila operatives doing the same things hundreds or thousands of times every day. Like the case of the TNC-owned tire factories in Nigeria (Adikibi 1983), in the typical Mexican maquila only the most senior technicians from the parent company have a vision of the whole productive process and they teach discrete parts of it to the Mexican technicians, who pass on discrete parts of what they know to the supervisors who are responsible for ensuring that the workers properly carry out their given tasks. However, as the COMO team and Peña have discovered, there are opportunities within this system for some workers and technicians to exercise independent judgment and to intervene at some level in the productive process. This suggests that all technology relocation presents the possibility of some technology anchorage, in the form of transmission of skills and the transfer of workable technology from its controllers to those employed to work with the products and processes in which it is embodied. The reformation of capitalism does not generally permit the transfer of the technological monopolies of the TNCs to potential competitors. The criterion of genuine technology transfer cannot be satisfied within the maquila or any other fdi structure.

## Conditions of Work

Much has been written on the exploitation of workers, especially women workers, in the maquilas. It is rarely clear whether we are to understand this as "super exploitation" of workers by the maquilas, whether the mere fact of foreign ownership constitutes exploitation in itself, or whether the industries in which the maquilas are typically concentrated tend to be more exploitative than other industries. My own position is that capitalism is exploitative insofar as it expropriates surplus value for private profit from those who are creating it, though no satisfactory alternative for creating wealth has yet been made to work at the societal level. Under some circumstances the nationality of capital makes a difference, and it is important to note that the structure of foreign-owned industry usually does differ from domestically owned industry. There are at least five day-to-day conditions of work that are relevant in this context, namely wages, job security, hours worked, workplace facilities, and health and safety at work.

Mexican maquila workers and professional staff earn far less than their counterparts in comparable U.S. factories. This is certainly one meaningful interpretation of exploitation. Another meaningful interpretation is to compare maquila workers with workers in domestically owned Mexican industry, both in the border regions and elsewhere. Maquila workers along the border earn higher wages than maquila workers in the interior, though it is less certain that maquila workers earn higher wages than nonmaquila workers in the same places. The federal minimum wage level is higher in the border areas where most of the maquilas are located than the rest of Mexico, with the exception of Mexico City and a few other areas. However, the rate of inflation has tended to be higher along the border than elsewhere in Mexico. Without a thorough knowledge of the typical maquila worker's shopping basket compared with the shopping basket of the typical nonmaquila worker, one cannot say whether the maquila worker is better or worse off than the worker in a Mexican nonmaquila factory or in any other occupation. It is, nevertheless, unlikely that maquila workers are much better off than other workers in Mexico or those who cross the border to find jobs. When, in 1987, the Mexican government increased the minimum wage by 23 percent while the rate of inflation was more like 100 percent, *TPN* suggested to maquila managers that they could protect the standard of living of their employees by "setting up a clothing exchange in the plant . . . Buy some bulk food items such as flour, beans, potatoes, etc., and distribute those among your employees. Also free meals in the plant can help" (January 1987:20). Pranis (1987) reports that since at least 1985, maquilas in the lower Rio Grande valley have been giving their workers small food basket allowances adjusted for devaluation. The Mexican government was forced to institute quarterly increases in minimum wage rates to deal with the desperate economic situation. Few objective observers, therefore, would agree with Michie when he asserts, after estimating the average maquila worker's wage as the equivalent of 75 to 80 cents an hour plus benefits worth about 40 cents, "What you have to keep in mind is that in Mexico, that's a very good wage" (quoted in Vrazo 1986). Cheap labor, of course, is the rationale of the maquila industry.

[214]

Job security raises some very interesting issues precisely because the maquiladoras have often been branded with the label of "runaway industries," and there have been several notorious cases of U.S. maquilas slipping silently away in the dead of night to avoid paying Mexican workers their legal entitlement of severance money (Baird and McCaughan 1979). The "runaway maquilas" have tended to be concentrated geographically, and to some extent sectorally, but most of the maquilas that started up in the 1970s were still in production in the 1980s, with the notable exception of a group of clothing maquilas in Tijuana, many of which closed down and opened up under different names. While this did cause major disruptions and considerable hardships to the workers of Tijuana, it is the exception rather than the rule in the history of the maquila industry. The fact remains that in the 1970s there were about 100,000 new jobs created by the maquila industry, and in the 1980s the maquilas have created at least an additional 150,000 jobs, most of these on the border. While we cannot be certain that indigenous border industries would not have created a quarter of a million new jobs since 1970, it is extremely unlikely. Indeed, most commentators argue that the maquila industry has been responsible for considerable multiplier effects on the border economy.

Job security also involves the position of the individual worker. Gambrill (1984), Carrillo and Hernández (1985), Valdés-Villalva (in Gibson and Corona Rentería 1985), and others describe temporary labor contracts (where maquilas employ workers on probation at less than the minimum wage, work them for the statutory permitted period, then fire them or offer them a further temporary contract), and illegal termination of workers whose productivity had dropped due to eye strain and job stress after years of service. These exploitative practices tended to take place in maquilas where there were no unions, and were typical of the years when there were dozens, sometimes hundreds of applicants for each maquila job. While abuses continue, job security is now more assured for most maquila workers.

In the hours worked per week there are no substantial differences between the maquila industry and Mexican industry as a whole. However, the intensity of the crisis in the frontera norte may be forcing maquila workers to work even longer hours to support themselves and their families. Research in Juárez indicated that, "workers supplement their income by working extra hours—26 percent of them; by holding other jobs—12 percent of them; by working in a family shop—6 percent; by having their spouses, parents and/or children work—35 percent" (George 1986:22).[26] The advantage of having maquila jobs available is tempered by the increasing lack of a decent living wage that maquila work offers.

Workplace facilities such as nurseries for children, subsidized meals, and sports tend to be a function of plant size. The average number of employees per maquila is around 250, more than double Mexican industry as a whole, which suggests that maquila workers are no worse off than other Mexican workers. A few individual maquilas and maquila industrial parks run nurseries and day care centers, some in conjunction with the Mexican social security service, but this is not yet widespread in the industry. Most of the Fortune 500-type maquilas and some of the facilitator groups consciously try to create positive corporate images through good workplace facilities, social events, and sports teams, which helps to attract and hold labor. Local maquila associations organize thriving leagues in a variety of sports, and the maquila industry holds a well-attended annual "maquiolimpiada" with teams from all over Mexico.[27]

On the other side of the coin, the maquila industry has its share of irresponsible management and dangerous processes. The strict U.S. codes on health and safety at work and environmental protection laws, particularly in California, have played their part in encouraging some U.S. manufacturers to establish maquilas in Mexico. In 1985, *Bridge over the Border* reported two such cases. A film processing company closed down its plant after being cited by the California Occupational Safety and Health Administration, and moved over to Mexicali to continue its dangerous practice (June–July 1985:1, 4); and the prestigious GTE Communications Corporation moved a department from its plant in Albuquerque to Juárez after 64 GTE workers filed compensation cases against the company for chemical poisoning (September–October 1985:1, 5). The relocation of electronic assembly work from California's Silicon Valley, where such problems are very well documented, suggests that there are other similar cases. The American Friends Service Committee has also reported on a variety of health and safety issues in the shrimp processing maquilas in Matamoros, cited by the U.S. Food and Drug Administration: "Workers generally are left uninformed as to any possible dangers coming from the chemicals, metals, and other materials they are using" (*Newsletter*, February 1981:5–6). While it is difficult to assess the exact incidence of production related disease and injury, several studies document health and safety hazards in the maquila industry (for example, Carrillo and Jasis 1983; Cleary 1981). Some types of electronic assembly and fabrication are known to be hazardous, and the maquila industry has plenty of them. The inadequacy of Mexican industrial health and safety legislation and factory inspection makes life even more hazardous for some maquila workers.

The experience of the maquila industry in the 1980s has had the effect of turning the question of "conditions of work" upside down. Turnover rates have been so high that some have begun to wonder why the industry has such difficulty in retaining its labor force. Monthly turnover in Juárez increased from 2.5 percent in 1981 to 6.1 percent in 1983. This was said to be "worrying" because it produced a "negative image from the promotional point of view" (Alderete 1983:V:1). The turnover rate varies from maquila to maquila, from time to time, and from location to location, but educated guesses suggest that in Juárez since 1985 it has been about 8 to 10 percent per month on the average, the highest of any of the main maquila locations, though Tijuana is not far behind (see *MN*, August 1986:9). "Poaching" of labor is common, and in Juárez recruiting agents for some maquilas are to be seen at the gates of others.

There are three main explanations for labor turnover, and none of them excludes any of the others. The first is that the maquilas, particularly since the devaluation and inflation of recent years, do not provide a living wage for most of their workers. As I noted earlier in the discussion on wages, the rate of inflation along the border has tended to be high and so this added pressure on subsistence for maquila workers and their families does make it more likely that the workers would go to the trouble of leaving one job and finding another even to secure very marginal improvements in pay and conditions.[28]

A second explanation involves the distance between the plants and workers' housing. Commentators in Juarez commonly report on the long and expensive journeys that many maquila workers are forced to make twice daily, and sometimes more frequently where there are children to look after, to keep their jobs (for example, Fernández-Kelly 1983: chapter 8; Staudt in Young, ed., 1986: chapter 5). There is no doubt that there is some truth in all of this, and it is not only in Mexico that workers quit their jobs for this reason. Nevertheless, it is unlikely that this is the whole truth, though the housing explanation is one that does serve the interests of the maquila owners insofar as they cannot be held directly responsible for it.

The third explanation of turnover is the mind numbing nature of maquila work. Juárez has been the major site for research on this question along the border and two views, which we can label the "discontented" and the "contented" worker theses, have emerged. Peña, one of the main proponents of the "discontented" worker thesis, has outlined a theory of maquila worker solidarity which distinguishes between trade union organized resistance, of which there is little, and informal shop floor resistance, of which he (and others such as Carrillo and Hernández 1985) have found considerable evidence. In particular, Peña has analyzed the phenomenon of *"tortuósidad"* (working at tortoise pace) as a strategy that maquila workers in Juárez have developed to cope with the nature of their work (in Ruiz and Tiano, eds., 1987: chapter 6). The logical connection between the "discontented" worker thesis and turnover is straightforward. If the evidence on lack of labor unrest, particularly the

[217]

absence of strikes in the industry, is to be believed, then it is difficult to accept that the nature of the work could be responsible for the high level of turnover. However, if, as Peña and others argue, the absence of trade union organized resistance obscures massive informal labor resistance, like tortuósidad, then this would indicate that the maquilas in Juarez are full of "discontented" workers, and high turnover becomes much more understandable.

The "contented" worker thesis is a product of the promotional efforts of the public and private maquila facilitators and the Mexican government in its attempt to sell the maquila program on the basis of a cheap and cooperative labor force. However, there has been some academic research support for the notion of the "contented" worker, particularly from researchers based at UTEP and in close contact with the maquila industry. Lucker's studies on attitudes toward maquila work and on the problem of turnover found that the workers in two coupon sorting plants in Juárez were on the whole quite happy with their jobs and that some even considered the work "entertaining" (Lucker and Álvarez 1984). Another UTEP researcher who quotes Lucker and others and finds the evidence of low job satisfaction among maquila workers unconvincing is Stoddard (1987:51–52). However, both Lucker and Stoddard confuse social satisfaction at the workplace, which Peña and others have documented, and job satisfaction, a quite different phenomenon. It may also be the case that there are differences between the pressures of work which Peña and most other maquila researchers have documented all along the border, and the coupon sorting plants that Lucker studied, where precision quality requirements such as are to be found in electronics and some needle trade maquilas, would not be the same. Lucker's own study of turnover which aimed to assess costs rather than reasons was, significantly, carried out in a wire harness assembly plant (Lucker 1987). The problem for the "contented" worker thesis is, simply, to explain the rate of labor turnover. If maquila workers are, on the whole, happy with their work and the financial rewards of flitting from one maquila to another are rather minimal, then we should expect a low rate of turnover. There is no evidence to suggest that the wage differentials between maquilas are substantial enough to explain fully monthly turnover rates of 10 percent and more. This is the strength of the "discontented" worker thesis, for in combination with rates of pay barely at survival level, workers who are in any case unhappy with their jobs, though glad to have the social solidarity of a workplace and friends on the production line, will be more willing to shop around for slight improvements.[29] There is indirect evidence that the maquilas themselves are not unaware of these factors, for many maquilas will reengage workers who have left, but usually only once or twice. It is difficult to see how the turnover rate can be drastically reduced without higher wages all round; obviously selective wage rises will exacerbate the problem, and as we have already seen, there appears to be no direct relationship between city wage levels and turnover rates.

There is, however, an alternative view on turnover, that has at least the merit of explaining why the employers appear to be less worried about it than might be expected. This view accepts that there is a high initial turnover in the maquila industry, but argues that this only affects a small proportion of new workers whose initial training costs can be comfortably written off. It is often said that once a maquila worker has stayed for a few months it is unlikely that she or he will leave in the short- or medium-term. These are the workers for whom the solidarity of the workplace may outweigh the minimal benefits of finding another maquila job. A survey of maquila related manufacturers suggests that after a high initial turnover the maquila industry "experiences a lower turnover rate than its U.S. counterpart" (USITC 1988:5–3). If this is true, then that fraction of the workforce that is not affected by excessive turn-over, presumably including most of those who have gained skills and/or qualifications in the industry, is more than sufficient to counteract the economic costs of the turnover that does occur on the margins.

This suggests that there is not much in it for maquila management to improve pay and conditions more than they have to. The improvements that have come have been because of management's wish or need to attract and hold on to workers in conditions of artificial labor shortages. Higher wages, job security, hours of work, plant facilities, and health and safety at work, where they have happened, have mostly been in the gift of management rather than won as any part of the struggle for the rights of the workers to a better standard of living and a more humane workplace. In this sense, and with few exceptions, the maquila industry in Mexico has not made any dramatic contributions to the welfare and dignity of the Mexican working class, but neither can it be fairly accused of reducing that welfare and dignity to any appreciable extent. In terms of the criterion of work conditions on the creation of development zones along the border, the net effect of the maquila industry has been more or less neutral.

## Distribution and the Class Struggle

Maquila workers, like all Mexican workers, have suffered a decline in real standards of living over the past few years, while the profits of the TNCs have increased substantially. Every plunge in the dollar value of the peso appears to herald a new surge in maquila startups. The decline of the peso has hit the maquila worker on the border particularly hard because Mexican border communities have always looked to the U.S. for many of their household purchases. Mexican alternative products have often been unavailable to the border consumer, too expensive, of inferior quality, or even disguised imports from the U.S. However, it would not be true to say that the maquila workers are the poorest groups in their localities or nationally. This is, of course, a very complex question both at the level of the household, where it involves the maquila worker and her (or his) extended family (often on both sides of the border), and the state, where it involves the revenues that the cities along the border derive from the maquila industry and state revenues from the industry. Equitable distribution, therefore, comprises a series of complicated comparisons. Maquila workers will have to be compared with the nonmaquila worker first along the border, and then in the interior of Mexico. The maquila working-class will also have to be compared with the maquila bourgeoisie. And finally, the ways in which the Mexican state deals with the communities of the frontera norte will have to be assessed.

The Mexican professionals and comprador bourgeoisie along the border have done very well because of the maquilas. Industrial park development, and legal and commercial services for the maquila industry, have created a new class of wealthy Mexican maquila facilitators (and, of course, U.S. maquila facilitators too). This phenomenon has been noted with increasing frequency in the last decade, and it merely confirms what rational expectation would lead any student of Mexican political and social structures to predict. The frontera norte may be far from Mexico City, but it is still in Mexico. Baird and McCaughan succinctly describe the membership of the "political cliques" that ran the BIP in its first decade: "a local government official, lawyer, accountant, banker, customs broker, labor contractor and in most cases the owner of factory land and buildings. U.S. businessmen from industrial development committees and chambers of commerce from nearby U.S. cities also usually form part of this clique" (1975:9).[30] What the maquila industry had to do if it was to succeed on a more permanent basis was to create a bourgeoisie to build a capitalist industrial culture that could serve its needs along the border. Howard Boysen, a major facilitator in San Diego/Tijuana, put this neatly when he said that the maquilas produce "middle-class men who are learning skills of programming and management, buying houses, educating their children, and limiting the size of their families" (in *National Journal*, 7 July 1979). This was not just a view from north of the border. It is confirmed by González Baz, of the Paso del Norte maquila industry law firm: "Maquiladoras have made the difference for the border. . . .For the first time in history there is a solid, strong middle class here" (in *Oakland Tribune*, 29 September 1982:B–8). And Whiteford, in his study of the Mexicali valley, argues that the maquila industry created an "emerging regional bourgeoisie . . . able to acquire considerable wealth and power as the program [BIP] expanded" (in Rosenthal-Urey, ed., 1986:34).

This "border ruling class" differs considerably from the traditional landed oligarchies. The maquila ruling class is, first, a new bourgeoisie in a recognizably Western capitalist sense and, second, it is also a comprador class dependent on the presence of foreign capital for its own existence and survival. This does not necessarily make it any less patriotic or even chauvinist in its practice or ideology, for in Mexico there are many economic nationalists who have no scruples about stealing public funds, and there are many compradors who genuinely try to put foreign investment to use in the development of their country.[31] Salas-Porras, in her path-breaking studies of the effects of the maquilas on Mexico's regional bourgeoisie, argues that this "border ruling class" has at least two distinctive characteristics that can be directly related to the growth of the maquilas. The base of this class is in services for the maquilas rather than productive investment in the plants themselves; and the members of this class exploit the peculiar "private-public sector" symbiosis that exists in Mexico in their own interests against the public interest (1986, 1987). She draws attention to the favorable terms on which state-owned facilities are made available to private maquila facilitators for the benefit of the maquilas, a paradigm case of the triple alliance between TNCs, state and comprador elements. It is for this reason that Tamayo has argued that the "nationalization of the 'political class' at the border" is necessary if national integration is to be achieved (in Gibson and Corona Rentería, eds., 1975:91).

Every ruling class requires subordinate classes to rule. The maquila industry has effectively replaced or supplemented the underclasses that were created by mines, land, and cattle along the border, some of which were themselves created by U.S. business interests, with an industrial proletariat. As Whiteford puts this in uncompromising terms, "the assembly-plant workers are thus the urban counterpart to [Mexicali's] landless rural laborers: both groups are non-unionized, poorly paid, and deprived of the social benefits of economic development in the Mexicali region" (in Rosenthal-Urey 1986:34).

Maquila workers are certainly poorly paid, but whether they are "deprived of the social benefits of economic development" is more controversial. Little research has been carried out comparing maquila workers with the general population, but what has been done reveals a complex picture. Staudt has analyzed data (from the 1980 Juárez Household Survey) on 223 households with maquila workers as members and 1,013 households without a maquila worker member. The area in which maquila workers were unquestionably better off than nonmaquila workers related to their access to health care, because all maquila workers are legally entitled to the benefits of the Mexican Social Security System. Although many of the differences between the samples were quite small (for example 50 percent of nonmaquila households were in debt while 58 percent of the maquila households were in debt), the overall trend of the findings justifies the conclusion that maquila households "tend to have more expenses and get less 'return' on their income than other households. They exhibit a tendency to live beyond their means, a pattern partly determined by employment and related costs of transportation. Unemployment is a greater problem in maquila households, aggravating their uncertainty" (Staudt in Young, ed., 1986:104–105, and passim). This conclusion is consistent with high turnover where even marginal improvements in material conditions (for example, a cheaper journey to work, a small increase in bonuses) would be enough to cause maquila workers to change jobs.

The distribution of costs and benefits will always be extremely difficult to assess with any degree of accuracy, and here I wish only to indicate that it cannot be unequivocally claimed that the maquila industry has brought anything like general prosperity to the frontera norte although it has certainly brought specific prosperity to many maquila facilitators. It would be utopian to believe that if the maquila industry had not created a new Mexican border comprador bourgeoisie then the "people" or the maquila workers themselves would have derived all the benefits that the maquila industry has undoubtedly brought. If the Mexican bourgeoisie had not cashed in on the industry, then the economically dominant strata north of the border would have taken even more out of it than they already have. Some argue that the creation of an indigenous "modernizing" bourgeoisie is essential for development, and as long as the Mexican government and the economic classes that run the country chose to follow an ELIFFIT-type strategy, then the border bourgeoisie that runs the maquilas will be comprador in character.

This connection between state policy and the border bourgeoisie is the conduit along which national and local interests run, sometimes in parallel, sometimes in veiled opposition, and sometimes in open conflict. While one cannot baldly assert that where the Mexican state has recycled the public revenues from the frontera norte these have promoted the interests of border industrial and commercial property developers, there is evidence to support this view. Herzog argues that "state intervention in Tijuana has not so much served to improve the quality of life in disadvantaged neighborhoods in the city, as it has to expand economic infrastructure in a few strategic locations." A meagre 6.5 percent of the budget in this period went to public housing in what was one of the world's fastest growing cities (Herzog 1989:327, 329).[32] Tijuana is, of course, not unique in this regard, either along the border, or in Mexico, or in the First, Second, or Third Worlds, but the phenomenon of a widening gap between the relatively rich and the relatively poor is nonetheless real all along the border. For example, Campbell Saavedra (in Flores Garza et al. 1986) notes an increasing tendency to polarization in and around Juárez into poor and rich sections, and the same can be said for many other Mexican border cities.

In terms of the criterion of equitable distribution, therefore, it is quite impossible to sustain the argument of the public and private maquila facilitators on both sides of the border that the maquila industry has brought prosperity and economic security to the people of the frontera norte. It is clear that some social strata have indeed benefited, but the balance of costs and benefits between the maquila owners and the vast majority of the workforce has been inequitable both with respect to the conditions of Mexican labor and with respect to labor in the U.S. At best, labor in the maquilas is not worse off than labor in Mexican domestic industry, where the distribution of costs and benefits, like elsewhere, is heavily in favor of the employers, whether private or public or parastatal. Aside from the effects of the much expanded infrastructure in the border cities (which has failed to keep pace with expanding population), the communities of the frontera norte have not derived many benefits from redistribution of state revenues earned by the maquila industry, and it can even be argued that they have paid a disproportionate amount of the costs of the maquila program because of their distinctive vulnerability to the continual peso devaluations which have guaranteed the "success" of the maquila industry, at least since 1982.

The six criteria of the transition from an economic zone to a development zone, the measures of the extent to which dependency reversal is being achieved, give no simple answers. Even in spatially circumscribed zones, like export processing industrial parks, it has proved to be very difficult to answer such questions. Therefore, the complexities that have been revealed in the spatially and functionally expanded maquila "zones" along the Mexican-U.S. border, and in the interior, should come as no surprise. In the next, concluding, chapter the results of this analysis will be evaluated in the context of the reformation of capitalism in Mexico and elsewhere in the Third World.

# Notes

1. "What began in 1982 was not just a short-term financial crisis precipitated by rising international interest rates and falling oil prices, but rather a much more fundamental economic and political crisis" (Cornelius 1986:1).

2. For example, from the U.S., "A star performer—maquiladoras do it again" (*Business Mexico*, February 1986:76–95); "Tijuana Flourishes as Mexico Withers" (*New York Times*, 18 May 1987); and from Mexico, "Las Maquiladoras, Salvación de Tijuana" (*Tabloide*, 16–20 September 1985); "Importancia de Maquiladoras" (*El Mexicano*, 22 October 1987:2A, 3B).

3. Edelberg's (1976) discussion of problems of procurement in the Mexican auto industry in the 1960s is of great relevance to the maquila industry in the 1980s. Bennett (in Rosenthal-Urey 1986) demonstrates that much of the "local content" of the "Mexican" auto industry is controlled by the TNCs.

4. See the report in *CONCAMIN*, the magazine of the *Confederación de Cámaras Industriales*, #657 (16 July 1976:28).

5. The sixth inputs show was held in Juárez in November 1987, with 500 Mexican exhibitors. Other border states, for example Nuevo León, are beginning to put on their own shows.

6. An image attested to by the colloquial phrases used to describe the maquilas, for example, "*plantas golondrinas*" (swallow, i.e. transient, plants); "*empresas que huzen*" (runaway shops); and "*industria sobre ruedos*" (industry on wheels).

7. "General Motors is trying to find more dedicated suppliers in Mexico but is not being too successful" and these are precisely the reasons why (interview with Packard maquila manager in Juárez reported in *TPN*, June 1986:10). Similarly, Irigoyen (1987) argues that Mexico's failure to sell materials to the maquila industry is not due to lack of things to sell or to inefficiency, but to a lack of credit that would permit Mexican firms to operate at their optimum capacity.

8. There are indications that this is beginning to happen. See the reports of a meeting in Querétero organized by a major maquila TNC which resulted in "a reliable supply of Mexican components at competitive quality and prices"; and the Technical Seminar Program brought to the maquilas by a zinc die caster from Mexico City (Arbitman et al. in Lee, ed., 1988:114).

9. This story was relayed to me several times as I traversed the border, suggesting that it is true but perhaps unique. More common are stories of maquila managers who go to the Juárez inputs show, contact potential suppliers, and never hear from them.

10. An enterprising local journalist, Daniel Cavazos, tells the story of one of these local suppliers, a plastics firm, that has built up a $4 million business supplying local maquilas in less than two years (in *Brownsville Herald*, 1 March 1987:1D, 4D).

11. Of the 55 maquilas authorized to sell in Mexico in 1987 (see chapter 3, note 27 above) about two-thirds appeared to be selling intermediate industrial goods.

12. For example, in a successful joint venture where GM "brought in enough money to get the business going. You need to prime the pump" (*TPN* June 1986:10). On the legal differences between maquilas and joint ventures see Davis (1985: part 2).

13. It can be argued that not all linkages are desirable and that some can be very damaging for the local economy. See Grunwald (in Gibson and Corona Rentería 1985); and the discussion (with reference to Ireland) in McAleese and McDonald (1978). This is not yet a problem for the maquila industry.

14. This methodological refinement reduced at a stroke a $1 billion value added total of 1979, claimed at the time, to around $640 million. INEGI (1988: table 1) adjusts all the data to take account of these changes, from 1975. For a critique of the INEGI methodology see González-Arechiga (1987).

15. Though rather less than might have been expected, as is argued in an unusually critical front page article in *El Financiero* stressing the negative effects of continuing peso devaluation on maquila industry revenues (Muñoz Ríos 1987).

16. For example, "Brownsville businessmen believe that at least 50 percent of this money [dollar transfers to banks in Matamoros for maquila wages] is spent in

Brownsville" (*Brownsville Briefing Book* 1987:II:2), $36 million in 1986 (updated to $54 million in 1987).

17. Hamer (in Lee, ed., 1988:53) estimates that 15 percent to 20 percent of "top positions" in foreign-owned maquilas are filled by Mexicans.

18. However, Dr. Valdés of COLEF in Juárez has stated (in Gardner 1987) that she had come across only three cases of former maquila employees setting up their own businesses.

19. The study was done under the auspices of *El Centro de Orientación de la Mujer Obrera* (COMO), an independent organization of women many of whom were maquila workers. Part of the research design involved a three-day conference, in which 450 women took part, to explain the nature of the inquiry (*Centro de Orientación de la Mujer Obrera* 1984:18–20). For a history of COMO, see Staudt in Ruiz and Tiano, eds., (1987: chapter 7).

20. Piore and Sabel (1984:322, note 19) point out that Henry Ford, "observed that assembly-line workers in his plants constantly devised small but significant improvements in tooling." There are many other examples of this in industrial history.

21. For a detailed account of the recommended training procedures in the maquilas of Juárez see Quiñones Ramos (1986).

22. Thus, according to a facilitator quoted in *El Fronterizo*, the maquila industry "continuously offers workers the means to achieve supervisory positions rather than remain in a low-paying, dead-end job" (in *U.S.-Mexico Report*, Nov.2–Dec.4, 1983:10).

23. Anyone who doubts this proposition is invited to look at the promotional materials issued by maquila parks, shelter operators, and industrial development authorities on both sides of the border. The phenomenon is not restricted to the maquila industry or to Mexico. For a penetrating discussion see Adikibi (1983) on the Nigerian tire industry. Adikibi uses the term "technology anchorage" for *genuine* technology transfer.

24. Interviews were carried out in all these maquilas in 1986 and 1987. There are many more that could be cited.

25. 806/807 prohibits fabrication, but many maquilas do it. Some, like Aerotech Matamoros, simply pay the duty involved as it does not come to very much and avoids problems with U.S. customs. For comprehensive analysis of this issue, see Watkins (1987).

26. A larger survey in 1987 found that 16 percent of male and 2 percent of female maquila workers had second jobs (Brannon and Lucker 1988:17). Overtime working is common in most maquilas.

27. These and other events are regularly reported in local maquila publications, and in *Ensamblador*, the national maquila magazine, published by CNIME in Spanish and English.

28. Diario de Juárez (20 April 1988:1–B) reports that substantial numbers of maquila workers are choosing to desert the maquilas and cross the border to earn dollars, many illegally. This, and similar reports, would tend to support the "low wages" theory.

29. This sentiment is well expressed by a maquila worker quoted by Vera (1981:8): "I get no satisfaction from the work itself, the company offers me no stimulation, the satisfaction lies in the women I get to work with."

30. This is both an accurate description and an excellent guide to research on the various fractions of the maquila ruling class. My own work, as chapters 4 to 7 illustrate, is indebted to it.

31. To this extent, therefore, I agree with Sklar's (1976) critique of the comprador phenomenon. As should be clear, I use comprador in the sense of anyone who accepts the ELIFFIT strategy, for which see chapter 1, above.

32. Ugalde (in Ross, ed., 1978:111–112) similarly argued that the Mexican government usually took much more out of the frontera norte than it put in, PRONAF not excluded.

# 10

# The Reformation of Capitalism and the Future of the Maquilas

Development, if it happens at all, happens in particular places at particular times. Most Third World governments have open door policies of one type or another and foreign involvement, whether through investment or aid, is generally seen to be necessary for economic growth to take place. One link between economic growth and development is forged or broken in the struggle between those promoting the interests of transnational capital and those promoting the interests of the host populations. These interests may coincide in the short-term, but in the struggle for global domination they are fundamentally antagonistic in the long-term. The six criteria for the creation of a successful development zone identify the concrete processes involved in turning economic growth into development. In the wider arena of global capitalism, development zones are the places in which claims of the virtues of "production sharing" can be put to the test and, by extension, they can serve as case studies for the distribution of costs and benefits between the rich and the poor and those caught between, promised by the doctrines of the reformation of capitalism. The six criteria on which to evaluate these claims permit a certain degree of measurement and quantitative comparison, but the end result is also based on some fundamental assumptions about the mechanics of development and its relationship to human dignity, in both a moral and a pragmatic sense. Thus, the assertions that linkages, foreign exchange retention, personnel upgrading, genuine technology transfer, good work conditions, and equitable distribution (all suitably hedged to avoid total naivety), will contribute positively to development and to justice and fairness for everyone involved, underlies the whole analysis.

## The Maquila Strategy Reconsidered

Seen in this light, it makes little sense to ask whether the frontera norte or Mexico is better off or worse off as a result of the maquilas. As I have argued, the maquila program was part of a development strategy (ELIFFIT), ambiguous at first, and now more consistent with Mexico's entry into the GATT. The great hopes on which the maquila strategy rests, namely that Mexico could supply substantial quantities of material inputs to the maquila industry, backward linkages, and that it could derive massive virtually free technology spinoffs and genuine technology transfers, have not been realized. The Mexican government has tailored its maquila rhetoric, if not its policies, to these ends. If the central argument of this book is correct, then the Mexican government's hopes are based on a faulty understanding of the ideology and practice of "production sharing." It is possible that the frontera norte and Mexico as a whole would have been better off without the maquilas in the first place, but only if a completely different development strategy had been pursued. My own view is that this is not only possible but probable, and that the structure of the global capitalist system in its contemporary phase of reformation has inhibited Mexico's choices, and the choices of many other Third World countries.[1] However, given the gradual evolution of the ELIFFIT strategy in Mexico over the past 20 years, and the challenge that comprador political and economic elites have successfully mounted against the entrenched forces of political chauvinism and economic nationalism, the maquila program was a natural and logical strategy. What began as a tactic in the mid-1960s to bring some foreign investment to the frontera norte has become in the 1980s a central part of a full-blown strategy for the industrial modernization of Mexico.

It is in this sense that the emphasis on the maquilas in the *Wall Street Journal* "Special Advertising Supplement" (of 23 December 1985) should be understood: "The in-bond industry provides Mexico with jobs, foreign exchange, access to technology, and a motor for industrial growth. As a result, the de la Madrid administration has made maquiladoras the centerpiece of the plan to modernize the Mexican industrial plant and boost nonpetroleum exports."[2] This is exactly what many Mexicans—and not only those on the left—most fear. This fear is summed up in the idea of the "maquilization of Mexico" and the threat that the whole of Mexico is becoming a maquila country. The government is clearly aware of this fear and of the potential for the crystallization of political opposition around issues such as the comprador and colonialist nature of the U.S.-dominated maquila industry. Government ministers and the official union movement have been mobilized to refute the idea that transnational business is converting Mexico into a country of maquilas.[3]

The opposition is not so much concerned with the size of the maquila industry as with its nature and its impact on Mexican economy and society. It is difficult to argue with the fact that new maquilas mean more jobs in Mexico, even if these jobs are not of high quality, and few call for the outright abolition of the maquila industry. Rather, the view current among most Mexican critics mirrors that of the early 1970s, namely that the maquilas are "a necessary evil for an underdeveloped society." The changing material circumstances of the industry since the early 1970s, in particular the explosive growth in maquila jobs in the mid-1980s, meant that the maquila industry became impossible to ignore as it had been in the past, even in the frontera norte. The political debate over the maquilas links up, in a manner that is clearly uncomfortable for the government of the PRI, with two critical issues that have long been smoldering in Mexico. First, the implication of the idea of "un país maquilador" is that as a cheap labor source for U.S. industry, Mexican pride is damaged without sufficient economic recompense, and so the country is suffering a double exploitation.[4] Second, the maquila industry is now frequently being blamed for many of the social ills that afflict the cities of the frontera norte. In both the academic literature (see, for example, Fernández-Kelly 1983) and in newspapers and magazines, the presence of the maquilas and the alien values they are said to imbue are identified as threatening to the social fabric of Mexican life, and particularly the integrity of the Mexican family. Domínguez Qintana (1987), for example, holds the maquila industry—"another kind of Yanqui imperialism"—to be partly responsible for the rise in juvenile delinquency, drug addiction, disintegration of the family, and other social ills in Ciudad Juárez. While it is difficult to find direct evidence of a causal link between the maquilas and these problems, there is a section of the Mexican public that does accept such connections.

The paradox remains that it is quite possible to hold these views, yet also accept that the frontera norte would undoubtedly be greatly worse off in some respects today if the maquilas had bypassed the border cities. This is a common but no less painful paradox of development and underdevelopment. The frontera norte stands at a crucial geographic and strategic crossroads in the path to capitalist reformation. The significance of the development zones that have at best been only partially created along the border, is their permanent promise of future benefits. This persuades the Mexican government to continue and to extend participation in the system of "production sharing" while picking up the crumbs available in the present. Comprador elements do not require such persuasion, and they are in the ascendence. The U.S. economy, though in decline relative to some of the economies of Asia and Europe, is still the single most important economy and purveyor of economic values, in the widest sense, in the world. This gives a peculiar salience to the border and the maquila industry. The reformation of capitalism did not start and will not end in these borderlands, but what is taking place there reveals the likely structure and prospects of relations of dependency, dependent development, and dependency reversal between rich and powerful societies and poor and weak societies.

The maquila strategy, therefore, can be realistically evaluated both in terms of what is presently on offer and what is presently not on offer. There is nothing, in principle, to prevent the Mexican government from unilaterally ending the maquila program by withdrawing the in-bond privileges, or raising the minimum wage to a level that the industry would be unwilling to sustain, or introducing minimum "local content" requirements that most maquilas would be unwilling or unable to satisfy, or restricting maquilas to projects genuinely in the interests of Mexican industrial development. However implausible this all sounds, it is not beyond the bounds of reason to speculate that all these measures could be part of a radical strategy to delink the economy and society of the frontera norte, and ultimately the whole of Mexico, from its dependence on the economy and society of the U.S. There are many who would object to this formula, who would argue that the relationship between Mexico and the U.S. is one of "interdependence" rather than "dependence." Weintraub, for example, in his "Introduction" to a recent volume on the subject, puts this very well: "Conflict is inevitable when two countries are so inter-dependent. This conflict is sharpened because this interdependence is asymmetrical: Mexico depends more on the United States than the reverse" (in Weintraub, ed., 1986:3).[5] The asymmetry is evident in the maquila industry as it is at present organized, not only between the communities and workers of the Mexican borderlands and those of the borderlands of the United States, but also between the needs of transnational capital and the developmental needs of the frontera norte, as I have tried to define them through the six criteria of transition to development zones. Where these needs are not being largely met it is unlikely that the maquila industry is satisfying the developmental needs of Mexico as a whole.

Within a radical, new, perhaps genuinely "interdependent" Mexican development strategy based on a more autonomous approach to external economic relations, the maquila industry might disappear altogether or it might look quite different. It could hardly remain the same. My purpose here, thankfully, is not to work out the details of such an alternative strategy but only to argue that, however unlikely it sounds, there is nothing in principle to prevent a sovereign Mexican government from pursuing it. The major reason why the scenario is unlikely, even fantastic, is that Mexico is thoroughly locked into the ELIFFIT strategy, and because Mexico plays such a central role in the reformation of capitalism as it is being worked out between the countries of the capitalist center and those of the Third World.

This being the case, the question of whether or not the maquila strategy is "a good thing" for the frontera norte and for Mexico as a whole, must be redefined. This redefinition must address the issue of whether the Mexican side of the maquila industry is taking full advantage of the logic and practice of "production sharing." As the analysis of the Border Trade Alliance campaigns showed, this issue has economic, political, and ideological dimensions for both the U.S. and Mexico. In export processing zones all over the Third World, the fear that by striving to increase its benefits the host country will "kill the goose that lays the golden eggs" is constantly being expressed. In Mexico, in 1982, when maquila wages in dollar terms were rising rapidly above those in Asia, this was precisely the word that was spreading along the border. The point here, of course, was not wages as such, but the peso-dollar relationship. Since then, the process of devaluation that was established in 1982 has silenced such talk. Few now argue either way that Mexico can improve its position through the mechanism of wages. Indeed, as I have already noted, the maquila managers claim that the low wages in the industry are due to the policy of the Mexican government in depressing official minimum wages in order to reduce inflationary pressures elsewhere in the economy.

Are we, then, to conclude that the reformation of capitalism provides no space for the maquila industry to develop, or that dependency reversal is impossible along the border? The answer to this must be no, but it is a consequence not of the strengths of the maquila industry or the Mexican state, but of the weaknesses inherent in the countries of the capitalist core. In particular, U.S. capitalism is itself vulnerable to the process of the reformation of capitalism.

## The Future of the Maquilas

Global capitalism is a peculiar system insofar as it has effects that can be analyzed systemically, although its constituent parts are typically trying to destroy, or at least eliminate, one another. Sovereign states in the Third World can choose whether or not they wish to have any part in this apparent anarchy though the cultural (or, to be more accurate, ideological) apparatus of capitalism makes it difficult and some would say impossible for any but the most remote societies to isolate themselves entirely from it. In a multitude of small and big ways, then, global capitalism makes the countries of the Third World offers that they cannot refuse. This is what is happening in Mexico.

What I have labeled the "reformation of capitalism" is a series of processes at work within this global system as it tries to regulate the relations between the countries of the capitalist center and those of the Third World. Underlying this is the well-founded belief that TNCs depend on the continual increase in international trade for their survival as instruments for the accumulation of capital. The Third World is of importance for two main reasons. The globalization of production is increasingly taking place in the countries of the Third World, and this is particularly the case with the rapid spread of "production sharing" and other similar arrangements that have been analyzed under the rubric of the new international division of labor. Second, although there are still large minorities in all First World countries whose basic above-subsistence demands (like automobiles, domestic appliances, and so on) have not yet been met, it is in the Third World where the mass consumer markets of the twenty-first century will have to be found. The TNCs will be seeking to satisfy not only these demands, but the demands for materials, components, capital goods and services that will be necessary to produce the consumer goods.

This, then, is the deeper significance of the adoption of the ELIFFIT strategy by the governments and ruling strata of most of the countries of the Third World. The strategy of export-led industrialization fueled by foreign investment and technology, in brief, comes with considerable cultural and ideological baggage. TNCs, like Third World governments, do have choices, but the choices of each can only be properly comprehended within the realm of necessity. For the TNCs, by definition, transnational enterprise is their very existence, but they do have choices about what and how much, if anything, actually to produce offshore or in the Third World. Third World governments, like all governments, must protect their sovereignty, but they do have choices about how to distribute or redistribute the social product, and how to deal with foreign investment.

In the case of the maquila industry, for both the TNCs and the Mexican government, choice has been turned into necessity, and this is a direct consequence of how the reformation of capitalism works through the ELLIFIT strategy. The TNCs that have followed the maquila strategy, as we have seen, invariably claim that it has been "forced" upon them as a necessary response, often to "unfair" foreign competition from cheap labor producers. Nevertheless, there are those who argue that the "necessity" of offshore relocation in a Mexican maquila or elsewhere is not for survival, but part of the eternal search for higher profits. By the nature of the case, it is difficult to demonstrate a priori that increased investment for enhanced technology would save more U.S. jobs than relocation in a maquila, but it is an option that has been insufficiently explored.[6] Further, there are those who argue that enhanced technology in the U.S. is beginning to spell the end for "production sharing" in the Third World. If this correctly interprets current trends, then the reformation of capitalism will be very short-lived. Grunwald points out that automated equipment is already in use in assembly plants in the Third World, and this is certainly true for some of the maquilas along the U.S.-Mexico border and in the interior. "Nevertheless," Grunwald argues, "it would take an enormous improvement in the economic efficiency of automation to offset the economies derived from the vast, inexpensive, and easily trainable labor pool of the developing world" (Grunwald and Flamm 1985:253). When automation does become economically viable on a massive scale, jobs will be lost in both the First and the Third Worlds, but we cannot write off the capacity of some Third World countries to capture some at least of the high-skill jobs that remain. This is a product specific question and one on which new technology still has surprises in store. Sanderson (1987) argues that these trends could mean the demise of the maquilas, and that the labor intensive aspects of electronic component fabrication and assembly need not last forever. Such ideas are being discussed seriously in Mexico. Sánchez (*El Financiero*, 30 May 1985) asserts that the coming of robots could have a disastrous effect on maquila employment and that many corporations in the U.S., Japan, and elsewhere are rapidly developing robotic processes which could make redundant many of the tasks that maquila workers presently perform. Similarly, José Giral, a prominent Mexican industrialist, has argued that Mexico is becoming "maquilized" at the worst possible time, namely when U.S. industry is becoming increasingly automated (*UnomasUno*, 10 March 1987).

These are, indeed, important considerations, but they are not beyond criticism. First, as Sanderson herself shows, estimates for the time it will take for the automation of most of the electronic processes that are presently performed by hand in the maquilas range from 5 to 15 years (Sanderson 1987: tables 2 and 3), and so many branches of the industry are probably secure until the end of the twentieth century. Second, as everyone acknowledges, the costs of automation are enormous and there are certainly many industrial processes that could be automated that are still done by human hand. Third, the argument that automation will destroy "production sharing" in the Third World because it will dispense with the need for cheap labor ignores the very real probability that new processes and products will come along to replace those whose production has been automated.

It is not only the prospect of automation that threatens the maquila industry, but the prospect that, under certain circumstances, U.S. labor could once again become competitive with labor in countries like Mexico. Some U.S. companies may be having second thoughts about moving production overseas to low-cost locations. Zenith persuaded its workforce in Springfield, Missouri, to accept an 8.1 percent pay cut in 1987 and a pay freeze through 1989. For this, Zenith committed itself to keep the Springfield factory open for at least five years.[7] This is certainly significant, but the question for the maquila industry is, how significant? In 1987 Zenith, with about 22,000 jobs in Mexico and 12,000 jobs in the U.S., brought 200 jobs back to Springfield that had gone to Mexico in 1985. The company also canceled plans for the relocation of 600 more jobs from the U.S. to Mexico. There is no evidence that this is anything more than a small readjustment by the corporation to make the reformation of capitalism work most efficiently for itself.

The Mexican government also has choices. Nevertheless, now that the country owes more than $100 billion to foreign banks,[8] there is considerable pressure on the government to raise as much hard currency as possible in order to service the debt. This makes it important, even for those who are not entirely convinced of the transcendental value of the ELIFFIT strategy as it is expressed for Mexico in the maquila industry, to investigate the possibility that Mexico could make more out of the maquilas than it is presently doing. There is, obviously, a fine balance to be achieved here. There are many other sites in the Third World to which disgruntled maquila owners could relocate without very great inconvenience. It would be a high risk strategy for the Mexican government to call the bluff of the maquilas in any future crisis, but if Mexico can work out how to relate its demands to the actual facts of life of those who run the maquilas, then some gains might be won.

The six criteria for the transition from an economic zone to a development zone suggest some ways in which this might be achieved. The first and most obvious mechanism for increasing Mexico's share of the maquila industry lies in the area of backward linkages. As I argued in chapter 9, the logic of transnational production either encourages, permits, or forbids backward linkages. With the experience derived over decades from local content requirements in those domestic industries in which TNCs are active, principally the auto industry, the Mexican government might target certain backward linkages that transnational production appears to encourage. Repeated claims by some sections of the maquila industry that nothing would please them more than to be able to purchase materials and components in Mexico, and in particular in the frontera norte, should be taken at face value. In order to make such a policy work, more positive incentives must be given to Mexican manufacturers to produce what the maquilas require. Tax breaks, as are on offer at present, are clearly not enough. It should not be beyond the wit of either Mexican planners or maquila managers to agree to a mutually satisfactory formula for mandatory local content if and only if supplies are available at an acceptable price, quality, and delivery. Only when this can be negotiated will sufficient numbers of Mexican producers be persuaded to enter this market. The high level of idle plants in Mexico, and the lucrative maquila inputs market, would suggest that this policy of selective local content is at least worth a try. If it succeeds, then Mexico's share of the benefits will rise, and as long as prices can be kept down, the TNCs might not feel the loss of the 806/807 tariff advantages that would ensue. If it fails, then Mexican planners will gain useful information about how "production sharing" and manufacturing industry in Mexico are working. It may also encourage more joint ventures in the maquila industry.

Although Mexico's "share" of the maquila industry is more than its foreign currency earnings, they are an important part of it. As precise figures are not available, one can do no more than speculate that the decline in the dollar value of the peso, which drags down the value added that Mexico earns from maquila activities, is to some extent compensated by the reduced propensity (or ability) of maquila workers to spend their wages in the U.S. There is always room for a little more tax and utility revenue to be extracted from foreign-owned enterprises, and Mexico has been extremely modest in its demands in these respects. Mexico can ask for more while making sure not to load the straw that breaks the camel's back. Mexico's treatment of the maquila industry has a long way to go before this happens.[9]

One area that no one has seriously investigated is the facilitator's profit. Without access to company accounts it is, of course, impossible to calculate exactly, but many items in a maquila budget are matters of public knowledge and one can make estimates of the rest.[10] In 1988, shelter operators charged their clients between $3.50 and $4.00 per hour per worker on average, while maquila wages were about $1.00 per hour. Labor is normally paid for fifty-two weeks for what is effectively a forty-nine-week year. Factory rent is about $4.00 per square foot per annum in the main border towns. About 35,000 square feet would be sufficient for 200 workers. The shelter operator also pays insurance, utilities, maintenance, and janitorial costs. An estimate of the annual budget of a shelter operator with a labor force of 200 might look like this:[11]

| A. Revenue | |
|---|---:|
| 200 workers x 48 hours x 49 weeks x $3.75 | $1,764,000 |
| | |
| B. Production Costs | |
| Wages (200 x 48 x 52 x $1.00) | $499,200 |
| Rent (35,000 sq.ft. x $4) | 140,000 |
| Utilities | 60,000 |
| Insurance | 10,000 |
| Maintenance | 25,000 |
| Janitorial | 10,000 |
| Professional Services | 15,000 |
| Other Business Expenses | 10,000 |
| Total Production Costs | $769,200 |
| **Operating Income** | **$994,800** |

Technical and administrative staff are budgeted for separately at cost, paid by the client. Allowing generously for head office expenses, I estimate that the facilitator must clear around fifty cents per hour per worker from a 200 employee maquila, about half a million dollars per year. Relative to the wages of the workers who are producing the products, this must seem to be a grossly exploitative relationship, though it is important to remember that these superprofits are only possible because the U.S. and other foreign client firms are prepared to pay the going rate for these operations. The corporations at the end of the line must be making substantial profits too, or else they would not be involved in the maquila industry, but their profits are less visible than those of the facilitators.

The facilitators argue that without them, Mexico would have fewer maquilas, and tens of thousands of maquila workers would be less liable to have industrial employment. This is undoubtedly true to some extent. The real points at issue here are whether a Mexican government agency *could* effectively do the job of the facilitators, and *would* it plow the profits back into Mexican development in some form. The issue of the wage exploitation of the maquila workforce in general is a separate, though related, and certainly just as important question.

The upgrading of personnel is one area in which the maquila industry has registered some progress. In order to capitalize on this the Mexican government could give positive incentives to ex-maquila staff, technicians, and operatives who wished to establish enterprises

[235]

on their own or joint ventures. There would seem to be definite scope for such people in the provision of backward and possibly even forward linkages with the maquila industry. Closely tied in with such possibilities is the genuine transfer of technology. Mexico's law on the control and registration for the transfer of technology and on patents and trademarks specifically includes the maquila industry (see Davis 1985: chapter 8), but the law itself merely sets up a registry for technology that has been introduced into the country. This is extremely unlikely to result in genuine technology transfer, and there is no way that the Mexican government can coerce the TNCs to share their technology if they do not want to do so. The TNCs will only agree to share their technology when it is obsolete, or when by doing so they can be sure of reaping even greater profits. Joint ventures between partners that have maquila industry experience would appear to be the most appropriate way of tackling this problem.

There is no doubt that the Mexican government could raise wages in the maquila industry rather more substantially than they have been doing, through the mechanisms of the minimum wage and the wage zones. Maquila wages have always been above the minimum level, though mostly not by much. Maquila owners have a good deal of slack between the level of dollar wages that have been offered since 1982 and present levels, and wages could increase in the industry somewhat without forcing out any but the most marginal producers. The level of minimum wages has historically been used by the industry as a ceiling rather than a floor, but this has not stopped maquilas in one place paying more than those in another. Were the maquilas to double the wages of their workers unilaterally, this might disrupt the Mexican labor market and bring down the wrath of the government. However, smaller adjustments have been frequently made without these consequences, and the present level of actual average wages could be increased without difficulty.[12] One can also argue, albeit indirectly, that the facilitators' profits are such as to suggest that Mexico could take a bigger share of the industry through wages without endangering its survival. Higher maquila wages might also be popular north of the border insofar as they would lead to more Mexican consumer spending in U.S. border cities.

There is another potential source of benefits opening up for the Mexican government, namely the growing interest that non-U.S. based foreign companies are beginning to show in the maquilas. Apart from the increase in plants and jobs (and possibly new types of products and processes) that this might bring, such maquilas could eventually act as a counterbalance to the overwhelming influence that the large U.S. maquilas presently wield. This could conceivably give Mexico some bargaining advantages. Though they are as yet few, there is certainly some interest being shown by Asian, Canadian, and European companies.[13] The potential for Mexico in backward linkages could be substantial, for these companies might be interested in buying materials and components from Mexico as an alternative to shipping them in from home. However, this is by no means a foregone conclusion, as some East Asian suppliers to Japanese maquilas have followed their customers and established themselves in the maquila industry, particularly in Tijuana, thereby cutting out both Mexican and U.S. suppliers. At present, Mexico offers nothing that would encourage such maquilas to buy what they need locally, and very little to Mexican manufacturers who might supply their needs.

The Mexican authorities, therefore, could decide to try to take more out of the industry by administrative means or by incentives to Mexican manufacturers to encourage linkages, or both. They also have choices in the realm of distribution, either directly through increasing the share of Mexican labor by raising wages, or indirectly by recycling more of the benefits that they do derive from the industry to target groups in Mexico. Here Mexico is undoubtedly caught in a familiar vicious circle where wage inflation and price inflation seem to chase each other endlessly. In 1987, minimum wages were increased four times. Prices rose even more rapidly, and between January 1986 and September 1987, real wages declined from about 76 percent of their 1983 value to about 56 percent (*MN*, September 1987:11). The "Economic Solidarity Pact" introduced in 1988 shows that the government has some room to maneuver, but not much. It would be absurd to argue that the reformation of capitalism has brought Mexico to this point through its encouragement of the ELIFFIT strategy. However, it would be naive to ignore the fact that Mexico's present problems do throw up valuable commercial and logistical opportunities for the TNCs operating along its borders. To the extent that this is true, it is also true that the maquila industry in Mexico and "production sharing" all over the Third World are useful for transnational capital in its attempts to globalize production. But there is no point in being a producer unless there are consumers able and willing to buy what is being produced. It is at this point that the faint glimmer of a key contradiction can be seen in the gloom. The producing classes, of whatever kind, can only become consuming classes on the basis of their income and wealth. The consumption of the wealthy in the Third World is strictly limited by their absolute small numbers, though individual cases often tend to deceive. Those on moderately high incomes in most Third World countries, likewise, are not sufficiently numerous to support the mass production of consumer and producer goods to which the TNCs are geared in their domestic and offshore operations. The popular masses in the Third World have to be turned into mass consumers if the system is to survive in its present form. This means higher wages for Third World workers to give them more purchasing power to buy the products of the TNCs as well as the products of the domestic producers who rely on materials, components, technology, and financial and other services from the TNCs. But higher wages is precisely what the TNCs from the countries of the capitalist center have all the time been trying to avoid by the globalization of production and "production sharing."

This study of the maquila industry along the Mexico-U.S. border might have been expected to suggest a way out of this dilemma. What it has done is to illustrate how the maquila strategy connects with what has been happening to global capitalism in the last few decades. Within Mexico's current development strategy, the maquilas have achieved a measure of success, and on top of that it is certainly possible for Mexico to squeeze a little more out of the maquila industry without destroying it entirely. However, the maquila strategy itself is not the only nor even a sure path to development. The end of the maquila industry as we know it would be extremely painful for the frontera norte and for the border communities of the U.S., but in the long-term unless the Mexican government and the TNCs can work out ways of transforming it into a more potent instrument for the development of Mexico and the advancement of its people, Mexico is better off without it.

## Notes

1. I shall take up these wider questions in a forthcoming study, provisionally entitled *The Reformation of Capitalism*, that compares the developmental effects of transnational capital in China, Egypt, Ireland, and Mexico.

2. The quotation is from Joe Keenan's informative contribution to the supplement, "Phenomenal Growth in Mexican Maquiladora Industry."

3. See "Un País Maquilador" (*La Jornada*, 28 March 1985); "No se pretende convertir a México en país maquilador" (ibid., 27 November 1985) for a government response; and "Apoya la CTM el impulso a maquiladoras en la frontera" (ibid., 8 November 1986) on CTM support for government policy.

4. See "Senala de PSUM la desventaja de las maquiladoras con capital extranjero" (*UnomasUno*, 2 June 1985) and "Debate político sobre el desarrollo" (ibid., 23 July 1987).

5. This is more or less how I have been using the idea of "dependence" throughout this book. As Jávier Alejo says, this is a "peculiar interdependence" (in Weintraub, ed., 1986:245).

6. The Trico example (*see* chapter 6) is a case in point, though, as opponents of the move suggested, the company appeared to take the easy way out of its dilemma. For an innovative proposal on how the U.S. might resolve these problems, namely through more craft-based production and "yeoman democracy", *see* Piore and Sabel (1984), a thesis as stimulating as it is vague.

7. See Harry Bernstein, "U.S. Companies may be Rethinking Their Export of Jobs," *Los Angeles Times* (15 April, 1987). Bernstein mentions that General Electric and Honda are both taking tentative steps along the same path.

8. I am not alone in being very uncomfortable with this formulation. The questions of where this money went and of corruption within the Mexican polity and economy, which should be central to a critique of Mexico's development strategy, are rarely posed. It is worth noting here that the maquila industry is *said* to be almost entirely free from corruption and graft.

9. A report by Wharton Econometric Forecasting Associates of Pennsylvania, dated May 1988, seen after this was written, estimates that Mexican value added will reach $2 billion in 1991.

10. The dispersed nature of the maquilas and the special requirements of many manufacturers make for a wide variation in contracts. For a useful discussion of what facilitators typically offer, see José Luis Barraza (in Lee, ed., 1988:99–102).

11. I am indebted to several maquila operators, particularly Terri Cardot of AIM, Don King of 3D Company, and Bill Wolfe of Translink, Brownsville, and also to Peter Pranis of the Council for South Texas Economic Progress, for help with this "budget." However, what follows are entirely my own estimates.

12. In fact, the opposite is happening. An "Economic Solidarity Pact" has more or less frozen wages, prices, and the exchange rate, and has reduced inflation. It remains to be seen whether the new president, Salinas de Gortari, will be able to hold this line.

13. *El Financiero* printed several interesting pieces on this in 1987. These included articles on firms from Japan (7 January:28); Canada (26 January:42); South Korea (17 February:28); Britain (2 April:32); and Taiwan and Hong Kong (10 April:35). See also an article on the 19 Japanese maquilas on the border in 1987, and the potential for Taiwanese, Korean and European maquilas (in *Christian Science Monitor*, 5 October 1987:1, 5).

# 11

# The Maquila Industry in the 1990s

When the manuscript of the first edition of this book was completed in mid-1988 there were already clear signs that the political economy of Mexico was changing in fundamental ways. In the four years since then, President Salinas and various groups of outward-oriented Mexican capitalists and officials (including those with maquila interests) have brought Mexico to the point at which the U.S. government and corporations talk openly about enshrining these changes in the constitution of Mexico in order to ensure their permanence. The main mechanism through which this is being achieved is the Mexico-U.S. (and Canadian) North American Free Trade Agreement (NAFTA), which I take to be the most important influence on the future of the maquila industry and, indeed, the Mexican economy, in the early 1990s. The head of the Business Roundtable's Mexico Working Group is on record as saying that the organization, composed of the heads of the 200 largest TNCs in the United States: "favors a free trade pact to 'lock into law' the measures taken by Mexican President Salinas to liberalize the Mexican economy."[1] This is clearly the view of both governments.

The maquila industry itself has not changed dramatically since 1988, although the economic, political, and ideological conditions under which it operates are undergoing dramatic changes. This is mainly due to the impacts of the NAFTA process on the maquila industry, not forgetting that the maquila industry itself has also had some impact on the debate and campaign over the NAFTA, an issue I take up elsewhere (see Sklair 1992).

The virtual collapse of Mexican domestic demand during the worst years of the crisis of the 1980s meant that Mexican factory owners were desperate for any type of business, and some took on subcontracts with U.S. corporations under the maquila rules, what the

1989 government decree, the Decreto para el Fomento y Operación de la Industria Maquiladora de Exportación, calls "idle capacity maquilas" (*Diario Oficial*, 22 December 1989: article 3, VIII). The dramatic events in Eastern Europe and the former Soviet Union in the last few years combined with problems in the U.S. economy to deflect the attention of potential maquila investors away from Mexico at the turn of the decade. The second half of 1990 was so bad in some places that talk of a crisis in the maquila industry was heard.[2] INEGI reported that between December 1990 and January 1991 the number of plants declined by 67 (the first such decline for many years) and more than 6,000 employees lost their jobs (though slight reductions in the workforce, mainly around Christmas time, are not unusual). The most recent data confirm that plant and job losses have been recovered since then and, indeed, the number of people employed in maquilas topped half a million (500,664) in May 1992. Table 11.1 documents some changes in the maquila industry since 1988.

The 1989 decree provides encouragement for the maquilas to make the transition from simple product assembly for export to more substantial manufacturing for the domestic market. The tendency of some maquilas to upgrade from assembly to manufacturing has undoubtedly begun to happen in recent years, but it is uncertain whether, under the conditions that NAFTA is likely to create, the maquilas will become more like Mexican domestic industry or Mexican domestic industry will be "maquilized" (Husson 1991).

The main issue for the maquila industry in the 1990s has been the proposal to establish a North American Free Trade Agreement between Mexico and the United States and Canada, to complement the agreement between the U.S. and Canada which came into force in 1989. The fact that the Mexican and U.S. governments and most sections of the dominant classes in Mexico and the maquila industry on

Table 11.1
Changes in the maquila industry, 1988–92.

| YEAR | NUMBER OF PLANTS | NUMBER OF EMPLOYEES | WOMEN AS % OF TOTAL OPERATIVES | TECHNICIANS AND STAFF AS % OF TOTAL WORKFORCE |
|------|--------|-----------|------|------|
| 1988 | 1,279 | 329,413 | 64.2 | 18.9 |
| 1989 | 1,518 | 393,658 | 61.8 | 18.9 |
| 1990 | 1,818 | 441,126 | 60.6 | 19.2 |
| 1991 | 1,819 | 431,694 | 60.6 | 20.0 |
| 1992 | 2,042 | 486,210 | 59.6 | 19.6 |

NOTE: all figures are for January of given year.
SOURCE: INEGI data.

both sides of the border should have committed themselves so whole-heartedly to the NAFTA process is further evidence for the central argument of this book, namely, that the ELIFFIT strategy of development, of which the maquila industry is a key element, will progressively integrate Mexico ever more closely into the global capitalist economy and society. The NAFTA is a logical consequence of the reformation of capitalism. The most prominent landmarks along this road for Mexico are the accession to the GATT in 1986, the liberalization of foreign investment, and the Free Trade Agreement with the U.S. and Canada.[3] The transformation of Mexico from one of the most protectionist and inward-oriented economic regimes into what the major institutions of global capitalism disarmingly call an "open economy" is well under way. As Barkin (1990:1) argues in his challenging critique of this unfolding strategy, "Mexico's economy has been literally turned inside out."

## The Impact of NAFTA

Before getting into the details of how NAFTA is likely to affect the maquila industry (and vice versa), it is important to clarify exactly what is at stake and to explain why, in the words of a big business coalition lobbyist in Washington: "we've never had a trade issue that has been this hot" ("U.S.-Mexico trade pact excites Capitol Hill lobbyists," *Wall Street Journal*, 25 April 1991). For the Mexican government of President Salinas, the NAFTA clearly represented a chance (perhaps the last chance) for the country to establish itself as an economic power. For the more globally oriented fractions of the Mexican capitalist class the NAFTA is a wonderful opportunity to make permanent the gains they have achieved under Salinas. Unlike the comprador class of the dependency theorists, the local wings of what I have labeled the "transnational capitalist class" (TCC) of global system theory[4] act like a class that believes it can fulfill its own economic destiny as part of a global capitalist system that rewards those who can play the system on a global scale. The Mexican wings of the TCC, therefore, are not mere dupes of hegemonic "American capital" but sometimes valued partners and sometimes serious competitors of TNCs, some of which happen to be domiciled in the United States (see Salas-Porras 1992). As Chanona (1991) argues, the NAFTA is perceived in Mexico to offer both partnership and competitive opportunities for Mexican capitalists in North America and elsewhere in the global capitalist sphere of operations—the world![5]

Herminio Blanco, chief Mexican trade negotiator, has said: "the entire industrial geography in North America is going to change" if NAFTA succeeds. The expectation is that high productivity combined with rock-bottom wages will turn Mexico into "a Korea but with an even wider industrial base" (in the words of Kodak Mexicana President Spieler). The *Washington Post* quotes an unnamed administration official: "There is a deep personal commitment [between U.S. and Mexican officials] driving this free trade agreement." And so it is no surprise that Mexico City's business elite are wheeling and dealing to exploit the NAFTA. The bottom line for the corporations is that a successful NAFTA is likely to reach Mexico's "untapped consumers," for, ever since the GATT deal in 1986, the "Mexican middle class has been on a consumer binge for U.S. products, sweeping in imports of Pampers and Miller's beer. Trade pact boosters now claim this demand for the small stuff will spill over into big-ticket purchases of cars, refrigerators, and washing machines" (all cited in Baker 1991). This expresses nicely, if anecdotally, the links between the transnational corporations, the transnational capitalist class, and the culture-ideology of consumerism.

## The Maquilas and NAFTA

The implementation of NAFTA would probably leave the maquilas relatively unaffected in the short term for the simple reason that the operation of the maquila industry under present conditions is more or less functionally equivalent to a free trade agreement for the U.S.-Mexico border region. While a report in *El Financiero Internacional* (7 September 1992:4) bluntly predicts "NAFTA to end Maquila Program," most commentators argue that the maquilas are likely to survive NAFTA.[6] This is also the position of the Mexican government, as expressed, for example, in a SECOFI booklet, "La industria maquiladora de exportación y el Tratado de Libre Comercio," of October 1991.

The main effects of NAFTA would be felt in the rest of Mexico, the nonborder sectors of the economy, where the maquila industry has penetrated to a much lesser extent. As has been shown in the previous chapters, it is the maquila industry's location at or near the U.S. border that constitutes its crucial "comparative advantage." U.S. corporations with maquilas on the border can supply their plants with greater efficiency than is normally the case with interior maquilas, particularly as just-in-time techniques are increasingly introduced. They can also have their U.S. staff commuting across the border on a daily basis, which permits them and their families to continue to live in the United States.

The creeping "maquilization of Mexico" under NAFTA—in which all of Mexico's industry, wherever situated, would benefit from maquila privileges while the restrictions of maquila operations gradually disappear—would probably have little immediate impact on most of the maquila industry. Conditions in the interior would have to improve dramatically for the maquilas to abandon the border en masse. On present evidence, *push factors* (congestion and labor shortages in Mexican border cities) are more likely to force maquilas deeper into Mexico than *pull factors* (cheaper and more plentiful labor), but this has not yet happened to any great extent. By 1992 nonborder maquilas accounted for around 27 percent of plants and employees, compared with about 20 percent in 1988 (see table 7.2 above).[7] Recognizing the primacy of "comparative locational advantage" of the border, we can move to consideration of the likely impacts of NAFTA on the maquila industry in terms of my six criteria of development.

## The Six Criteria Evaluated

1. **Linkages.** Backward linkages are still very meagre in the maquila industry. On average, maquilas purchase only around 2 percent of their total inputs in Mexico, and so the maquila factories make almost no contribution to the growth of local industry, or indeed industry anywhere in Mexico. In order to assess the likely impact of NAFTA, it is useful to recall the argument that the logic of transnational production either *forbids*, *permits*, or *encourages* backward linkages (see pp. 199–202). This is particularly critical as just-in-time inventory control is introduced into the maquilas. The reasons why U.S. maquilas do not buy Mexican components and materials are also often cited by Japanese companies as the reasons why *they* do not buy U.S. components for their plants. Some Japanese maquilas have, in fact, brought their own component suppliers from Asia to Mexico.[8]

While NAFTA will provide Mexican industry with the *incentives* to be more competitive, it is not at all clear to what extent it will *actually have this result*. Without substantial financial and material supports from the Mexican government, augmenting those that are already being introduced, it is difficult to see how Mexican manufacturers could substantially improve their prospects of supplying the maquila industry. In any case, NAFTA might well disqualify some incentives as contrary to "free trade."

One possible scenario is that the Mexican government could introduce domestic content requirements in the maquila industry, or in selected sectors of the industry. This is the strategy that has had some interesting results in autos and auto parts, the latter accounting for about one-quarter of current value added in the whole maquila industry. Well over half of all the auto parts exported from Mexico come, in fact, from the maquilas. While the Mexican auto parts industry is, by most measures, a success story, the most profound consequence of this success has been its almost total "external dependence" (the phrase is from Zapata et al. 1990:77) on U.S., European, and Japanese auto manufacturers in terms of markets and technologies. It is unlikely that domestic content requirements in other maquila sectors (for example, consumer electronics and electrical tools) would have significantly different results. However, it could be argued that the Mexican economy is already so dependent on the health of the U.S. economy that such measures will not make much difference. NAFTA generally legislates for *North American* rather than Mexican local content in any case.

Where backward linkages have been established, the problem for Mexico is that "local" usually means the U.S. side of the border. Particularly in California and Texas, it is U.S. rather than Mexican firms that take advantage of the opportunities opening up for local suppliers. The trade magazines of the maquila industry, for example, *Twin Plant News*, *Border\*Trax*, and *Maquila Magazine* (subsequently retitled *Voice of Free Trade*), are full of advertisements for U.S.-based maquila suppliers trade shows.

All is not entirely gloomy for Mexican suppliers, however. The story of how Honeywell, which has 2,500 maquila workers, is overcoming its sourcing problems is instructive. Production materials decisions are usually taken by U.S. procurement staff, who are reluctant to change vendors because of cultural-language barriers, location problems due to overconcentration of Mexican industry, scarcity of vendors, logistical doubts, quality requirements, and negative past experiences (Díaz 1990). Mexican vendors, Díaz argues, need to become more competitive and communicate more effectively. In 1989 Honeywell created a procurement office in Mexico City which buys plastic-injection parts, metal stamped parts, PCBs, cardboard, solder, cable assemblies, magnet wire, polystyrene packaging, transformers, etc., in Mexico. With other U.S. companies, Honeywell formed a multicompany working group. It remains to be seen how successful these initiatives will be for Honeywell and the extent to which they spread to the rest of the maquila industry. It is important to recognize that such supplies can be bought either in Mexico or in the United States (or a third country), and in the absence of large increases in business one party's gain is the others' loss. To this extent, sourcing is a zero-sum game.[9]

Though neither the frontera norte nor the rest of Mexico appears at this time to be picking up much in the way of backward linkages, the southwest of the United States looks to be in a better position to do so.[10] This is, of course, consistent with the logic of production sharing and is very much connected with the struggle to secure the maquila industry and NAFTA from the attacks of their enemies in the United States. Coalitions of AFL-CIO activists and rustbelt politicians attack the maquilas and NAFTA as destroyers of manufacturing jobs in the United States, and the promoters continue to argue that U.S. jobs are protected precisely because U.S. materials and components are assembled in the maquilas. As I argued above, this defense relies on the inability of Mexico to produce these materials and components, a position that Mexican and U.S. maquila promoters must obscure when presenting their case in Mexico! There is nothing in NAFTA in itself that will give Mexico a decisive advantage in this respect. Nevertheless, its proponents argue that NAFTA will increase economic activity, particularly the manufacturing of the types of goods that the maquilas produce, to such an extent that large numbers of extra suppliers jobs would be created in both countries. This is an extremely optimistic scenario, and present trends suggest that the United States' gain would be Mexico's loss, or vice versa. In a revealing passage, a U.S. government agency states: "In the long run, and assuming that an FTA does not result in the equalization of wages and health, safety, and environmental standards, U.S. firms may accelerate the process of producing more finished machinery and equipment in Mexico" (United States International Trade Commission 1991:xv).

2. **Foreign Currency.** Mexico's foreign currency earnings from the maquila industry derive from two main sources: maquila purchases of Mexican inputs and the dollars exchanged to pay wages and salaries. Mexican to total inputs have hovered around 2 percent for some years, so as the industry expands, the total of dollars earned from backward linkages does too. However, the bonanza in foreign currency earnings that hopeful commentators have predicted from this source has not yet materialized.

What of maquila wages and salaries? The main problem here is the leakage of dollars back to the United States as workers change pesos for dollars to spend in the United States. It is clear from data on border transactions that some Mexicans are spending lots of dollars in the shopping malls of U.S. border cities, but the probability is that, since 1982, there are not many maquila operatives among them. As I reported in chapter 9, various researchers have begun to tackle this problem. Dollars flowing back to the United States from the maquila industry must be mainly from salaried personnel, whose numbers are increasing faster than production workers. *Border\*Trax* (July 1991:25) gives salaries for about one hundred professional positions in the maquilas. For example, the range for Cost Accountant is $25–35,000; Technical Writer, $26–34,000; Systems Analyst, $36–44,000; Industrial Nurse, $31–39,000; Purchasing Manager, $46–58,000; QC Engineer, $29–37,000; and Maintenance Engineer, $28–32,000. Few production workers take home more than U.S. $60 per week (see Carrillo 1991; Sander and Mendoza 1990).[11]

NAFTA is likely to have considerable, if unpredictable, effects on patterns of consumer spending and foreign currency retention in Mexico and thus the welfare of maquila workers. Because of lower overheads, Mexican retailers might benefit from freer entry of U.S. consumer goods, and, ultimately, consumers in Mexico might enjoy lower prices as a result. NAFTA has already encouraged U.S. retailers to expand in Mexico.[12] In a similar fashion, U.S. retailers might benefit from increased imports of cheaper Mexican goods.

The prospect of exporting many more consumer goods to Mexico is an important part of the NAFTA agenda for the U.S. government and the corporations that pushed hard for the extension of "free trade" in North America. The oft-cited market size of six trillion dollars and 360 million consumers (about 85 million of whom are in Mexico) is the prize for which the NAFTA contestants are competing. That this is also the agenda of the Mexican president has been publicly stated. The goal of NAFTA is "to spur enough economic activity south of the border to raise Mexican wages," Salinas explained in a recent conversation. This would increase Mexican workers' purchasing power, providing a larger market for U.S. goods and generating new jobs for U.S. workers (*Washington Post*, 15 April 1991). The 1989 decree suggests that the maquilas themselves might help supply the domestic market.

3. **Upgrading of Personnel.** Maquilas have, of course, great incentives to employ Mexican managers and technicians. In response to shortages of trained personnel, many maquilas have institutionalized contacts with Mexican universities, colleges, and technical institutes. Maquilas and colleges (on both sides of the border) provide facilities for on-the-job training for students in the technical and administrative fields. Of the 43 education centers studied by Carrillo's team (1991:V) over half had maquila-related courses, and many of the teachers were maquila employees. Maquilas continue to recruit Mexican executives from Mexico City, Monterrey, and other industrial centers, and salaries along the border for top positions in the maquilas are said to be among the best in Mexico. *Border\*Trax* (July 1991:25) asserts that "Mex-

ican National Senior Professional salaries have jumped to equal or surpass their equivalent U.S. professional salaried technical and management positions." While Sander and Mendoza (1990) (and the present writer) do not go this far, they agree that the trend is certainly in this direction. Mobility within the maquila, for Mexican staff, has also been on the increase in recent years. In Carrillo's (1991) sample of 358 plants, about 20 percent of the workforce had received technical or professional training within the maquilas; in general, the larger the plant, the greater the likelihood of training. The demand for Mexican professional staff regularly outstrips the supply and salaries appear to have risen as a result.

It is in this area that we might expect substantial indirect impacts of NAFTA on the maquila industry. NAFTA would increasingly "open up" the Mexican economy to global standards and practices, through expanded influence of North American corporations, management schools, retailing, etc., a process that is, of course, well under way. The maquila industry, which has since its inception been a transmission belt for such influences, would undoubtedly continue to be so, and its social power and prestige could be expected to rise as its role as a pioneer for the modernization and globalization of the Mexican economy and society is increasingly appreciated. However, if NAFTA were to lead to an intensification rather than a solution of Mexico's problems, the status of the maquila industry and its leading personnel would suffer.

4. **Technology Transfer.** The likelihood that technology relocation will result in genuine technology transfer is a conceptual as much as an empirical question, and we must consider to whom, exactly, the technology is being transferred.[13] This is a subject on which much has been written but many disagreements remain. In the electronics sector of the maquila industry there is certainly more than simple assembly being carried out. Wilson (1990a) cites several good examples from her research on the maquilas of Guadalajara, and in Ciudad Juárez, SMT de Mexico's publicity material (1990) illustrates surface mount technology with state-of-the-art Fuji equipment, including a GSP-II Screen printer and two CP-III Chip Placers. Grupo Chihuahua, the Mexican corporation that owns SMT, formed the company out of two leading El Paso/Ciudad Juárez facilitators in 1990.

Recent research indicates the complexity of this question, with notable contributions from Brown and Domínguez (1989); Carrillo (1990); González and Ramírez (1989, and 1990: part 3); Mungaray (1990); Shaiken (1990); and Wilson (1990a, 1990b). This research mostly displays measured optimism that Mexican industry in general and the maquilas in particular can take some advantage of the new high-technology opportunities offered by foreign investment, though evidence that this is currently taking place to any significant degree is, to quote Brown and Domínguez (1989:221), "partial and selective." Even Wilson, a strong proponent of the new (high-tech) maquila industry found that only 12 percent of her maquila sample in Guadalajara and 20 percent in Monterrey (both notably high-tech centers) used computer-controlled production machinery to a substantial degree (1990b: table 9.1). The maquila industry is a very fruitful site for research into the *differences* between technology relocation, technology transfer, and the division of labor and organization of production on the shop floor.

NAFTA in itself is unlikely to cause substantial changes in technology transfer to the maquilas, though some of the global forces that lie behind NAFTA—in particular the complex phenomena of the "microelectronic revolution" and "computer integrated manufacturing"—are already highly significant for the future of the maquila industry and, indeed, offshore industries all over the world. I return to this issue below.

5. **Conditions of Work.** There has been a good deal written on the conditions of workers, especially women workers, in the maquilas. Most of the research presents a rather negative picture of the maquilas, but there is agreement that most workers are glad to have the jobs even though the jobs themselves are far from ideal (Pearson 1991). Careful studies based on original research of women in the maquilas in Chihuahua by Reygadas (1992) and in Mexicali by Tiano (n.d.) push this debate significantly forward.

The Flagstaff Institute, contracted by the State of Sonora's public-private development agency in association with the Technical Institute in Hermosillo, carried out research on the question and identified three main findings: maquila workers held remarkably positive feelings about the industry; border workers got more in wages than interior workers, and workers in the same plants received very different benefits; and the human relations function most needs to be improved, especially in the interior (see *Twin Plant News*, March 1990:52, 55–56). Despite the smallness (54 respondents) and skew of the sample (too many supervisors), this is an interesting piece of research.

Four day-to-day conditions of work are particularly relevant in assessing the likely impacts of NAFTA on the maquilas: (i) wages, (ii) job security, (iii) hours worked, and (iv) workplace facilities.

(i) *Wages.* There is no doubt that Mexican maquila workers (and some salaried staff, for that matter) are highly exploited compared with workers (and staff) in comparable U.S. factories. However, this is not necessarily the case if we compare maquila workers with workers in domestically owned Mexican industry, both in the border regions and elsewhere. While the federal minimum wage level in the border areas where most of the maquilas are located is the highest in Mexico, the proportion of workers who earn only or slightly above the minimum wage has traditionally been greater in the maquila industry than in the indigenous sector, though fringe benefits in the maquilas are often considerable (see Carrillo 1991; Tiano n.d.).

Further, the cost of living in some of the main maquila centers tends to be higher than elsewhere in Mexico. While the rate of inflation declined from 160 percent in 1987 to under 30 percent in 1991, there is little evidence that the lot of Mexican workers in general (see La Botz 1992: chapter 1) or the maquila workers in particular (Sánchez 1990b) actually improved in the 1980s.[14] However, labor from even lower-paying Mexican industries has been attracted to the maquilas. For example, workers and technicians engaged in rebuilding Mexican railways are reported to have gone to work in maquilas for better benefits and wages (see *Diario de Juárez*, 22 May 1989).

It is unlikely that NAFTA will have any substantial upward impact on maquila wages in the short term. The maquilas will rely on their labor cost advantages over U.S. and other offshore plants to survive and prosper. Former U.S. secretary of labor Ray Marshall is not alone when he argues that, under NAFTA, real wages in the United States would tend to fall (as they have been doing recently) toward the Mexican level, rather than Mexican wages rise to U.S. levels (in La Botz 1992: introduction).

(ii)  *Job security.* Job security is an issue precisely because the maquiladoras have not shaken off the image of "runaway plants." And, of course, some maquilas did close down in the winter of 1990–1991. However, in the long term maquilas are not any more likely to close than comparable plants in Mexico, the United States, or, indeed, anywhere else. To the recently redundant U.S. auto or apparel or electronics worker, industries would appear to be running away from the United States, not Mexico!

NAFTA may have some consequences for job security insofar as common legislation might eventually be enacted to give workers greater protection from the dislocation effects of trade policies. Gunderson and Hamermesh (in Reynolds et al. 1991) estimate that those workers who lose their jobs due to "free trade" between Canada and the United States will experience a 10–15 percent wage cut in subsequent employment.[15] Women workers and black workers are most likely to be adversely affected. These authors argue that compensation to such workers would disarm the opponents of NAFTA and buy off labor opposition. Making such estimates and proposals for Mexico is a daunting task, but this bullet might have to be bitten one day if, as some suggest, NAFTA destroys the part of Mexican industry that is globally uncompetitive.

(iii)   *Hours of work.* In hours worked per week there are no substantial differences between the maquila industry and Mexican industry as a whole. However, economic conditions in the frontera norte may be forcing maquila workers to work longer hours to support themselves and their families. The distinct advantage of having a maquila job is tempered by the increasing lack of a decent living wage that it offers. It is in *Twin Plant News* (a pro-maquila "booster" magazine), not in some anti-maquila tract, that we read: "the cost of a basket of products and services considered the absolute minimum required to allow a blue-collar worker to subsist is considerably more than the average maquila operator can afford" (Sander and Mendoza 1990:34). Sander and Mendoza do point out that benefits and recent wage increases reduce the *deficit* from three-quarters to half of a tolerable wage. To live properly, then, maquila workers would need to have at least two jobs. It is possible that NAFTA could eventually bring in legislation to harmonize working hours in the three countries, but this is not likely to happen in the near future.

(iv)   *Workplace facilities.* Safety provisions, childcare, subsidized meals, recreation, etc., tend to be a function of plant size and sector rather than ownership. The number of studies documenting health hazards in the industry is growing rapidly. Although some new, revisionist research suggests that women working in the maquilas may not, in fact, suffer more health problems than other groups of women in Mexico (see Guendelman and Jasis n.d.), the damning conclusions of studies like Moure-Eraso et al. 1991 are rather more common. This is a highly controversial issue.

The central focus of recent criticism of the maquilas is on the wider environmental questions. In recognition of this relatively new phenomenon—that is, the *visibility* as well as the actuality of the maquila industry as a hazardous industry—the following section will deal specifically with environmental issues.

6.   **Environment.**[16] Dan Pegg, then president of the Border Trade Alliance, was moved at a meeting in 1989 to reject the "constant attacks" on the maquila industry for encouraging immigration of undocumented workers, taking away U.S. jobs, and causing toxic waste hazards. "None of the above claims is supported by any concrete evidence," he said (as reported in *El Universal*, 4 September 1989:12).

While the issues of encouraging undocumented workers and destroying U.S. jobs may still be contentious, there can be no doubt of the truth of the claim that the maquila industry causes toxic waste hazards. Even the highly cautious EPA/SEDUE Integrated Environmental Border Plan concedes: "the total amount of hazardous wastes produced by maquiladoras is still not known and is believed to be significantly higher than the recorded values" (United States Environmental Protection Agency/Secretaría de Desarrollo Urbano y Ecología 1992:III-20). This is clearly a euphemistic way of saying that no one knows how much toxic waste the maquilas dump illegally, but it is certainly a lot!

Maquilas are not the only source of environmental hazards along the border, but it is the maquila industry that has been targeted for serious and at times ferocious criticisms from the opponents of NAFTA. The tremendous growth of electronics maquilas due to the relocation from California's Silicon Valley and other centers of production, where problems of chemical poisoning and toxic wastes are very well documented (Gassert 1985), suggests that similar problems for maquila workers and their communities are likely. Electronics is not, of course, the only maquila sector which raises health, safety, and environmental problems (see Sánchez 1990a; Perry et al. 1990).

From 1982 until 1992 the administrative responsibility for the environment in Mexico lay with the Secretaría de Desarrollo Urbano y Ecología (Ministry of Ecology and Urban Development, SEDUE), which tended to prioritize housing and urban development over environment and ecology. In 1983, in recognition of growing environmental concerns at the border, the U.S. and Mexican governments signed the La Paz Agreement, designed to control pollution generated by the maquilas, among others (see Mumme and Nalven 1988). Widely seen as ineffective, the La Paz Agreement was overtaken by the NAFTA negotiations and a SEDUE/EPA border environmental plan, whose first draft, issued in August 1991, attracted a torrent of criticism. Responding to the criticism, SEDUE and EPA published an improved version of the plan, which is now the basic framework for binational environmental management along the border (see Rich 1992).

In the meantime, Mexico promulgated a new environmental law (the Ley General de Equilibrio Ecológico y la Protección al Ambiente) which gave a more important role to local and state governments. However, it is doubtful if sufficient resources are available to carry out and enforce all the excellent environmental improvements that the law dictates. In 1992 SEDUE was abolished and some of its functions taken over by a powerful new Ministry of Social Development (SEDESOL), responsible for the key Solidarity Program. It is as yet uncertain whether this will mean increased or reduced priority for environmental issues.

Nevertheless, NAFTA brought environmental issues *in the maquila industry* to the top of the political agenda in the 1990s. The maquila industry has been fully subject to Mexican pollution law only since 1989, and it may be no coincidence that public anxiety about the environmental hazards posed by the industry intensified around this time. Leslie Kochan, of the Oregon Department of Environmental Quality, researched these issues for the AFL-CIO and her 1989 report, a searing indictment of the record of the maquila industry, received widespread publicity. While the motives of the AFL-CIO in publishing the report have been questioned by the maquila industry (the argument is that the labor movement is clearly more interested in protecting U.S. jobs than in protecting the border environment), its substance and its sources appear soundly based. The issue is not whether there is environmental hazard along the border—there clearly is—but how to quantify it, and to what extent the maquila industry is directly and/or indirectly responsible for it.[17] Some of the research cited in Kochan's report is, at best, ambiguous on this latter question and it must be acknowledged that while some, perhaps many, maquilas are serious polluters, many are not, and there are also many other sources of environmental hazard along the border. Maquila supporters become understandably agitated when blamed for all environmental hazards along the border. Nevertheless, many seem unable or unwilling to grasp the connections between uncontrolled maquila growth and the hazards that arise due to the combination of this growth with infrastructural inadequacies (see Sklair 1993). In any case, that the industry is responsible for some types of environmental hazard—for example, water contamination (see Lewis et al. 1991), illegal dumping of toxic wastes (Sánchez 1990a), and inadequate protection of the workforce (Moure-Eraso et al. 1991)—can hardly be denied. In a typical case, residents of the Barreal area in Ciudad Juárez protested that a local maquila working with glass fiber was polluting the atmosphere with carcinogenic materials. Complaints were filed with SEDUE and other agencies, but with no apparent results (see *El Fronterizo*, 7 May 1989).

Several institutions, including the premier Mexican border research center, El Colegio de la Frontera Norte (COLEF), have documented the huge discrepancy between the large amounts of toxic materials entering Mexico for use in the maquilas and the small amounts of toxic wastes returning to the United States, as required by law. Ciudad Juárez maquilas are said to produce many tons of toxic wastes per annum and dump most of them in the Rio Grande. A COLEF survey showed that only 20 out of 772 border maquilas reported returning toxic wastes to the United States, though 87 percent of these maquilas used toxic materials (see Kochan 1989; USEPA/SEDUE 1992: III, 18–22). A common practice, reportedly, is for maquilas to sell old chemical drums to employees who sometimes use them for water storage. The media are beginning to link birth deformities, cancer, and other health risks along the border with maquila toxic wastes.[18]

There is little doubt that some U.S. manufacturers have established maquilas in order to escape strict U.S. environmental regulations, including the expensive toxic waste regulations. For example, furniture manufacturers from Los Angeles have established maquilas in Baja California to escape legislation on solvents emissions (see General Accounting Office report, GAO/NSIAD-91-191 of 1991). In March 1988, when the new General Law on Ecological Equilibrium and Environmental Protection came into force, SEDUE was charged to administer it. However, supporters (Lowery 1990) and opponents (Kochan 1989) of the maquila industry agreed that SEDUE had too few inspectors and lacked the basic equipment to enforce the law along the border, let alone in the rest of Mexico. Despite recent reinforcement of the service, much of the opposition to NAFTA between Mexico and the United States has focused on the widespread belief that Mexico will not be able to enforce its current environmental legislation properly.[19] It is notable that since the law came into effect, maquila spokespersons, particularly in Mexico, have become increasingly conscious of the damage that a bad environmental image could do to the future prospects of the industry.[20]

It is probable that NAFTA might eventually lead to the imposition of higher standards in the environmental realm than can be realized in Mexico. NAFTA is bound to raise many questions about the possibility that its unintended consequence will be to export dangerous and polluting industries to Mexico through an ever-widening open door. It is worth remembering that both Mexico City and Washington, where the laws are made, are a long way from the U.S.-Mexico borderlands, where the environmental hazards of the maquila industry are most likely to be felt. This general argument can, of course, be used by those who wish to tighten up environmental regulations to protect people and the environment as well as by those who wish to relax the regulations to retain polluting industries in the United States or elsewhere (see Leonard 1988).

The final balance sheet on the six criteria of development under NAFTA is, unsurprisingly, far from conclusive. The (usually unspoken) assumption on which most of the pro-NAFTA case has rested is that NAFTA will inevitably bring increased prosperity for all the partners. This can be seen as a rather more general version of the production-sharing premise on which much of the pro-maquila industry argument rested in the 1970s and 1980s. Without NAFTA, the maquila industry is likely to continue much as before, with increasing pressure to locate new plants in the interior or in new sites along the border. With NAFTA, the prospects are that a general "maquilization of Mexico" will lead to the end of the maquilas as we know them although the "border industries" will survive. On March 20, 1992, Jaime Serra Puche inaugurated Mexico City's first maquila industrial park with the statement that the Federal District welcomes maquilas because they are "modern, nonpolluting, and labor intensive" (quoted in *La Jornada*, 21 March 1992). So the implication is not that the maquilas will become more like Mexican industry but that Mexican industry will become more like the best maquilas (see Husson 1991). It is in this sense that the "maquilization of Mexico" becomes a distinct development strategy.

## The "Maquilization of Mexico" and the End of the Maquilas?

The NAFTA as presently conceived by the transnational corporations that dominate it, and perhaps even by some sections of the transnational capitalist class in Mexico, is likely to have the paradoxical consequence of making the maquila industry as such redundant by "maquilizing" much of Mexico, though the precise effects on the frontera norte are not so clear-cut. Here I focus on two interrelated aspects of this: the extent to which Mexico can aspire to be a high-tech competitive producer in the global economy, and the impacts on labor of Mexico's role in a North American (and perhaps eventually a continental American) economy and society within a single free trade area.

## High-Tech Maquilas: Leading Edge or Misleading Edge?

The high-tech trade balance of the United States in 1981 was plus $26.6 billion on exports of $60.3 billion, with every major category of goods in surplus (communications equipment and computers were $7.7 billion in surplus; office machines, $6.8 billion; plastics and synthetic resins, $4.2 billion); by 1986 this had turned into a deficit of $2.6 billion (aircraft and parts, minus $15.1 billion; professional and scientific instruments, minus $2.9 billion; and engines, turbines, and parts, minus $0.8 billion). Only communications equipment and computers, typical maquila products (plus $9.1 billion) were still in substantial surplus (Sewell and Tucker et al. 1988: chapter 1). While the effects of an overvalued dollar on the growing total trade deficits ($39.6 billion in 1981, $170 billion in 1986) cannot be ignored, many argue that the United States is facing fundamental problems in this respect (see Office of Technology Assessment 1990) despite recent reductions in the deficit achieved through increased exports of manufactured goods, notably to Mexico.

The "new technological revolution" based on microelectronics is already beginning to revolutionize production through computer-aided manufacturing and design (CAD/CAM) and numerical control manufacturing technology in many industries. New materials are replacing traditional raw materials (silicon optic fibers for copper in telephone cables, plastics and composites in cars, graphite-epoxy composites in airplanes, ceramics in jet engines).[21] Nevertheless, many argue that: (i) most of this is potential rather than actual and, at best, will take a very long time to come to much; and (ii) its implications for maquila-type industries are not so drastic.

(i) Anderson, writing on the machine tool industry, argues that CAD/CAM is a bit of a myth and speaks of the "wall separating design engineering from manufacturing. The computer systems used by the two departments are usually incompatible and the efforts to design for ease or economy of manufacturing minimal" (in Hicks 1988:63). It is probable that this judgment is valid beyond the machine tool industry. Anderson opines that the control system for the factory of the future is "computer integrated manufacturing" (CIM), though this is still some way off for most practical purposes.

Anderson's argument rests as much on political economy as on technology. While the rate of change might have speeded up recently, in general U.S. investors go for quick profits in preference to large investments and uncertain profits later. Technology tends to advance by small increments because the more you want to invest, the higher up the company you need to go. This is an argument that is often made in debates over U.S. competitiveness, and it is clearly the case that the theoretical or even practical existence of new technology is a necessary but by no means sufficient condition for its use in production. Offshore sourcing in cheap labor zones in general and the maquila industry in particular bear eloquent testimony to the truth of this proposition. NAFTA as proposed will not necessarily alter this.

This connection between technology and political economy is also to be observed in an industry that is central to the maquilas, autos and auto parts. Between 1979 and 1983 at least one-third of the 1.4 million jobs in the U.S. auto parts industry were lost, some entirely and some to maquilas. The supplier firms of the major auto assemblers could be halved as rationalization to a Japanese tiered structure takes its toll. "The Big Three have increased their levels of offshore sourcing of parts, components, and raw materials, a trend that is likely to continue."[22]

There are certainly some examples to suggest that quality and performance now outweigh short-term prices in winning maquila contracts. However, specialists also predict, for example, that wiring harnesses are likely to be replaced by multiplexing in steering columns and doors, so much more simplified wiring will be possible (Flynn and Cole, in Hicks 1988). If this is correct, then many tens of thousands of maquila-type jobs will certainly be lost in Mexico and elsewhere, irrespective of local efforts.

(ii) How has the "new technological revolution" affected the maquila industry in the last few years? Each main maquila center has its own models of state-of-the-art technology where the "revolution" appears to be upgrading rather than destroying the maquila industry (for some examples, see p. 212 above), and this trend does appear to be on the increase. Maquila researchers have reached no consensus on three key questions: How representative are these maquilas? Do they bring genuine technology transfer? How likely is NAFTA to increase or decrease their numbers?

In light of available evidence my own answers are as follows. These cases are, as yet, quite unrepresentative of the maquila industry in Mexico as a whole, but they do illustrate what is possible. As my discussions on technology transfer suggest, a definitive answer to the second question is difficult to find. Much of the research, as I have argued, fails to distinguish clearly enough between technology relocation, technology transfer, and the division of labor on the shop floor. Wilson, an advocate of the view that technology transfer is creating a "new" type of maquila, has done research on 71 maquilas on these questions. She writes: "The maquiladora industry is finding a role in the new competitive strategy of flexible production. Computer-controlled machinery is being used to mold plastic components, wire computer keyboards, insert chips on printed circuit boards, and weld and paint metal. About 20 percent of the maquiladora plants surveyed here . . . [have] just-in-time inventory methods, multiskilling of production workers and job rotation, worker participation in problem diagnosis, machine maintenance and quality control, continuous quality control and error prevention, and statistical process control" (Wilson 1990b: 151).[23] This is a formidable agenda, but in what measure does it demonstrate technology transfer, technology relocation, and the reorganization of the workplace?

Carrillo and his team at COLEF surveyed over 350 maquilas in Tijuana, Ciudad Juárez, and Monterrey (in the electronics, auto parts, and garment sectors). More than three-quarters of the workforce were workers with no qualifications, unskilled labor; between 6 and 10 percent were workers with qualifications; between 7 and 10 percent were technicians and supervisors. In auto parts and electronics, the most high-tech maquila sectors, fully 75 percent and 76.6 percent of the workers were classed as unskilled (in the typically low-tech garment maquilas, 87.2 percent were classed as unskilled). Of the five most important activities of direct labor, assembly work scored highest in all locations (44.7 percent of the labor force in Ciudad Juárez, 49.6 percent and 54.3 percent in Monterrey and Tijuana (Carrillo 1991: 38–44). It is possible that management artificially classes some skilled workers as unskilled to keep their wages low, but I do not think that this can alter the conclusion that a significant transfer of high technology and high-tech jobs has yet to occur.[24]

The third question, how likely is NAFTA to increase or decrease the number of maquilas, suggests that high-tech maquilas might represent a genuine threat to U.S. plants and the jobs of the operatives, technicians, engineers, and managers in them. It is difficult to demonstrate a priori that increased investment for enhanced technology is more economically efficient if it takes place in a U.S.-owned plant in the United States or in Mexico. The more basic question of whether or not it is worth investing in technology to save U.S. jobs, rather than relocating for cheap maquila labor, has been insufficiently explored.[25]

The argument that enhanced technology in the United States and elsewhere is already beginning to spell the end for production sharing in general and the maquila industry in particular has been labeled the "reverse comparative advantage" thesis, namely, that the new technologies could mean the demise of the maquilas, and that the labor-intensive aspects of electronic component fabrication and assembly need not last forever. As I argued in chapter 10, estimates for the time it will take for the automation of most of the electronic processes that are presently performed by hand in the maquilas range from 5 to 15 years, and thus many branches of the industry are probably secure until well into the next century. Further, the costs of automation are enormous and there are certainly many industrial processes that could be automated that are still done by human hand. Turning the conventional argument on its head, Rafael Maynez, a manufacturing engineer in a Ciudad Juárez maquila, declares that "Mexico's cheap labor makes automation a very poor investment" and that *mechanization*, whose "goal is to eliminate the need for operator skill in the production process" will ensure prosperity for the maquilas (Maynez 1991). And finally, the view that automation will destroy production sharing in the Third World because it will dispense with the need for cheap labor ignores the probability that new processes and products will come along to replace those whose production has been automated.

[258]

Nevertheless, there are reported job losses in Mexico due to the fact that these new technologies are generally capital rather than labor intensive. For example, robotization at the much publicized Ford plant in Hermosillo is said to have been responsible for a 60 percent reduction in employment.[26] And this is where the technical debate about technology and the maquila industry becomes a political economy argument and a concrete struggle about what happens to labor in Mexico and the United States under the changes likely to be brought about by NAFTA.

## Labor, the Maquila Industry, and NAFTA

The experience of the maquila industry in the 1980s turned the question of labor supply upside down. Turnover rates have been so high that some began to wonder why the industry had such difficulty in retaining its labor force. The turnover rate varies from maquila to maquila, from time to time, and from location to location. "Poaching" of labor has been common, and in Ciudad Juárez recruiting agents for some maquilas are to be seen at the gates of others. This is one reason why some new maquilas are reluctant to locate in maquila parks.

NAFTA raises the prospect that by leveling the playing field U.S. labor could once again become competitive with labor in countries like Mexico, particularly if there really did turn out to be a genuine labor shortage in the maquila industry (a view I dispute in pp. 156–80, above). In the economic conditions of the late 1980s, some U.S. companies appeared to be having second thoughts about moving production out of the country to low-cost locations. Zenith, for example, persuaded its workforce in Springfield, Missouri, to accept an 8.1 percent pay cut in 1987 and a pay freeze through 1989. In exchange, Zenith committed itself to keep jobs in the United States. General Electric and Honda (U.S.) and others were reported to be taking tentative steps along the same path. However, in October 1991 Zenith announced the end of TV production in the United States and its transfer to Mexico in 1992.[27]

There is also evidence to suggest that maquila management is increasing pressure on maquila workers. We might speculate that there is a hidden agenda behind this pressure, namely, to reinforce the conditions under which Mexico's "cheap labor comparative advantage" can be best exploited under NAFTA when, according to most analysts, "cheap labor" will be Mexico's main contribution to the North American partnership. For example, in 1989, during a local maquila dispute, fifteen U.S. plants threatened to pull out of Reynosa. In a manner reminiscent of the 1970s (see 56ff. above) these maquilas also said they would let 800 U.S. companies planning to invest in Mexico know all about it (*El Universal*, 5 August 1989). As in previous decades, the 1990s have seen struggles between labor and management, and between official and unofficial union factions.[28]

Maquila and other workers inside and outside the official labor unions have been organizing to protect their interests should NAFTA happen, and there is growing evidence to suggest that the urgency of the Mexican government to conclude NAFTA has been translated into pressure on the labor force. Agapito González, the veteran maquila leader in Matamoros (see pp. 121–22, above) was arrested at the end of January 1992 during a dispute over maquila wages. Edward Cody, a *Washington Post* reporter, explained that Salinas had heard complaints about González during a meeting with a business group. A "senior government official, speaking with reporters on condition he not be named, said the government has proof that González was not paying taxes on his landholdings in Matamoros. But he acceded to suggestions that the arrest also was tied to efforts to improve the business climate in Mexico" (in "Mexican ruler tightens reign on labor: Prominent union leader arrested in midst of contract negotiations," *Washington Post*, 28 February 1992). There is little doubt that serious labor disputes and labor victories over wages and conditions in the maquilas could have thrown a wrecking spanner in the NAFTA works (see Nauman 1992).

While in no way comparable to the level of transnational organization of the maquila owners and managers, the workers are also beginning to organize across borders (see Fox 1992; Gutiérrez-Haces 1992; Sklair 1992). A Trinational Workers' Network on NAFTA was established in Detroit in April 1991 to mobilize the labor movement (reported in *Correspondencia* [San Antonio], Fall 1991:22; see also Red 1991). The opponents of NAFTA (particularly those in the labor movement) have called for the introduction of progressive social policies for the workplace to be written into NAFTA, and in the unlikely event of anything like this happening the maquilas would have to undertake expensive upgrades to higher standards. Mexico's "cheap labor" attraction would, under such circumstances, quickly evaporate and some maquila-type jobs would go elsewhere.

NAFTA as presently conceived will not go along this path. However, if pressure to build trade sanctions into NAFTA to secure better working conditions for Mexican labor does eventually succeed—a rather large *if*, in my view—then the maquila industry, along with the rest of Mexican industry, might well find its costs of production rising. While this would not adversely affect the border locational advantage of the maquilas, it would adversely affect their cheap labor advantage for most producers. Mexico would become less attractive to the more labor-intensive assembly enterprises, and the maquila industry would suffer. As has been argued above, some technical upgrading of the industry, insofar as it is based on relatively cheap labor, would not significantly alter this conclusion.

The contradiction for global capitalism, well illustrated in the Mexican case, is that if the TNCs expect to sell large quantities of their consumer goods in countries like Mexico, then there have to be mass markets of prosperous workers to buy them. For this to be possible, the workers need to be paid relatively high wages and be encouraged to spend their wages on these goods. The encouragement certainly exists through what I label the "culture-ideology of consumerism" (Sklair 1991a), but the high wages do not, for the most part. NAFTA, with its assumption and heartfelt hope that all-around prosperity will inevitably follow the creation of a North American "free market," is just one regional attempt to resolve this global contradiction. In Mexico, as in many other industrializing countries, much of the new foreign investment is "geared only toward the highest income bracket, while wage figures from the National Statistics Institute indicate the majority of Mexicans are steadily losing purchasing power" ("Mexican economy picks up, and so does foreign investment," *Associated Press*, 30 March 1992). And, ominously, Mexico's foreign debt, after a brief reduction, is rising back to $100 billion.

What difference will NAFTA make to the capacity of the United States to retain jobs and the capacity of Mexico to create jobs? As I have argued throughout, NAFTA *in itself* will be less important than other more general factors, notably the health of the U.S. and global economies and the technological development of modern industries.[29] For example, if wire harness assemblies could be economically automated, tens of thousands of maquila jobs would be wiped out. However, it would not be correct to deduce from this either that NAFTA is irrelevant or that the maquila industry is doomed.

In the words of one Mexican commentator, "offshore assembly plants will likely be a permanent and growing characteristic of the world economy."[30] The weight of evidence suggests that NAFTA will do little to change this in the foreseeable future. This leads to the conclusion that while the *general* pattern of U.S.-Mexican economic relations will continue much as before, we still need to keep an open mind on the outcomes for specific products inside and outside the maquila industry. Less than one year after the U.S.-Canada FTA began, it is reported that both countries had around 2,000 requests from firms and organizations to reduce tariffs more quickly (Crookell 1990: chapter 6). The number of firms and organizations requesting that tariffs be retained or raised is not reported. There is clearly a great deal of hard negotiating to be done, pressure to be withstood, deals to be made, before all sections of Mexican and U.S. opinion go willingly into NAFTA. There are also pressures to extend NAFTA to include environmental, labor and health, and safety standards, all of which would impact the maquila industry.

The view that a fully implemented NAFTA will eventually bring the demise of the maquila industry by "maquilizing" the whole of Mexico ignores the crucial comparative advantage of the border location for U.S. corporations (and foreign corporations in the United States). If wages were to rise precipitously along the border relative to wages in the interior, or if the infrastructural and congestion problems in the border cities became intolerable, then it is possible that foreign investors might flock in greater numbers to the interior. But then they might also be tempted to other low-wage areas like the Caribbean, other parts of Latin America, or, of course, Asia.[31] The maquila industry promoters have successfully sold the advantages of the border over "a slow boat to China" and a high-wage United States for many years. For example, stories like that of AT&T relocating its mobile phone repair facilities from Singapore to Mexico, saving four months in turnaround time (*Washington Post*, 17 May 1992), and those relating the repatriation of apparel and similar subcontracting to Mexico and the United States from Asia (*Business Week*, 1 July 1992) are beginning to be commonplace.

However, competition from Asia and elsewhere is not all that threatens Mexico and the maquila industry. If, as Weintraub argues, U.S. protectionism is going to increase rather than decrease, then NAFTA is politic for Canada and Mexico. The Mexican *apertura* (open door policy) signifies a profound change of which the GATT decision and NAFTA negotiations are expressions: "a half century of internal development as the only engine of growth is being jettisoned." On this analysis, Mexico has little alternative but to make the best out of any NAFTA that it can negotiate.[32]

The gamble of technological upgrading in the United States, for lower production costs, bigger profits, retention of higher-value domestic jobs, or all three, hinges on the willingness of U.S. corporations to transfer their technology. Views on this differ dramatically. On the one hand: "large multinational corporations, which are based in the developed countries, have two strong incentives for restricting developing countries' access to new technologies [short life cycle of new technologies and the increasing costs of research and development]" (María y Campos, in Reynolds et al. 1991:208); and on the other: "it is in the fundamental *economic* interest of the United States and its leading industrial sectors to promote a process of technological development in the Third World that fosters growing demand for micro-electronics innovations" (Castells and Tyson 1988:90–91). These views appear to be incompatible, but then advanced capitalism faces many global contradictions.[33]

The great unanswered question is whether NAFTA will further open up the whole of North America to the global economic system or whether it will lead to a Fortress North America. The future of the maquila industry and the likely impact of NAFTA on its contribution to Mexico's economic development depend rather more on the answers to these larger questions than on any specific deals that Mexican and U.S. (and Canadian) NAFTA negotiators might or might not carve out.

## Notes

1. The quotation is from "U.S., Canada, Mexico begin free-trade talks," *Washington Post* (13 June 1991). NAFTA was concluded by the representatives of the United States, Mexico, and Canada in August and signed by the three leaders in December 1992. At the time of this writing the details and possibly the entire status of the agreement are yet to be finalized by the legislatures of the respective countries. The victory of Bill Clinton in the U.S. presidential election in 1992 might force some changes in the NAFTA, but the pressure for North (and, perhaps, eventually Continental) American economic integration is inexorable. For a summary of the legislative processes for NAFTA in the three countries, see *Business Mexico*, July 1991, pp. 142–45.

2. See "Maquiladora growth rate drops sharply," *San Diego Tribune* (11 October 1990). Some of the most prominent maquila facilitator firms—for example, Howard Boysen's IMEC (see pp. 90–91 above)—did not survive this downturn.

3. The negotiations over NAFTA have generated a large number of publications, for example, Driscoll de Alvarado and Gambrill 1992; Rey Romay 1992; Reynolds et al. 1991; Hufbauer and Schott 1992; and the listings in United States International Trade Commission 1991: appendix D. See also the special issue of *Revista Mexicana de Sociología* (July–September 1991), "El Tratado de Libre Comercio y la Frontera Norte."

4. For a full exposition of "global system theory" and the roles of the transnational corporations, transnational capitalist classes, and culture-ideology of consumerism, see Sklair 1991a.

5. On the Mexican opposition to NAFTA, see Red 1991; *Trabajo* 1991. While one researcher argues that NAFTA: "has generated the most heated debate between the specialists, political and union representatives and public opinion itself" in Mexico (Jordy Micheli, in *Trabajo* 1991:1), another argues: "In Mexico there has hardly been a national debate" (Fox 1992:8). For the anti-NAFTA campaign in the United States, see Thorup 1991; Sklair 1992.

6. For example, Székely and Vera (1991). The *El Financiero Internacional* report quoted a maquila industry spokesman who was referring to the NAFTA item that "programs [of duty exemptions or refunds] will be eliminated by January 1, 2001." Technically this does mean the end of the maquila program, but the *actual* consequence is that most of Mexican industry will be able to operate under "maquila" conditions.

7. This is an issue that has been simmering in the maquila community for many years (see chapter 5 above). For example, *El Universal de Cd. Juárez* (25 November 1988) reported that Ciudad Juárez had frozen a request for 12 new maquilas outside industrial parks. Such maquilas, often in residential areas, are frequently said to cause traffic,

pollution, and other problems. In Ciudad Juárez in October 1991, a SEDUE spokesperson "clearly stated that new border growth will be restricted and that off-border growth will be encouraged" (*Maquiladora Newsletter*, October–November 1991:2). I take up the issue of border infrastructure in Sklair 1993.

8. Tax-break and subsidized borrowing schemes have been introduced to stimulate local production of inputs for the maquila market. U.S. and Mexican Customs data indicate their value at billions of dollars annually. It should be noted that since the first edition of this book was published, items 806/807 of the U.S. Tariff Code have been renumbered as 9802.00.60 and 9802.00.80, and the Code has been modified.

9. The ongoing problems of "rules of origin" are relevant here as the NAFTA negotiators and their critics have been quick to point out. For a legalistic account, see Hufbauer and Schott (1992: chapter 8), and for a well-illustrated journalistic account, "Is it American? Here's an easy way to tell," *Business Week* (16 March 1992). This arcane issue has formidable material consequences—Honda of Canada received a bill from the U.S. government for U.S. $17 million back duties on 19,000 Civics exported from Canada to the United States when a rules-of-origin judgment went against them.

10. For example, the Exhibitors' List for the Sixth Annual Borderlands Tradeshow in 1992, the largest maquila suppliers event, had only *three* identifiable Mexican companies out of 250 exhibitors (*Twin Plant News*, February 1992:65–66), though the *Twin Plant News 1992 Sourcebook* does list many more potential Mexican suppliers. See also *Business Week* (12 November 1990), "Is free trade with Mexico good or bad for the U.S.?"; and "How Virginia lost jobs to Texas, Mexico," *Washington Post* (5 May 1991). It is worth noting that maquilas in the interior tend to purchase more Mexican inputs than those on the border (see Carrillo 1991; Wilson 1990b).

11. Very rough calculations from INEGI data for May 1992 indicate that *average* weekly wages are about U.S. $52 for maquila operatives, $140 for technicians, and $215 for staff. The minimum wage for maquila workers in Ciudad Juárez in November 1991 was 64 cents per hour, about U.S. $31 for a 48-hour week.

12. J.C. Penney, for example, is to invest $100 million in five new stores in Mexico (*Twin Plant News*, September 1992:8).

13. For a very clear discussion of the various types of technology transfer between institutions with measurably different levels of technology (specifically high-tech TNCs and their lower-tech foreign partners), see United Nations 1987.

14. The National Maquila Council has argued that 20,000 new houses need to be built on the border just to accommodate new maquila workers, commenting: "The reason for immigration of Mexican border workers to the U.S. is not the lack of employment but the lack of housing, water, electricity, and transportation services" (*El Día*, 22 July 1989). The "tent city" occupied by maquila workers in downtown Ciudad Juárez in the summer of 1988 and frequent mass media images of the shacks in which many of them live bear witness to this.

15. For a good discussion of the implications of the U.S.-Canada FTA, see Campbell 1991. Jeff Faux, of the Economic Policy Institute, points out that the United States International Trade Commission in February 1991 estimated that 73 percent of U.S. workers would experience income declines under NAFTA, though it promptly withdrew this figure (see "Are we ready for a U.S.-Mexico trade revolution? No," *Washington Post*, 14 April 1991). United States International Trade Commission Publication 2326 (October 1990) records the widespread view that NAFTA would hurt U.S. workers, particularly the less skilled. It is significant that in September 1992 the U.S. labor secretary was the first administration official to estimate potential NAFTA job losses in the United States ("Trade pact's job toll put at 150,000," *San Diego Union Tribune*, 11 September 1992).

16. In the original formulation of the six criteria, *distribution* was the final one. I have replaced this with *environment* for two reasons. First, environmental problems have become for many critics the central issue of the maquilas since the late 1980s and now demand discussion in their own right. Second, I now see *distribution* more clearly in the context of the class struggle as the framework within which these criteria need to be discussed, rather than one of the criteria as such.

17. For a good discussion of the main issues, see Sánchez 1990a, 1990b; Texas Center for Policy Studies 1990. Evidence is accumulating that these problems are on the

increase along the border, for example, in the excellent video about the nonmaquila Stepan Chemical plant in Matamoros (Day 1992). In June 1992 EPA established an Annual Border Environmental Assembly to counteract criticisms. I give a more detailed analysis of environmental hazard and the maquilas in Sklair 1993.

18. See, for example, "Disfigured children, distressed parents; suit filed against U.S. firm over alleged effects of pollution in Mexican border region," *Washington Post* (15 October 1991), on the "Mallory children," deformed due to toxics from a now-closed maquila; and the four-part series "The Free-Trade Dilemma: the environmental costs of a U.S.-Mexico pact," in *Los Angeles Times* (17–20 November 1991). Moure-Eraso et al. 1991 is a particularly vivid account of maquila-induced hazard in Tamaulipas/South Texas.

19. On SEDUE see Mumme 1992 and the GAO report "Assessment of Mexico's Environmental Controls for New Companies" (August 1992). Hearings on the SEDUE/ EPA Draft Border Environmental Plan held in nine U.S. border cities in 1991 attracted over 150 groups and individuals (see Kelly 1991; Rich 1992).

20. Alejandro Bustamante, president of the National Maquila Council, called on the government to regulate maquilas, "so that they will no longer cause pollution problems for the surrounding population. There have already been numerous complaints about this" (reported in *UnomasUno*, 11 March 1989). See also regular environment features in *Border*Trax, Maquila: Voice of Free Trade*, and *Twin Plant News*, and coverage in *U.S.-Mexico Free Trade Reporter* and *NAFTA Monitor*. I consider this issue in more detail in Sklair 1993.

21. See Sewell, "The Dual Challenge: Managing the Economic Crisis and Technological Change," in Sewell and Tucker et al. 1988. Sewell also includes bioengineering (genetically engineered vaccines, and new food production techniques). There is certainly potential for the maquilas in some of these new industries.

22. M. Flynn and D. Cole, "U.S. Auto Industry: Technology and Competitiveness," in Hicks 1988:113. Shaiken (1990) and Zapata et al. (1990) are also very instructive on this topic.

23. For a rather different point of view, see "Mexico's Silicon Valley: A Myth," *El Financiero Internacional* (13 April 1992:9). Wilson distinguishes assembly, manufacturing, and flexible production maquilas and argues in terms of the "Fordist/post-Fordist" debate. She concludes that maquila flexible producers are a "caricature of post-Fordism" (1990a:51). In my view, maquilas tend to mix these three types of production, and, therefore, the Fordist/post-Fordist analysis confuses rather than illuminates maquila-type strategies.

24. I am very grateful to Jorge Carrillo for an early copy of this report though he is, of course, in no way responsible for my interpretation of the data. In general, Mexican researchers are rather more optimistic about technology transfer in the maquilas than they used to be.

25. On the "cheap labor over technology" decision by Trico Products Corporation to relocate from Buffalo, New York, to a maquila in Matamoros, see pp. 122–27 above. Schoepfle 1991 is an excellent account of the impact of the maquilas on U.S. labor.

26. See M. de María y Campos, in Reynolds et al. 1991. In the Shenzhen Special Economic Zone (China's "maquila industry"), the automation of Sanyo electronics plants led to more rather than fewer jobs, at least in the short term (Sklair 1991b:204).

27. See "U.S. companies may be rethinking their export of jobs," *Los Angeles Times* (15 April 1987); and "TV-Maker Zenith will move assembly operations to Mexico," *Washington Post* (30 October 1991). For an interesting discussion of the same points in the apparel industry, see "U.S. garment makers come home," *New York Times* (10 August 1991:D1, 7), a rather misleading title as will be discovered if the piece is read carefully.

28. For an indictment of the official labor movement, see La Botz 1992, and compare the article by Arturo Romo (education secretary of the CTM), "Brothers, not enemies of American workers," *Washington Post* (19 May 1991), extolling the virtues of labor-government cooperation in Mexico, conditions in the maquilas, and CTM support for NAFTA. Williams 1991 is a useful guide to recent labor organization in the maquilas.

29. As Gruben shows, this is a truly global process. He argues that maquila workers "compete with workers in Asia just as much as they compete with U.S. workers" (1990:27). For further analysis of these issues, see Sklair 1991a.

30. S. Trejo Reyes, "Labor Market Interdependence between Mexico and U.S.," in Reynolds et al. 1991:248. While I certainly agree with this view, there are many who do not.

31. The president of the National Maquila Council made this point in a campaign to streamline maquila administration. Competition for Mexico's maquilas, he said, now comes from Guatemala, Haiti, and the Dominican Republic (reported in *Summa*, 22 July 1989). For a convincing analysis of the Caribbean challenge, see Schoepfle and Pérez-López 1990.

32. The quote is from Weintraub, "Trade Policy in North America: Where Do We Go from Here?" in Reynolds et al. 1991:271. Weintraub, a long-time advocate of "free trade" with Mexico, argues plausibly that Mexico does not want to be left out of a NAFTA but is very nervous about going in. For a detailed discussion of the Mexican position, see Chanona 1991.

33. And this is precisely the issue I take up in my *Sociology of the Global System* (Sklair 1991a).

# Bibliography

Adikibi, O. (1983). "The Transfer of Technology to Nigeria: the Case of Tyre Production." Chapter 2 in C. Kirkpatrick and F. Nixson, eds., *The Industrialisation of Less Developed Countries*. Manchester: Manchester University Press.

Alderete Muñoz, Manuel (1983, 1985). *Imagen de la industria maquiladora*. Chihuahua: Desarrollo Económico del Estado de Chihuahua, two editions, mimeo.

Amozurrutia C., Jesús (1987). "Industria maquiladora Mexicana y generación de empleo." Nuevo León: Universidad Autónoma de Nuevo León, Facultad Económia, thesis.

Andonaegui, Miguel Angel (1985, December 10). "La cultura que genera la industria maquiladora." *ABC*.

Anker, R. and C. Hein, eds. (1986). *Sex Inequalities in Urban Unemployment in the Third World*. London: Macmillan.

Baerreson, Donald (1971). *The Border Industrialization Program of Mexico*. Lexington: Heath.

Baird, Peter and Ed McCaughan (1975, July–August). "Hit and Run: U.S. Runaway Shops on the Mexican Border." *North American Congress on Latin America [NACLA] Report*.

—— (1979). *Beyond the Border*. New York: NACLA.

Bassols Batalla, Angel (1972). *El noreste de México, un estudio geográfico-económico*. México D.F.: Universidad Autónoma de México.

Bath, C. Richard (1982, August). "Health and Environmental Problems: The Role of the Border in El Paso-Ciudad Juárez Coordination." *Journal of Inter-American Studies and World Affairs*, 24, 375–392.

Beebe, Michael (1987, March 8–12). "Mexico: the Border Industry." *Buffalo News*.

Bermúdez, Antonio J. (1968). *Recovering our Frontier Market. A Task in the Service of Mexico*. México D.F. [Translation by Edward Fowlkes of *El Rescate del Mercado Fronterizo*. Mexico City: Eufesa, 1966].

Birkhead, Frank (1984, August 24). "Remarks for Form-O-Uth, Inc.'s 50th Anniversary Celebration." McAllen, Texas: McAllen Industrial Board, mimeo.

Blanco Mejia, J. (1983, November). "La maquila no puede ser base del desarollo industrial." *Economía informa*, 110, 13–16.

Bluestone, Barry and Bennett Harrison (1982). *The Deindustrialization of America*. New York: Basic Books.

Boggs, S. Whittemore (1940). *International Boundaries*. New York: Columbia University Press.

Bojórquez, Felizardo (1987, January 2). "Discriminatoría política económica del gobierno." *El heraldo*, A–6.

Border Trade Alliance (1987). "Maquiladora Impact Survey: Findings and Conclusions." El Paso: Department of Marketing, University of Texas, and Foreign Trade Association, mimeo.

Brannon, Jeff and William Lucker (1988). "The Impact of the Mexican Economic Crisis on the Demographic Characteristics of Maquiladora Labor Supply." El Paso, University of Texas, mimeo.

Briggs, Vernon (1973). "The Mexico-United States Border: An Assessment of the Policies of the United States upon the Economic Welfare of the Chicano Population."

Austin: University of Texas, Institute of Latin American Studies, Conference on Economic Relations between Mexico and the United States, mimeo.

—— (1984). *Immigration Policy and the American Labor Force*. Baltimore and London: The Johns Hopkins University Press.

*Brownsville Briefing Book/Border Trade Alliance* (1987). Brownsville, Texas: Chamber of Commerce, mimeo.

Bryan, González Vargas, González Baz, Delgado y Rogers (1984). "The Mexican In-Bond Industrial Program." Ciudad Juárez: Bryan, et al., mimeo.

Bustamante, Jorge (1975). "El programa fronterizo de maquiladoras: observaciones para una evaluación." *Foro internacional*, 16:2, 183–204.

Bustamante, Jorge and G. Martínez (1979, Fall). "Undocumented Immigration from Mexico: Beyond Borders but Within Systems." *Journal of International Affairs*, 33, 265–284.

Cárdenas, Gilbert (1979, November–December). "Mexican Illegal Aliens in the San Antonio Labor Market," *Texas Business Review*, 187–191.

Carrillo, Jorge (1985). *Conflictos laborales en la industria maquiladora*. Tijuana: CEFNOMEX.

Carrillo, Jorge and Alberto Hernández (1985). *Mujeres fronterizas en la industria maquiladora*. Mexico City: SEP/CEFNOMEX.

Carrillo, Jorge and Monica Jasis (1983, June). "La salud y la mujer obrera en las plantas maquiladoras. El caso de Tijuana." *Enfermería Hoy*, 4, 20–33.

Castellanos, Alicia (1981). *Ciudad Juárez: La vida fronteriza*. México D.F.: Editorial Nuestro Tiempo.

*Centro de Orientación de la Mujer Obrera* (1984). "Primer taller de análisis sobre aprendizaje en la produción y transferencia de technología en la industria de maquila de exportación." Ciudad Juárez: CEFNOMEX, mimeo.

City of El Paso (1971). "Community Renewal Program, Economic Studies." El Paso: Urban Research Group, mimeo.

Cleary, Amity (1981). "A Comparative Analysis of Occupational Health and Safety Issues in the Electronics Industry: Silicon Valley, California, Ciudad Juárez, Mexico." Santa Cruz, University of California, Senior thesis.

Clement, Norris and Louis Green (1978, Winter). "The Political Economy of Devaluation in Mexico". *Inter-American Economic Affairs*, 32, 47–75.

Clement, Norris and Stephen Jenner (1987). "Location Decisions Regarding Maquiladora, In-Bond Plants Operating in Baja California, Mexico." San Diego: San Diego State University, Institute for the Regional Studies of the Californias, mimeo.

Cockcroft, James D. (1986). *Outlaws in the Promised Land: Mexican Immigrant Workers and America's Future*. New York: Grove Press.

COLEF/Center for U.S.-Mexican Studies (continuing). *Guía internacionale de investigaciones sobre México/International Guide to Research on Mexico*. Tijuana/San Diego: COLEF/University of California.

Corbridge, S. (1986). *Capitalist World Development*. London: Macmillan.

Cornelius, Wayne (1982, Summer). "Interviewing Undocumented Immigrants: Methodological Reflections Based on Fieldwork in Mexico and the U.S." *International Migration Review*, 16, 378–411.

—— (1986). *The Political Economy of Mexico Under de la Madrid: The Crisis Deepens, 1985–1986*. San Diego: Center for U.S.-Mexican Studies, University of California.

Corona, Rodolfo (1986). *Evaluación de los Datos Censales de 1980. Población Residente y Migración en Baja California*. Tijuana: CEFNOMEX.

Corwin, Arthur, ed. (1978). *Immigrants and Immigrants: Perspectives on Mexican Labor Migration to the United States*. Westport: Greenwood.

Coyle, Laurie, G. Hershatter, and E. Honig (1980). "Women at Farah: An Unfinished Story." In M. Mora and A. de Castillo, eds., *Mexican Women in the United*

*States: Struggles Past and Present.* Los Angeles: Chicano Studies Research Center, University of California.

Davila, Alberto, R. Schmidt, and G. Ziegler (1984, May). "Industrial Diversification, Exchange Rate Shocks, and the Texas-Mexico Border." *Federal Reserve Bank of Dallas, Economic Review*, 1–9.

Davis, Reginald (1985). *Industria Maquiladora y Subsidiarias de Co-Inversión. Régimen Jurídico y Corporativo.* México D.F.: Cárdenas.

Demaris, Ovid (1970). *Poso del Mundo: Inside the Mexican American Border.* Boston: Little Brown.

Derossi, F. (1970). *The Mexican Entrepreneur.* Paris: OECD.

Dillman, C. Daniel (1970). "Commuter Workers and Free Zone Industry along the Mexico-United States Border." *Proceedings, Association of American Geographers*, 2, 48–51.

—— (1970a). "Urban Growth along Mexico's Northern Border and the Mexican National Border Program." *Journal of Developing Areas*, 4, 487–508.

—— (1983, February). "Assembly Industries in Mexico: Contexts of Development." *Journal of Inter-American Studies and World Affairs*, 25, 31–58.

Dobken, J. Chris (1984, March 16). "Mexican In-Bond Industry: Infrastructure Requirements." Chihuahua City: AMCHAM Maquiladora Seminar, mimeo.

Domínguez Qintana, José (1987, January). "La empresa maquiladora: otra modalidad del imperialismo yanqui." *Tarahumara*, [Chihuahua], (89), 35.

Doran, Charles, George Modelski, and C. Clark, eds. (1983). *North/South Relations: Studies of Dependency Reversal.* New York: Praeger.

Drucker, Peter (1977, March 15). "The Rise of Production Sharing." *Wall Street Journal.*

—— (1980). *Managing in Turbulent Times.* London: Heinemann.

Edelberg, Guillermo S. (1976). *The Procurement Practices of the Mexican Affiliates of Selected U.S. Automobile Firms.* New York: Arno Press.

El Paso Chamber of Commerce (1987). *Maquiladoras.* El Paso: Chamber of Commerce, mimeo.

Elson, Diane and Ruth Pearson (1981, Spring). "Nimble Fingers Make Cheap Workers: An Analysis of Women's Employment in Third World Export Manufacturing." *Feminist Review*, 8, 87–107.

Ende, A. Van de and H. Haring (1983). "Sunbelt Frontier and Border Economy: A Fieldwork Study of El Paso." El Paso: University of Texas, Center for Inter-American and Border Studies, mimeo.

Erb, R. and S. Ross, eds. (1981). *United States Relations with Mexico.* Washington and London: American Enterprise Institute for Public Policy Research.

Ericson, Anna-Stina (1970, May). "An Analysis of Mexico's Border Industrialization Program." *Monthly Labor Review*, 12, 33–40.

Evans, James and Dilmus James (1979, Spring). "Conditions of Employment and Income Distribution in Mexico as Incentives for Mexican Migration to the United States: Prospects to the End of the Century." *International Migration Review*, 13, 4–24.

Evans, Peter (1979). *Dependent Development: The Alliance of Multinational, State, and Local Capital in Brazil.* Princeton: Princeton University Press.

Fajnzylber, Fernando and Trinidad Martínez Tarrago (1976). *Las empresas transnacionales: expansión a nivel mundial y proyección en la industria mexicana.* México D.F.: Fondo de Cultura Económica.

Farías Negrete, J. (1969). *Industrialization Program for the Mexican Northern Border.* México D.F.: Banco Comercial Mexicano.

Fernández, Raúl (1977). *The United States-Mexico Border.* Notre Dame: Notre Dame University Press.

Fernández-Kelly, María Patricia (1983). *For We Are Sold, I and My People: Women and Industry on Mexico's Northern Frontier.* Albany: State University of New York Press.

Flores Garza, F., E. Estrada F., W. Campbell Saavedra (1986). "Economía fronteriza enfocada a la industria maquiladora." Ciudad Juárez, Universidad Autónoma de Ciudad Juárez, mimeo.

Fouts, S. C. (1973). "Mexican Border Industrialization: An Analogy and a Comment." Austin: University of Texas, Institute of Latin American Studies, Conference on Economic Relations between Mexico and the United States, mimeo.

Friedmann, John and Clyde Weaver (1979). *Territory and Function.* London, Edward Arnold.

Frobel, F., J. Heinrichs, and O. Kreye (1980). *The New International Division of Labour.* Cambridge, Cambridge University Press.

Galarza, Ernesto (1964). *Merchants of Labor: The Mexican Bracero Story.* Charlotte: McNally and Loftin.

Gambrill, Monica Claire (1984, Winter–Summer). "El Sindicalismo en las Maquiladoras de Tijuana." *Campo Libre,* 11, 119–132.

Ganster, Paul, ed. (1987). "The Maquiladora Program in Tri-National Perspective: Mexico, Japan, and the United States." San Diego State University: Institute for the Regional Studies of the Californias, mimeo.

Gardner, David (1987, July 31). "The Rich Pickings in America's Backyard," *Financial Times.*

George, Edward (1986, July). "Impact of the Maquilas on Manpower Development and Economic Growth on the U.S.-Mexico Border." Montreal: North American Economics and Finance Association, Conference.

Gereffi, Gary and Donald Wyman (1987, Spring). "Determinants of Development Strategies in Latin America and East Asia." *Pacific Focus,* 2, 5–33.

Gibson Lay James and Alfonso Corona Rentería, eds. (1985). *The U.S. and Mexico: Borderland Development and the National Economies.* Boulder: Westview Press.

Goldfinger, Nat (1985, August). "Statement." In *Subcommittee on Multinational Corporations, Committee on Foreign Relations.* Washington: U.S. Congress.

González-Arechiga, Bernardo (1985). *Vinculación fronteriza a Estados Unidos y su cambio con la crisis.* Tijuana: CEFNOMEX.

González-Arechiga, Bernardo, ed. (1987). "Desarrollos nuevos de la industria maquiladora y sus estructuros sectoriales de importación y exportación." Tijuana: COLEF, mimeo.

González Salazar, Roque, ed. (1981). *La frontera del norte: integratión y desarrollo.* México D.F.: COLEF.

Goodwin, Leslie (1980). "Discover Foreign Trade Zones—and Increase Profits!" *Made In Mexico,* 3:2, 14–17.

Grunwald, J. and K. Flamm, eds. (1985). *The Global Factory: Foreign Assembly in International Trade.* Washington: Brookings.

Hale, Carl (1965). "Industrial Development Corporations in Texas." *Federal Reserve Bank of Dallas, Business Review,* Part 1, February, 3–9; Part 2, March, 3–9.

Hall, Thomas (1986, June). "Incorporation in the World-System: Toward a Critique." *American Sociological Review,* 51, 390–402.

Hansen, Niles (1981). *The Border Economy: Regional Development in the Southwest.* Austin: University of Texas Press.

Herzog, Lawrence (1985). "City Profile–Tijuana." *Cities,* 2, 297–306.

—— (1989). *Where North Meets South: Cities, Space and Politics on the United States-Mexico Border.* Austin, University of Texas Press.

Hirschman, Albert O. (1958). *The Strategy of Economic Development.* New Haven and London: Yale University Press.

Horowitz, Rose (1986, August 26). "Yucatan Targeted for In-Bond Plants; Low-Cost Surface Transport Vital." *Journal of Commerce and Commercial,* 1A, 3A.

House, John W., (1982). *Frontier on the Rio Grande: A Political Geography of Development and Social Deprivation*. Oxford: Oxford University Press.

Hymer, S. (1975). "The Multinational Corporation and the Law of Uneven Development." In H. Radice, ed. *International Firms and Modern Imperialism*. Harmondsworth: Penguin.

Iglesias, Norma (1985). *La flor mas bella de la maquiladora*. México D.F.: SEP/CEFNOMEX.

Industrial Development Commission of Mexicali (continuing). *Manufacturing in Mexicali*. Mexicali: Industrial Development Commission, mimeo.

INEGI (1988). *Estadística de la industria maquiladora de exportación 1975–1986*. México D.F.: Secretaria de Programación y Presupuesto.

Irigoyen, Alejandro (1987, January 24). "Insuficientes, los insumos que reciben las maquiladoras del País." *Excelsior*.

Jamail, M. (1981). "Voluntary Organizations along the Border." In S. Kaufman Purcell, ed., *Mexico-United States Relations*. New York: Academy of Political Science.

Jenkins, Rhys (1984). *Transnational Corporations and Industrial Transformation in Latin America*. London: Macmillan.

Konig, Wolfgang (1981). "Effectos de la actividad maquiladora fronteriza en la sociedad mexicana." In R. González Salazar, ed. op. cit.

Kras, E. S. (1987, July). "Maquiladora Management Problems of Working in Two Cultures." *Maquiladora Newsletter*, 14–16.

Ladman, J. (1975). "The Development of the Mexicali Regional Economy: An Example of Export Propelled Growth." Tempe: Arizona State University, College of Business Administration.

Lall, Sanjaya (1980). *The Multinational Corporation*. London: Macmillan.

Lazes, Peter (1986). "Trico Product Corporation Studies." New York: Cornell University Programs for Employment and Workplace Systems, mimeo.

Lee, Thomas P., ed. (1988). *In-Bond Industry/Indústria Maquiladora*. México D.F.: Administración y Servicios Internacionales, S.A.

Lim, Linda (1985). *Women Workers in Multinational Enterprises in Developing Countries*. Geneva: International Labour Organization.

Lindquist, Diane (1986, December 6). "Expo-Maquila at Acapulco Called a Success." *San Diego Union*, E1, 2.

López, David (1969, June). "Low-Wage Lures South of the Border." *AFL-CIO Federationist*, 1–7.

Lucker, G. W. (1987, Spring). "The Hidden Costs of Worker Turnover: A Case Study in the Maquiladora Industry." *Journal of Borderlands Studies*, 2, 93–98.

Lucker, G. W. and A. Alvarez (1984, Summer). "Exploitation or Exaggeration: A Worker's-Eye View of 'Maquiladora' Work." *Southwest Journal of Business and Economics*, 1, 11–18.

Macarthy, P. with O. Franco (1983). "National Income, Wages and Hours of Work in Mexico—An Historical Analysis." Paisley: College of Technology, mimeo.

Martínez, Oscar (1978). *Border Boom Town: Ciudad Juárez since 1848*. Austin: University of Texas Press.

Maxfield, Sylvia and Ricardo Anzaldua M., eds. (1987). *Government and Private Sector in Mexico*. San Diego: Center for U.S.-Mexican Studies, University of California.

McAleese, D. and D. McDonald (1978). "Employment growth and the development of linkages in foreign-owned and domestic manufacturing enterprises." *Oxford Bulletin of Economics and Statistics*, 40, 321–339.

McAllen Industrial Board (continuing). "Mexico's Border Industrialization Program for U.S. Manufacturers at Reynosa, Tamps." McAllen: Industrial Board, mimeo.

McClelland, E. (1979, July). "U.S.-Mexico Border Growth Back on Fast-Growth Track." *Federal Reserve Bank of Dallas, Voice*, 3–9.

McClintock, W., comp. (continuing). *Maquiladora Directory*. El Paso: Mexico Communications, mimeo.

Mendelowitz, A. (1986, December 10). "Statement on Commerce Department Conference on Mexico's Maquiladora Program." Washington: General Accounting Office, U.S. Government.

Mendoza Berrueto, Eliseo (1982). "História de los programas federales para el desarrollo económico de la frontera norte." In M. Ojeda, ed., op. cit.

Mexico, Government of (1979). *National Industrial Development Plan*. London: Graham and Trotman. [Translation of *Plan nacional de desarrollo industrial* (1979)].

México, SIC (1968). *Programa de industrialización de la frontera norte de México* México. D.F.: Dirección General de Indústrias.

—— (1971). *Mexican Border Industrialization Program*. México D.F.: SIC.

Mier y Teran, Enrique (1984, April). "Domestic Inputs to the In-Bond Industry." *Maquiladora Newsletter*, 2–7.

Miller, M. (1982). *Economic Growth and Change Along the U.S.-Mexican Border*. Austin: University of Texas Bureau of Business Research.

Mitchell, Jacqueline (1977). "Preliminary Report on the Impact of Mexico's Twin-Plant Industry Along the U.S.-Mexican Border." El Paso: Organization of U.S. Border Cities, mimeo.

Mungaray L., Alejandro (1983, August). "Contradicciones en la desarrollo de las maquiladoras en Tijuana." *Economía informa*, 107, 25–31.

Mungaray L., Alejandro and Patricia Moctezuma M. (1984, January–April). "La disputa del mercado fronterizo, 1960–1983." *Estudios fronterizos*, 1, 89–112.

Muñoz Ríos, Patricia (1987, March 16). "Menos divisas por maquiladoras. Disminuye la derrama por las devaluaciones diarios del peso." *El Financiero*, 1, 31.

Muñoz, Victor (1987, August 25). "Outline of testimony submitted on behalf of the Texas AFL-CIO Twin Plant Task Force." El Paso: Central Labor Union, mimeo.

de Murguia, Valdemar (1986). *Capital Flight and Economic Crisis: Mexican Post-Devaluation Exiles in a California Community*. San Diego: Center for U.S.-Mexican Studies, University of California.

Nash, June and Maria Patricia Fernández-Kelly, eds. (1983). *Women, Men and the International Division of Labor*. Albany: State University of New York Press.

Nash, June and Helen Safa, eds. (1985). *Women and Change in Latin America*. New York: Bergin and Garvey.

Negrete M., José (forthcoming). *Integración e industrialización fronteriza: el caso de la Cd. Industrial Nueva Tijuana*. México D.F.: COLEF.

Noriega Verdugo, Sergio (1982). *La mujer trabajadora en Baja California: una apreciación estadística*. Tijuana: Cuadernos de Ciencias Sociales.

Ojeda, Mario, ed. (1982). *Administración del desarrollo de la frontera norte*. México D.F.: El Colegio de México.

Overstreet, Daphne, ed. (1981). *An "Offshore" Manufacturing Opportunity. Production Sharing and the In-Bond Industry from an Arizona-Sonora Perspective*. Nogales, Arizona: U.S.-Mexico Business Information Service.

Passel, J. and K. Woodrow (1984, Fall). "Geographic Distribution of Undocumented Immigrants: Estimates of Undocumented Aliens Counted in the 1980 Census by State." *International Migration Review*, 18, 642–671.

Patrick, J. Michael and R. S. Arriola (1987, April). "The Economic Impact of Maquiladoras on Border Development: Rio Grande Valley Case Study—Some Preliminary Findings." El Paso: Western Social Science Association Meetings.

Peach, James (1984). "Demographic and Economic Change in Mexico's Northern Frontier: Evidence from the X Censo General de Población y Vivienda." Las Cruces: New Mexico State University, Center for Latin American Studies, mimeo.

Pearce, J. and J. Gunther (1985, September). "Illegal Immigration from Mexico: Effects on the Texas Economy." *Federal Reserve Bank of Dallas, Economic Review,* 1–12.

Peña, Devon (1981). "Maquiladoras: A Select Annotated Bibliography and Critical Commentary on the United States-Mexico Border Industry Program." Austin: University of Texas, Center for the Study of Human Resources, mimeo.

—— (1984, Winter–Summer). "Skilled activities among assembly line workers in Mexican-American border twin plants," *Campo Libre*, 11, 189–207.

Piore, M. and C. Sabel (1984). *The Second Industrial Divide: Possibilities for Progress.* New York: Basic Books.

Pranis, Peter (1987, February). "Historical Comparisons 1981–1985. Border Zone Maquiladora Wages versus Selected Manufacturing Wages in Other Countries." McAllen: Council for South Texas Economic Progress, mimeo.

Price, J. (1973). *Tijuana: Urbanization in a Border Culture.* Notre Dame: University of Notre Dame Press.

Prock, Jerry (1983, Winter). "The Peso Devaluations and Their Effect on Texas Border Economies." *Inter-American Economic Affairs*, 37, 83–92.

Quiñones Ramos, Raúl (1986, September). "Importance of Personnel Training in the Maquiladora Industry." *Maquiladora Newsletter*, 10–16.

Ray, Nancy (1986, November). "Is Otay Mesa the Hong Kong of the Future?" *Los Angeles Times*, 1, 10.

Reifenberg, S. (1986, July 1). "Contract Assembly on the Mexican Border." *Electronic Business*, 114–116.

Reynolds, Clark (1970). *The Mexican Economy: Twentieth Century Structure and Growth.* New Haven and London: Yale University Press.

Richards, John (1964). *Economic Growth in El Paso, Texas, 1950–1962.* El Paso: Texas Western College, Bureau of Business and Economic Research.

Rosenthal-Urey, I., ed. (1986). *Regional Impacts of U.S.-Mexican Relations.* San Diego, Center for U.S.-Mexican Studies, University of California.

Ross, Stanley, ed. (1978). *Views Across the Border.* Albuquerque: University of New Mexico Press.

Rubio del Cueto, E. (1974, August 16). "Desarrollo y perspectivas de la industria maquiladora." *Concamin*, 17–19.

Ruiz, Vicki and Susan Tiano, eds. (1987). *Women on the United States-Mexico Border: Responses to Change.* Boston and London: Allen and Unwin.

Salas-Porras, Alejandra (1986, April). "Maquiladoras and the Sociopolitical Structure in the Northern States of Mexico: Chihuahua, Sonora and Baja California." Reno: Association of Borderlands Scholars Meeting.

—— (1987) "Maquiladoras y burguesia regional." *El Cotidiano* (numero especial 1), 51–58.

Sanders, T. (1986). "Maquiladoras: Mexico's In-Bond Industries." Indianapolis: Universities Field Staff International, no.15.

Sanderson, Susan (1987). "Automated Manufacturing and Offshore Assembly in Mexico." In Cathryn Thorup, ed., *The United States and Mexico: Face to Face with the New Technology.* New Brunswick and Oxford: Transaction Books.

Sawers, L. and W. Tabb (1984). *Sunbelt/Snowbelt. Urban Development and Regional Restructuring.* New York: Oxford University Press.

Scheinman, Marc N. (1987, Summer). "The Role of Banking in the Financing of the Maquiladora Industry." México D.F.: Proceedings of the North American Economics and Finance Association.

Scott, Bruce and George Lodge, eds. (1985). *U.S. Competitiveness in the World Economy.* Boston: Harvard Business School Press.

Seligson, Mitchell A. and Edward J. Williams (1981). *Maquiladoras and Migration: Workers in the Mexico-United States Border Industrialization Program*. Austin: University of Texas Press.

Shafer, Robert Jones (1973). *Mexican Business Organizations: History and Analysis*. Syracuse: Syracuse University Press.

Sklair, Leslie (1985). "Shenzhen: A Chinese 'Development Zone' in Global Perspective." *Development and Change*, 16, 571–602.

—— (1988). *Maquiladoras: Annotated Bibliography and Research Guide to Mexico's In-Bond Industry*. San Diego: Center for U.S.-Mexican Studies, University of California.

—— (1988a). "Foreign Investment and Irish Development: A Study of the International Division of Labour in the Midwest Region of Ireland." *Progress in Planning*, 29:3, whole issue.

—— (1988b). "The Costs of Foreign Investment: The Case of the Egyptian Free Zones." In E. Kedourie and S. Haim, eds., *Essays on the Economic History of the Middle East*. London: Frank Cass.

—— (1988c). "Metatheory, Theory and Empirical Research in the Sociology of Development and Underdevelopment." *World Development*, 16:6, 697–709.

Sklar, Richard (1976, September). "Postimperialism. A Class Analysis of Multinational Corporate Expansion." *Comparative Politics*, 9, 75–92.

Sprinkle, R. (1986) "Project Link: An Investigation of the Employment Linkage Between Ciudad Juárez and El Paso." El Paso, University of Texas, mimeo.

Stockton, William (1986, January 19). "Mexico's Grand 'Maquiladora' Plan." *New York Times*, F4.

Stoddard, E. (1987). *Maquila: Assembly Plants in Northern Mexico*. El Paso: Texas Western Press.

Stoddard, E., R. Nostrand, and J. West, eds. (1983). *Borderlands Sourcebook: A Guide to the Literature on Northern Mexico and the American Southwest*. Norman: University of Oklahoma Press.

Stokes, Bruce (1987, June 20). "Mexican Momentum." *National Journal*, 1572–1578.

Suárez-Villa, Luis (1985, September). "Urban Growth and Manufacturing Change in the United States-Mexico Borderlands: A Conceptual Framework and an Empirical Analysis." *Annals of Regional Science*, 19, 54–108.

Tamayo, Jesús and José Luis Fernández (1983). *Zonas fronterizas. (México-Estados Unidos)*. México D.F.: Centro de Investigación y Docencia Económicas.

Tiano, Susan (1986). "Women and Industrial Development in Latin America (Review Essay)." *Latin American Research Review*, 21:3, 157–170.

Tocups, Nora (1980, Fall). "City growth and cooperation along the U.S.-Mexican border." *Georgia Journal of International and Comparative Law*, 10, 619–644.

Turner, Roger (1983, November 28). "Mexico Turns to Its In-Bond Industry as a Means of Generating Exchange." *Business America*, 27–33.

Unger, Kurt (1985, May). "El comercio exterior de manufacturas modernas en México. El papel de las empresas extranjeras." *Comercio Exterior*, 35, 431–443.

United Nations Centre on Transnational Corporations (1988). *Transnational Corporations in World Development*. New York: UNCTC.

United States Congress (1986). *Hearings. Commerce Department's Promotion of Mexico's Twin Plant Program*. Washington: Subcommittee on Economic Stabilization of the Committee on Banking, Finance, and Urban Affairs.

—— (1987). *Maquiladora Impact on U.S. Jobs and Trade Competition with Japan*. Washington: Subcommittee on Commerce, Consumer, and Monetary Affairs of the Committee on Government Operations.

United States Department of State (continuing). "Airgram." Mexico City: U.S. Embassy.

[274]

United States International Trade Commission (1986). *The Impact of Increased United States-Mexico Trade on Southwest Border Development*. Washington: USITC.

—— (1988) *The Use and Economic Impact of TSUS Items 806.30 and 807.00*. Washington: USITC.

United States Tariff Commission (1970). *Economic Factors Affecting the Use of Items 807.00 and 806.30 of the Tariff Schedules of the United States*. Washington: USITC.

Urquidi, Victor L. and Sofia Mendez Villarreal (1978). "Economic Importance of Mexico's Northern Border Region." In S. Ross, ed., op. cit.

Van Waas, Michael (1981). "The Multinationals' Strategy for Labor: Foreign Assembly Plants in Mexico's Border Industrialization Program." Stanford University: Ph.D. dissertation.

Vera, Beatriz Eugenia (1981, January). "The Impact of Wage Labor on Women's Lives." *Boletín Informativo* (American Friends Service Committee), 8–10.

Vernon, Raymond (1971). *Sovereignty at Bay: The Multinational Spread of U.S. Enterprises*. New York: Basic Books.

Villalobos C., Liborio (1973). "Foreign Assembly Industries in Mexico: A Necessary Evil of an Underdeveloped Society." Austin: University of Texas Institute of Latin American Studies, Conference on Economic Relations between Mexico and the United States.

Vrazo, Fawn (1986, November 4). "Mexican Expo Loses U.S. Backing. Show Was to Encourage Businesses to Move South." *Philadelphia Inquirer*, E01.

Watkins, Al (1985). "The Texas-Mexico Twin Plants System: Industry and Item 807.00 of the United States Tariff Schedules." *Texas Tech Law Review*, 16, 963–987.

Weintraub, Sidney, ed. (1986). *Industrial Strategy and Planning in Mexico and the United States*. Boulder: Westview Press.

Wende, Charles (1969). "How I Established a Twin Plant." In *International Twin-Plant Seminar*. Cd. Juárez: U.S./Mexico Border Cities Association.

Wilhelm, Robert (1987, April). "In-Bond Manufacturing in Mexico: Update 1987." El Paso: Western Social Science Association Meeting, mimeo.

World Bank (continuing). *World Development Report*. New York: Oxford University Press.

Worthy, James (1984). *Shaping an American Institution: Robert E. Wood and Sears, Roebuck*. Urbana and Chicago: University Press.

Wright, H. (1971). *Foreign Enterprise in Mexico: Laws and Policies*. Chapel Hill: University of North Carolina Press.

Xirau Icaza, J. and M. Díaz (1976). *Nuestra dependencia fronteriza*. México D.F.: Fondo de Cultura Económica.

Young, Gay, ed. (1986). *The Social Ecology and Economic Development of Ciudad Juárez*. Boulder: Westview.

# Additional Bibliography

Baker, S. (1991). "Mexico, A New Economic Era—The Rush to Free Trade May Create a Unified North American Economy." *Business Week*, November 12.

Barkin, David (1990). *Distorted Development: Mexico in the World Economy*. Boulder: Westview.

Brown, Flor and Lilia Domínguez (1989). "Nuevas tecnologías en la industria maquiladora de exportación." *Comercio Exterior*, 39, 2:215–23.

Campbell, Bruce (1991, May). "Beggar Thy Neighbor." *NACLA Report on the Americas*, 24, 6:22–29.

Carrillo, Jorge, ed. (1990). *La nueva era de la industria automotriz en México*. Tijuana: COLEF.

——— (1991). "Mercados de trabajo en la industria maquiladora de exportación." Tijuana: COLEF, for Dirección General de Empleo.

Castells, Manuel and Laura Tyson (1988). "High-Technology Choices Ahead: Restructuring Independence." In John Sewell et al. op. cit.

Chanona, A. (1991). "The Political Economy of Economic Integration: The North American Free Trade Agreement." Colchester, Essex: University of Essex.

Crookell, Harold (1990). *Canadian-American Trade and Investment under the Free Trade Agreement*. New York: Quorum Books.

Day, M. (1992). *Stepan Chemical: The Poisoning of a Mexican Community*. San Antonio: Coalition for Justice in the Maquiladoras. Videotape.

Díaz, O. (1990, March). "Sourcing in Mexico." *Twin Plant News*, 90–91.

Driscoll de Alvarado, Barbara and M. Gambrill, eds. (1992). *El Tratado de Libre Comercio*. Mexico City: UNAM.

Fox, Jonathan (1992, Spring). "Agriculture and the Politics of the North American Trade Debate." *LASA Forum*, 23, 3–9.

Gassert, Thomas (1985). *Health Hazards in Electronics: A Handbook*. Hong Kong: Asia Monitor Resource Center.

González-Aréchiga, Bernardo and José Carlos Ramírez (1989). "Productividad sin distribución: Cambio tecnológico en la maquiladora mexicana (1980–1986)." *Frontera Norte*, 1, 97–124.

González-Aréchiga, Bernardo and José Carlos Ramírez, eds. (1990). *Subcontratación y empresas trasnacionales: Apertura y restructuración en la maquiladora*. Tijuana: COLEF/Fundación Friedrich Ebert.

Gruben, William (1990, January). "Mexican Maquiladora Growth: Does It Cost U.S. Jobs?" *Federal Reserve Bank of Dallas, Economic Review*, 15–29.

Guendelman, Sylvia and Mónica Jasis (n.d.). "Health Consequences of Maquiladora Work: Women on the U.S.-Mexican Border." *American Journal of Public Health*, forthcoming.

Gutiérrez-Haces, Teresa (1992, September). "The Challenge of Free Trade for Unions and Workers." Presentation at the XVII International Congress of the Latin American Studies Association, Los Angeles.

Hicks, Donald A., ed. (1988). *Is New Technology Enough? Making and Remaking U.S. Basic Industries*. Washington, D.C.: American Enterprise Institute.

Hufbauer, Gary and Jeffrey Schott (1992). *North American Free Trade: Issues and Recommendations*. Washington, D.C.: Institute for International Economics.

Husson, M. (1991, May–June). "La maquiladorización de la industria mexicana." *El Cotidiano* 7, 41, 3–13.

Kelly, Mary (1991). "Facing Reality: The Need for Fundamental Changes in Protecting the Environment along the Border." Austin: Texas Center for Policy Studies.

Kochan, Leslie (1989). *The Maquiladoras and Toxics: The Hidden Costs of Production South of the Border*. Washington, D.C.: AFL-CIO.

La Botz, Dan (1992). *Mask of Democracy: Labor Suppression in Mexico Today*. Boston: South End Press, for the International Labor Rights Education and Research Fund.

Leonard, H. (1988). *Pollution and the Struggle for the Global Product*. Cambridge: Cambridge University Press.

Lewis, Sanford, Marco Kaltofen, and Gregory Ormsby (1991). *Border Trouble: Rivers in Peril*. Boston: National Toxic Campaign Fund.

Lowery, S. (1990, May). "Environmental Services: A Growing Priority." *Twin Plant News*, 45–48.

Maynez, Rafael (1991, June). "Mechanization." *Twin Plant News*, 63, 65.

Moure-Eraso, R. et al. (1991). "Back to the Future: Sweatshop Conditions on the Mexico-U.S. Border." Lowell, Mass.: University of Lowell/Work Environment Program.

Mumme, Stephen (1992). "System Maintenance and Environmental Reform in Mexico." *Latin American Perspectives*, 19, 1, 123–43.

Mumme, Stephen and Joe Nalven (1988, Spring). "National Perspectives on Managing Transboundary Environmental Hazards: The U.S. Mexico Border Region." *Journal of Borderlands Studies*, 3, 39–68.

Mungaray, Alejandro (1990). *Crisis, automatización y maquiladoras*. Mexicali: Universidad Autónoma de Baja California.

Nauman, T. (1992, September 7). "Is Labor Law Losing Teeth in Face of Free Trade?" *El Financiero Internacional*.

Office of Technology Assessment (1990). *Making Things Better*. Washington D.C.: OTA.

Pearson, Ruth (1991). "Male Bias and Women's Work in Mexico's Border Industries." In Diane Elson, ed., *Male Bias in the Development Process*. Manchester: University of Manchester Press.

Perry, D. et al. (1990). "Binational Management of Hazardous Waste: The Maquiladora Industry at the U.S.-Mexico Border." *Environmental Management*, 14:4, 441–50.

Red Mexicana de Acción Frente al Libre Comercio (1991). *Libre comercio o explotación libre?* Mexico City: RMALC.

Rey Romay, Benito, ed. (1992). *La integración comercial de México a Estados Unidos y Canadá: ¿Alternativa o destino?* Mexico City: Siglo Veintiuno/UNAM.

Reygadas, L. (1992). *Un rostro moderno de la pobreza: Problemática social de las trabajadoras de las maquiladoras de Chihuahua*. Chihuahua: Ediciones del Gobierno del Estado de Chihuahua.

Reynolds, Clark, Leonard Waverman, and Gerardo Bueno, eds. (1991). *The Dynamics of North American Trade and Investment: Canada, Mexico and the United States*. Stanford, Calif.: Stanford University Press.

Rich, Jan Gilbreath (1992). "Planning the Border's Future: The Mexican-U.S. Integrated Border Environmental Plan." Austin: U.S.-Mexican Policy Studies Program, University of Texas at Austin.

Salas-Porras, Alejandra (1992). "The Free Trade Agreement and the Process of Corporativization of the Largest Economic Groups in Mexico," mimeo.

Sánchez, Roberto (1990a). "Otra manera de ver la maquiladora: Riesgos en el medio ambiente y la salud." In Bernardo González-Aréchiga and J.C. Ramírez, eds., op. cit.

—— (1990b, July–December). "Condiciones de la vida de los trabajadores de la maquiladora en Tijuana y Nogales." *Frontera Norte*, 2, 153–81.

Sander, Guillermo and F. Mendoza (1990, May). "Compensation Overview." *Twin Plant News*, 34–37.

Schoepfle, Gregory (1991, January–June). "Implications for U.S. Employment of the Recent Growth in Mexican Maquiladoras." *Frontera Norte*, 3, 25–54.

Schoepfle, Gregory and Jorge Pérez-López (1990). "Employment Implications of Export Assembly Operations in Mexico and the Caribbean Basin." Washington, D.C.: Commission for the Study of International Migration and Cooperative Economic Development.

Sewell, John and Stuart Tucker et al. (1988). *Growth, Exports, and Jobs in a Changing World Economy: Agenda 1988.* New Brunswick, N.J.: Transaction Books.

Shaiken, Harley (1990). "Going Global: High Technology in Mexican Export Industry." Final Report. Washington, D.C.: Office of International Economic Affairs, U.S. Department of Labor.

Sklair, Leslie (1991a). *Sociology of the Global System.* Baltimore, Md.: Johns Hopkins University Press, and London: Harvester.

—— (1991b). "Problems of Socialist Development: The Significance of Shenzhen Special Economic Zone for China's Open Door Development Strategy." *International Journal of Urban and Regional Research*, 15, 197–215.

—— (1992, September). "The Transnational Capitalist Class in Mexico and the USA: Some Evidence from NAFTA." Paper presented at the XVII International Congress of the Latin American Studies Association, Los Angeles.

—— (1993). "Global System, Local Problems: Transnational Corporations and Environmental Hazards in the Mexico-U.S. Borderlands." In H. Main and W. Williams, eds., *Environment and Housing in Third World Cities.* London: Belhaven Press.

Székely, Gabriel and Oscar Vera (1991, Summer). "What Mexico Brings to the Table: Negotiating Free Trade with America." *Columbia Journal of World Business*, 26, 2.

Texas Center for Policy Studies (1990). "Overview of Environmental Issues Associated with Maquiladora Development along the Texas-Mexico Border." Austin: TCPS.

Thorup, Cathryn (1991, Summer). "The Politics of Free Trade and the Dynamics of Cross-Border Coalitions in U.S.-Mexico Relations." *Columbia Journal of World Business*, 26, 2:12–27.

Tiano, Susan (n.d.). *Patriarchy on the Line: Labor, Gender and Ideology in the Mexican Maquila Industry.* Philadelphia, Penn.: Temple University Press, forthcoming.

*Trabajo* (1991, Winter–Spring). "Debate: Tratado de Libre Comercio," entire issue.

United Nations (1987). *Transnational Corporations and Technology Transfer: Effects and Policy Issues.* New York: U.N. Centre on Transnational Corporations [E.87.II.A.4].

United States Environmental Protection Agency/Secretaría de Desarrollo Urbano y Ecología (1992). *Integrated Environmental Plan for the Mexican-U.S. Border Area (First Stage, 1992–1994).* Washington, D.C.: USEPA/SEDUE.

United States International Trade Commission (1991). *The Likely Impact on the United States of a Free Trade Agreement with Mexico.* USITC Publication 2353. Washington, D.C.: USITC.

Williams, Edward (1991). *The Unionization of the Maquiladora Industry: The Tamaulipan Case in National Context.* San Diego: Institute for Regional Studies of the Californias, San Diego State University.

Wilson, Patricia (1990a). "Maquiladoras and Local Linkages: Building Transaction Networks in Guadalajara." Working Paper No. 32. Washington D.C.: Commission for the Study of International Migration and Cooperative Economic Development.
———— (1990b). "The New Maquiladoras: Flexible Production in Low Wage Regions." In Khosrow Fatemi, ed., *The Maquiladora Industry: Economic Solution or Problem?* New York: Praeger.
Zapata, Francisco, T. Hoshino, and L. Hanono (1990). *Industrial Restructuring in Mexico: The Case of Auto Parts.* Tokyo: Institute of Developing Economies.

# About the Author

Leslie Sklair was born in Glasgow, Scotland in 1940. He received his Ph.D. in sociology at the London School of Economics in 1969, and is presently senior lecturer in sociology there. He has lectured extensively in Europe and the United States, and was a visiting research fellow at the Center for U.S.-Mexican Studies, University of California, San Diego, from August 1986 to May 1987, from where he carried out most of the field research for this book. He is on the editorial board of the *British Journal of Sociology*, and has been a consultant to the United Nations Centre on Transnational Corporations. His publications include *The Sociology of Progress, Organized Knowledge*, and several monographs and articles resulting from the research project of which this book is a part. He is married, has three daughters, and lives in London.

# Index

[286]

Vrazo, Fawn 191n, 214

wages 6, 22n, 24, 42n, 58–60, 65, 67, 72, 75n, 80, 84, 96, 99, 122, 126, 137n, 142–3, 148, 161–2, 169, 171, 178–9, 203–5, 214, 218–19, 225n, 230, 236–8
*Wall Street Journal* 8, 45, 74n, 132, 227
Warwick Electronics 51–2, 197
Watkins, Al 225n
Weintraub, Sidney 229, 238n
Wende, Charles 56
Westinghouse 105, 149, 212
Whirlpool 51, 74n
Whiteford, Scott 92, 96, 221
Whitworth, C. C. 74n
Wilhelm, Robert 95
Western Maquila Trade Association 84, 87, 187
Wolf, Richard 123, 124

Wolfe, Bill 239n
Wolff, Alan 2, 8
Woo Morales, Ofelia 191n
Wood, R. E. 50, 74n
work conditions 20, 93–4, 150–2, 173, 213–19
working class 13, 160–43, 172, 184, 206, 220–3
Worthy, James 50, 74n
Wright, H. 22n

Xirau Icaza, J. and M. Diaz 26

Young, Gay 160, 217, 222
Yucatan 112, 143, 145, 153

Zaragoza 143
Zenith 57, 120, 122, 127, 132–6, 138n, 148, 155n, 233